MOON HANDBOOKS®

YOSEMITE

SECOND EDITION

ANN MARIE BROWN

© ANN MARIE BROWN

AVALON TRAVEL

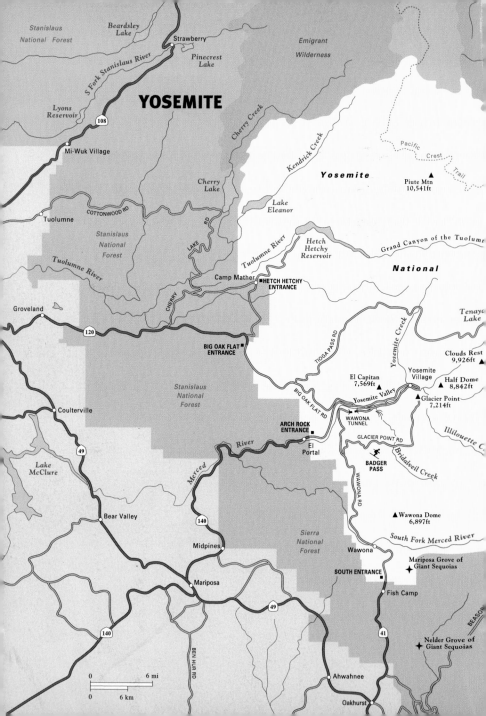

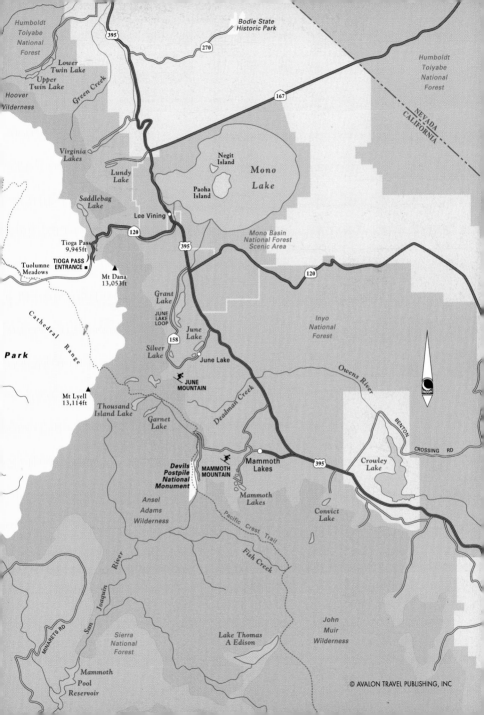

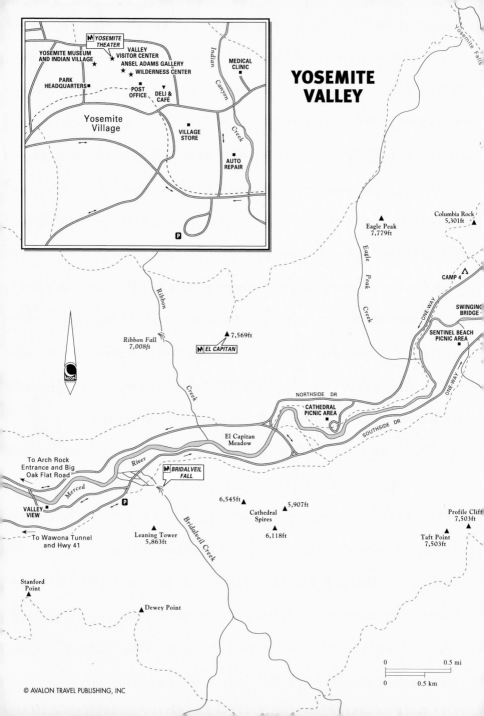

YOSEMITE VALLEY

Inset map — Yosemite Village:

YOSEMITE THEATER

YOSEMITE MUSEUM AND INDIAN VILLAGE

PARK HEADQUARTERS

VALLEY VISITOR CENTER

ANSEL ADAMS GALLERY

WILDERNESS CENTER

MEDICAL CLINIC

POST OFFICE

DELI & CAFE

Yosemite Village

VILLAGE STORE

AUTO REPAIR

Main map labels:

Yosemite Falls

Columbia Rock 5,301ft

Eagle Peak 7,779ft

CAMP 4

SWINGING BRIDGE

SENTINEL BEACH PICNIC AREA

Eagle Peak Creek

Ribbon Creek

Ribbon Fall 7,008ft

7,569ft

EL CAPITAN

NORTHSIDE DR

CATHEDRAL PICNIC AREA

SOUTHSIDE DR

ONE-WAY

El Capitan Meadow

To Arch Rock Entrance and Big Oak Flat Road

Merced River

BRIDALVEIL FALL

VALLEY VIEW

To Wawona Tunnel and Hwy 41

Leaning Tower 5,863ft

Bridalveil Creek

6,545ft

Cathedral Spires

5,907ft

6,118ft

Profile Cliff 7,503ft

Taft Point 7,503ft

Stanford Point

Dewey Point

MOON

0   0.5 mi

0   0.5 km

© AVALON TRAVEL PUBLISHING, INC

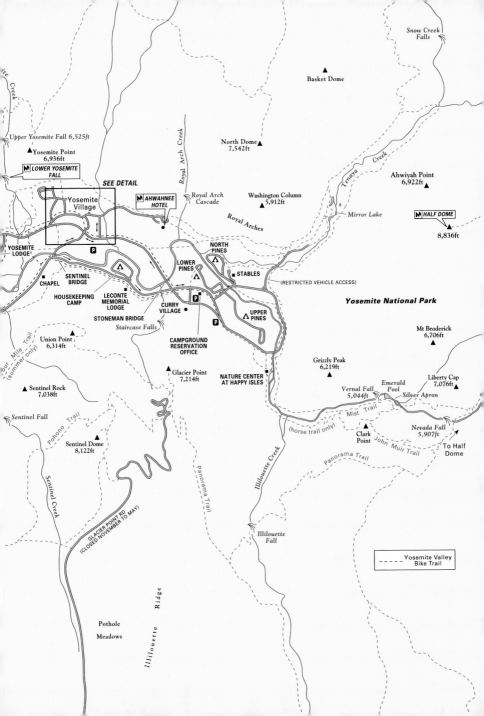

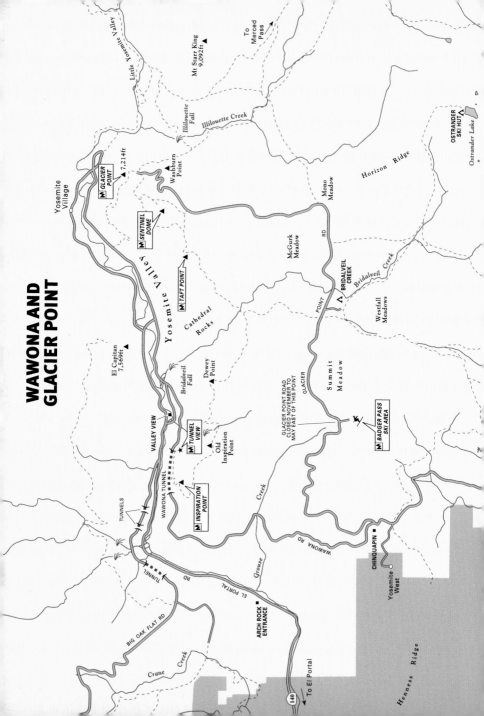

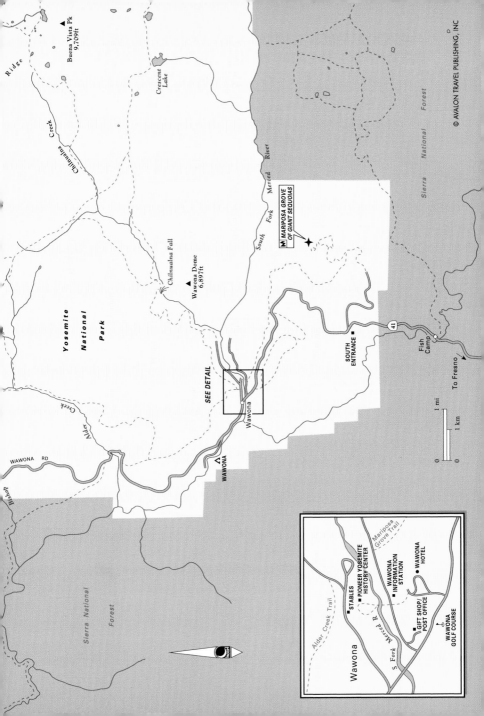

© AVALON TRAVEL PUBLISHING, INC

Buena Vista Pk
9,709ft

Ridge

Chilnualna Creek

Crescent Lake

South Fork Merced River

Sierra National Forest

MARIPOSA GROVE
OF GIANT SEQUOIAS

Chilnualna Fall

Wawona Dome
6,897ft

Yosemite National Park

SEE DETAIL

41

Fish Camp

SOUTH ENTRANCE

To Fresno

Wawona

Alder Creek

WAWONA RD

WAWONA

Bishop

0   1 mi

0   1 km

Sierra National Forest

N

Wawona

Alder Creek Trail

STABLES

PIONEER YOSEMITE HISTORY CENTER

Mariposa Grove Trail

S Fork Merced R

WAWONA INFORMATION STATION

WAWONA HOTEL

GIFT SHOP/ POST OFFICE

WAWONA GOLF COURSE

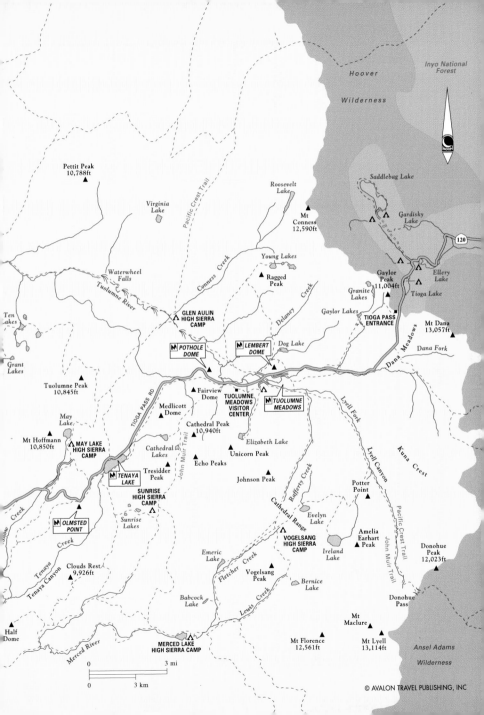

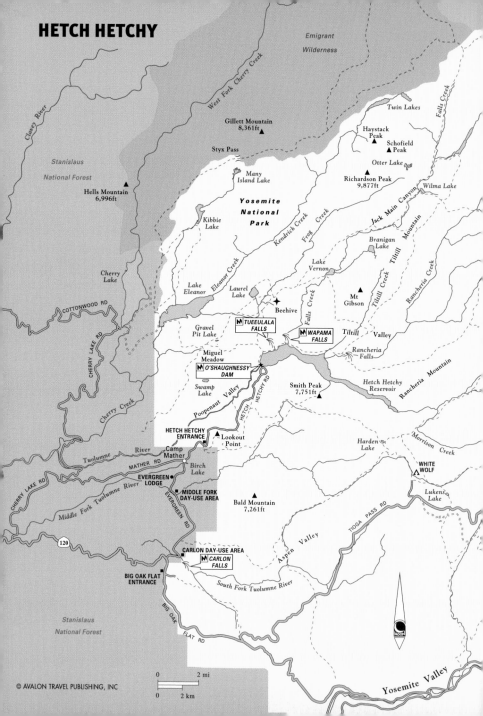

HETCH HETCHY

Clavey River

Emigrant Wilderness

West Fork Cherry Creek

Falls Creek

Twin Lakes

Gillett Mountain 8,361ft ▲

Haystack Peak ▲

Schofield ▲ Peak

Styx Pass

Stanislaus National Forest

Many Island Lake

Otter Lake

Richardson Peak 9,877ft ▲

Wilma Lake

Hells Mountain 6,996ft ▲

Yosemite National Park

Kibbie Lake

Kendrick Creek

Frog Creek

Jack Main Canyon

Tiltill Mountain

Branigan Lake

Lake Vernon

Rancheria Creek

Cherry Lake

Lake Eleanor

Eleanor Creek

Laurel Lake

Mt Gibson ▲

COTTONWOOD RD

Beehive

Gravel Pit Lake

Ⓜ **TUEEULALA FALLS**

Falls Creek

Ⓜ **WAPAMA FALLS**

Tiltill

Tiltill Creek

Valley

CHERRY LAKE RD

Miguel Meadow

Ⓜ **O'SHAUGHNESSY DAM**

Rancheria Falls

Swamp Lake

Poopenaut Valley

HETCH HETCHY RD

Hetch Hetchy Reservoir

Rancheria Mountain

Cherry Creek

Smith Peak 7,751ft ▲

HETCH HETCHY ENTRANCE

HETCH HETCHY RD

▲ Lookout Point

Harden Lake

Morrison Creek

Tuolumne River

Camp Mather

MATHER RD

Birch Lake

△ **WHITE WOLF**

CHERRY LAKE RD

EVERGREEN LODGE

■ **MIDDLE FORK DAY-USE AREA**

EVERGREEN RD

Middle Fork Tuolumne River

Bald Mountain 7,261ft ▲

Lukens Lake

TIOGA PASS RD

120

Aspen Valley

CARLON DAY-USE AREA

Ⓜ **CARLON FALLS**

BIG OAK FLAT ENTRANCE

BIG OAK FLAT RD

South Fork Tuolumne River

Stanislaus National Forest

MOON

0   2 mi

0   2 km

© AVALON TRAVEL PUBLISHING, INC

Yosemite Valley

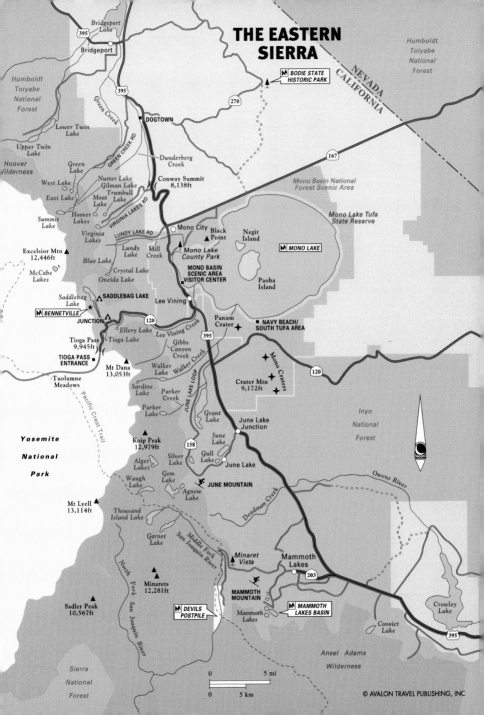

CONTENTS

Discover Yosemite

Explore Yosemite

Yosemite Valley 24

Wawona and Glacier Point 47

Tioga Pass and Tuolumne Meadows 66

Know Yosemite

MAPS

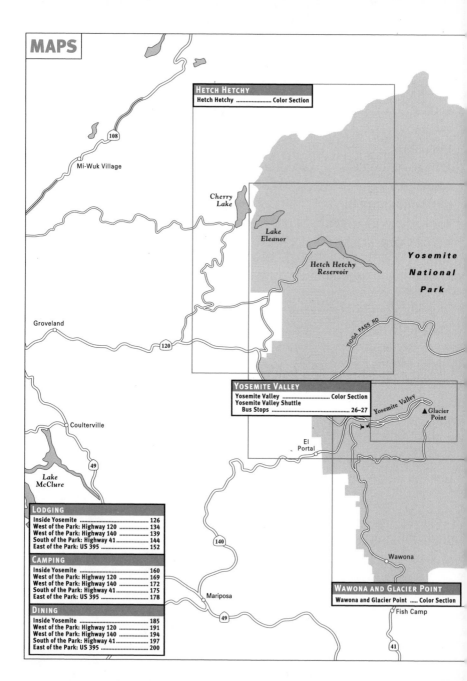

HETCH HETCHY
Hetch Hetchy .... Color Section

Mi-Wuk Village

Cherry
Lake

Lake
Eleanor

Hetch Hetchy
Reservoir

Yosemite

National

Park

Groveland

120

TIOGA PASS RD

Coulterville

49

YOSEMITE VALLEY
Yosemite Valley .... Color Section
Yosemite Valley Shuttle
  Bus Stops 26–27

Yosemite Valley

▲Glacier
Point

El
Portal

Lake
McClure

140

Wawona

WAWONA AND GLACIER POINT
Wawona and Glacier Point ..... Color Section

Mariposa

Fish Camp

49

41

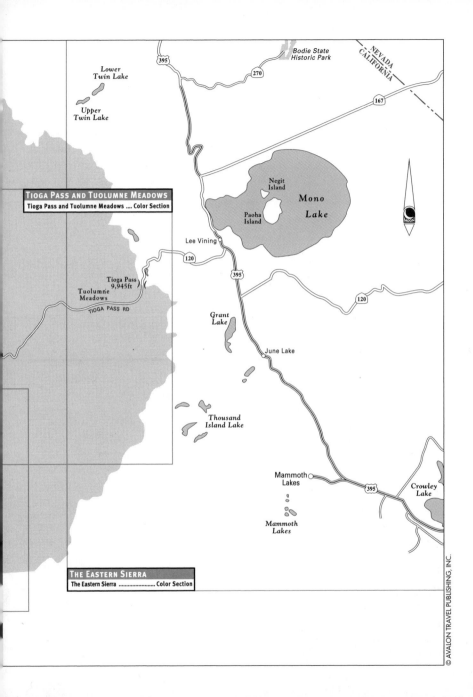

Lower
Twin Lake

Upper
Twin Lake

Bodie State
Historic Park

NEVADA
CALIFORNIA

395

270

167

Negit
Island

Mono
Lake

Paoha
Island

Lee Vining

120

Tioga Pass
9,945ft

Tuolumne
Meadows

TIOGA PASS RD

395

120

Grant
Lake

June Lake

Thousand
Island Lake

Mammoth
Lakes

395

Crowley
Lake

Mammoth
Lakes

MooN

© AVALON TRAVEL PUBLISHING, INC.

Discover Yosemite

© ANN MARIE BROWN

Plunging waterfalls, stark granite, alpine lakes, pristine meadows, giant sequoia trees, and raging rivers—you'll find them all in Yosemite National Park. From Yosemite Valley's famous water- falls—three of which are among the tallest in the world—to the towering granite domes and glistening meadows of Tioga Pass, Yosemite is a place that can only be described in superlatives. At 1,200 square miles and 750,000 acres, the park is nearly the size of Rhode Island, and one of the most popular national parks in the United States. Currently Yosemite plays host to approximately 3.4 million visitors per year, or as many as 20,000 people a day on the busiest summer holidays.

Set aside as a national park in 1890, Yosemite is a place that is synonymous with scenery. The seven-mile-long Yosemite Val- ley is known the world over as an incomparable natural wonder, with its 3,000-foot granite walls and leaping waterfalls. It is esti- mated that more than half of the park's visitors see only Yosem- ite Valley when they travel to Yosemite—even though the Valley makes up less than one percent of the park. Beyond the Valley lies the pristine high country of Tioga Pass Road and Tuolumne Meadow's large subalpine expanse, bordered by precipitous mountain summits and granite domes. To the northwest lies Hetch Hetchy, a reservoir in a valley considered to be a twin of Yosemite Valley. To the south is Glacier Point with its picture-postcard vistas, and the marvels of the Mariposa Grove of Giant Sequoias—the largest living trees on earth. The park has 260 miles of roads that allow even the most casual visitor a look at these highlights.

In addition to all its scenic beauty, Yosemite is a park that is ideally suited for outdoor recreation. From skiing to horseback riding, from camping to hiking, the vast majority of Yosemite travelers come to this park to play outside in its mountain landscape. Even those who have never set foot on a trail before are inspired to go for a hike. And why not? With more than 800 miles of paths to walk, hikers can choose from short-and-easy jaunts to world-class destinations like Sentinel Dome and Vernal Fall, intense treks to the summits of Half Dome or Clouds Rest, or a wealth of moderate trails in between the two extremes. One thing is certain—every trail in Yosemite leads to a destination well worth the effort required to reach it.

Last but certainly not least, Yosemite is a park for nature study. Whether you are captivated by the secrets of its glacier-carved rocks, the poetry of the evening light on Half Dome, or the adorable antics of a chipmunk at your campsite, you'll find that a visit to Yosemite sparks a deep sense of curiosity and wonder about the natural world. It has done so for as long as humans have inhabited its landscape; it will continue to do so for as long as we continue to preserve, protect, and cherish it.

As early as 1928, the Secretary of the Interior reported that the heavy influx of visitors to Yosemite "has caused serious congestion and brought about conditions similar to those encountered in a small city." Imagine what that same Secretary would say today, when park visitation has grown to well over three million people per year.

Key to optimizing your experience in Yosemite is planning your visit for the least crowded months of the year, or at least being prepared for crowds if you show up in the high season (June to September). First-time visitors, especially those who come to the park without lodging or camping reservations, are often disappointed by the cramped conditions in Yosemite Valley. Jammed parking lots, parades of hikers on trails, and long lines at entrance stations, restrooms, and eating establishments can seriously detract from one's ability to enjoy the scenic splendor.

Fortunately, you don't have to suffer this experience. Yosemite is open 24 hours a day, 365 days a year, and has much to offer in every season of the year. Visitors can enter the park any time of the day or night without prior notice or reservations, but those hoping to stay overnight or longer in the park will do best by having lodging or camping reservations secured well before their arrival. In general, summer weekends are the busiest days and best avoided, especially in Yosemite Valley. When school is in session—from September through May—the crowds lessen substantially, except for holiday weekends.

No matter when you go, it's unwise to travel to Yosemite at any time of year without checking on current conditions. Weather, rockfalls, fire, and other natural occurrences in this constantly changing landscape can affect driving routes and lodging options and necessitate altering your trip plans. To get up-to-the-minute information on the park, phone 209/372-0200, or visit the official National Park website for Yosemite: www.nps.gov/yose. By phone and at the park website, you can request to have maps and information about Yosemite mailed to your home. If you wish to write to Yosemite, the address is P.O. Box 577, Yosemite National Park, CA 95389.

Several other websites and phone numbers can help you plan your trip. For park accommodations, tours, events, and organized activities, contact the park concessionaire, DNC Parks and Resorts at Yosemite, 559/252-4848, 559/253-5676, or www.yosemitepark.com. For campground reservations within the park, call the campground reservations office (800/436-7275, or 301/722-1257 if you are outside the United States) or visit the website: http://reservations.nps.gov.

PARK FEES AND PASSES

Arriving at one of Yosemite's entrance gates, you stare in confusion at the list of prices and fee options for entering the park. A long line of cars waits behind you. The ranger asks for 20 bucks; you fork it over. She hands you a map and smiles as you drive through. Did you do the right thing?

Maybe. The entrance fee to Yosemite National Park is $20 per vehicle (car, RV, truck, etc.). The fee is good for a seven-day stay. You are given a receipt to keep, which you must show any time you pass through one of the park's five entrance stations. If you are staying in the park for more than a day or so, you will most likely go through the entrance stations a few times. Don't misplace that receipt.

But Yosemite also has other fee options, which might be more economical for you. If you buy a Yosemite Pass for $40, you are given a plastic card (it looks like a credit card) that is good for entrance to Yosemite National Park for one year. If you will go to Yosemite more than once in a year, this is an obvious choice.

An even better choice may be the National Parks Pass, which costs $50. That buys you a plastic card good at all national parks across the United States for one year. With 14 national parks and preserves in California alone, and most of them costing $10 or $20 to enter, this is an excellent value.

And last but not least, if you arrive in a bus, the fee is $10 per individual. A $10 fee also applies to those who arrive on foot, on a bicycle or motorcycle, or even on a horse!

WHEN TO GO

Which season is best in Yosemite? Each month of the year has its own myriad charms. The summer months, from June to October, are the only time that the entire park, including the high country (Glacier Point and Tuolumne Meadows), is open and accessible. Road closures and openings vary somewhat from year to year depending on snow levels, but in most years all park roads are open by early June. Yosemite Valley and the northwest and southern region of the park are accessible year-round. Hetch Hetchy may also be open year-round, depending on snow levels.

Spring is a wonderful time for visiting Yosemite Valley, when its famous waterfalls are at their peak flow. First-time visitors would do well to time their initial Yosemite trip for April or May, when the Valley is at its most photogenic, the waterfalls are shimmering whitewater cascades, and the summer crowds have not yet arrived. Accommodations are relatively easy to come by at this time, except for Saturday nights.

Autumn is also a fine time to visit Yosemite, even though most of the Valley's famous waterfalls, except for dependable Bridalveil, have run dry by midsummer. The lack of falling water is compensated for by the show of fall colors on the Valley floor and the chance for solitude in this well-loved park.

The quietest season in Yosemite is winter. Lowest visitation levels are recorded from November to March, except for around the holidays. And there is plenty to do in Yosemite in winter: see Yosemite Valley or the groves of giant sequoias crowned in snow, ice skate on an outdoor rink with Half Dome as a backdrop, and ski, snowboard, and take part in other winter sports at Badger Pass.

Weather

The majority of Yosemite National Park is blessed with typical Sierra summer weather: warm, clear days with temperatures in the 70s and low 80s (Fahrenheit), and cool nights with temperatures in the 40s and 50s. Some parts of Yosemite are at lower elevations and are 10–20 degrees hotter; these include Yosemite Valley (4,000 feet in elevation) and the Hetch Hetchy region (3,800 feet in elevation).

In winter, some park entrances and roads close due to snow. Glacier Point Road and Tioga Pass Road (Highway 120 East) are closed usually from late October until early June. The Hetch Hetchy Road and Mariposa Grove Road are also occasionally closed for snow. Because the timing of snowfall and snowmelt vary greatly from year to year, always phone the park for a road and trail update before planning your trip. Also be forewarned that in winter, chains may be required on any park road at any time.

In Yosemite Valley, which stays open year-round, winter days average 30°F–55°F, and nights will often drop below freezing. Snow falls in Yosemite Valley a few times each winter, but it usually does not last more than a week or two. Accumulations above one or two feet are rare. Rain is fairly common in winter but unusual between May and October.

WHAT TO TAKE

If you're visiting Yosemite for the first time, you may be surprised to find that the Valley has all the amenities of most small cities. Within a few square miles, you'll find grocery stores, restaurants, lodgings, and even an auto garage, hair salon, medical facility, post office, and jail. This means that if you are staying in or near the Valley, you can leave almost everything at home except for the clothes on your back. Anything you need, you can buy in the Valley or in the small towns surrounding the park.

Far and away the most important item you can bring on your Yosemite vacation is a reservation for lodging or a campsite. Show up without a reservation, especially in the busy season from May through September or during the winter holidays, and you could face an ordeal.

A few personal items to pack along are hiking boots or sturdy shoes for walking, and a small day pack or fanny pack. Even people who have never hiked a trail in their entire life are often inspired to take a walk in Yosemite.

Too many of them end up wearing gold lamé sandals as they trudge up the granite stairsteps of the Mist Trail. Sturdy shoes or hiking boots are far more comfortable, and a lot safer. A small day pack or fanny pack is useful for holding a bottle of water, a snack, and your camera. Even if you don't go for a hike, you'll probably meander around the Valley floor during some part of your visit, and these items will come in handy.

It's also wise to bring a variety of clothing for layering. Weather changes constantly in the Sierra Nevada Mountains; it's smart to pack rain gear, jackets, and clothes for both warm and cool weather—even though you may spend your entire vacation in nothing but shorts and a T-shirt.

The general rule of thumb for summer trips to the park: Bring warm clothes for evenings (especially if you're camping) and layers for daytime. Carry rain gear in late summer, when afternoon thunderstorms are common. Spring and fall are cooler, so pack warmer layers.

For winter trips to Yosemite, always carry chains for your car tires, even if you have a four-wheel-drive vehicle. Although Yosemite's roads are kept plowed in winter (except for those roads that are closed completely for the season), chains can be required on any park road at any time. It is far less expensive to buy chains for your personal or rental car at a big-box store in a large city (Wal-Mart–type stores carry chains, as well as auto supply stores) than it is to buy or rent them near the park.

WHAT TO DO

At 1,200 square miles, Yosemite is a big park—so big that it can be daunting for first-time visitors. Here's where to go in the park to find popular features and recreation opportunities:

Waterfalls: Yosemite Valley or Hetch Hetchy Valley (but don't wait until August, when the mighty waterfalls dwindle to a trickle—visit in April, May, or June).

Giant Sequoias: Wawona's Mariposa Grove is the largest and most popular sequoia grove. Along Highway 120, you'll find Merced Grove (near Big Oak Flat) and Tuolumne Grove (near Crane Flat).

Day-Hiking Trails: The most popular, and crowded, trails are located in Yosemite Valley. A vast selection of day-hiking trails, many offering a better chance at solitude, are found on Glacier Point Road and in the Tioga Pass Road/Tuolumne Meadows area. For the fewest crowds, head for the Eastern Sierra region just outside of Yosemite National Park.

Backpacking Trails: The majority of backpackers set out from Tuolumne Meadows or Yosemite Valley. Much less traveled backpacking trails are found in the Hetch Hetchy region and in the south part of the park, near Wawona.

Rock Climbing: The centerpiece for rock climbing in Yosemite is Yosemite Valley, where granite walls tower thousands of feet high. Tioga Pass Road is also popular for climbers, especially in the areas near Tenaya Lake and Tuolumne Meadows.

Horseback Riding: Stables offering guided horseback rides are located in Yosemite Valley, Wawona, Tuolumne Meadows, and at several locations in the Eastern Sierra.

Yosemite History: A good introduction to park history can be found at the Pioneer Yosemite History Center in Wawona and in and around the Yosemite Valley Visitor Center.

Alpine Lakes: Tioga Pass Road offers access to the greatest number of Yosemite lakes, both by car and on foot. The Eastern Sierra, just east of Tioga Pass, is also marked by an abundance of lakes.

Fishing: Best bets for fishing are in Wawona, along Tioga Pass Road, and in the Eastern Sierra. Many consider the Eastern Sierra to be the trout capital of California.

Bicycling: If you are bringing a bike, be sure to ride the Yosemite Valley bike path in Yosemite Valley. Riding on national park hiking trails is forbidden, but mountain biking opportunities are plentiful in the Eastern Sierra.

Scenic Drive-to Overlooks: No visitor should miss taking in the spectacular views from three drive-to overlooks in Yosemite National Park: Glacier Point at the east end of Glacier Point Road, Inspiration Point at Wawona Tunnel, and Olmsted Point on Tioga Pass Road.

YOSEMITE VALLEY

Yosemite Valley is the centerpiece of Yosemite, and the place where the vast majority of visitors spend most of their time. It is also the busiest part of the park, especially in the summer months, though the Valley is open and accessible year-round. The Valley offers the greatest number of organized activities of any area of the park: from nature walks to evening slide shows, from ice skating to photography seminars, from Indian basket-making to rock climbing, as well as numerous hiking trails. The majority of the park's visitor services—lodgings, restaurants, and campgrounds—are also found in Yosemite Valley.

Yosemite's world-famous waterfalls drop from both the north and south Valley rims. El Capitan, the largest single piece of granite rock on earth, is found in the Valley. And Half Dome, one of the most frequently photographed landmarks in the park, is also located here. For visitors who want "something to do" on their vacation, Yosemite Valley is the place to be.

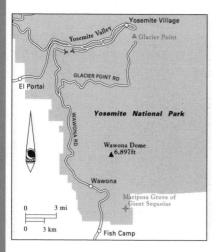

WAWONA AND GLACIER POINT

Two major tourist destinations are found in the southern part of Yosemite near the settlement of Wawona: the Mariposa Grove of Giant Sequoias and Glacier Point. The Mariposa Grove is the largest and most famous of Yosemite's three sequoia groves, boasting several hundred of the big trees. Glacier Point is a high drive-to overlook that offers what many consider to be the best views in the West. The commanding vista takes in all the major granite landmarks of Yosemite Valley and the surrounding high country. For many park visitors, it is the single most memorable spot in Yosemite. Several hiking trails begin at Glacier Point and along Glacier Point Road.

History lovers will enjoy Wawona, with its historic buildings at the Pioneer Yosemite History Center and 19th-century hotel. Across the road from the hotel is a nine-hole golf course, an unusual feature in a national park. Fishing and swimming holes are found on the South Fork of the Merced River, which runs through Wawona.

The Wawona area is open and accessible year-round, although snow frequently covers the area in winter. Glacier Point is closed each year from approximately late October to mid-June.

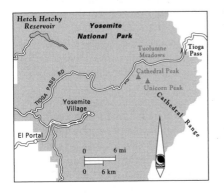

TIOGA PASS AND TUOLUMNE MEADOWS

The Tuolumne (pronounced too-ALL-um-ee) Meadows region is the centerpiece of a huge High Sierra playground for hikers and backpackers, as well as for visitors who simply want to sit at a picnic table and enjoy its scenic beauty. At an elevation of 8,600 feet, Tuolumne Meadows is one of the most photographed regions of Yosemite, its wide, grassy expanse bounded by a series of high granite domes and peaks. Trails here lead to alpine lakes set below the spires of Cathedral and Unicorn Peaks, to a series of roaring waterfalls on the Tuolumne River, and to the summits of lofty granite domes with commanding vistas of the high country.

This region comprises Yosemite's high country, a pristine alpine area that is only accessible a few months of the year, usually from mid-June until late October. Visitor services are few and far between here, but hikers, campers, and nature lovers will be in their element.

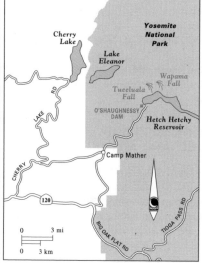

HETCH HETCHY

Of the five park entrance stations, Hetch Hetchy gets the fewest number of cars passing through day after day. That's largely because it is devoid of visitor services; there are no visitor centers, restaurants, hotels, or even car campgrounds here. Why the lack of development? Because Hetch Hetchy, a granite-walled valley similar in appearance to but slightly smaller than Yosemite Valley, was flooded in 1923 to create a water supply for the city of San Francisco. It was the tragic end of a long fight for naturalist John Muir, who tried in vain to save Hetch Hetchy from the big city politicians.

Despite human's best efforts to destroy it, Hetch Hetchy remains beautiful. Hetch Hetchy's waterfalls still spill over its massive cliffs, and imposing granite palisades stand guard over the valley. Wildflowers blossom in the understory of ponderosa pines and incense-cedars. Many park visitors make day trips to Hetch Hetchy to admire the enormous O'Shaughnessy Dam or hike along the edges of its reservoir. Backpackers use Hetch Hetchy as a jumping-off point for long trips into the Yosemite backcountry.

Hetch Hetchy is open and accessible year-round, although snow often blankets the area in winter.

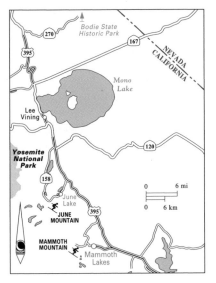

EASTERN SIERRA

The Eastern Sierra is an outdoor-lover's playground: skiers and snow-boarders swoosh down mountain slopes, hikers and mountain bikers explore miles of trails, anglers cast into crystal-clear streams and rivers, scenery lovers and photographers enjoy alpine lakes backed by granite cliffs. The region hosts two major mountain resorts, Mammoth Lakes and June Lake, and unusual destinations such as Bodie State Historic Park, a historic gold rush ghost town; and Mono Lake, a 700,000-year-old saline lake.

The Eastern Sierra is accessible year-round. However, since the land lies just east of Tioga Pass along the U.S. 395 corridor, it cannot be accessed in the winter and spring months by traveling through Yosemite as Tioga Pass is generally closed from late October to mid-June.

If You Only Have One Day

There is a famous story about a Yosemite visitor who goes up to a park ranger and asks, "I'm only visiting the park for one day. How should I spend my time?"

And the ranger replies, "If I only had one day in Yosemite, I would sit right down and have myself a good cry."

Certainly it's not ideal to spend only one day in Yosemite, but if that's the way your vacation is scheduled, you better dry your tears and get busy.

First, you'll need to limit your travels to one small portion of the park. For most visitors, the portion of choice is Yosemite Valley. During the busy season, it's smart to park your car in the Valley as soon as possible after your arrival and choose from these transportation options: (1) pay for a guided tour on the open-air tram that leaves from Yosemite Lodge; (2) rent a bicycle at Yosemite Lodge or Curry Village and ride the paved bike paths in the Valley; or (3) design your own tour of the Valley by walking and riding the free Valley shuttle bus. The option you choose will determine your itinerary.

The open-air tram tours travel all over the Valley and are narrated by an interpreter. You're not stuck in an enclosed bus; you're out in the open, smelling the Valley air and getting a much better view than you'd have from your car windshield. Tours last about two hours and are highly informative.

A great way to get introduced to Yosemite Valley is to take a narrated tour on an open-air tram.

On a bicycle, you can easily visit Lower Yosemite Fall and Mirror Lake (you'll park your bike at the trailheads for both destinations and walk a short distance). You can also tour a large expanse of the Valley, including stops at the visitor center and Yosemite Village or Curry Village for water and snacks.

On foot, and by taking short hops on the free Yosemite Valley shuttle bus, you can see all of the Valley's famous sights. However, this requires a little more map-reading and planning than the other options.

If possible, leave enough time in your one Yosemite day to take a drive to Glacier Point. You can do so in your own car, or ride the tour bus that leaves from Yosemite Lodge. The ideal time to be at Glacier Point is at sunset, when Half Dome turns pink from the bottom up, but the view from the point will knock your socks off at any time of day.

To capture the essence of Yosemite, try to squeeze in at least one hike during your stay. A few easy-to-moderate hikes recommended for short-stay visitors are the trails to May Lake and Lembert Dome on Tioga Pass Road, and the trails to Sentinel Dome and Taft Point on Glacier Point Road. In Yosemite Valley, make sure you take the short walks to Lower Yosemite Fall and Bridalveil Fall (each walk is less than a half mile). If you have a little more time in the Valley and don't mind hiking with a crowd, take the spectacular Mist Trail to the top of Vernal Fall.

The Hardcore Hiker

You've come to Yosemite with a purpose. You have one week of vacation time and you want to hike all of the park's most notable trails—a worthwhile mission, to be sure. Okay, lace up your boots, fill your pack with snacks and water, and let's get started.

Day 1

Better begin with something fairly easy, since you'll probably need to adjust to the high mountain altitude. Go to Yosemite Lodge first thing in the morning and pay for a one-way ticket on a tour bus to Glacier Point. The bus will drop you off at the point and you'll hike the Panorama Trail and Mist Trail back down to Yosemite Valley. The 8.5-mile one-way hike is mostly downhill, but that doesn't make it easy. Your knees will get a workout with 3,200 feet of descent along the way, plus one uphill stretch, which gains 760 feet over 1.5 miles. But the scenery makes it all worthwhile. You'll hike past three major waterfalls—Illilouette, Nevada, and Vernal—and through miles of picture postcard–quality Sierra scenery.

Day 2

You're feeling good. Better do another high-elevation hike, just to make sure your lungs are ready for your big Half Dome day (tomorrow). Head up to Tuolumne Meadows and take the classic high-country hike to Cathedral Lakes. This 7.4-mile round-trip has a 1,000-foot elevation gain on the way to two glacial cirque lakes, which are set below 10,840-foot Cathedral Peak. Don't forget your camera. The scenery, needless to say, is stunning.

Day 3

Okay, you're ready for Half Dome. Start as early in the morning as you can, because you have 17 miles ahead of you and a whopping 4,800 feet of elevation gain. This hike is no picnic, but complaining or whining is unbecoming of a

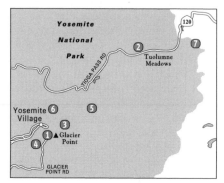

hiker of your stature. Start at Happy Isles (ride the free shuttle bus or walk there from Curry Village) and proceed up the Mist Trail past Vernal and Nevada Falls. Above Nevada Fall, take the left turnoff for Half Dome. The trail is relatively easy to follow from this point (you've completed about half of the ascent already) until you reach the infamous steel cables that run up the back of the dome. It takes two hands and two feet to haul yourself up the cables, ascending 440 feet of nearly vertical granite.

Day 4

An easy day is in order here. You've earned it. Today you'll put together a smorgasbord of short hikes from Glacier Point Road. Start with the trails to Sentinel Dome and Taft Point, both 2.2-mile round-trips that begin at a trailhead one mile before the end of the road. Then, if you still feel energetic, hike to McGurk Meadow from its trailhead farther west on Glacier Point Road (7.5 miles from the Chinquapin turnoff). It's only one mile to the pristine meadow, so you might as well continue another 2.5 miles to Dewey Point,

© ANN MARIE BROWN

From the summit of North Dome, Half Dome looms in the background.

one of the most fantastic viewpoints of Yosemite Valley possible in the park.

Day 5

Time for another epic hike. The summit of Cloud's Rest beckons, and it's 1,000 feet higher than Half Dome, with an even better view. The hike is 14 miles round-trip from the Sunrise Lakes Trailhead on Tioga Pass Road. The good news is that the total elevation gain is only 2,300 feet, so it's much easier than Half Dome. The final summit ascent travels along a series of granite "pancakes" and is downright breathtaking. Be sure to stop at Sunrise Lakes for a swim on your way back to the trailhead. Ah, that cold water feels good on your weary body.

Day 6

So many hikes, so little time. Your week is coming to a close and you haven't yet climbed North Dome, Half Dome's neighbor—right across Tenaya Canyon. This 9.0-mile round-trip is going to seem easy after all you've done so far, but wow—the North Dome view is sublime. It offers the best possible perspective on Half Dome of any summit in the park, plus a chance to visit Indian Rock, the only granite arch in Yosemite.

Day 7

It's your last day in Yosemite, and time to prove your worth as a true mountaineer. You're heading for the 13,053-foot summit of Mount Dana, and after a week of hiking, the high elevation is no longer a problem for you. The grade on this trail, well, that's a different matter. This rather brutal hike gains 3,100 feet spread out over a mere three miles. It's slow going, to say the least. Start at the Tioga Pass entrance station and hike southeast on the obvious use trail. You'll climb all the way to Dana Plateau at 11,600 feet, where it's wise to take a rest. Another mile and 1,500 feet of elevation gain await, but the hard work is completely worth it. Your reward is one of the finest views in the Sierra, encompassing Mono Lake, Ellery and Saddlebag Lakes, Tuolumne Meadows, and an untold wealth of high peaks. After a week like this, it's time to pat yourself on the back for being such a fine mountaineer.

You may be enthralled by Yosemite's scenery—waterfalls leaping thousands of feet over granite cliffs, giant sequoias as wide as your living room, delicate wildflowers painting grassy meadows with a kaleidoscope of color—but your kids may be a tougher audience. Let's face it, children like different stuff than adults like. And as much as we try to expose our kids to adult fun, sometimes it's a good idea to cater to a kid's idea of fun. Fortunately, there are plenty of family-friendly activities in Yosemite. Here's a five-day itinerary that includes lots of fun kid stuff:

Day 1

In the morning, rent bikes at the Curry Village Recreation Center and ride around Yosemite Valley. With 12 miles of smooth, level paths to pedal, bikes are a great equalizer between children and adults. If your kids are too young to ride on their own, parents can rent bikes with kid trailers attached. When you return the bikes to Curry Village, trade them in for an inflatable raft, life jackets, and paddles. You'll put in to the Merced River near Curry Village, then float three miles downstream, where a shuttle bus returns you to your starting point. For dinner, get an extra-large pizza at Curry Village and sit outside on the patio. (Bike rentals are available most of the year; rafting is usually only possible in June and July when the river is at a safe level and flow.)

Day 2

Go for a hike. But forget the crowded trails on the Valley floor, and head instead for the quieter

The Yosemite Valley bike path is one of the best ways to get around the Valley. If you didn't bring your bike, you can rent one at Yosemite Lodge or Curry Village.

© ANN MARIE BROWN

trails off Glacier Point Road. The easy trails to Taft Point and Sentinel Dome make good family hikes; each one is only 2.2 miles round-trip. After your hike, get a hot dog or baked potato at the Glacier Point Snack Stand to replenish the kids' calorie stores, then hang around and gaze at the view from Glacier Point. If you pack along a picnic, you can have dinner at Glacier Point, then stay for the sunset and evening ranger talk. On many nights, amateur astronomers set up telescopes for stargazing.

Day 3

Experience the ultimate in family bonding by signing up the whole brood for an introduction to rock climbing class. Yosemite Mountaineering School guides offer instruction suitable for beginners of all ages. After an exhausting but fun day learning the basics of climbing, go see a live show at the Yosemite Valley Theater (kids' tickets are discounted).

Day 4

Take a drive to the south end of the park, where even the most jaded kids will be duly impressed by the size of the giant sequoias in the Mariposa Grove. If your kids don't want to hike, buy tickets for the open-air tram that tours the big trees (again, kids' tickets are discounted). After being suitably awed by the sequoias, take a trip through history at the Pioneer History Center in Wawona. Kids will love the carriage rides in horse-drawn wagons. Finish out the afternoon with a swim in the South Fork Merced River. If it's a Sunday, head to the Wawona Hotel for the weekly barbecue dinner and dance outside on the lawn. Kids of all ages will want to take part in the square dance; even novice "do-si-doers" will figure out the basics in no time.

Day 5

Sign up for a two-hour morning horseback ride at the Yosemite Valley Stables. Then, head for the Yosemite Art Center in Yosemite Valley and have the kids take part in free children's watercolor classes, held every Tuesday and Sunday afternoon. Finish out the day by heading to El Capitan Meadow, where with a pair of binoculars your kids can watch the rock climbers on El Cap.

People come from all over the world to get a negative ion fix from the plentiful waterfalls in Yosemite National Park. But there's a catch: Show up in mid- to late summer and your waterfall fantasies may be all dried up. Waterfall aficionados should time their Yosemite visit for April, May, or June, the months during which 75 percent of the high country's snowmelt occurs, producing powerful cascades of water. Here is a suggested five-day spring waterfall tour:

Day 1

Start with Yosemite Valley's waterfalls, which are easily seen by walking, driving your car, riding the free Yosemite Valley shuttle bus, riding a bike, or any combination of the above. Bridalveil Fall and Lower Yosemite Fall are obvious must-sees, but don't miss some of the Valley's lesser known falls. At the overlook for Bridalveil Fall, turn directly around and you'll see Ribbon Fall pouring off the north rim of the valley. Look for Sentinel Fall on the south canyon wall, roughly across from Yosemite Falls, just west of Sentinel Rock. Behind Curry Village, Staircase Falls skips its way down the stair-stepped cliff below Glacier Point. If you have time, drive partway up the Big Oak Flat Road toward Crane Flat, where Cascade Falls drops just west of the tunnels. Or visit its final drop to the Valley floor near Cascades Picnic Area, 2.8 miles east of the Arch Rock entrance on Highway 140.

Day 2

Hike the Panorama Trail from Glacier Point down to Yosemite Valley (it's an 8.5-mile one-way trek; you'll need to catch the tour bus at Yosemite Lodge in the morning to deliver you to the trail's start). Just two miles downhill from Glacier Point you'll come to the lip of 370-foot Illilouette Fall. Keep going and an hour or so later you'll reach the brink of Nevada Fall, then finally Vernal Fall. It is an absolutely dizzying experience to stand at the railing-lined overlooks on top of these two falls and stare down into the powerful plunge of white water below.

Day 3

Head to Hetch Hetchy Valley to see its spectacular free-leaping falls. Tueeulala and Wapama Falls can be seen via an easy-to-moderate 4.8-mile round-trip hike along the edge of Hetch Hetchy Reservoir. Park near the dam, walk across it, then follow the trail through a tunnel and along the north edge of the reservoir. You'll cross over the flow of both falls on a series of sturdy bridges.

Day 4

Drive to the south part of the park to see a few lesser-visited falls. Hike the 8.0-mile round-trip trail to Chilnualna Falls located near Wawona.

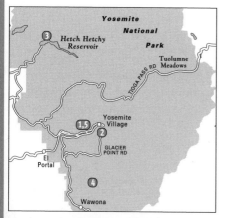

Chilnualna Falls

Day 5

Waterfall lovers can't leave Yosemite without a trip to the top of the highest waterfall in North America, 2,425-foot Yosemite Falls. Start hiking at the trailhead behind Camp 4 and after 3.6 miles and 2,700 feet of elevation gain, you're at the railed overlook that is perched alongside the brink of this behemoth.

For waterfall fans who are unlucky enough to miss the prime falling-water season in Yosemite, there's still hope. July and August park visitors can enjoy a waterfall-laden hike along the Tuolumne River that leads past four falls: Tuolumne, California, LeConte, and finally Waterwheel. The trailhead is found on Tioga Pass Road near Lembert Dome and Soda Springs, and the trail is not usually accessible until July 1 each year, due to snow and wet conditions. This epic hike is a whopping 16 miles round-trip, but with only 1,900 feet of elevation change. The good news is that you don't have to hike the entire distance to enjoy some of the falls—the first one (Tuolumne) is located only 4.5 miles from the trailhead.

Many seasoned Yosemite visitors insist that the best time to see the park is in winter. Rates drop considerably at park lodgings. Crowds are nonexistent. Think you'll miss out on Yosemite's scenic beauty by visiting in the colder months of the year? Just take a look at some of Ansel Adams' photographs and you'll see that Yosemite in winter is incredibly beautiful.

Day 1

Go snowshoeing. No experience is required; snowshoeing is as easy as walking, and rentals cost only a few bucks an hour. Rent a pair of snowshoes at Curry Village, Badger Pass Ski Area, or Crane Flat gas station. Beginners can snowshoe amid the giant sequoia trees at the Merced Grove, Tuolumne Grove, or Mariposa Grove. More experienced snowshoers can head out from Badger Pass to Dewey Point, a seven-mile round-trip, or follow one of several other marked snowshoe/cross-country ski trails from Badger Pass or Crane Flat. If you don't want to set out on your own, join a ranger-guided snowshoe walk. After a day playing in the white stuff,

head to the Ahwahnee Bar for appetizers and a warm cocktail, then choose a comfy seat in one of the Ahwahnee's public rooms and read a book by a blazing fire.

Day 2

Go sledding in the morning and ice skating in the afternoon. Several snow-play areas are located near Crane Flat (Highway 120/Big Oak Flat entrance). Bring along a garbage can lid or a cheap plastic saucer and for a few brief moments, you'll feel like a kid again. Then head to Curry Village for an afternoon skate session, where you can practice your figure eights with a head-on view of Half Dome. Can't skate? Then sit

© ANN MARIE BROWN

Sledding is the perfect low-tech winter activity and is fun for all ages.

by the warming hut's fire pit and treat yourself to a cup of hot chocolate, while you watch other skaters perform triple camels... or just fall down. Top off the day with a pizza at Curry Village or a more formal meal at Yosemite Lodge's Mountain Room. Try to squeeze in an evening ranger talk or slide show.

Day 3

Call in sick to work so your weekend becomes a three-day weekend. Start your day by taking a brief early morning walk around the floor of Yosemite Valley. During most of the winter, the Valley is usually snow-free. The Valley's paved bike trails make easy walking even when they are covered with a few inches of snow. Get out and about before the sun gets too high and you may get to see the ice cone that forms around Yosemite Falls on cold winter nights. Most sunny days the cone melts off completely by 9 or 10 A.M., so an early start is critical. Then go skiing or snowboarding at Badger Pass, one of the mellowest ski resorts in the entire Sierra. Lift lines? High-priced lift tickets? No such thing here. If you don't feel like driving on snow-covered roads, you can take the shuttle bus to Badger Pass from Yosemite Lodge. If you don't know how to ski or snowboard, Badger's 85 acres of slopes are the perfect place to learn. Lessons are offered daily. Or, keep it simple—go "snow tubing" on the Badger Pass hills. It's just like sledding, only safer, because you are cushioned by a big, billowy inner tube.

All this snow play is going to fire up your appetite, so stop in at the burger joint at Badger Pass for some après-ski sustenance. Then head back down to Yosemite Valley for drinks and a seat around the fire at the bar at Yosemite Lodge.

Explore
Yosemite

Yosemite Valley

Seven miles long and one mile across at its widest point, Yosemite Valley is a mélange of verdant meadows bisected by the clear Merced River. It is powerful waterfalls plunging thousands of feet over sheer granite walls. It is the forested home of a rich tapestry of wildlife, including black bears, mule deer, and chipmunks.

It is also the home of several hundred people who are employed in the park, or married to someone who is, and many thousands more who visit each day. It is a small city with sewage lines, garbage collection, a dentist's office, jail, courtroom, auto garage, and church.

The Valley is the centerpiece of Yosemite, and the place where the vast majority of visitors spend most of their time. It offers the greatest number of organized activities of any area of the park, ranging from nature walks to evening slide shows, from ice skating to photography seminars, from Indian basket-making to rock climbing. Without question, there is something for everyone in Yosemite Valley.

Must-Sees

Look for **M** to find the sights and activities you can't miss.

M Bridalveil Fall: The most dependable waterfall in Yosemite Valley, 620-foot Bridalveil flows year-round, even in the dry late summer and fall months. A 200-yard walk will take you to an overlook point below the falls. In the spring and early summer, prepare to get wet from the billowing spray (page 30).

M El Capitan: Towering 3,000 feet above the floor of Yosemite Valley, El Cap is the undisputed king of the granite monoliths, and a mecca for daredevil rock climbers. Get a good look at "The Chief" from the meadow at its base (page 30).

M Lower Yosemite Fall: Upper, Lower, and Middle Yosemite Falls combined make up the highest waterfall in North America, at a prodigious 2,425 feet. It's a strenuous hike to reach the top of the upper fall, but the base of the lower fall can be visited via an easy, level stroll of a few hundred yards. Bring your rain gear from April to June; the fall's spray will leave you soaked (page 30).

M Ahwahnee Hotel: It costs a bundle to spend the night here, but it is completely free to wander amid the "public rooms" of this splendid 1920s-era hotel. Check out the stained glass windows, historic Yosemite paintings and drawings, and Native American baskets, then buy a drink at the bar and pretend you're rich enough to stay here (page 30).

M Half Dome: Your first look at this sheared-off granite dome always comes as a surprise, even though you've undoubtedly seen its image hundreds of times on postcards, calendars, and Ansel Adams prints. Nothing says "Yosemite" quite like this odd-shaped granite icon. Hardcore hikers can trek to its summit and stand atop its bald pate; everybody else can admire it from below or nearby (page 32).

M Yosemite Theater: For only a few bucks, you can take in some live theater in a small, intimate auditorium almost every summer evening, and most weekends in winter. The various shows depict slices of Yosemite and California history and are both entertaining and informative (page 45).

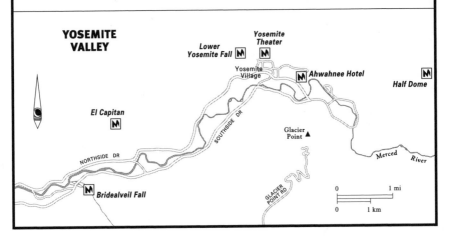

Exploring Yosemite Valley

WEATHER AND SEASONS

Yosemite Valley is open year-round, and its weather is dependably mild. Summer days and nights are usually warm and dry, with temperatures reaching 80°F to 90°F during the day and 50°F to 60°F at night. Autumn and spring are generally 10 to 20 degrees cooler. Winter daytime temperatures average 30°F to 55°F, and nights will often drop below freezing. Snow falls in Yosemite Valley typically a few times each winter, but it usually does not last more than a week or two. Rain is much more common in winter than snow.

VISITOR CENTER

The largest of the park's visitor centers is located in Yosemite Valley. Unfortunately, first-time visitors can have a difficult time finding it because it is not found along a main road or day-use parking lot. If you ride the free Valley shuttle bus, you can access the visitor center by getting off at stop numbers 5 or 9. (When you disembark, the bus driver will point you in the right direction.) If you are driving your car, leave it at the day-use parking lot by the Yosemite Village Store, then walk northwest (go around or through the store, then past the Degnan's Deli complex, post office, wilderness center, and Ansel Adams Gallery), and reach the visitor center in about 200 yards.

The Valley Visitor Center (209/372-0298) is open daily 9 A.M.–6 P.M. in summer (may be shorter hours in winter). It has natural history displays, including a glass-enclosed stuffed black bear standing on its hind legs, audiovisual programs, a well-stocked bookstore, and staff on hand to answer questions. Charts are posted with current road closures and openings and the status of campsite availability throughout the park.

A National Park Service–sanctioned 23-minute film, *The Spirit of Yosemite,* is shown in an auditorium behind the visitor center every half hour. The film explains some of the basics about Yosemite's geology and history but mostly consists of a lot of very beautiful videography. A separate video called *One Day in Yosemite* is available in English, French, German, Spanish, and Japanese. It's more informative, giving suggestions on how to get the most out of a short visit.

Next door to the Valley Visitor Center is the **Yosemite Museum,** where an Indian Cultural Exhibit interprets the life of the Miwok and Paiute Indians from 1850 to the present. On display are Indian deerskin dresses and dance regalia, as well as natural fiber and beaded baskets. Rotating works of local artists are on display in the Museum Gallery, and a gift shop features local American Indian arts and crafts. Behind the museum is the Indian Village of Ahwahnee, a year-round outdoor exhibit of local Native American culture. This

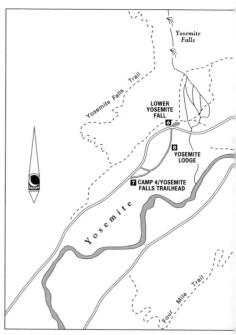

exhibit is an excellent way to teach children about the Indians who once lived in Yosemite Valley. Visitors can walk among several traditional dwellings and watch demonstrations on native skills, such as basket-weaving and beadwork. A self-guided trail leads through the village, called "The Miwok in Yosemite."

Across the street from the Museum is the **Yosemite Valley Cemetery,** where many notable people from the Valley's history are buried, including Galen Clark, Yosemite's first guardian; George Anderson, the man who first climbed Half Dome; and three members of the Hutchings family, including Florence Hutchings, the first white child born in Yosemite. You can purchase a copy of a guide to the cemetery at the Valley Visitor Center.

SHUTTLES AND TOURS

Free shuttle buses transport visitors around the Yosemite Valley floor year-round. To get a seat on one of these buses, simply stand at one of the shuttle stops, then wait a few minutes until one shows up. Shuttles run daily 7 A.M.–10 P.M. in summer and shorter hours in winter. During the busy summer season, it is highly recommended that once you arrive in the Valley, you park your car and use the free shuttles. All of the Valley's sights are accessible via the shuttle.

Tour buses and trams are also available for a fee. Buy tour tickets at the Yosemite Lodge Tour Desk (inside the lodge; 209/372-1240), Curry Village Tour Desk, or Yosemite Village ticket kiosk (outdoors next to the Village Store). In the summer, tours fill up, so reserve in advance if possible. The Yosemite Lodge Tour Desk has the longest hours (8 A.M.–8 P.M.); stop in during the evening to make your plans for the next day, or show up first thing in the morning when it opens. All tours depart from Yosemite Lodge.

A choice of tours is available: The year-round **Valley Floor Tour** is a two-hour, 26-mile interpretive tour through the Valley that takes place in an open-air tram in summer and an

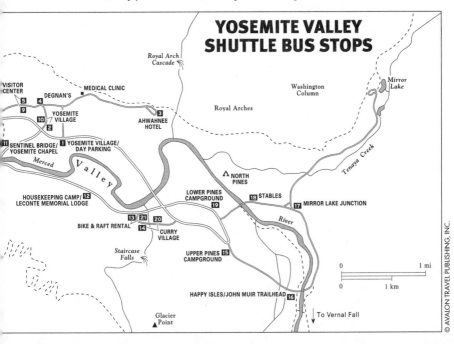

YOSEMITE VALLEY SHUTTLE BUS STOPS

Royal Arch Cascade

VISITOR CENTER
MEDICAL CLINIC
DEGNAN'S
Washington Column
Mirror Lake
Royal Arches

YOSEMITE VILLAGE
AHWAHNEE HOTEL

SENTINEL BRIDGE/ YOSEMITE CHAPEL
YOSEMITE VILLAGE/ DAY PARKING
Merced
Valley
Tenaya Creek

NORTH PINES

HOUSEKEEPING CAMP/ LECONTE MEMORIAL LODGE
LOWER PINES CAMPGROUND
STABLES
MIRROR LAKE JUNCTION
River

BIKE & RAFT RENTAL
CURRY VILLAGE

Staircase Falls
UPPER PINES CAMPGROUND

HAPPY ISLES/JOHN MUIR TRAILHEAD
To Vernal Fall

Glacier Point

0   1 mi
0   1 km

© AVALON TRAVEL PUBLISHING, INC.

ANSEL ADAMS: YOSEMITE VISIONARY

One of Yosemite Valley's most famous residents was Ansel Adams, the great photographer who captured Yosemite, and many other national parks and beautiful landscapes, in complex and delicate shades of black and white. Although most people are familiar with Adams's famous photographs, fewer realize that the man had another well-developed talent: He was a concert-quality pianist. He met his wife, Virginia Best, because her father, painter Harry Best, owned one of only two pianos in Yosemite Valley and allowed Adams to practice there. Virginia and Adams were married in 1928 at Best's Studio, which is today the Ansel Adams Gallery. When Harry Best died, he passed the studio on to his daughter and son-in-law.

Adams made his first trip to Yosemite when he was only 14 years old. It was 1916, and his parents gave him a Box Brownie camera that he used to take his first pictures of Yosemite. A few years later he moved to the Valley to run the Sierra Club's LeConte Memorial Lodge. He led hikes throughout the Valley and into the backcountry and, in doing so, developed a deep understanding of the nuances of light and shadow in the Sierra. Later he worked as a commercial photographer, shooting pictures for the Curry Company. Many of these images—of skiers and toboggan riders—are on display at the Ahwahnee Hotel.

Adams' love of the camera won out over his musical ability, and over the years he started to shoot and sell more of his own artistic work. He was also a great conservationist and used his talent to photograph places that needed to be brought to the attention of the federal government for protection and preservation. In 1934, he was elected to the Sierra Club Board of Directors, a position he held for 37 years. Soon after, the National Park Service hired him to photograph several national parks.

Adams and his wife continued to live in Yosemite Valley until the 1960s, when they moved to Carmel, California. The great photographer died in April 1984, but visitors can still find his spirit, and his photographs, at the Ansel Adams Gallery in Yosemite Valley.

enclosed bus in winter. Most tours include a drive up to Tunnel View, located just before the entrance to the Wawona Tunnel, which many consider to be one of the finest vistas in the park. Along the way, a tour guide remarks on the park's unique geology and history ($22 adults, $17 children).

The Moonlight Tour is a two-hour evening tour offered on full moon nights from spring to fall (about five nights each month). Hot chocolate is provided; this tour also takes place in an open-air tram. A Twilight Tour is available on summer weekends; it departs at 5:30 P.M.

Other tours leave from Yosemite Lodge and travel to highlights outside the Valley. A half-day excursion on a large enclosed tour bus leads to Glacier Point (June–Nov.). Some visitors ride this bus to Glacier Point, then hike back down to the Valley. The first bus of the day leaves at 8:30 A.M. Round-trip prices are $33 for adults and $26 for children; one-way is half price. A sunset tour to Glacier Point is also offered.

A similar bus tour is offered from Yosemite Valley to Tuolumne Meadows (July through Labor Day). Visitors can take an all-day round-trip excursion ($23 adults; $16 children), or ride one-way and then hike back down to the Valley. (This is usually done as an overnight backpacking trip.)

The Yosemite Grand Tour is a full-day tour (spring to fall) that travels from Yosemite Valley to Glacier Point, then on to the Mariposa Grove of Giant Sequoias ($60 adults, $33 children). Take your own boxed lunch with you or purchase the tour and meal package, which includes lunch at the Wawona Hotel. If you bring your own lunch, you can eat it outside on the lawn at the Wawona.

SERVICES

Shopping and Supplies

Some people just have to go shopping—it doesn't matter where they are. If you fall into that category, you'll find some excellent browsing and/or buying opportunities at these Valley establishments.

Yosemite Village: The **Village Store** (209/372-1253) is a huge general merchandise store that has an amazing selection of groceries and just about everything else you can think of, from camping supplies and hiking socks to clothing to magazines. If you need a watermelon or an inflatable mattress, you can get one here. Plus, the store has a convenient parking lot right out front, and it's open late—until 10 P.M. in summer.

Behind the Village Store, the **Village Sport Shop** is the place to go for a fishing license or a new pair of hiking shoes. Over at Yosemite Lodge, the **Yosemite Lodge Gift and Grocery Store** is a convenient choice if you need an extra sweatshirt or some shaving cream. It also carries enough snacks, beverages, and picnic supplies to hold you over until supper.

If you need to buy someone a gift from Yosemite, you have several choices: The **Yosemite Museum Store** has Native American arts and crafts, plus related books on the subject. In the Degnan's Deli complex, **Habitat Yosemite** sells sculpture, stuffed animals, jewelry, music, videos, wind chimes, and just about anything else with a very loose connection to Yosemite. A similar shop at Yosemite Lodge is called the **Nature Shop.**

Next to the Valley Visitor Center you'll find the **Ansel Adams Gallery** (209/372-4413, www.anseladams.com), which houses a large selection of limited-edition prints and signed photographs by Ansel Adams himself, plus the work of other accomplished Yosemite artists, photographers, and craftspeople. If you'd rather take your own pictures than buy somebody else's, the gallery has an expansive collection of film, photography supplies, and camera and tripod rentals. Photography workshops are available. The gallery is open 9 A.M.–6 P.M. daily.

The Ahwahnee: At the **Ahwahnee Gift Shop,** you can purchase the Ahwahnee's very own china (a fresh set, not the one they just used for the last dinner seating). In addition, the shop has a large and varied selection of Native American art and jewelry and Yosemite art and photographs. The neighboring **Ahwahnee Sweet Shop** has more than just sweets; it's also a good bet for wines, picnic foods, film, and greeting cards.

Curry Village: For outdoor enthusiasts, the **Curry Village Mountain Shop** is a miniature version of REI or Adventure 16. This store is the real McCoy. If you've considered buying the newest kind of water purifier or the latest high-tech sleeping bag, they'll know all about them here. Prices are about the same as you'd find at any high-quality outdoor store. Curry Village also has a small grocery store, but for serious groceries, it's best to head to the Village Store.

And finally, if your shopping is of a more practical nature, there's always the **Housekeeping Camp Store,** which carries just the basics. If your cooler is out of ice, you'll find it here. If you need a few postcards, you can get those, too. If you want much else, you better head over to Curry Village or Yosemite Village.

Gas

There is no gas station in Yosemite Valley. The closest gas stations are at El Portal (12 miles) or Crane Flat (15 miles); at both spots you can pay at the pump 24 hours a day with a credit card. If your car runs out of gas in Yosemite Valley, you can get emergency gas from the **Village Garage** (209/372-8320).

Banking Services/ATM

There are no banks located in Yosemite Valley, but several automated teller machines (ATMs) are available. In Yosemite Village, there is a Bank of America ATM south of the Village Store, and an independently operated ATM inside the Village Store. In Yosemite Lodge, there is an independently operated ATM near the main registration area. In Curry Village, there is an ATM inside the grocery store.

DRIVING TOUR

Because of traffic congestion, a driving tour of the Valley is not recommended, especially in the summer months. Instead, ride the free Valley shuttle bus, or take an organized tour in an open-air tram. Or, for the more energetic, tour Yosemite Valley on the seat of a bike—your own two-wheeled steed or a rental bike obtained from Yosemite Lodge or Curry Village.

SIGHTS

The following Yosemite Valley sights are listed from west to east along the Valley floor:

Bridalveil Fall

This 620-foot waterfall is easily reached by a quarter-mile walk from the well-signed parking lot just past the Highway 41 turnoff from the Valley. The view of the fall from the west end of the parking area is stunning, and it will inspire you to take the short, paved walk to an overlook near the base of the fall. There, in spring and early summer, you will get drenched from Bridalveil's billowing spray.

El Capitan

The largest single piece of granite rock on earth, El Capitan (The Chief) towers 3,000 feet above the Valley floor. It is arguably the most famous rock-climbing site in the world. You can get a good look at this granite behemoth from El Capitan Meadow alongside Northside Drive. Many park visitors hang out in lawn chairs in this meadow, binoculars in hand, watching the daring climbers inch their way up El Cap's sheer face.

Yosemite Chapel

The Yosemite Chapel is the oldest of all the public structures still in use in Yosemite. Built under the sponsorship of the California State Sunday School Association, the small New England–style chapel held its first service on June 7, 1879. It was built near the base of the Four-Mile Trail but

was moved here in 1901. All Yosemite visitors are invited to attend services at the chapel. Non-denominational services are held Sunday mornings at 9:15 A.M. and Thursday evenings at 7 P.M. The chapel can be accessed via shuttle stop 11. For more information, phone 209/372-4831.

Lower Yosemite Fall

No visit to Yosemite Valley would be complete without a walk to the base of Lower Yosemite Fall, the bottom section of the highest waterfall in North America. The entire waterfall is 2,425 feet high; the lower section is 320 feet. It's an easy stroll of only a quarter mile to one of the most thrilling sights in Yosemite. The trail starts right across the park road from Yosemite Lodge (shuttle stop number 6).

LeConte Memorial Lodge

Built by the Sierra Club in 1903, this beautiful stone building served as the Valley's first public visitor center. It was moved from its original location in Curry Village to its present site east of the Yosemite Chapel (shuttle stop number 12). The lodge is named for Joseph LeConte, a geologist and Sierra explorer. The Sierra Club holds evening programs in summer at the lodge; they are open to all visitors and are free of charge. Phone 209/372-4542 for program details.

Ahwahnee Hotel

This National Historic Landmark in Yosemite Valley is an attraction even for people who aren't spending the night there. The Ahwahnee has several "public rooms" where you can wander around and appreciate the hotel's 1927 architecture, designed by Gilbert Stanley Underwood, stained glass windows, Native American tapestries and baskets, Turkish Kilim rugs, and paintings and artifacts from Yosemite's history. Take a walk around the Great Lounge, peek into the grand Dining Room, and buy a drink at the bar or a souvenir in one of the Ahwahnee's shops. There is a small parking lot located at the end of Ahwahnee road, or take the shuttle to stop number 3.

YOSEMITE'S WATERFALLS

Yosemite is a park well known for superlatives. Among its many bragging rights, the park's waterfalls are perhaps most famous and revered. Most geographers agree that in the list of the world's 10 tallest waterfalls, Yosemite Valley scores two positions: 2,425-foot **Yosemite Falls** at number five and 2,000-foot **Sentinel Fall** at number seven. Yosemite Falls also holds the undisputed title of the tallest waterfall in North America.

Other, less famous Valley falls boast their own impressive statistics: **Ribbon Fall** at 1,612 feet holds the title of tallest free-leaping waterfall in Yosemite Valley. Unlike Yosemite Falls, Ribbon's cascade never touches the granite wall behind it; its fall is unbroken or "free-leaping." Ribbon Fall ranks among the world's 20 tallest waterfalls.

If you want to see Yosemite Valley when its granite walls are graced by the white plumes of gushing waterfalls, you must time your trip carefully. Many a first-time Yosemite visitor has shown up in August or September and questioned why the Park Service has "turned off" the waterfalls.

Unlike at New York's famous Niagara Falls, the bureaucrats are not in charge of the water flow in Yosemite—Mother Nature is. Because the Valley's waterfalls are mostly fed by snowmelt in the high country above the Valley rim, the waterfalls are at their fullest flow in spring and early summer. Approximately 75 percent of the high country's snowmelt occurs in April, May, and June. These three months are prime time for waterfall viewing.

By late July, Yosemite Falls may be only a dribble, or it may be completely dry. Water flows year-round in only a few of the Valley's famous falls—**Bridalveil Fall, Vernal Fall, and Nevada Fall**—but their flow in late summer can be as little as five percent of what it is from April to June.

Perhaps to compensate for its ephemeral nature, Yosemite Falls has a few tricks up its sleeve that may be seen by lucky Valley visitors. In winter, a giant ice cone forms at the base of Upper Yosemite Fall. Composed of frozen spray and fallen chunks of ice, the ice cone can sometimes grow to a height of 300 feet. And on full moon nights in spring, a "moonbow" will sometimes appear around the base of Lower Yosemite Fall.

Although with the combined forces of Bridalveil, Yosemite, Vernal, and Nevada Falls, the Valley is the undisputed best place in the park for waterfall viewing, other regions of the park have their own worthy cataracts. If you're a serious waterfall lover, there's a travel strategy just for you in the *Discover* chapter.

Happy Isles

A lesser known visitor center in Yosemite Valley is found at Happy Isles (shuttle bus stop number 16). The small interpretive center has family-oriented exhibits on the natural history and geology of the Valley, including wildlife dioramas and interactive displays. Short nature trails lead from the center, including one that explores evidence of the great rockslide of 1996—a slide that completely devastated this region of the park. Happy Isles is also the trailhead for the famous hikes to Vernal and Nevada Falls and to Half Dome.

Mirror Lake

It is not hard to imagine how Mirror Lake got its name. When the lake is at its fullest, it reflects a lovely mirror image of Mount Watkins, a granite summit named for one of Yosemite's earliest photographers. The brief interpretive loop trail at Mirror Lake gives you a look into Yosemite's natural history and also its history as a world-famous park. The lake is actually a pool on Tenaya Creek that is slowly filling with sediment. By late summer each year, it looks more like a meadow than a lake, although the first winter rains fill it to the brim once more. In the 1880s the lake was dammed and a bathhouse was built on its edges; park visitors floated around its surface in small rowboats. Reach Mirror Lake's trailhead by taking the shuttle bus to stop number 17.

⋈ Half Dome

Probably the most famous icon of Yosemite is the sheared-off granite dome known as Half Dome. There are several places on the Valley floor to get a good look at this odd-looking granite formation. One is at Mirror Lake, or on the trail just beyond it, where you are standing at its base. Another is at Stoneman Meadow, across the road from Curry Village. This is a fine spot to watch the sun set on Half Dome if you can't make it up to Glacier Point. Other good spots include Tunnel View, just above the Valley on Highway 41, and almost any other high point in the park.

Recreation

HIKING

From the floor of Yosemite Valley, it's hard to fathom that hikers can scale its massive granite walls and ascend to the top of Glacier Point or the brink of Yosemite Falls. It's difficult to comprehend that a trail could take you within a few feet of Vernal or Nevada Fall without sending you tumbling into its spray, or to the polished summit of Half Dome without careening you off the edge. But the well-built trails of Yosemite Valley make these destinations accessible, despite how daunting they may look. Hiking in and around the Valley reveals so many geological and natural wonders that it is often more an exercise in suspending disbelief than in physical exertion. You just have to experience it for yourself to believe it.

So, have a hearty breakfast, fill up your water bottles and your day pack, and set out on the trail. You won't be sorry.

Upper Yosemite Fall

- Distance: 7.4 miles round-trip
- Duration: 4–5 hours
- Rating: Strenuous
- Elevation Change: 2,700 feet
- Shuttle Stop: 7
- Trailhead: Camp 4
- Directions: From Yosemite Village, drive west on Northside Drive 0.75 mile to the Yosemite Lodge parking lot on the left. Park and walk across the road to Camp 4. The Upper Yosemite Fall Trailhead is located between the parking lot for Camp 4 and the camp itself.

At 2,425 feet, Yosemite Falls is the highest waterfall in North America and the fifth highest in the world. That's why hundreds of park visitors hike this strenuous trail every day in the spring and summer. There's no feeling quite like standing at the waterfall's brink and realizing you've conquered a landmark of this magnitude.

Still, if you tucker out on this demanding climb to Upper Yosemite Fall, just remember that you always have a fallback position: you can hike only 1.2 miles one-way to the Columbia Point viewpoint, with more than 100 switchbacks and a total gain of 1,200 feet, then call it a day. The view of Yosemite Valley from Columbia Point is a stunner, and plenty of people who planned on hiking to Upper Yosemite Fall turn around here and still leave satisfied.

Those who push on are also rewarded. After a level section and then a short descent, the trail switchbacks up and up until—at 3.7 miles, and a total 2,700-foot climb—you reach the brink of Upper Yosemite Fall. Make sure you take the cutoff trail on your right to reach the falls overlook; the main trail doesn't go there. From its lip you have an amazing perspective on the waterfall's plunge, and the Valley floor far below.

If this trip hasn't provided you with enough exertion, continue another .75 mile, crossing the bridge above the falls, to Yosemite Point (6,936 feet above sea level), where you get a stunning view of the south rim of the Valley, Half Dome and North Dome, and a look at the top of Lost Arrow Spire, a single shaft of granite jutting into the sky.

© ANN MARIE BROWN

If you tire out on the long climb to the top of Upper Yosemite Fall, you can always turn around at Columbia Point, 1.2 miles from the start, which offers a tremendous view of Yosemite Valley.

Eagle Peak

- Distance: 13.4 miles round-trip
- Duration: 6–8 hours
- Rating: Very strenuous
- Elevation Change: 3,800 feet
- Shuttle Stop: 7
- Trailhead: Camp 4
- Directions: From Yosemite Village, drive west on Northside Drive 0.75 mile to the Yosemite Lodge parking lot on the left. Park and walk across the road to Camp 4. The Upper Yosemite Fall Trailhead is located between the parking lot for Camp 4 and the camp itself.

If you seek more of a challenge than the day hike to Upper Yosemite Fall, the trail to Eagle Peak delivers the same stunning destinations as the shorter trip—Columbia Point and Upper Yosemite Fall—plus an additional three miles one way to a lookout atop the highest rock of the Three Brothers formation. Not only can you see all of Yosemite from Eagle Peak, but on rare, extremely clear days you can also see the mountains and foothills of the Coast Range, 100 miles to the west.

Follow the trail notes for the hike to Upper Yosemite Fall, then after taking the spur trail to the fall's brink, backtrack .25 mile to the trail junction for Eagle Peak Trail. Follow Eagle Peak Trail northwest for 1.5 miles, then hike south for one mile through Eagle Peak Meadows. At a trail junction with El Capitan Trail, bear left for a .5-mile ascent to your final destination—the summit of Eagle Peak, elevation 7,779 feet. After completing this trip, you'll never view the Three Brothers the same way again.

Lower Yosemite Fall

- Distance: 0.5 mile round-trip
- Duration: 30 minutes
- Rating: Easy
- Elevation Change: 50 feet
- Shuttle Stop: 6
- Trailhead: Lower Yosemite Fall or Yosemite Lodge
- Directions: From Yosemite Village, drive west on Northside Drive .75 mile to Yosemite Lodge. Unless you are staying at the lodge, parking is difficult in this area, so riding the shuttle bus is recommended. The shuttle bus

DAY HIKING ESSENTIALS

Aside from the shoes on your feet, it doesn't take much equipment to go day hiking. While backpackers must concern themselves with tents, sleeping pads, pots and pans, and the like, day hikers have an easier time of it. Still, too many day hikers set out carrying too little and get into trouble as a result. Here's a list of essentials every well-equipped day hiker should carry:

1. **Food and water.** Water is even more important than food, although it's unwise to get caught without a picnic, or at least some edible supplies for emergencies. If you don't want to carry the weight of a couple water bottles, at least carry a purifier or filtering device so you can obtain water from streams, rivers, or lakes. Never, ever drink water from a natural source without purifying it. The microscopic organism *Giardia lamblia* may be found in backcountry water sources and can cause a litany of terrible gastrointestinal problems. Only purifying or boiling water from natural sources will eliminate *Giardia*.

   The new water bottle–style purifiers, such as those made by Exstream, are as light as an empty plastic bottle and eliminate the need to carry both a filter and a bottle. You simply dip the bottle in the stream, screw on the top (which has a filter inside it), and squeeze the bottle to drink. The water is filtered on its way out of the squeeze top.

   What you carry for food is up to you. Some people go gourmet and carry the complete inventory of a fancy grocery store. If you don't want to bother with much weight, stick with high-energy snacks like nutrition bars, nuts, dried fruit, turkey or beef jerky, and crackers. The best rule is to bring more than you think you can eat. You can always carry it back out with you, or give it to somebody on the trail who needs it.

   If you're hiking in a group, each of you should carry your own food and water just in case someone gets too far ahead or behind.

2. **A Yosemite map.** Never count on trail signs to get you where you want to go. Signs get knocked down or disappear with alarming frequency, due to rain, wind, or park visitors looking for souvenirs. Ideally, you should carry a more detailed map than the free one given out at park entrance stations. A variety of maps are for sale at park visitor centers and stores. Suggested hiking maps include those published by Tom Harrison Maps or Trails Illustrated.

3. **Extra clothing.** On Yosemite's trails, conditions can change at any time. Not only can the weather suddenly turn windy, cloudy, or rainy (it can even snow!), but your own body conditions also change: You'll perspire as you hike up a sunny hill and then get chilled at the top of a windy ridge or when you head into shade. Because of this, cotton fabrics don't function well in the outdoors. Once cotton gets wet, it stays wet. Generally, polyester blend fabrics dry faster. Some high-tech fabrics will actually wick moisture away from your skin. Invest in a few items of clothing made from these fabrics and you'll be more comfortable when you hike.

   Always carry a lightweight jacket with you, preferably one that is waterproof and wind-resistant. If your jacket isn't waterproof, pack along one of the $2, single-use rain ponchos that come in a package the size of a deck of cards (available at outdoors stores or drug stores). If you can't part with two bucks, carry an extra-large garbage bag. In cooler temperatures, or when heading to a mountain summit even on a hot day, carry gloves and a hat as well.

4. **Flashlight.** Just in case your hike takes a little longer than you planned. Mini-flashlights are available everywhere, weigh almost nothing, and can save the day. A popular variety

are the tiny "squeeze" LED flashlights, about the size and shape of a quarter, which you can clip on to any key ring. Some turn on and off with a small switch, so you don't have to squeeze them for extended periods. (The Photon Micro-Light is a popular brand.) Whatever kind of flashlight you carry, make sure the batteries work before you set out on the trail. Take along an extra set of batteries and an extra bulb, or simply an extra flashlight or two. You never know when the darn things will run out of juice.

5. **Sunglasses and sunscreen.** You know the dangers of the sun, and the higher the elevation, the more dangerous it is. Wear sunglasses to protect your eyes and sunscreen with a high SPF on any exposed skin. Put on your sunscreen 30 minutes before you go outdoors so it has time to take effect. If you are going to hike a lot in Yosemite, you might want to invest in a good wide-brimmed hat. Wearing lip balm with a high SPF is also a smart idea.

6. **Insect repellent.** Several kinds of insect repellent now come with sunscreen, so you can combine items 5 and 6 and put on one lotion instead of two. Many types of insect repellent have an ingredient called DEET, which is extremely effective but also quite toxic. Children should not use repellent with high levels of DEET, although it seems to be safe for adults. Many other types of repellent are made of natural substances, such as lemon oil. What works best? Everybody has an opinion. If you visit White Wolf's meadows in the middle of a major mosquito hatch, it often seems like nothing works except covering your entire body in mosquito netting. For typical summer days outside of a hatch period, find a repellent you like and carry it with you.

7. **First aid kit.** Nothing major is required here unless you're fully trained in first aid, but a few supplies for blister repairs, an ace bandage, an antibiotic ointment, and an anti-inflammatory medicine such as ibuprofen can be valuable tools in minor and major emergencies. If anyone in your party is allergic to bee stings or anything else in the outdoors, carry their medication.

8. **Swiss Army-style pocket knife.** Carry one with several blades, a can opener, scissors, and tweezers.

9. **Compass.** Know how to use it. If you don't know how, take a class or get someone to show you.

10. **Emergency supplies.** Ask yourself, "What would I need if I had to spend the night outside?" Aside from food, water, and other items previously listed, here are some basic emergency supplies that will get you through an unplanned night in the wilderness.

   • *A lightweight space blanket.* Get a blanket or sleeping bag made of foil-like Mylar film designed to reflect radiating body heat. These can also make a great emergency shelter and weigh and cost almost nothing.

   • *A couple packs of matches and a candle.* Keep these in a waterproof container (or ziploc bag), just in case you ever need to build a fire in a serious emergency.

   • *A whistle.* If you ever need help, you can blow a whistle for a lot longer than you can shout.

   • *A small signal mirror.* It could be just what you need to get found if you ever get lost.

11. **Fun stuff.** These items aren't necessary, but they can make your trip a lot more fun: a wildflower and/or bird identification book, a small pair of binoculars, a fishing license and lightweight fishing equipment, and an extra pair of socks (these can feel like heaven halfway through a long hike).

will drop you off at the official Yosemite Fall trailhead, which is a bus stop along Northside Drive (no parking available here).

It's so short you can hardly call it a hike, and the route is perpetually crawling with people. Still, the trail to Lower Yosemite Fall is an absolute must for visitors to Yosemite Valley. When the falls are roaring with snowmelt in the spring and early summer, they never disappoint even the most seasoned hiker.

The Lower Yosemite Fall Trail received a major face-lift in 2004. The old parking lot was removed, the trail was extended so that it now makes a pleasant loop, and new, modern restrooms and facilities were added. The only problem is that now that the parking lot is gone, most visitors can't figure out where to leave their car and start the hike. Your best bet is to ride the shuttle bus from other points in the Valley, which will deposit you at the "new" Yosemite Fall Trailhead, which is an attractive log structure right alongside Northside Drive (no parking here). If you want to drive your own car, you'll have to leave it in the Yosemite Lodge parking lot (good luck finding a space in the summer months). Either way, once you get started the trail is simple enough to follow. With about 10 minutes of walking, you are standing at the footbridge below the falls. In the spring you can get soaking wet from the incredible mist and spray. By late summer, on the other hand, the fall often dries up completely. If at all possible you should plan your trip for sometime between April and June. Seasoned waterfall lovers visit on full moon nights in spring, when they are sometimes treated to the appearance of "moonbows" in the lower fall.

Mist Trail to Top of Vernal Fall

- Distance: 3.0 miles round-trip
- Duration: 1.5–2 hours
- Rating: Moderate
- Elevation Change: 1,050 feet
- Shuttle Stop: 16
- Trailhead: Happy Isles
- Directions: From the Arch Rock Entrance Station on Highway 140, drive 11.6 miles east to the day-use parking lot at Curry Village.

Board the free Yosemite Valley shuttle bus to Happy Isles, stop number 16. In winter when the shuttle does not run, you must hike from Curry Village, adding two miles to your round-trip. Trails may be closed in winter; call to check on weather conditions.

This is a hike that every visitor to the Valley should take, even if it's the only trail they walk all year. Despite how crowded the trail inevitably is, this is a world-class hike to one of the most photographed waterfalls in the world. Make your trip more enjoyable by starting as early in the morning as possible, before the hordes are out in full force.

Start by taking the free Yosemite shuttle bus to the trailhead at Happy Isles. (Or you can add on an extra mile each way by hiking from the day-use parking area in Curry Village to Happy Isles.) The partially paved route is an easy 500-foot climb to the Vernal Fall footbridge, then a very steep tromp up the seemingly endless granite staircase to the top of the falls. Although many people hike only to the footbridge, 0.8 mile from Happy Isles, it's definitely worth the extra effort to push on another 0.5 mile to reach the top of Vernal Fall.

Doing so means ascending another 500 feet on the Mist Trail's famous granite stairway, which frames the edge of Vernal Fall. You will come so close to the plunging spray that you may feel as if you are part of it. Sometimes you are—hikers are frequently drenched in spray and mist, particularly in springtime. Remember to bring a rain poncho if you don't like getting wet.

When you reach the fall's brink, you can stand at the railing and watch the dizzying flow of rushing whitewater as it tumbles downward. This is a trip you have to do at least once in your life.

Mist and John Muir Loop to Nevada Fall

- Distance: 6.8 miles round-trip
- Duration: 3–4 hours
- Rating: Strenuous
- Elevation Change: 2,600 feet

- Shuttle stop: 16
- Trailhead: Happy Isles
- Directions: From the Arch Rock Entrance Station on Highway 140, drive 11.6 miles east to the day-use parking lot at Curry Village. Board the free Yosemite Valley shuttle bus to Happy Isles, stop number 16. In winter when the shuttle does not run, you must hike from Curry Village, adding two miles to your round-trip. Trails may be closed in winter; call to check on weather conditions.

You can hike either the John Muir Trail or the Mist Trail to reach Yosemite's classic Nevada Fall, but the best choice is to make a loop out of it by hiking up on the Mist Trail, then down partway or all the way on the John Muir Trail. Both trails join above and below Nevada Fall, so you have some options. By hiking uphill rather than downhill on the Mist Trail's treacherous granite staircase, you can look around at the gorgeous scenery every time you stop to catch your breath. The John Muir Trail is somewhat less scenic, especially in its lower reaches, so save it for the way back downhill.

Start at Happy Isles and follow the signed trail to the footbridge over the Merced River, below Vernal Fall. After crossing the bridge, stay close along the river's edge on the Mist Trail for 1.2 miles to the top of Vernal Fall. If it's spring or early summer, make sure you bring your rain gear for this stretch, or you'll get drenched by spray.

Catch your breath at the top of Vernal Fall, then continue along the river's edge, still following the Mist Trail. In 0.5 mile the path crosses the river again, then climbs another steep mile to the brink of Nevada Fall. Total elevation gain to the top of the 594-foot-tall falls is 2,600 feet. It's a strenuous ascent, but when you get to walk this close to two world-class waterfalls, who's complaining?

For your return trip, cross the footbridge above Nevada Fall and follow the John Muir Trail to loop back. As you descend, check out the great view of Nevada Fall with Liberty Cap in the background. This is one of the most famous scenes in Yosemite Valley.

HALF DOME'S FIRST MOUNTAINEERS

Anyone making the epic trek to the bald summit of 8,836-foot Half Dome will find themselves at some point in their journey wondering about those who have gone before. Perhaps the most interesting of the Half Dome mountaineers is the man who did it first—despite Josiah Whitney's claim that the summit would never be conquered. "Never has been, and never will be trodden by human foot," said the famous geologist in 1868.

The man who proved Whitney wrong was George Anderson, a Scotsman who worked in Yosemite Valley as a laborer from 1870 until his death in 1884. In October 1875 he drilled holes and inserted a series of bolts and pegs into the hard granite on the dome's back side. Upward he worked, standing on each new bolt as he drilled in the next, a few feet higher. At 3 P.M. on October 12, he made it to the top, then carefully made his way back down. A few days later he ascended Half Dome again, this time with a huge coil of rope on his back. He knotted one end to a bolt on the summit, then started downward and secured the remainder of the rope to each of the bolt "stairsteps." This rope ladder was the predecessor of today's steel cables.

Within a few weeks, several other brave souls made the ascent to the summit of Half Dome, using Anderson's rope ladder to pull themselves up. Galen Clark and John Muir were two of the first dozen people, as well as pioneer woman Sally Dutcher, who goes down in history as the first woman to climb Half Dome.

Note that you can cut back over to the Mist Trail at Clark Point, just above Vernal Fall, if you so desire. That way you get a second chance to see Vernal Fall and hike the Mist Trail's granite staircase.

Mirror Lake Loop
- Distance: 4.6 miles round-trip
- Duration: 2 hours
- Rating: Easy

- Elevation Change: 80 feet
- Shuttle Stop: 17
- Trailhead: Mirror Lake Junction
- Directions: From the Arch Rock Entrance Station on Highway 140, drive 11.6 miles east to the day-use parking lot at Curry Village. Board the free Yosemite Valley shuttle bus to Mirror Lake Junction, stop number 17.

Thousands of Yosemite visitors walk to Mirror Lake every day in summer, but the vast majority of them miss the best part of this hike. Sure, the lake itself is interesting to see, especially in early summer when its still waters produce a lovely reflective image of the granite domes above. But if you leave the lake behind and head back a mile or more into Tenaya Canyon, you will find quiet, solitude, and the kind of nature experience that most visitors seek in Yosemite.

To start the hike, ride the free shuttle from Curry Village parking lot to Mirror Lake Junction. (Or walk there, if you wish, adding 1.5 miles round-trip to your hike.) From the bus stop, walk 0.5 mile on pavement to Mirror Lake and check out the interpretive signs at its edges. Then follow the foot trail up Tenaya Creek for 1.5 miles, circling back when you reach the footbridge. Views of Half Dome, Mount Watkins, and neighboring granite walls are spectacular, and the forested creek canyon presents an intimate amphitheater in which to view them. Find a boulder somewhere, have a seat, and take in the show.

Half Dome

- Distance: 17.0 miles round-trip
- Duration: 8–10 hours
- Rating: Very strenuous
- Elevation Change: 4,800 feet
- Shuttle Stop: 16
- Trailhead: Happy Isles
- Directions: From the Arch Rock Entrance Station on Highway 140, drive 11.6 miles east to the day-use parking lot at Curry Village. Board the free Yosemite Valley shuttle bus to Happy Isles, stop number 16.

No argument about it, Half Dome is one of

those once-in-your-life-you-gotta-do-it hikes. Just be sure you know what you're in for before you set out on this epic trail. You're in for 17 miles round-trip, a 4,800-foot elevation gain, and an unbelievable amount of company. During the summer about 500 people a day make the trek to Half Dome's summit. The vast majority do it as a day hike, not a backpacking trip (although that is an option if you can get a permit). All day-hikers should be sure to bring a load of water and food with them. You'll be handing it out to others who are not so well prepared, as well as gulping it down yourself.

Follow either the John Muir Trail or the Mist Trail from Happy Isles to the top of Nevada Fall, then go left and enter Little Yosemite Valley, where backpackers make camp. At 6.2 miles the John Muir Trail splits off from the Half Dome Trail and you head left for Half Dome. Everything usually goes smoothly until you reach the steel cables that run 200 yards up the back of the dome, at which point you'll start praying a lot and wishing there weren't so many other hikers on the cables with you. Do some soul-searching before you begin the cable ascent—turning around is not an option once you're halfway up. Pick up a pair of old work gloves from the pile at the base of the cable route; you'll need them to protect your hands as you pull yourself up the cables. It takes two hands and two feet to haul yourself up 440 feet of nearly vertical granite. Unless you somehow managed to get here before the rest of the Half Dome hopefuls, the going will be slow as you wait for the masses ahead to make the ascent. When you reach the top, the views are so incredible that you forget all about your tired arms and feet.

Inspiration and Stanford Points

- Distance: 7.6 miles round-trip
- Duration: 4 hours
- Rating: Strenuous
- Elevation Change: 2,250 feet
- Trailhead: Wawona Tunnel
- Directions: From the Arch Rock Entrance Station on Highway 140, drive 6.3 miles east and turn right at the fork for Highway 41/Wa-

wona/Fresno. Continue 1.5 miles to the parking lots on either side of the road just before the Wawona Tunnel. The trailhead is on the left (south) side of the road.

Many consider the view from Inspiration Point at the entrance to the Wawona Tunnel to be one of the finest scenes in Yosemite—a wide panorama of Yosemite Valley, El Capitan, Half Dome, and Bridalveil Fall. If you like this view, you might want to see more of it by taking this hike from the trailhead at the vista point parking lot. The Pohono Trail leads uphill on a moderately steep grade until at 1.3 miles it reaches the "old" Inspiration Point. This is where the road to Yosemite Valley went through in the days before the Wawona Tunnel, and the view is now largely obscured by trees. Keep climbing, however, because with another 1,000 feet of elevation gain, you will cross Meadow Brook and reach the left cutoff trail for Stanford Point. You're 3.8 miles from the trailhead and you've climbed 2,200 feet, but your reward is an eagle's-eye view of the valley floor, 3,000 feet below, and a vista to the east of Half Dome and all its granite cousins. This stretch of the Pohono Trail is a dependable workout, and the trail is never crowded with hikers.

Bridalveil Fall

- Distance: 0.5 mile round-trip
- Duration: 30 minutes
- Rating: Easy
- Elevation Change: None
- Trailhead: Bridalveil Fall
- Directions: From the Arch Rock Entrance Station on Highway 140, drive 6.3 miles east and turn right at the fork for Highway 41/Wawona/Fresno. Turn left almost immediately into the Bridalveil Fall parking lot.

Bridalveil Fall is right up there with Lower Yosemite Fall as a must-do walk for visitors (including non-hikers) to Yosemite Valley. Like that other famous waterfall walk, the path to Bridalveil Fall is paved with people. But the best thing about this waterfall is that unlike other falls in Yosemite Valley, Bridalveil runs

year-round. It never dries up and disappoints visitors. The walk to its overlook is short and nearly level; the trail delivers you to a small viewing area about 70 yards from the fall. You can look straight up and see Bridalveil Creek plunging 620 feet off the edge of the south canyon wall. In high wind the fall billows and sways; if you are lucky you might see rainbows dancing in its mist. Another bonus is that your position at the Bridalveil overlook is such that if you do an about-face, you have an excellent view of Ribbon Fall flowing off the northern Yosemite Valley rim. Ribbon Fall is the highest single drop in the park at 1,612 feet, but it only flows in the earliest months of spring.

Four-Mile Trail

- Distance: 9.6 miles round-trip
- Duration: 5–6 hours
- Rating: Strenuous
- Elevation Change: 3,200 feet
- Trailhead: Four-Mile
- Directions: From the Arch Rock Entrance Station on Highway 140, drive 9.5 miles east to the Four-Mile Trailhead, located next to mile marker V18 on the right side of Southside Drive. Park in the pullouts along the road.

Although the vast majority of Yosemite visitors get to Glacier Point by driving there, your arrival at this dramatic overlook is somehow made more meaningful if you get there under your own power. That means hiking the Four-Mile Trail all the way up from the Valley floor, gaining 3,200 feet in 4.8 miles—not four miles, as the name indicates. The trail is partially shaded and makes a terrific day hike with an early-morning start. A bonus is that in the summer months the snack stand on Glacier Point is open during the day, so you can hike to the top with a light day pack, then order whatever you want for lunch. Go ahead, have the chili dog—the hike back is all downhill.

From Glacier Point you have unobstructed views of just about every major landmark in Yosemite Valley, most notably Half Dome, Basket Dome, Yosemite Falls, Vernal and Nevada Falls, and the Valley floor far, far below you.

BACKPACKING

Although most of the hiking trails in Yosemite Valley are used mainly by day-hikers, several trails begin in the Valley and lead out of it to overnight camping destinations. Far and away the most popular of these is the busy trail from Happy Isles. Every day in summer, a swarm of day-hikers follows the trail to Vernal and Nevada Falls, and many continue on for the long trek to Half Dome.

Backpackers can make the trip to **Half Dome** easier by splitting it into two days. A designated camp is located at Little Yosemite Valley, 4.7 miles from the start and about 3.5 miles from Half Dome's summit. Permit reservations for this trail are nearly impossible to come by, and you might not want to have one anyway: Little Yosemite Valley is one zoo of a backpacking camp. A better option is to continue past this camp on the John Muir Trail—heading toward **Tuolumne Meadows**—or follow the other fork toward **Merced Lake.** Backpackers are permitted to set up camp as long as they are two miles from Little Yosemite Valley, and either of these options offers some spectacular scenery.

If you want to get farther away from people, take the **Snow Creek Trail** from the Mirror Lake area up and out of the Valley. Of all the pathways that ascend to the Valley's high walls, this one is the steepest. It heads up switchbacks toward Snow Creek, then gains the north rim of the Valley near North Dome and Basket Dome. You must travel at least four miles beyond the Valley floor before camping.

Although you can't camp at the top of Yosemite Falls, you can take a backpack trip up the **Yosemite Falls Trail,** visit the waterfall's exhilarating brink, and then continue on to **Eagle Peak, El Capitan,** or **North Dome.** As long as you are four miles from the Valley floor and one mile from the top of Yosemite Falls, you can make camp.

No matter where you decide to go, remember that if you want to strap on a backpack and spend the night in Yosemite's wilderness, you must have a permit (209/372-0308).

Also keep in mind that backpackers should always use hard plastic bear canisters to store their food for overnight trips. Hanging food from a tree is ineffective in Yosemite.

BIKING

The **Yosemite Valley bike path** is the best way to escape the car trap in the Valley. With 12 miles of smooth, paved bike paths to ride, you can see the entire Valley without once having to worry about where to park. Didn't bring your bike? No problem; you can rent one at Yosemite Lodge or Curry Village Recreation Center (209/372-1208 or 209/372-8319) for about $8 per hour. They have bikes for men, women, and children, plus baby strollers and three-wheel strollers. Helmets come with all rentals. Remember that bikes are not allowed on any dirt trails in Yosemite Valley; keep your bike on the paved paths and roads and you won't risk getting a ticket.

You can start your bike tour of Yosemite Valley from just about anywhere. The bike path runs right by the Yosemite Lodge and Curry Village and parallels the stretch of Northside and Southside Drive that runs between the two lodging facilities. If you wish, you can make stops at the trailheads for Lower Yosemite Fall and Mirror Lake. Remember that if you are on a rental bike, you are not permitted to ride your bike down the hill from Mirror Lake; there are too many pedestrians in this area, and the park's insurance company wants to make sure no one gets hurt. Go ahead and ride your bike up this hill, then park it in the bike rack and take a walk around Mirror Lake. Then walk your bike back down. When you reach the flat stretch at the bottom, go ahead and start pedaling.

One of the best lengths of the looping bike path is on the western end, where it crosses the picturesque Swinging Bridge over the Merced River and provides a straight-on view of billowing Yosemite Falls. Now isn't this better than driving a car?

ROCK CLIMBING

Yosemite is well known as a mecca for rock climbers. But even experienced climbers who

© ANN MARIE BROWN

Miniaturized rock climbers and very big walls—that's the way the equation works for Yosemite Valley climbers.

have tackled high walls in parks and public lands near their homes are sometimes daunted when they get their first look at Yosemite Valley's massive vertical walls. If you don't have experience with granite crack climbing or traditional climbing, you might want to consider **Yosemite Mountaineering School and Guide Service** (209/372-8344), which conducts seminars and classes for beginning, intermediate, and advanced climbers from mid-April–Oct. each year. Classes meet daily at 8:30 A.M., and equipment rentals are available. Private guided climbs are available for up to three people and start at $221 per day. The school is located in the Curry Village Mountain Shop.

If you decide to set out on your own, be aware that the limited number of "easier grade" climbs in Yosemite are quite popular. If you don't start early in the morning, you will be forced to wait in line. The greatest number of climbers hit the Valley in May, and then again in September and October. The walls are less crowded in the summer, when the temperatures are high.

Experienced climbers visiting the Valley for the first time should head for the **Royal Arches** (just east of the Ahwahnee Hotel), the southeast face of **Half Dome,** and a climb known as "Munginella" near **Yosemite Falls.** These climbs are mostly rated 5.6 and 5.7, but many find them more difficult than their ratings indicate. El Capitan is *definitely* not recommended for first-timers, even the "experienced" ones.

Those who enjoy **bouldering** will find plenty of it on the rocks around Camp 4. Other popular bouldering areas are found near Cathedral Rocks (directly across from El Capitan, on the south side of the Valley and just east of Bridalveil Fall) and the Ahwahnee Hotel.

If you'd rather watch rock climbers than be a rock climber, congratulate yourself on your level-headedness and head to El Capitan Meadow, where with a pair of binoculars you can watch the slow progress of climbers heading up the face of **El Capitan.** Ever since this 3,000-foot rock face was conquered in the 1950s, a succession of bold climbers have inched their way to the top. **Swan Slab** across from Yosemite Lodge (between the Lower Yosemite Fall parking lot and Camp 4) is another good place to watch climbers strut their stuff.

RAFTING

On any warm early-summer day in Yosemite you can take a drive up to Glacier Point, look down over its mighty edge, and see a flotilla of rafters drifting lazily downstream on the Merced River. Lazily? Yes indeed. This is not river rafting as most people think of it. "River meandering" would be a better term.

Still, rafting is one of the greatest ways to see Yosemite Valley in early summer—no traffic jams, no watching out for pedestrians, just lying on your back, trailing a few fingers in the water and gazing up at the granite walls as you float by. Sadly, the rafting season in Yosemite Valley is painfully short. The water level isn't usually low enough to be safe until late May or early June, and the season ends when the river gets too low and the rafts start scraping the river bottom, which is usually in late July.

Inflatable rafts are rented at Curry Village Recreation Center, which is open daily 10 A.M.– 4 P.M. ($13.50 per person; rafts can hold up to six people); the put-in point is nearby. Rental rafts come complete with life jackets and paddles, although you are unlikely to need either one. You float three miles downstream, then ride a shuttle bus back to your starting point. The whole adventure takes three to four hours. Children under 50 pounds are not permitted on rafts. For more information on raft rentals, phone 209/372-8319.

While you're out on the water, remember to protect the beautiful Merced River. If you choose to disembark, do so only on sandy beaches or gravel bars. Stay away from vegetated streambanks to protect the delicate riparian habitat.

If, on the other hand, you'd like to try true, shoot-the-rapids, adrenaline-pumping, thrills-and-chills river rafting, you need only drive a few miles outside of Yosemite Valley to the section of the Wild and Scenic **Mer-**

ced River below El Portal. This is one of the most popular river rafting runs in the Sierra, mostly because it packs a whole lot of excitement into a one-day trip. The 16 miles of river below El Portal include several Class IV and Class III rapids, interspersed with calm sections where rafters can catch their breath. For one-day trips, the put-in is near Red Bud Picnic Area and the take-out is at Railroad Flat, below Briceburg Visitor Center. Some two-day trips are also offered by local outfitters, most running from Red Bud to Lake McClure, but these are for more experienced rafters. Adventurous beginners and intermediates can handle the one-day trip on the Merced.

The rafting season begins around mid-May, depending on snow runoff. Several private companies offer rafting trips daily from May through July, when the water level usually drops too low. Trips include lunch, parking, wetsuits when the water is cold, and a round-trip bus shuttle to and from the river. For more information, contact Zephyr Whitewater, 800/431-3636 or www.zrafting.com; Whitewater Voyages, 800/488-7238, or whitewatervoyages.com; or OARS Inc., 800/346-6277 or www.oars.com.

FISHING

Planning on going trout fishing in Yosemite Valley? Don't waste your time. Oh, sure, plenty of people drop a line in the Merced River, then sit down and admire the scenery. But if you want to actually catch fish, head to any other area of the park, or just outside the park boundaries, and you'll have a lot greater chance at success. The **Merced River in Yosemite Valley** has been hit with a ton of fishing pressure over the course of many decades, and the few trout that live here are wary and smart.

At one time, however, fish were plentiful in Yosemite Valley. The Ahwahneechee Indians who lived in the Valley ate native rainbow trout as a major part of their diet. When white settlers arrived in the Valley, they saw that its river fishing prospects were an opportunity to lure

© ANN MARIE BROWN

This lazy rafting trip on the Merced River doesn't involve any whitewater, but it's a fun way to see Yosemite Valley.

in tourist dollars. By the late 1800s, brown, brook, and cutthroat trout were planted in the Merced River, much to the delight of the white sport fishermen who frequented the Valley. The cutthroat and brook trout didn't last, but the browns did.

To make the planting of fish easier, in 1926 a hatchery was built at Happy Isles, and it operated until 1959. Many thousands of rainbow and brown trout were raised at that hatchery and released in the park. During the Great Depression, hundreds of families camped and lived in the Valley and ate trout every day. It cost only a few dollars to stay the entire summer in the park, and the fish were free.

Today, the waters of Yosemite Valley are home to some of California's most challenging brown trout, plus a small population of native rainbows. Although the planting of brown trout was suspended throughout the entire park in 1948, brown trout still thrive in the Merced and are occasionally caught, but only by the wiliest of anglers. Generally the best luck is had very early in the morning or just before nightfall.

By 1971 all fish plants were discontinued in Yosemite's streams and rivers, and the number of fish including native rainbow trout declined dramatically. With more and more visitors coming to Yosemite Valley in the 1970s and 1980s, and few of them practicing catch-and-release fishing, the trout population never recovered. Today the remaining native rainbow trout are protected by catch-and-release-only regulations. Brown trout may still be taken because they are a non-native population.

If you decide to fish in Yosemite Valley, make sure you know the rules. Trout season runs from the last Saturday in April until November 15 in all park rivers and streams. (Yosemite's lakes may be fished year-round, but it isn't easy to get to them through 10 feet of snow.) A valid California fishing license is required for all anglers 16 and older and must be visibly displayed on an outer layer of clothing above the angler's waist. Licenses can be purchased at the Village Sport Shop in Yosemite

Village, the Wawona Store, and the Tuolumne Meadows Store.

From Happy Isles downstream to the Pohono Bridge, no bait fishing is allowed—it's artificial flies and lures with barbless hooks only. The same applies as the river leaves the park, from the Pohono Bridge downstream to the Foresta Bridge in El Portal. All rainbow trout must be released; a limit of five brown trout may be taken per day. No fishing is permitted from park bridges.

To learn more about the history of fishing in Yosemite Valley, or to get some tips on how to go about it, join the 90-minute seminar called "How to Catch Fish at Yosemite," led by a Yosemite Concession Services naturalist. This walk-and-talk lesson departs from the Village Sport Shop (209/372-1286) on summer days.

If you're willing to drive a few miles out of the park on Highway 140, fishing opportunities abound. The Merced River below Yosemite, from El Portal to the Briceburg area, is filled with beautiful wild rainbow trout. Much of the river is a designated native trout area, which means only barbless hooks are permitted, and fishing is catch-and-release only. Guided fishing trips and fly-fishing instruction in the Merced River are offered by **Yosemite Guides,** 209/379-2231, 877/425-3366, or www.yosemiteguides.com. The company provides full-day fly-fishing trips that include lessons, equipment, and lunch. The first person pays $225, and each additional person pays $50. Half-day trips are also available.

If you would rather fish the Merced on your own, the El Portal area just outside the Arch Rock entrance is best in the autumn. Flies with barbless hooks are required. Anglers can also head farther west on the river to the Briceburg Visitor Center. Cross over the river on the old bridge, then leave your car near one of the primitive campgrounds. You can hike along the dirt road (the old bed of the Yosemite Railroad) as far as you wish, then drop your line in any large and inviting pool. Brown and rainbow trout are found in these waters. Since this is a designated wild trout area, all the usual rules apply.

SWIMMING

From mid-July to late September, plenty of swimming holes can be found along the Merced River's sandy beaches on the Valley's east end, especially near Housekeeping Camp and the Pines campgrounds in an area called **Sentinel Beach.** The sandy bars found here are ideal for lounging by the river and also the most ecologically sound spots for entering and exiting the water. In the interest of protecting the Merced's fragile shoreline, always stay off grassy, meadowy areas.

In spring and early summer, swimming anywhere in the Merced River is a very bad idea— the current can be much stronger than it looks. All summer long the same goes for the pools above Vernal and Nevada Falls, Ilillouette Fall, and Upper Yosemite Fall. Although the water looks tempting after a hot and sweaty hike, even in late summer the current above these waterfalls can be deceptively swift—even deadly.

Guests staying at Yosemite Lodge and Curry Village can enjoy the use of their swimming pools free; nonguests can use the pools for a $2 fee. The Ahwahnee Hotel also has a swimming pool, but it is off-limits to nonguests.

HORSEBACK RIDING

Feeling aerobically challenged? Let Trigger do the walking for you. **Yosemite Valley Stables** offers horseback rides April–Nov., in a variety of prices and configurations. Two-hour and four-hour rides ($40–55) depart daily; all-day rides and pack trips can also be arranged ($80 and up). The two-hour ride, the most popular among park visitors, heads up and around Mirror Lake. The four-hour ride climbs out of the Valley on the John Muir Trail to scenic Clark Point, between Vernal and Nevada Falls. The all-day ride heads to Glacier Point or Half Dome.

For half-day and all-day rides, saddlebags are provided, in which you can store your picnic lunch, water, a camera, a jacket, and maybe a carrot or an apple for Trigger, since he's doing all the work. Children must be at least seven years old and 44 inches tall. Helmets are required for all riders and are available free of charge. The maximum a rider may weigh is 225 pounds. The stables are located in Yosemite Valley, right next to the entrance to North Pines Campground (shuttle stop number 18). Phone 209/372-8348 for reservations.

WINTER SPORTS

From early Nov.–March, weather permitting, Curry Village's outdoor **ice skating rink** is open daily (209/372-8341). Where else can you practice your figure eights with a head-on view of Half Dome? Sessions are held in the afternoons and evenings on weekdays and from morning until evening on weekends ($7 adults, $5 children). Ice skate rentals are available for $3–4. If you find yourself falling down more often than performing graceful pirouettes, head for the warming hut's fire pit and snack stand and treat yourself to a cup of hot chocolate. The skating rink has a long history in Yosemite Valley; it was built in 1928 by the Yosemite Park and Curry Company.

Snowshoe rentals are available at the Curry Village Mountain Shop. The Valley rarely has enough snow for snowshoeing except in the canyon beyond Mirror Lake. You may have to carry your snowshoes as you walk up the paved road to the lake, then strap them on when you hit the trail. A four-mile loop can be made from Mirror Lake up Tenaya Canyon. It's a delightful surprise to see this area so quiet and serene, compared to the summer when it is crowded with tourists.

Alternatively, you can take your rental snowshoes up to the **Tuolumne or Merced Groves of Giant Sequoias** and meander among the giants. If you don't want to snowshoe by yourself, check the free Yosemite newspaper for guided events. In the winter months, park rangers often lead snowshoe walks in the Valley or in the groves.

Also, if you are staying in Yosemite Valley but would like to take advantage of the downhill skiing and snowboarding opportunities at **Badger Pass Ski Area** on Glacier Point Road, know that you don't have to drive your car and risk icy conditions on the roads. Buses leave from Yosemite Lodge every morning and return in the afternoon.

ENTERTAINMENT AND EVENTS

The wealth of ranger programs, educational seminars, and events in Yosemite Valley is enough to make the average visitor's head spin. There is simply no way to do it all, so leaf through your free copy of the Yosemite newspaper and see what most appeals to you. The following is a sampling of what is available:

Ranger Talks and Walks

Ranger walks take place every day in Yosemite Valley. Typical subjects include Yosemite's Native Americans, bears, trees, and geology. Walks leave from various locations—campgrounds, visitor center, Happy Isles, other Valley trailheads—at around 10 A.M. and 2 P.M. each day. Ranger-led sit-down talks are held year-round at the Lower Pines Campground Amphitheater at 7 P.M. on Saturday. Check the Yosemite weekly newspaper for locations.

Evening Programs

Led by people other than park rangers, evening programs include slide shows, films, and talks on subjects ranging from Ansel Adams to rock climbing to the building of the Ahwahnee Hotel. Evening programs are usually going on simultaneously at the Curry Village Amphitheater and Yosemite Lodge Amphitheater. Most programs start at 7:30 or 8:30 P.M. Information, times, and locations for these talks are published in the Valley newspaper and posted at the Visitor Center.

LeConte Memorial Lodge Programs

Run by the Sierra Club, the LeConte Memorial Lodge (shuttle stop 12, 209/372-4542) offers a variety of evening programs in summer, many with a conservation bent. Typical offerings include slide shows and talks on John Muir, Hetch Hetchy Valley, Frederick Olmsted, and more general programs on national

parks. LeConte Lodge also runs a series of programs geared toward children and families. Call ahead or check the free Yosemite newspaper for a schedule.

Yosemite Theater

A variety of programs are scheduled at the Yosemite Theater, but actor **Lee Stetson** always steals the show. Stetson has been portraying naturalist John Muir at the Yosemite Theater for more than 20 years. He acts out some six different rotating programs. In each one he puts on a convincing Scottish brogue and becomes the voice of Muir for an hour or so. The theater sets the scene perfectly: it is small, intimate, and casual enough for hiking boots.

Stetson's wife, Connie, has her own show at the Yosemite Theater. **Connie Stetson** plays Sarah Hawkins, a pioneer woman contemplating her fourth marriage after her first three husbands have died.

The theater is located behind the Valley Visitor Center. Tickets are $8 for adults and $4 children 12 and under, available at any tour desk in Yosemite. You can also buy them outside the theater right before showtime, providing that seats are still available. Shows are year-round.

Photography Walks

The Ansel Adams Gallery sponsors one- and two-hour photography walks a few mornings each week. A photography walk is a guided walk with an experienced photographer/teacher. The "walkers" carry their cameras with them and learn how to take better Yosemite landscape/nature photos. The walks are free and available year-round, but space is limited. Sign up at the gallery or phone 209/372-4413.

Art Activity Center

At the east end of Yosemite Village, next to the Village Store, is the Art Activity Center (209/372-1442), where, unbeknownst to most park visitors, free art classes are offered from spring to fall each day, 10 A.M.–2 P.M. Art supplies are sold at the center. Classes include such topics as nature sketching, watercolors, and silk-screening.

Winter Events at the Ahwahnee

Heading the bill each winter at Yosemite's grand Ahwahnee Hotel is the annual **Bracebridge Dinner,** a lavish 17th-century English Christmas celebration featuring more than 100 minstrels and a seven-course feast. The event, a loose adaptation of an episode from Washington Irving's *Sketch Book,* has been held every year at the Ahwahnee since 1927. The three-hour program features Middle Age music, Renaissance rituals, traditional yuletide decorations throughout the dining room, and plentiful food, song, and mirth. Even though a seat for this extravaganza costs more than $300, tickets sell out fast. For reservations, phone 559/252-4848 or visit www .yosemitepark.com. Seats for Bracebridge usually sell out the spring before but, through cancellations, sometimes become available later.

Although the annual Bracebridge Dinner is the most famous, other popular winter events at the Ahwahnee Hotel include the Vintners' Holidays and Chefs' Holidays, in which California's finest winemakers and chefs strut their stuff. An annual New Year's Eve dinner and dance is also held, in which guests ring out the old and ring in the new in classic Ahwahnee style. Reservations for this black-tie event are available by lottery; phone 559/252-4848 or visit www.yosemitepark.com.

Wawona and Glacier Point

To the Native Americans who traveled between the foothills and Yosemite Valley, Wawona was the halfway point on their journey. They called it Pallachun, meaning "a good place to stay." This popular Indian encampment later became the site of a wayside inn built by Galen Clark. Today it is home to the historic Wawona Hotel and a private community of homes, many of which can be rented by park visitors. Now, as then, Wawona is a good place to stay.

It's also a good place to visit, with fishing and swimming holes in the South Fork of the Mer-ced River, an excellent hiking trail to Chilnu-alna Falls, the natural spectacle of the Mariposa Grove of Giant Sequoias, and an opportunity to get a glimpse back in time at the Pioneer Yosemite History Center. Plus, Wawona offers convenient access to Glacier Point, home of what may well be the grandest viewpoint in the West. The commanding vista from Glacier Point takes in all the major granite landmarks of Yosemite Valley and the surrounding high country. For many park visitors, it is the single most memorable spot in Yosemite.

Must-Sees

Look for **M** to find the sights and activities you can't miss.

M **Tunnel View and Inspiration Point:** The breathtaking vista of Yosemite Valley from Inspiration Point was made famous by an Ansel Adams photograph. See it via an easy 10-minute drive from the Valley floor (page 51).

M **Glacier Point:** This spectacular 7,214-foot granite precipice overlooks Yosemite Valley, Half Dome, and the High Sierra. For many park visitors, the view from Glacier Point is the highlight

© ANN MARIE BROWN

Taft Point

of their Yosemite vacation. If you can time it right, don't miss watching the sunset from here (page 51).

M **Sentinel Dome and Taft Point:** Two short hikes to these two overlook points start at the same trailhead, just one mile west of Glacier Point. Both hikes are short and easy enough for families to handle; each is 2.2 miles round-trip (page 52).

M **Badger Pass Ski Area:** Only winter visitors to Yosemite will get to experience the joys of Badger Pass, which include short or nonexistent lift lines, relatively inexpensive lift tickets, and plenty of recreation options for non-skiers (page 53).

M **Mariposa Grove of Giant Sequoias:** Yosemite's largest grove of giant sequoia trees, the largest living trees on earth by volume, is found near the southern entrance to the park. Casual visitors can wander through the lower grove to see some of the largest and most famous trees; more serious hikers can trek to the upper grove as well. Those who don't want to walk at all can opt to ride on an open-air tram (page 54).

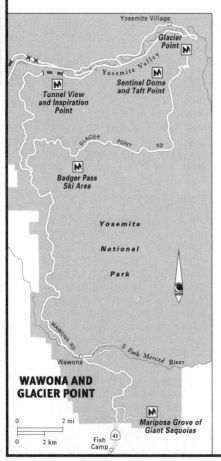

Exploring Wawona and Glacier Point

WEATHER AND SEASONS

The settlement of Wawona and the Mariposa Grove of Giant Sequoias share approximately the same elevation (5,000 feet) and the same weather: warm, mild days and cooler nights. Summer temperatures reach the mid-80s (Fahrenheit) during the day and drop into the 50s at night. Both areas receive a few feet of snow in winter, which often closes the road to the Mariposa Grove. (Still, this is a fine time to strap on your snowshoes or skis and enter the grove under your own power.) Highway 41 stays open year-round, but remember to carry chains for travel in the winter season.

Glacier Point, at 7,214 feet elevation, is covered with deep snow and most of its road is closed late Oct.–late May each year. This snowpack is cause for celebration at Badger Pass Ski Area, however, six miles east on Glacier Point Road (the road is plowed to the ski area, but you should carry chains at all times). Temperatures at Glacier Point during the summer and fall months are generally mild, ranging between 60°F and 80°F during the day, and 40°F to 60°F at night. Thunderstorms occur occasionally, most often on August afternoons.

VISITOR CENTER

The Wawona Information Station has two locations: in Hill's Studio at the Wawona Hotel and at the Pioneer Yosemite History Center in Wawona. Both stations provide information on interpretive activities and programs in the southern portion of the park. Books, maps, and wilderness permits are available. In summer, a museum is open in the upper portion of the Mariposa Grove of Giant Sequoias, with exhibits that detail the fascinating ecology of the big trees.

SHUTTLES AND TOURS

During the summer months, a free shuttle bus runs from the Wawona Store to the Mariposa Grove. Unless you are visiting the grove very early in the morning, before the daily crowds arrive, you should ride the shuttle and avoid the hassle of trying to park your car at the grove.

Once you are in the grove, you can elect to take the **Mariposa Big Trees Tram Tour** (209/375-1621), a one-hour interpretive tour in an open-air tram (daily, spring to fall, weather permitting). The first tram leaves from the Mariposa Grove parking lot at 9 A.M. and the last one departs at 5 P.M. Trams run every 15–20 minutes, and you may disembark at any point and reboard the tram later. Many people ride the tram uphill to the upper grove and museum and then hike back downhill. Buy tour tickets in advance at the Yosemite Lodge Tour Desk (inside the lodge, 209/372-1240), or the Curry Village or Yosemite Village ticket kiosks. Tickets can also be purchased at the Mariposa Grove ($16 adults, $10 children).

Also note that if you are staying in Yosemite Valley, you can leave your car there and ride a tour bus to the Mariposa Grove and/or Glacier Point. Phone the Yosemite Lodge Tour Desk for details.

A private company outside the park also provides bus tours to the southern portion of the park. **Yosemite Sightseeing Tours** (559/658-8687, www.yosemitetours.com) takes visitors from Oakhurst, Bass Lake, and Fish Camp to the Mariposa Grove, Wawona's Pioneer Yosemite History Center, Glacier Point, and even Yosemite Valley. Guides provide a running commentary on the sights; frequent photo stops are made. Fees are $58–66 for adults.

SERVICES
Shopping and Supplies

The **Wawona Store** (summer hours 8 A.M.–8 P.M., shorter winter hours) is a surprisingly well-stocked grocery store where you'll find all the necessary picnic and camping supplies, plus film and batteries for your camera, postcards, and the like. An ATM is also available, and a

YOSEMITE MOUNTAIN SUGAR PINE RAILROAD

Although most visitors to Yosemite take tours on foot, or by bus or open-air tram, a more unusual tour can be taken on a vintage narrow-gauge steam train.

Just three miles south of the park in Fish Camp is the home of the Yosemite Mountain Sugar Pine Railroad, an attraction that brings to life memories of long-gone logging camps. On the same route that sturdy flumes once transported lumber from Fish Camp to Madera, visitors today can ride an authentic narrow-gauge steam train, called the Logger, through scenic woodlands.

Along the four-mile stretch of track, beautifully restored and maintained engines pull cars with benches carved from giant trees through a wooded stretch of Sierra National Forest. In days gone by, this was the train that carried massive sugar pine logs into the mills, to be sawed into timbers and boards to build the growing local communities. The narrated ride lasts about one hour and often includes a stop in the forest where riders can enjoy a picnic and a stroll. You might want to keep an eye on your wallet, though; on warm summer evenings you have to watch out for masked bandits who stage hold-ups on horseback—complete with blazing six-shooters.

Tours usually leave daily 11 A.M.–3:30 P.M. in summer. On Wednesday and Saturday nights, a 6 P.M. train ride comes complete with a New York steak barbecue dinner and music and singing around a campfire. Also available are daily tours on Jenny railcars, powered by antique Model A Ford gas engines. The railcars were once used to provide transportation for logging and track repair crews.

For more information, or to reserve a seat on the Logger, contact Yosemite Mountain Sugar Pine Railroad, 56001 Highway 41, Fish Camp; 559/683-7273; www.ymsprr.com.

post office is right next door. Another small grocery store is about a mile east on Chilnualna Falls Road, in the residential area of Wawona.

The **Wawona Golf Shop** (209/375-6572, summer hours 9 A.M.–5 P.M., shorter winter hours) offers no surprises: it has golf equipment and rentals, clothing, and film. A snack stand allows hungry golfers the chance to fuel up before hitting the green. The shop is located at the end of the Wawona Annex by the hotel.

After driving all the way out to Glacier Point, you may be happy to find the **Glacier Point Snack Stand and Gift Shop** (summer hours 9 A.M.–7 P.M., closed the rest of the year). The shop is housed in a handsome log cabin and has a variety of souvenir-type trinkets, plus a good selection of guidebooks on Yosemite. Snacks and drinks are available at the snack stand in the same building.

Gas

Wawona has a gas station (near the Wawona Store) where you can pay at the pump 24 hours a day with a credit card. You can also buy gas a few miles outside the park in Fish Camp. There is no gas anywhere near Glacier Point.

DRIVING TOUR
Driving from Yosemite Valley

Plan on about one hour one-way for the drive from Yosemite Valley to Glacier Point. If you are continuing on to the Mariposa Grove, plan on another 30 minutes to backtrack down Glacier Point Road, plus about 30 minutes to the big trees. From Yosemite Valley, it is a 14-mile drive to Chinquapin junction, much of which leads through an area badly burned in a 1989 fire. With a left turn at Chinquapin (restrooms available here), it's 16 miles to Glacier Point, through some lovely forested terrain. After a visit to the scenic overlook (snacks and restrooms available), retrace your tire treads back down Glacier Point Road, then turn left (south) on Highway 41 and head for Wawona, 15 miles distant. Stop here if you wish and visit Wawona's Pioneer Yosemite History Center. A small store and restrooms are available. Then continue three miles farther south on Highway 41 to the left (east) turnoff for the Mariposa Grove of Giant Sequoias, located just before Yosemite's south entrance. The grove is two miles down this road. In the peak summer season, it is best to ride a free shuttle bus from the Wawona Store to the Mariposa Grove instead of driving your car. Traffic congestion can be quite severe on the Mariposa Grove entrance road and at its parking lot.

Driving from Yosemite's South Entrance

From Yosemite's southern entrance station, it is a two-mile drive to the Mariposa Grove of Giant Sequoias. (Turn right or east almost immediately after you pass through the entrance station.) After a hike or a tour through the trees, continue three miles north on Highway 41 to Wawona. From Wawona, it is a 15-mile drive to Chinquapin, then a right turn and a 16-mile drive to Glacier Point.

SIGHTS

⚑ Tunnel View and Inspiration Point

Don't miss this parking area as you drive out of the Valley on your way to Wawona or Glacier Point. (The turnout is just before you enter the Wawona Tunnel.) The vista of Yosemite Valley here is a standout; you may recognize it from a famous Ansel Adams photograph. The view of Bridalveil Fall, El Capitan, and Half Dome is sublime.

⚑ Glacier Point

Often referred to as "the grandest view in all the West," Glacier Point is a 7,214-foot overlook with a vista of Yosemite Valley, Half Dome and all its granite neighbors, and the High Sierra. The overlook area at Glacier Point was completely restored and refurbished in 1999, resulting in a beautiful amphitheater for evening ranger talks, an imposing log cabin that houses a snack stand and gift shop, a large and clean restroom, plus all the historic highlights of the point: the stone-constructed Geology Hut that faces Half Dome and the rock railings that look

view of Half Dome from inside the Geology Hut on Glacier Point

© ANN MARIE BROWN

UNDERSTANDING GIANT SEQUOIAS

Sierra redwoods, or *Sequoiadendron giganteum*, are the largest living things on earth by volume—not by height alone, but by a combination of height and girth. Whereas coast redwoods can grow 365 feet tall and up to 18 feet across, giant sequoias grow "only" 310 feet tall, but up to 30 feet across (or 12 feet in diameter). Imagine that a tree this large grows from a seed the size of a single flake of oatmeal.

The sequoia's immense girth often makes the strongest impression on visitors. Walking around the base of one of these giants is a slow task. If your hiking partner heads in one direction and you head in the opposite, it will be much longer than you expect until you meet on the far side.

The oldest sequoias are around 3,000 years old, but they are not the oldest trees on Earth. That honor goes to the ancient bristlecone pines that live east of Yosemite in the White Mountains, Death Valley National Park, and Nevada. (The oldest known bristlecone pine is 4,600 years old; the oldest known giant sequoia is a mere 3,200 years old.)

Giant sequoias once ranged across the globe, but now they are found only in a narrow strip of the western Sierra Nevada, 250 miles long and 15 miles wide, at elevations ranging from 4,000 to 7,000 feet. A total of 75 scattered groves are found in this belt. By all appearances, the sequoia seems to be slowly disappearing from the earth. Some of the Sierra's existing groves are quite healthy and will continue to reproduce,

most likely for many more centuries. Other groves have only a few older trees and not enough young ones to replace the ancients when they die. The northernmost groves of sequoias, such as a small grove in Placer County near Foresthill, California, seem to be in the greatest danger of extinction. The largest, healthiest groves of sequoias are located south of Yosemite in Sequoia and Kings Canyon National Parks and Giant Sequoia National Monument.

The big trees have many interesting characteristics, but one of their most unusual features is that their bark can grow up to two feet thick. This makes the sequoia extremely insect- and fire-resistant. In fact, fire is essential to the sequoia life cycle: it takes extreme heat to open up the sequoia cone and spread its tiny seeds along the forest floor. Sequoia seedlings survive best in a forest that experiences frequent small fires, which thin out competing trees and allow sunlight and other resources to go to the young sequoias. Animals also aid in the sequoia life cycle: The chickaree fells sequoia cones, drops them to the ground, then eats the fleshy part, leaving the cones' seeds to germinate on the forest floor.

Yosemite's three sequoia groves are each distinctly different in character. Here is a brief guide to their treasures:

Mariposa Grove: The largest and most popular of Yosemite's sequoia groves, this grove contains about 500 mature trees, each more than 10 feet in diameter, spread out over 250 acres. To

out over Vernal and Nevada Falls and the Merced River canyon. A big hotel once stood on top of Glacier Point, but it burned to the ground in 1969 and was never rebuilt.

Washburn Point

Located just .75 mile before Glacier Point on Glacier Point Road, Washburn Point has an equally dizzying view of Half Dome and the granite country of the High Sierra. Many visitors bypass this overlook in their hurry to get to Glacier Point, but Washburn Point is worth

a stop in its own right. Although it doesn't have much perspective on Yosemite Valley, it has the best possible view of Vernal and Nevada Falls. The overlook was named for the Washburn brothers, who owned the original Wawona Hotel and drove visitors by stagecoach to this spot in the 1870s.

Sentinel Dome and Taft Point

These two spectacular overlooks cannot be seen from the car; each requires a hike of 1.1 miles one-way. But if you have the energy and

hike around the entire Mariposa Grove is a six-mile trek that requires a good amount of climbing. For this reason, the National Park Service operates open-air, motorized tram tours for nonhikers. Some of the most spectacular trees can be seen by walking a much shorter loop, which passes the Fallen Monarch, the Grizzly Giant, and the California Tunnel Tree.

The Fallen Monarch, which fell more than 300 years ago, was made famous by an 1899 photograph of the U.S. Cavalry and their horses standing on top of it. The Grizzly Giant, the largest tree in this grove at 210 feet tall and 31 feet across at its base, is the most photographed sequoia in Yosemite. Its massive, gnarled branches appear to be sculpted by some unseen hand. One particularly impressive branch measures almost seven feet in diameter—larger than the trunks of most trees.

The California Tunnel Tree was tunneled in 1895 so stagecoaches could drive through. In the early 1900s it was used as a "substitute" for the more famous Wawona Tunnel Tree, located in the upper portion of the Mariposa Grove, which was frequently inaccessible due to winter storms. Today you can walk through the California Tree. The Wawona Tree collapsed in 1969 at the ripe age of 2,200 years. Most likely it died prematurely; the 26-foot-long, 10-foot-high tunnel carved into its base weakened its ability to withstand that year's heavy winter snowfall.

Merced Grove: The Merced Grove is Yosemite's quietest, least visited sequoia grove, accessible only by hiking three miles round-trip. Its 20 sequoias were "discovered" in 1833 by a group of explorers headed by Joseph Walker who were looking for the best route through the Sierra Nevada. Most likely, local Indian tribes had long known about the location of the big trees. (Some historians believe that the Walker Party passed through the Tuolumne Grove, not the Merced Grove, or possibly both groves, on their exploration. Members of the party reported seeing huge trees "16 to 18 fathoms around the trunk," which could have belonged to either grove.)

Tuolumne Grove: This grove of about 25 large sequoias is quite popular because of its convenient location near Crane Flat and the short walk required to reach its big trees. The Tuolumne Grove is situated along the old Big Oak Flat Road, a paved, six-mile historic road/trail that was open to cars up until 1993. The one-mile hike to the grove is downhill on the way in and uphill on the way back. The grove's biggest attraction is the Dead Giant, a sequoia stump that was tunneled in 1878 so that wagons, and later automobiles, could drive through. A short distance farther is a small picnic area, adjacent to a quarter-mile loop trail through the forest. One immense fallen tree in the Tuolumne Grove provides the opportunity to walk alongside a sequoia, and in doing so gain a solid appreciation for the massive height and girth of these trees.

can afford the time, either of these destinations will round out your trip to Glacier Point. Both trails lead from the same parking lot but head in opposite directions. Sentinel Dome, a granite dome at 8,122 feet, offers a breathtaking view of Yosemite Falls and a 360-degree panorama of granite peaks and domes. Taft Point's view is completely different: a head-on look at El Capitan and a stomach-churning view of the Yosemite Valley floor, 3,000 feet below. Hold on to the railing while you peer over it.

Badger Pass Ski Area

Although in the summer months, the turnoff for Badger Pass is unmarked and barely even noticeable, in the winter it is the most obvious (and only) destination on Glacier Point Road. The road is plowed for six miles, up to the ski area's driveway, but two feet beyond it is piled several feet high with snow.

If you want to travel farther on Glacier Point Road, the ski area is your trailhead, and your mode of travel will be skis or snowshoes. But there is also plenty to do right at Badger Pass, which has the distinction of being the oldest ski resort in California. The resort offers downhill skiing, cross-country skiing, snowshoeing, snowboarding, and "snow tubing," or sledding on inner tubes. Even if you don't feel like playing in the snow, Badger Pass is a fine place to go for lunch on a sunny winter's day—buy a hamburger and a soda, sit outside on the deck, and watch the legions of skiers carve S-turns through the white stuff.

Wawona Hotel and Golf Course

The historic Victorian-style Wawona Hotel makes a lovely sight alongside Highway 41 just south of Wawona. You can stop in for breakfast, lunch, or dinner, or just drop by for a look at the old photographs in the lobby area. Across the street from the Wawona Hotel is a real oddity for a national park—a nine-hole golf course (209/375-6572), complete with a pro shop! The historic golf course was built in 1917, and the National Park Service considers it a part of the cultural history of the park. If you feel like playing a round, greens fees are about $15 for nine holes, $24 for 18 holes.

Pioneer Yosemite History Center

A collection of historic buildings, many of which were relocated from other places in the park, the Pioneer Yosemite History Center in Wawona brings Yosemite's history to life. In the summer months, docents dress in period costumes and lead visitors on free tours inside the buildings. (You can walk around their exteriors on your own; an interpretive brochure is available.) The structures are from different periods of Yosemite's history—a U.S. Cavalry office, the bakery the Degnans used in the Valley to bake bread, a Wells Fargo station that served stagecoach passengers, and a few homesteads.

To reach the Pioneer Yosemite History Center, visitors cross the South Fork of the Merced River by walking through a covered bridge. The bridge was built in 1857 by the Washburn brothers, who established a tourist facility here in what later became Wawona. Although the elaborate bridge served a practical purpose—the covered deck and truss portion protected the bridge from the winter weather—it may

have been built more to satisfy the Washburns' longing for the familiar sights of their family home on the East Coast. The Washburn brothers owned the Wawona Hotel and most of the land in this area until 1932, when the National Park Service purchased it.

Mariposa Grove of Giant Sequoias

These magnificent ancient trees are the largest living things on earth, as measured by total volume. They are very big and very old. The giant sequoias you see in the Mariposa Grove, at the two other groves in Yosemite, and in other regions of the Sierra Nevada have been living since the beginning of Western history.

The Mariposa Grove is divided into two areas—upper and lower. Most casual visitors stroll through the lower grove, where several famous trees are found, or ride the open-air tram for a longer tour through both groves. A short walk from the parking lot, the Grizzly Giant is the showpiece of the Mariposa Grove—a tree that is 2,700 years old and, at 210 feet tall and 31 feet across, is the largest sequoia in the park. (It's not the largest sequoia in the world, however; that honor falls to the General Sherman Tree in nearby Sequoia National Park.)

More willing hikers will want to wander around both the upper and lower groves (six miles round-trip with a 1,200-foot elevation gain). The upper grove has an interesting museum (open in summer only) with exhibits on the history of this region and mankind's long fascination with the giant sequoia. The museum stands at the site of a cabin that belonged to Galen Clark, the first official guardian of Yosemite. Nearby is an unusual sequoia known as the Telescope Tree, whose hollowed-out trunk creates a telescoping effect if you stand inside it and look upward.

The Mariposa Grove is prone to overcrowding on summer days. Plan your visit for early in the morning or very late in the day to avoid long lines of cars. Or better yet, park at the Wawona Store and ride the free shuttle bus to the Mariposa Grove. RVs or trailers longer than 23 feet are not allowed on the road from 9 A.M. to 6 P.M. in summer; visitors with these types of vehicles must ride the free shuttle. Once you're in the grove, tram tours cost $16 for adults; taking a hike through the giants is free. In winter and early spring, the Mariposa Grove access road is not plowed of snow. Visitors can park near the park's south entrance station and snowshoe or walk two miles into the grove.

Recreation

HIKING

Day-hikers will find that the Glacier Point region offers a wealth of spectacular hikes that range from easy jaunts for families to longer treks for more seasoned hikers. Although the trails on Glacier Point Road are popular, hiking here sets you free from the masses of Yosemite Valley. The same is true for trails in the Wawona area, with the exception of the busy paths through the Mariposa Grove of Giant Sequoias.

The following eight hikes on Glacier Point Road are listed in the order that their trailheads appear along the road, assuming you are traveling from west to east (Chinquapin junction to Glacier Point). Following these eight trails are three hikes in the Wawona area.

McGurk Meadow and Dewey Point
- Distance: 2.0–7.0 miles round-trip
- Duration: 1–4 hours
- Rating: Easy to moderate
- Elevation Change: 300 feet
- Trailhead: McGurk Meadow
- Directions: From Highway 41, turn east on Glacier Point Road and drive 7.5 miles to the McGurk Meadow Trailhead on the left. Park in the pullout about 75 yards farther up the road.

Some trails seem to capture the essence of Yosemite, and the McGurk Meadow Trail is one of those. The trailhead is the first one you reach as you wind along Glacier Point Road to spectacular Glacier Point. It's worth a stop to take the short walk through a fir and pine forest to pristine McGurk Meadow, a mile-long meadow crossed by a footbridge over a small feeder creek. A quarter mile before the meadow the trail passes an old pioneer cabin, still standing in half-decent repair.

You can turn around at the meadow for a short and easy trip, or you can follow the trail until it connects to the Pohono Trail, which traverses Yosemite's south rim. An ideal destination is Dewey Point, a spectacular promontory with an unforgettable view of Yosemite Valley, located just off the Pohono Trail. That option turns this hike into a seven-mile round-trip.

Bridalveil Creek
- Distance: 3.2 miles round-trip
- Duration: 1.5 hours
- Rating: Easy
- Elevation Change: 70 feet
- Trailhead: Ostrander Lake
- Directions: From Highway 41, turn east on Glacier Point Road and drive 8.9 miles to the Ostrander Lake Trailhead on the right.

Maybe the best time to hike to Bridalveil Creek is immediately after visiting Bridalveil Fall. After a short walk from Glacier Point Road through a regenerated forest fire area, you wind up at the edge of Bridalveil Creek, a babbling brook that seems far too tame to produce the giant waterfall downstream. It's a great lesson for children, as is the abundance of new growth in the burned areas of the forest. To make the trip, follow the Ostrander Lake Trail from Glacier Point Road for 1.4 miles. This stretch is almost completely level and framed by colorful bunches of lupine in midsummer. Where the trail splits, take the right fork toward Bridalveil Creek. You reach it in less than 0.25 mile. The stream is so peaceful here that there is no bridge to cross—it's just an easy rock hop by midsummer. Pick a spot along its banks and

© ANN MARIE BROWN

Dewey Point on the Pohono Trail offers one of the finest viewpoints of Yosemite Valley.

spend some time counting the wildflowers, or watch the small, darting trout.

Ostrander Lake

- Distance: 12.5 miles round-trip
- Duration: 6–7 hours
- Rating: Strenuous
- Elevation Change: 1,600 feet
- Trailhead: Ostrander Lake
- Directions: From Highway 41, turn east on Glacier Point Road and drive 8.9 miles to the Ostrander Lake Trailhead on the right.

While many people take short day hikes from Glacier Point Road, a longer 12.5-mile trip to Ostrander Lake may better suit your taste. The trail is surprisingly easy considering the number of miles; the first half is quite level. Although many backpackers set up camp near Ostrander Lake's shores, it also makes a fine day-hiking destination. The wide blue lake, set at 8,580 feet, is the site of the stone Ostrander Ski Hut, used by cross-country skiers in the winter. Although the trail (really an old road) begins in a regenerated forest fire area, it traverses a typical high country landscape

of firs, pines, and, as you ascend, granite. You gain 1,600 feet along the way, most of it in the final three miles to the lake. The culmination of the climb occurs nearly six miles out as you reach the trail's highest point, a saddle on top of 8,700-foot Horizon Ridge. You are rewarded with excellent views of Half Dome, North Dome, Basket Dome, and Liberty Cap. This is a fine place to catch your breath. From here, the lake is less than 0.5 mile farther. On summer days, bring your swimsuit and a book and plan to spend a few hours on Ostrander's sand- and boulder-lined shore.

Sentinel Dome

- Distance: 2.2 miles round-trip
- Duration: 1 hour
- Rating: Easy
- Elevation Change: 400 feet
- Trailhead: Taft Point/Sentinel Dome
- Directions: From Highway 41, turn east on Glacier Point Road and drive 13.2 miles to the Taft Point/Sentinel Dome Trailhead on the left.

It's hard to believe you can get so much for

so little, but on the Sentinel Dome Trail you can. The granite dome is located about a mile west of Glacier Point, and its elevation is 1,000 feet higher than the point's. Views from the dome's summit extend a full 360 degrees. A short and nearly level walk leads you to the base of the dome, and a 100-yard climb up its smooth granite backside brings you to its summit. There you are greeted by stunning vistas in all directions, including an unusual perspective on Upper and Lower Yosemite Falls. This is one of the best places in Yosemite to watch the sun set. To make a longer excursion, you can easily combine this hike with the hike to Taft Point and the Fissures, which starts from the same trailhead but heads in the opposite direction.

Taft Point and the Fissures

- Distance: 2.2 miles round-trip
- Duration: 1 hour
- Rating: Easy
- Elevation Change: 250 feet
- Trailhead: Taft Point/Sentinel Dome
- Directions: From Highway 41, turn east on Glacier Point Road and drive 13.2 miles to the Taft Point/Sentinel Dome Trailhead on the left.

It's not so much the sweeping vista from Taft Point that you remember, although certainly you could say that the views of El Capitan, Yosemite's north rim, and the Valley floor are stunning. What you remember is the incredible sense of awe that you feel, perhaps mixed with a little fear and a lot of respect, as you peer down into the fissures in Taft Point's granite—huge cracks in the rock that plunge hundreds of feet down toward the valley. One of the fissures has a couple of large boulders captured in its jaws; they're stuck there waiting for the next big earthquake or ice age to set them free. After a brief and mostly forested walk, you come out to the metal railing at the edge of Taft Point's cliff, where you can hold on tight and peer down at the valley far, far below. If you have kids with you or anyone who is afraid of heights, be sure to keep a tight handhold on them.

Pohono Trail

- Distance: 13.0 miles one-way
- Duration: 6–8 hours
- Rating: Very strenuous
- Elevation Change: 4,300
- Trailhead: Glacier Point
- Directions: From Highway 41, turn east on Glacier Point Road and drive 15.7 miles to Glacier Point. Park and walk toward the main viewing area across from the cafe and gift shop. Look for the Pohono Trail sign about 150 feet southeast of the cafe, on your right.

If you can arrange a shuttle trip, the Pohono Trail from Glacier Point downhill to its end at Wawona Tunnel is worth every step of its 13 miles. The two ends of the trail have the best drive-to viewpoints in all of Yosemite, and in between you are treated to dozens of other scenic spots, including Sentinel Dome at 1.5 miles, Taft Point at 3.8 miles, and four bird's-eye lookouts over the valley floor: Inspiration, Stanford, Dewey, and Crocker Points. Starting at Glacier Point and ending at Wawona Tunnel, you'll cover a 2,800-foot descent, but there are some "ups" along the way, too, such as the stretch from Glacier Point to Sentinel Dome, and between Bridalveil Creek and Dewey Point. The trail stays on or near Yosemite Valley's southern rim the entire way except for one major detour into the woods to reach the bridge across Bridalveil Creek.

Bring along a good map, because many of the trail's best offerings are just off the main path. If you don't take the short spur routes to reach them, you'll miss out on some spectacular scenery. Note: The view of Yosemite Falls from the Pohono Trail in front of Sentinel Dome is the best in all of Yosemite. For best overall vista along the trail, it's a toss-up between Glacier Point, Taft Point, and Dewey Point.

Panorama Trail

- Distance: 8.5 miles one-way
- Duration: 4–5 hours
- Rating: Moderate to strenuous
- Elevation Change: 3,900
- Trailhead: Glacier Point

Wawona and Glacier Point

• Directions: From Highway 41, turn east on Glacier Point Road and drive 15.7 miles to Glacier Point. Park and walk toward the main viewing area across from the cafe and gift shop. Look for the Panorama Trail sign about 150 feet southeast of the cafe, on your right.

The Panorama Trail follows a spectacular route from Glacier Point to Yosemite Valley, heading downhill most of the way, but you must have a shuttle car waiting at the end or it's one heck of a long climb back up. A great option is to take the Yosemite Lodge tour bus for one leg of the trip; call 209/372-1240 to reserve a seat.

The aptly named Panorama Trail begins at Glacier Point, elevation 7,214 feet. You switchback downhill, accompanied by ever-changing perspectives on Half Dome, Basket Dome, North Dome, Liberty Cap, and, in the distance, Vernal and Nevada Falls. You will gape a lot. After passing Illilouette Fall and ascending a bit for the first time on the trip, continue eastward to the Panorama Trail's end near the top of Nevada Fall. Turn right to reach the top of the fall and have a rest at the overlook, then continue downhill on the Mist Trail on the north side of the river. After a view-filled descent along the north side of Nevada Fall, you'll cross the river in 1.4 miles and walk alongside lovely Emerald Pool on your way to the top of Vernal Fall. Enjoy the show here, then tromp down the granite staircase on the busy trail back to Happy Isles.

Note that the route has a 3,200-foot elevation loss over its course, but there is also a 760-foot climb after you cross Illilouette Creek. Also be forewarned that while the starting miles of the trip are quite tranquil, the final two miles by Vernal Fall can be a parade of people.

Illilouette Fall

• Distance: 4.0 miles round-trip
• Duration: 2 hours
• Rating: Easy to moderate
• Elevation Change: 1,200 feet
• Trailhead: Glacier Point
• Directions: From Highway 41, turn east

© ANN MARIE BROWN

Illilouette Fall is a 320-foot freefall that roars with snowmelt in early summer.

on Glacier Point Road and drive 15.7 miles to Glacier Point. Park and walk toward the main viewing area across from the cafe and gift shop. Look for the Panorama Trail sign about 150 feet southeast of the cafe, on your right.

Those who can't afford the time to hike the entire Panorama Trail should at least hike this out-and-back trip on the top portion of the route. Glacier Point is where you start, and the bridge above Illilouette Fall becomes your destination, but what happens in between is sheer magic. Hiking this upper portion of the Panorama Trail is like staring at a life-size Yosemite postcard. As you walk, you'll feel as if you've become one with the magnificent panorama of Half Dome, Basket Dome, North Dome, Liberty Cap, and far-off Vernal and Nevada Falls. The trail is downhill all the way to Illilouette Fall, which means you have a 1,200-foot elevation gain on the return trip. The path is extremely well graded, though, so even children can make the climb. After viewing the waterfall from a trailside overlook, walk another 0.25 mile and stand on the bridge perched just above its 370-foot drop.

Wawona Meadow Loop

- Distance: 3.2 miles round-trip
- Duration: 1.5 hours
- Rating: Easy
- Elevation Change: None
- Trailhead: Wawona Meadow
- Directions: From the park's south entrance station on Highway 41, drive north for two miles to the trailhead just south of the golf course and across the road from the Wawona Hotel.

Sometimes you just want to take a stroll in the park, and the Wawona Meadow Loop is exactly that. Many hikers ignore this trail because of its proximity to the Wawona Golf Course, but they are missing out on an easy, pleasant meander. On this level trail (a former stage road), you can see terrific wildflowers in early summer and enjoy the good company of butterflies as you take a lazy stroll. From the signed trailhead across the road from the Wawona Hotel, hike to your left on the dirt road, following the split rail fence. At the end of the meadow the old road crosses the stream and returns to the hotel on the north side of the golf course. If you wish, you can even bring your dog or ride your bike on this trail. If you're staying at the Wawona Hotel, you can hike from there, crossing the Wawona Road on your way out and back.

Chilnualna Falls

- Distance: 8.2 miles round-trip
- Duration: 4–5 hours
- Rating: Strenuous
- Elevation Change: 2,200 feet
- Trailhead: Chilnualna Falls
- Directions: From Highway 41 at Wawona, turn east on Chilnualna Falls Road. Drive 1.7 miles and park in the lot on the right side of the road. Walk back to Chilnualna Falls Road and pick up the single-track trail across the pavement.

Are you ready to climb? It's good to be men-

tally prepared for this hike, which includes a steady four-mile uphill, gaining 2,400 feet to reach the top of Chilnualna Falls. Pick a nice, cool day because this trail is in the lower-elevation part of Yosemite. Your nose will be continually assaulted with the intoxicating smell of bear clover, which together with manzanita and oaks makes up the majority of the vegetation along the route. Halfway up you get a great view of Wawona Dome (elevation 6,897 feet) from a granite overlook. This is a great place to take a break and stretch your hamstrings. Shortly thereafter you glimpse a section of Chilnualna Falls high up on a cliff wall, still far ahead. The trail leads above the brink of the fall's lower drop to a series of higher cascades. Keep hiking until you reach the uppermost cascade, which consists of five pool-and-drop tiers just 100 yards off the granite-lined trail. You'll want to spread out a picnic here before you begin the long descent back to the trailhead.

Mariposa Grove

- Distance: 2.0–6.4 miles round-trip
- Duration: 1–3 hours
- Rating: Easy to moderate
- Elevation Change: 400–1,200 feet
- Trailhead: Mariposa Grove
- Directions: From the park's south entrance station on Highway 41, turn east on the Mariposa Grove access road and drive two miles to the parking area. The road may be closed in winter. In summer, visitors are sometimes required to take a free mandatory shuttle bus to the Mariposa Grove parking lot. The shuttle bus leaves from the Wawona store.

The Mariposa Grove is the largest of the three groves of giant sequoias in Yosemite National Park. That's why in summer the parking lot fills up and people wait in line in their cars to see the hundreds of big trees here (and on the busiest days, you will be required to ride a shuttle bus to the trailhead). The star tree in the Mariposa Grove is the Grizzly Giant, with a circumference of more than 100 feet. At approximately 2,700 years old, it's one of the oldest known giant sequoias. If you want to see only the most famous trees in the grove, including the Grizzly Giant, take the well-signed two-mile hike through the lower grove and turn around at the signs pointing to the upper grove. If you hike the entire lower and upper grove, you will cover 6.4 miles of trail. One surprise to first-time visitors is the motorized open-air trams that run through the grove, which are ideal for people who don't want to hike. Some visitors choose to ride the tram to the top of the grove, then hike back downhill for a one-way trip of six miles.

BACKPACKING

Some of the best, and least crowded, backpacking opportunities in Yosemite are found in the southern portion of the park. Many excellent trips start in Sierra National Forest lands just outside the park boundary (Clover Meadow, Upper Chiquito, and Granite Creek), then head into the remote southern region of Yosemite—a land completely unreachable by car or day hiking. The most popular of these paths is the **Chiquito Pass Trail,** which leads to the Chain Lakes, Buena Vista Crest, and the Clark Range.

From Glacier Point Road, backpackers head to **Ostrander Lake,** or beyond it to Hart Lake. The **McGurk Meadow Trail** leads day hikers and backpackers to the meadow and beyond to Dewey Point; backpackers can set up camp near Bridalveil Creek on the Valley's south rim. Longer trips from Glacier Point Road's **Mono Meadow Trailhead** include a loop through Merced Pass and around the Buena Vista Crest, or a loop to the Ottoway Lakes, through the peaks of the Clark Range, and then north to Washburn Lake and Merced Lake.

A very popular trail for both day hikers and backpackers is the **Panorama Trail** from Glacier Point. While day hikers use this trail to drop down to the Valley, backpackers can use it as a route to Half Dome, or head out toward the Merced Lake High Sierra Camp.

From Wawona, backpackers can head up above Chilnualna Falls to **Buena Vista Peak.** A popular 40-mile, five-day loop in this region visits a series of high mountain lakes: Crescent, Johnson, Royal Arch, Buena Vista, and Chilnualna.

Your best bet for more information about backpacking trips in this region is the Wawona or Yosemite Valley wilderness permit offices (209/372-0740). Remember that to spend the night in Yosemite's wilderness, you must have a permit. Also understand that backpackers must take bear precautions. Ideally, you will use hard plastic bear canisters to store your food for overnight trips. Hanging food from a tree is ineffective in Yosemite, where the bears have long since smartened up to that routine.

If you'd rather have someone else plan and guide a backpacking trip for you, contact the **Southern Yosemite Mountain Guides** in Bass Lake (800/231-4575, www.symg.com).

BIKING

The challenge of riding **Glacier Point Road** calls to many a road cyclist each summer. Despite the fact that the road has a narrow-to-nonexistent shoulder and plenty of tourist traffic, almost every summer day cyclists pedal this road. If you leave your car at Chinquapin Junction and ride out and back to Glacier Point, you'll have a 32-mile round-trip with a 2,300-foot elevation gain. The toughest part of the trip is the initial two-mile climb back out from Glacier Point. Fortunately, you can fuel up with water and snacks at the Glacier Point snack stand (open summer only) before you ride out. If at all possible, plan this ride for a weekday, not a weekend, and the earlier in the day the better. The fewer cars you see on this narrow, steep road, the more you'll be able to enjoy the world-class scenery.

A much less obvious option for mountain bikers in the park is to ride the **Four-Mile Fire Road** that begins across from the Wawona Hotel. This old dirt road is one of the only "trails" in the park where bikes are allowed, although it is much more of a road than a trail. (It's a section of an old stagecoach route.) The scenery is pleasant, and the gentle grade will give you a chance to spin your wheels.

Many more mountain biking adventures are possible in the lands of **Sierra National Forest,** just south of Yosemite National Park. For more information about biking in the lands near Fish Camp, Oakhurst, and Bass Lake, contact the North Fork Ranger Station (559/877-2218). Another good source is **Yosemite Bicycle and Sport** in Oakhurst (559/641-2453, www .yosemitebicycle.com). Located behind the Mc-Donald's in town, the shop offers ride guides, morning and weekend group rides, mountain biking shuttles, and trail maps for those who want to set out on their own.

FISHING

You won't find an abundance of lakes on or near Glacier Point Road and Wawona, so most fishing takes place in streams and rivers. **Bridalveil Creek** near the campground of the same name offers a chance at catching brook trout. Brown and rainbow trout are also occasionally caught in this stream. **Illilouette Creek,** accessible by a downhill hike from Glacier Point on the Panorama Trail, is populated by rainbow trout. (Head upstream from the waterfall and bridge.)

The **South Fork Merced River,** which runs through Wawona, is popular with anglers. Just south of Wawona in Fish Camp lies **Big Creek,** a popular angling stream in early spring. Most people park by the Highway 41 bridge in Fish Camp, then fish downstream using flies and spinners. If you stay off the neighboring private property, you can work your way down the creek over a two-mile stretch.

The main lake in the southern region of Yosemite is **Ostrander Lake,** accessible via a long hike from Glacier Point Road. The lake is a popular backpacking destination and a dependable producer of brook trout. Rainbows are also sometimes taken. Like all other lakes in Yosemite, Ostrander has not been planted for many years, so the fish that live there are a self-sustaining population.

For a more serious fishing excursion, contact the **Southern Yosemite Mountain Guides** in Bass Lake (800/231-4575, www.symg.com).

They hold two-, three-, and five-day fly-fishing courses in Yosemite and the neighboring Ansel Adams Wilderness, with an emphasis on catch-and-release fishing. Everything is provided: rods, reels, flies, and even your fishing license. Your best bet may be to sign up for the three-day **Yosemite Fly Fishing School,** which covers casting techniques, fly selection, reading the water, entomology, tying your own flies, and everything else you need to know. You'll spend your days practicing your technique in the Merced and Tuolumne Rivers in Yosemite. If you don't want to take a class, you can hire a private guide to show you the secret fishing spots of the region.

Finally, no discussion of fishing in or near the southern part of the park would be complete without mentioning **Bass Lake.** The 1,000-acre lake located just outside of Oakhurst, or 14 miles from Yosemite's south entrance, is well loved by fishermen, even though they must share its lovely blue waters with water-skiers, jet skis, and boaters of every variety. Fishing is quite good at Bass Lake, but not necessarily for bass. Instead, trout fishing is popular in winter and spring, when the Department of Fish and Game drops in heavy plants of rainbows. In summer, people catch a little bit of everything: catfish, bluegill, bass, crappie, and trout. The lake level usually drops substantially by late summer, which hinders the lake's fishing as well as its scenic value.

SWIMMING

The **South Fork of the Merced River** in and around Wawona is rife with swimming holes and sandy beaches. Many swimmers jump in the river just upstream from the Pioneer History Center and its covered bridge, but an even better choice is the big, boulder-lined pool near Wawona's Swinging Bridge. Getting there requires about a mile walk up the dirt road from the Chilnualna Falls parking lot.

If you are a lake lover and willing to take a long hike, **Ostrander Lake** usually warms up enough for swimming by mid- to late summer. Hike to it from Bridalveil Creek Campground or the Ostrander Lake Trailhead on Glacier Point Road. If you'd prefer to get your feet wet somewhere that's a little easier to reach, the historic Wawona Hotel has a swimming pool, but it is for guests only.

HORSEBACK RIDING

There's no better way to get into the spirit of the Old West than to climb on a horse and ride off into the sunset. **Wawona Stables** offers horseback rides May–Oct. (although you'll have to leave earlier in the day, not at sunset). Two-hour and four-hour rides depart daily ($40–55); destinations include Chilnualna Falls or the high granite ridge above Wawona. All-day rides and pack trips can also be arranged ($80 and up). Saddlebags are provided for longer rides, in which you can store a picnic lunch, water, camera, and a jacket. Children must be at least seven years old and 44 inches tall. Helmets are required for all riders and are available free of charge. The maximum a rider may weigh is 225 pounds. The stables are located in Wawona, next door to the Pioneer Yosemite History Center. Phone 209/375-6502 for reservations.

Just two miles outside of the park, in Fish Camp, is **Yosemite Trails Pack Station** (559/683-7611, www.yosemitetrails.com). One-hour rides leave several times a day for a loop through the Sierra National Forest lands near the stables. A six-hour trip departs daily at 11:45 A.M. and heads to the Mariposa Grove of Giant Sequoias. All riders spend an hour in the grove, during which they can walk around the big trees or ride the tram. Then the group mounts up their horses and heads back to the stable. In winter, the pack station offers sleigh rides when the snow permits. Yosemite Trails is located on Jackson Road, 1.3 miles east of Highway 41 in Fish Camp.

WINTER SPORTS
Downhill Skiing and Snowboarding
If you want to take part in Yosemite's winter wonderland, head for **Badger Pass** for skiing, snowboarding, and "snow tubing," a low-tech

version of sledding in which snow-lovers slide down the slope in inner tubes. All equipment rentals are available; just wear your warmest clothes, carry chains in your car, and show up at Badger Pass. Ski season usually begins in late November, depending on snowfall. For an update on ski conditions, phone 209/372-1000 or 209/372-8444.

First opened in 1935, Badger Pass is billed as California's oldest ski resort. Downhill skiing was a relatively new sport in the United States, and so the resort hired a series of European ski instructors to teach the Swiss sport of skiing to clumsy Americans. Badger Pass was the proud owner of the West's first mechanical uphill lift, aptly called the Upski. In 1948, Nic Fiore, a Canadian, started teaching at Badger Pass. By the late 1950s he had become director of the ski school, and in the following years he made many important changes, such as adding T-bars and chairlifts. Today, five lifts service 85 acres of ski slopes. The resort emphasizes family-oriented skiing, and prices are substantially less than what you'll find at the ski resorts around Lake Tahoe ($40 all-day ticket). For the daily snow report, visit www.badgerpass.com.

In the winter months, Yosemite Lodge and the Wawona Hotel often offer stay-and-ski packages, with reduced lodging rates and lift tickets included in the package price. Phone Yosemite Reservations at 559/252-4848 or visit www.yosemitepark.com for availability.

Cross-Country Skiing and Snowshoeing
Cross-country skiers and snowshoers can also start their adventures at Badger Pass, and unless they are renting equipment, their adventures will be free of charge. Both groomed and ungroomed cross-country trails depart from the parking lot at Badger Pass. One of the most popular cross-country ski routes is to simply follow the groomed tracks on unplowed **Glacier Point Road.** Three miles of gliding brings you to Bridalveil Campground, where the Ghost Forest Loop leads through a dead stand of lodgepole pines. You can return to Glacier Point Road on Bridalveil Creek Trail.

Cross-country skiing lessons are available for beginners and intermediates as well as for those who wish to learn telemarking skills. To sign up for lessons, contact the **Yosemite Cross Country Ski Center** (209/372-8444) located at Badger Pass Ski Area.

The most popular of Glacier Point's snowshoe routes is the seven-mile round-trip to **Dewey Point.** Although skiers use this route as well, the vast majority of visitors on any weekend day are snowshoers, some who may be trying out their functional snow footwear for the first time. The well-marked, seven-mile loop route is basically level, with one good climb on the way out to Dewey Point. Plan on at least four hours for the loop; if the weather is nice, you'll want to hang out at Dewey Point for a while to enjoy its spectacular view of the Valley. (Bring a rubber mat or something to sit on, and plenty of snacks and drinks.)

Even if the **Mariposa Grove** Road is closed, cross-country skiers and snowshoers can glide up the road to the giant sequoias, then commune with the big trees while they are crowned in snow. This is one of the most glorious winter sights in all of Yosemite. Beginners will want to keep to the road and the trails in the lower grove; more advanced snowshoers and skiers can head to the upper grove.

Glacier Point Ski Hut

If you like the idea of an overnight stay at a cross-country ski hut but think that getting there may be beyond your abilities, the Glacier Point Ski Hut is for you. The distance to be covered on skis or snowshoes is a substantial 10 miles from where you leave your car, but the going is easy, and you have almost nothing to carry.

If you've driven to Glacier Point in summer, you've seen the Glacier Point Ski Hut, except that June–Oct., the impressive log building serves as a snack stand and gift shop. In winter, Yosemite Concession Services (YCS) removes the store shelves and cash registers and puts in bunk beds, then leads guided ski trips with an overnight stay at the hut.

The fact that the trip requires a guide makes it suitable even for beginners. Although YCS requests that you are at least an intermediate-level cross-country skier, plenty of beginners make the trip. It's doable because the 10-mile route from Badger Pass is on well-groomed track that follows Glacier Point Road all the way. With one guide in front of your group and one in back, everybody skis at their own pace and nobody gets left behind.

It's also doable for beginners because you carry almost nothing on your back. YCS issues each skier their own lightweight liner to stuff inside the hut's sleeping bags. You carry that and some water and snacks for the trip; the guides take care of the rest, including all meals and wine.

The minimum number of people for a night at Glacier Point Ski Hut is five; the maximum is 20. On weeknights, you and your family or friends can have the place to yourselves (plus your guides, of course). On weekends, you're likely to share the place with company, unless you managed to convince 19 friends to go with you. Reservations are required; phone 559/252-4848 or visit www.yosemitepark.com. For a one-night ski trip, the fee is $150–180 per person, including meals. For a two-night ski trip, the fee is $225–270 per person, including meals.

Ostrander Ski Hut

Unlike at Glacier Point Ski Hut, you have to work hard to earn your stay at Ostrander Ski Hut. The trip to the overnight hut is only for those who are strong and skilled enough to ski or snowshoe from the Badger Pass Ski Area 10 miles each way on mostly ungroomed track. But for those who make the snowy journey, the reward is a warm night in a two-story stone cabin perched on the edge of Ostrander Lake at 8,500 feet in elevation. This is a way of experiencing Yosemite that few people will ever know.

The Ostrander Ski Hut is operated by the Yosemite Association, a nonprofit educational organization. It's open each year from mid-December to mid-April, depending on snow conditions. The hut sleeps 25 people and has bunks, mattresses, a wood stove, solar lights, a kitchen

© ANN MARIE BROWN

Take a ride on a horsedrawn stagecoach wagon at the Pioneer Yosemite History Center and find out what traveling through Wawona was like in the old days.

with gas stove for cooking, and assorted cooking and eating utensils. For drinking water, you walk 100 feet down to Ostrander Lake, fill up a bucket, then bring it back and filter it.

You're on your own for your trek to Ostrander Ski Hut, so you must possess some winter backcountry skills. Skiers should be at least intermediate level and in good physical shape. You must carry quite a few items with you: sleeping bag, sleeping pad, head lamp, water filter, water bottle, snow emergency gear, food, and so on.

Even with all these prerequisites, reservations for Ostrander Ski Hut can be tough to come by. The hut is particularly popular with telemark skiers, as the slopes around the hut provide wonderful opportunities for this type of skiing. Making it even more attractive, the nightly fee is very low—a mere $25 per person. The Yosemite Association begins taking reservations in early November (209/372-0740). You must write to the Association (P.O. Box 545, Yosemite, CA 95389) to request a lottery form, then fill it out and send it in. If you can't get the dates you want, try phoning after December 1 to see if there are cancellations.

Your chances are much better midweek than on weekends.

ENTERTAINMENT AND EVENTS
Ranger Talks and Walks
Guided walks are held daily in summer in the southern area of the park. In the Mariposa Grove, 1.5-hour interpretive hikes leave from the grove parking lot twice a day in the summer and on autumn weekends at 10 A.M. These easy walks stay within the lower grove and are appropriate for hikers of all abilities. Once a day in summer, a ranger leads a tram tour to the upper grove, followed by a 2.5-mile hike back downhill. This walk is also rated as easy. At Glacier Point, rangers lead hikes to Taft Point and Sentinel Dome.

A list of ranger-led hikes in the Wawona and Glacier Point area is posted at the Wawona Hotel and the Wawona Campground. Or check the schedule in the free Yosemite newspaper.

Campfire Programs
The Wawona Campground holds a campfire program on Friday or Saturday nights dur-

ing summer only. A schedule is posted at the campground.

Pioneer Yosemite History Center

In Wawona, docents dress in period costumes and take visitors on tours inside Yosemite's historic buildings. On the south side of the History Center's covered bridge, horse-drawn stagecoach rides depart every 15–20 minutes from the stables. The 10-minute ride loops around Wawona and gives visitors a taste of what early-days transportation in Yosemite was like.

Rides are offered daily in summer only and cost $3 for adults, $2 children ages 3–12.

Glacier Point Sunset Talks and Star Programs

Evening ranger programs are held nightly in summer at the Glacier Point railing or amphitheater, usually at 7 P.M. Star programs are held on clear Saturday nights. A telescope is set up for viewing the heavens. Scheduled events are posted at Glacier Point and listed in the free Yosemite newspaper.

Tioga Pass and Tuolumne Meadows

One of the most photographed regions of Yosemite is Tuolumne Meadows, at 8,600 feet in elevation, with its wide, grassy expanse bounded by a series of high granite domes and peaks. This pristine meadow extends for more than two miles along the Tuolumne River and is considered to be the largest subalpine meadow in the entire Sierra Nevada. From its tranquil edges, trails lead in all directions—to the alpine lakes set below the spires of Cathedral and Unicorn Peaks, to a series of roaring waterfalls on the Tuolumne River, and to

the summits of lofty granite domes with commanding vistas of the high country. The Tuolumne Meadows region is the centerpiece of a huge High Sierra playground for hikers and backpackers, as well as for visitors who simply want to sit at a picnic table and wallow in the scenic beauty.

The regions on either side of the meadow, following the 39-mile length of Tioga Pass Road from Crane Flat to Tioga Pass, offer more wonders. Two giant sequoia groves wait to be explored—the Merced and Tuolumne

▌ust-Sees

Look for ▌ to find the sights and activities you can't miss.

▌ Olmsted Point: In a park rife with impressive overlooks, Olmsted Point may be the most impressive of them all. Seen from here are Clouds Rest, Tenaya Canyon, and an unusual side view of Half Dome, as well as a smorgasbord of high country peaks and passes (page 69).

▌ Tenaya Lake: This deep blue granite tarn is located right alongside Tioga Pass Road, enticing many drive-by sightseers to slam on the brakes and go for an impromptu swim in its frigid waters, or picnic along its sandy shores (page 70).

▌ Pothole Dome: Even nonhikers will enjoy the short walk to the top of this low granite dome on the western edge of Tuolumne Meadows (page 70).

▌ Tuolumne Meadows: The largest subalpine meadow in the Sierra Nevada, the grassy expanse of Tuolumne Meadows inspires awe in even the most jaded travelers. Numerous trails lead from its edges, but many visitors are happy just to stop their cars and stare at this pristine place. Here at 8,600 feet, the air is always pleasantly cool and comfortable (page 70).

© ANN MARIE BROWN

Tuolumne Meadows

▌ Lembert Dome: Hang out at the base of this granite monolith and watch the rock climbers strut their stuff on its steep vertical face. Or, take a 2.8-mile round-trip hike around to the sloping back side of the dome, then climb to the top for a thrilling view of the high country (page 79).

Tioga and Tuolumne

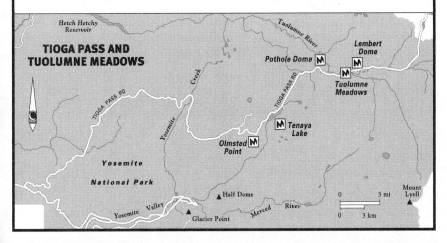

TIOGA PASS AND TUOLUMNE MEADOWS

Hetch Hetchy Reservoir

Tuolumne River

Lembert Dome

Pothole Dome ▌

Tuolumne Meadows

Creek

TIOGA PASS RD

TIOGA PASS RD

▌ Tenaya Lake

Olmsted ▌ Point

Yosemite

Yosemite National Park

Yosemite Valley

▲ Half Dome

Merced River

▲ Glacier Point

0   3 mi

0   3 km

Mount Lyell ▲

Groves—as well as meadows filled with wildflowers at Crane Flat and White Wolf. The drive-to vista at Olmsted Point provides an unusual view of Half Dome and a peek into the funneled granite walls of Tenaya Canyon. Just beyond the overlook, Tenaya Lake sparkles in the sunshine, dazzling visitors with its beauty.

Tioga Pass Road reaches the park's eastern boundary at 9,945-foot Tioga Pass, the highest-elevation highway pass through the Sierra Nevada. But the fun doesn't end there—the drive through its reaches and down to U.S. 395 is one of the most thrilling stretches of road in the West. Most of the 3,000-foot descent takes place without the aid of guard rails, so try your best to keep your eyes on the road and not on the spectacular mountain scenery.

Exploring Tioga Pass and Tuolumne Meadows

WEATHER AND SEASONS

Tioga Pass Road and the Tuolumne Meadows area are blanketed in a thick layer of snow usually from late Oct.–late May. That leaves a five-month window when Tioga Pass Road is usually open and visitors have access to this spectacular high country. Count on mild days and cool nights at these high elevations. It's rare to have daytime temperatures above 80°F, and nights will often drop down close to freezing.

VISITOR CENTER

The second largest of the park's visitor centers is located on the west end of Tuolumne Meadows, on the south side of Tioga Pass Road. Open in summer only, the visitor center (209/372-0263) is housed in a historic building that often has a cozy fire burning in the fireplace. Exhibits focus on the area's geology, wildflowers, wildlife, and ecology. A few displays interpret humans' relation to the Yosemite high country, including John Muir's perspective on the value of Yosemite as a national park. Books and maps are for sale. The visitor center is open daily 9 A.M.–5 P.M. from Tioga Pass Road's opening date until the end of September.

For visitors driving into the park through the Big Oak Flat entrance on Highway 120, a small information station is located 100 feet south of the entrance kiosk, on the west side of the road. A few books and maps are for sale, and wilderness permits are available.

SHUTTLES AND TOURS

During the summer months, a free shuttle bus runs along Tioga Pass Road, stopping at all major trailheads between May Lake and Tioga Pass. Check at the Tuolumne Meadows Visitor Center or at White Wolf or Tuolumne Lodge for a detailed schedule, or phone 209/372-1240.

SERVICES
Shopping and Supplies

Most gas station stores don't offer much besides a dozen different kinds of chips, but the **Crane Flat Gas Station** (at Crane Flat off Highway 120) has enough groceries for a camper to be able to cook dinner, plus a selection of guidebooks and aisles full of junk food. This store is a good bet for most anything you might need, and that's fortunate, because it's the only place around for many miles.

If you're staying at White Wolf or Yosemite Creek Campgrounds and you run out of, say, chocolate bars or insect repellent, you may be able to stock up at the **White Wolf Lodge Store** (8 A.M.–8 P.M. summer only). But be forewarned, this is a *really* small store (basically a closet with a walk-up window on the side of the White Wolf dining room). If you want anything more than the most basic items, you'll have to drive to Crane Flat or Tuolumne Meadows.

The latter has the most extensive shopping on Tioga Pass Road. In fact, there probably isn't anything they haven't crammed into the canvas tent that makes up the **Tuolumne Meadows Store** (8 A.M.–8 P.M. summer only) Groceries, camping gear, clothing items, guidebooks—you name it, it's probably there. A post office and the Tuolumne Meadows Grill—a dependable bet for breakfast and lunch—are right next door.

If you strike out everywhere else in Yosemite's high country, you can also drive a few miles out of the park to **Tioga Pass Resort** (two miles from Tioga Pass, 209/372-4471, 7 A.M.–9 P.M. summer only) or the **Tioga Gas Mart** (11 miles from Tioga Pass). The resort has basic items like firewood, snacks, and drinks; the gas mart has a very large, well-stocked store and cafe.

Gas

Gas is available at either end of Tioga Pass Road: at the **Crane Flat gas station** or 39 miles east at Tuolumne Meadows (at both, you can pay at the pump 24 hours a day with a credit card). If you are even farther east when the needle registers "E"—say, at the top of Tioga Pass—it might be smarter to drive downhill and out of the park rather than backtracking to Tuolumne Meadows. Your first chance for gas will be the **Tioga Gas Mart,** 11 miles from Tioga Pass, but it's downhill all the way.

Banking Services/ATM

There are no banking services on Tioga Pass Road, but if you drive east to Lee Vining you'll find ATMs at several establishments, including the Tioga Gas Mart.

DRIVING TOUR

Tioga Pass Road is a 39-mile scenic drive through red fir and lodgepole pine forest, past meadows, lakes, and granite domes and spires. Now a part of California State Highway 120, the road has an interesting history: It was built in 1882–83 as a mining road to service the silver mines in the Tioga Pass area. It was realigned and modernized in 1961.

If you are driving to Tioga Pass from Yosemite Valley, plan on about two hours from the

time you leave the Valley until the time you reach the Tioga Pass entrance station. It will take about 30 minutes to get to Crane Flat and the start of Tioga Pass Road, which is 20 miles from the main lodgings and campgrounds in Yosemite Valley via Big Oak Flat Road. At Crane Flat you'll find a gas station and small store for supplies.

From this 6,000-foot elevation, Tioga Pass Road slowly climbs its way through dense forests to the White Wolf turnoff at 14 miles. (A restaurant, small store, and restrooms are available in White Wolf.) In another dozen miles you reach the pullout for the spectacular vista at Olmsted Point; Tenaya Lake is two miles beyond. You have now left the thick stands of trees behind and entered a granite wonderland.

At world-famous Tuolumne Meadows, six miles beyond Tenaya Lake, you have another chance for gas and supplies (as well as plenty of chances to admire the scenery), then it's on to 9,945-foot Tioga Pass. This pass is the highest mountain pass you can drive through in California. Here the road exits Yosemite National Park and drops down to Mono Lake, the Eastern Sierra, and U.S. 395.

SIGHTS
White Wolf

Likely named for a Sierra coyote mistaken for a wolf, White Wolf is situated at 8,000 feet on an old section of the original Tioga Road. A drive-in campground and tent-cabin resort are located there, plus an excellent restaurant. The meadows around White Wolf usually display beautiful wildflowers in June and July.

Olmsted Point

Located just west of giant Tenaya Lake on Highway 120/Tioga Road, Olmsted Point offers a wide-open vista of Yosemite Valley's array of granite domes and cliffs, but from a much different vantage point than you have anywhere else in the park. First-time visitors may have trouble picking out Half Dome because it looks so different from this angle. Clouds Rest and the sky-scraping walls of Tenaya Canyon are also in full view. A quarter-mile trail from this vista point leads through a series of glacial erratics and gives a brief lesson in park geology. Marmots and pikas are often seen poking out from the rocks. If you walk or drive to the far eastern end of the turnout, you get an interesting look at Tenaya Lake and the multitude of granite domes and peaks beyond it.

Olmsted Point was named for Frederick Law Olmsted, one of Yosemite's first preservationists (and the man who designed New York's Central Park), and his son, Frederick Law Olmsted Jr., who worked as a planner in Yosemite National Park.

M Tenaya Lake

The last of the Ahwahneechee tribespeople were rounded up at Tenaya Lake, ending Native Americans' reign as the caretakers of Yosemite Valley. It's difficult to imagine that sad piece of history on a beautiful August day at Tenaya Lake, when the lakeshore's white sands are lined with picnickers and sunbathers. Plenty of people swim in Tenaya Lake, but the water is icy cold. This is a fine place to sit on the beach with a pair of binoculars and watch the rock climbers on Polly Dome, just across Tioga Pass Road. Picnic areas with fire grills are located on both ends of the lake.

M Pothole Dome

On the far western edge of Tuolumne Meadows lies a low granite dome that even young children can hike to. The parking pullout is on the north side of Tioga Pass Road, 2.2 miles west of Tuolumne Meadows Campground. An easy, short trail parallels the road for about 100 feet to a stand of trees; the dome lies just beyond. In less than 10 minutes from the time you get out of your car, you can be at the top, gazing at the fine view of Lembert Dome, Mount Dana, Mount Gibbs, and, of course, Tuolumne Meadows and its namesake river.

M Tuolumne Meadows

Situated at 8,600 feet above sea level, Tu-

olumne is the largest subalpine meadow in the Sierra Nevada, extending for more than eight miles. The meandering Tuolumne River cuts a swath through its grassy expanse. Perhaps more impressive than the wide meadow itself are the majestic granite domes and peaks that surround it. Although the meadow is so beautiful that it is tempting to wander into it, be sure to stay on designated paths. High-elevation meadows are extremely fragile and can be damaged by foot traffic.

Lembert Dome

This glacially polished rock is an example of a roche moutonnée, a dome that has one gently sloping side and one side that drops in a steep escarpment. The dome was named for Jean Baptiste Lembert, a homesteader who lived in Tuolumne Meadows in the mid-1880s. Lembert was something of a hermit who made his living by herding sheep and collecting insects to sell to museums. You may see rock climbers plying their trade on the highway side of Lembert Dome, but hikers can head around to the back side and walk right up to the summit.

Soda Springs and Parson's Memorial Lodge

Visitors who want to get a look at Tuolumne Meadows up close should take the short walk to Soda Springs and Parson's Lodge, on the north side of the meadow. Soda Springs is a permanent spring that produces a true carbonated water. The Sierra Club built the Parson's Memorial Lodge here in 1915. The trailhead is located right on Tioga Pass Road (just east of the Cathedral Lakes Trailhead), or you can hike there from the end of the dirt road past the Lembert Dome parking lot. Either 0.5-mile trail will give you a good look at the wildflowers, grasses, and sedges of the meadow, plus a glimpse into the area's history. You'll visit the site where John Muir and Robert Underwood Johnson discussed the idea of creating Yosemite National Park.

Recreation

HIKING

To truly experience Yosemite's high country, you simply have to go on foot. Armed with only a day pack full of supplies, you can set out on a trail and experience Yosemite on its own terms, as it is meant to be seen. The following hikes in the Tioga Pass Road and Tuolumne Meadows area are listed in the order that their trailheads appear on the highway, assuming you are traveling from west to east (Big Oak Flat entrance station to Tioga Pass).

Merced Grove

- Distance: 3.0 miles round-trip
- Duration: 1.5 hours
- Rating: Easy
- Elevation Change: 350 feet
- Trailhead: Merced Grove
- Directions: From the Big Oak Flat entrance station on Highway 120, drive southeast 4.3 miles to the trailhead on your right. Or, from

Crane Flat, drive west 3.7 miles on Big Oak Flat Road to the trailhead on your left.

Of the three giant sequoia groves in Yosemite—Merced, Tuolumne, and Mariposa—the Merced Grove is the smallest and least visited. Yet surprisingly, it offers the most pleasant hike. Generally the trail sees foot traffic only from people who enter Yosemite at the Big Oak Flat entrance and drive by this trailhead on their way to Yosemite Valley. The trail is a closed-off dirt road that is level and straight for the first 0.5 mile. Bear left at the only junction and head downhill through a lovely mixed forest of white firs, incense-cedars, ponderosa pines, and sugar pines. Azaleas bloom in early summer beneath the conifers' branches. You will reach the first sequoias, a group of six, at about 1.5 miles. More big trees lie in the next 100 yards. A total of only 20 sequoias are found in this grove, but because they grow very close together, they make a dramatic impression.

M Tioga and Tuolumne

© ANN MARIE BROWN

This old log cabin in Merced Grove sits across from some of the largest sequoias in the grove.

The largest sequoias are found directly across the road from a handsome old log cabin built as a retreat for the park superintendent. It is no longer used. Sit on its front steps and have a picnic while you admire the giant trees. Retrace your steps from the cabin, hiking gently uphill for your return.

Tuolumne Grove

- Distance: 2.5 miles round-trip
- Duration: 1.5 hours
- Rating: Easy
- Elevation Change: 550 feet
- Trailhead: Tuolumne Grove
- Directions: From the Big Oak Flat entrance station on Highway 120, drive southeast 7.7 miles to Crane Flat, then turn left to stay on Highway 120. Drive 0.5 mile to the Tuolumne Grove parking lot on the left.

Up until 1993 you could drive right in to the Tuolumne Grove of Giant Sequoias, but now the road is closed off and visitors have to

The Dead Giant in the Tuolumne Grove is a large stump that was tunneled in 1878 so stagecoaches, and later automobiles, could drive through.

hike in. The grove is found on the old Big Oak Flat Road, a paved, six-mile historic road/trail that is open to bikes and hikers (although bikes are a rarity here). This is a popular destination, so arrive early in the morning to have the best chance at solitude. Leave your car at the parking lot near Crane Flat and hike downhill into the big trees. It's one mile to the first sequoias.

The Tuolumne Grove's claim to fame is that it has one of the two remaining walk-through trees in Yosemite; this one is called the Dead Giant. It's a tall stump that was tunneled in 1878. Go ahead, walk through it—everybody does.

At a small picnic area, a half-mile trail loops around the forest. Make sure you save some energy for the trip back uphill to the parking lot; the moderate grade ascends 550 feet. The old paved road continues downhill beyond the grove all the way to Hodgdon Meadow Campground. Some people hike the entire six-mile distance, then have someone pick them up at Hodgdon Meadow.

Harden Lake

- Distance: 5.6 miles round-trip
- Duration: 3 hours
- Rating: Easy
- Elevation Change: 500 feet
- Trailhead: White Wolf
- Directions: From the Big Oak Flat entrance station on Highway 120, drive southeast 7.7 miles to Crane Flat, then turn left to stay on Highway 120. Drive 14 miles to the left turnoff for White Wolf. Turn left and drive one mile to the lodge and trailhead.

Harden Lake itself isn't much—by late summer, you'd be hard-pressed to call it a pond. But people come here for another reason, and that's to see the wildflowers that bloom in a region known as Harden's Gardens, about a quarter-mile beyond the lake. July is the most dependable month for the wildflower bloom. Views of the Grand Canyon of the Tuolumne River are another reward.

The trail follows White Wolf's gravel service road (a stretch of the original Tioga Road) past the campground entrance and across the Tuolumne River. Follow the obvious signs that point you through a few junctions to a blossom-filled marshy area. A few more steps and you're at the lake. If you haven't yet gotten your fill of the flower show, proceed a short distance farther and feast your eyes on Harden's Gardens.

Lukens Lake

- Distance: 1.5 miles round-trip
- Duration: 1 hour
- Rating: Easy
- Elevation Change: 300 feet
- Trailhead: Lukens Lake
- Directions: From the Big Oak Flat entrance station on Highway 120, drive southeast 7.7 miles to Crane Flat, then turn left to stay on Highway 120. Drive 16.2 miles to the Lukens Lake Trailhead parking area on the south side of the road. The trail begins across the road.

The Lukens Lake Trail is the perfect introductory lake hike for families in Yosemite National Park. A six-year-old could make the trip easily. A bonus is that the trailhead is on the western end of Tioga Road, so it's quickly reached from points in Yosemite Valley. The trail is 0.75 mile long, leading from Tioga Road up to a saddle, then dropping down to the lake. It winds through a dense red fir forest, filled with mammoth trees, then cuts across a corn lily–filled meadow to the edge of the shallow lake. If you time it right, you could see a spectacular wildflower show in this meadow. Swimming in Lukens Lake is highly recommended; by midsummer, this is one of the warmest lakes in the park.

If you want to take a longer trail to Lukens Lake, you can start from the trailhead at White Wolf Lodge and make a 4.6-mile round-trip.

North Dome

- Distance: 9.0 miles round-trip
- Duration: 4–5 hours
- Rating: Moderate to strenuous
- Elevation Change: 1,500 feet
- Trailhead: Porcupine Creek
- Directions: From the Big Oak Flat entrance station on Highway 120, drive southeast 7.7 miles to Crane Flat, then turn left to stay on

Indian Rock, the only granite arch in Yosemite, is found a short distance off the trail to North Dome.

Highway 120. Drive 24.5 miles to the Porcupine Creek Trailhead on the right, a mile past Porcupine Flat Campground.

There are those who say that climbing Half Dome is a bit of a disappointment, and not just because of the crowds. When you reach the top and check out the commanding view, the panorama of granite is not quite as awesome as you might expect, and that's because you can't see Half Dome—you're standing on it.

That's a dilemma that's easy to fix. If Half Dome is an absolute necessity in your view of Yosemite, climb North Dome instead, which offers a heart-stopping view of that big piece of granite. The route is not for the faint of heart, but when you are way up high looking down at Tenaya Canyon and across at Half Dome and Clouds Rest, well, you'll know why you came.

The main day hiker's route to North Dome begins at the Porcupine Creek Trailhead a mile east of Porcupine Flat Campground. A dirt access road shortly brings you to a proper trail, signed as Porcupine Creek. Continue straight at two possible junctions near the 2.5-mile mark, heading due south for North Dome. After the third mile your views begin to open up, providing fine vistas of North Dome and Half Dome and increasing your anticipation. At the trail junction at 4.5 miles, take the left spur for the final hike to North Dome's summit. Surprise—it's a downhill grade to reach it.

Hope you brought plenty of film with you; the view from the top is sublime. Half Dome appears close enough to touch—just across the canyon. Clouds Rest is a dramatic sight to the northeast. To the southwest you can see cars crawling along the Yosemite Valley floor. On your return trip consider taking the unsigned spur trail two miles from North Dome, at an obvious saddle. The spur leads a steep 0.25 mile to Indian Rock, the only natural arch on land in Yosemite. It's great fun to climb around on.

May Lake and Mount Hoffman

- Distance: 2.4–6.0 miles round-trip
- Duration: 1 hour to May Lake; 4 hours to Mt. Hoffman

- Rating: Easy to May Lake; strenuous to Mt. Hoffman
- Elevation Change: 500 feet to May Lake; 2,000 feet to Mt. Hoffman
- Trailhead: May Lake
- Directions: From the Big Oak Flat entrance station on Highway 120, drive southeast 7.7 miles to Crane Flat, then turn left to stay on Highway 120. Drive 26.6 miles to the May Lake Road turnoff on the left (near road marker T-21). Turn left and drive two miles to the trailhead.

Here's another hike you can take the kids on. It's an easy 1.2 miles to May Lake, tucked in below 10,850-foot Mount Hoffman. The trail's total elevation gain is only 500 feet, and better yet, it's downhill all the way home. If you want to turn the hike into more of an adventure, you can add on a climb to the sum-

© ANN MARIE BROWN

After bagging the peak of Mount Hoffman, hikers should take a moment to pose for photographs in front of the mighty summit and May Lake.

mit of Mount Hoffman, the exact geographical center of Yosemite National Park. Don't take younger kids (or out-of-shape adults) on that trek, though. It will add 1,500 feet of climbing in an extra two miles of trail, and reaching the actual summit requires scrambling skills and excellent footing.

May Lake is a round, blue lake set at 9,329 feet, with the granite walls of Mount Hoffman forming a very photogenic backdrop. A High Sierra Camp is located along the shore. The trail to the lake begins at the Snow Flat Trailhead two miles off Tioga Road. It passes through a lodgepole pine forest and climbs up granite-lined slopes, then drops down to the lake's southern shore. I *would* recommend swimming in May Lake, but unfortunately, it's not allowed; the lake is the water source for the High Sierra Camp.

Families will want to stop here and enjoy a picnic on the lakeshore, but ambitious hikers can head west around May Lake to its north side and follow an informal-use trail that leads to the summit of Mount Hoffman. Be forewarned that this is not an official park trail, and you need to exercise extreme caution because of loose rock and steep drop-offs. If you make it to the top, the 360-degree view is without peer, but you can't get there without some effort.

Clouds Rest

- Distance: 14.0 miles round-trip
- Duration: 7–8 hours
- Rating: Strenuous
- Elevation Change: 2,300 feet
- Trailhead: Sunrise Lakes
- Directions: From the Big Oak Flat entrance station on Highway 120, drive southeast 7.7 miles to Crane Flat, then turn left to stay on Highway 120. Drive 30.3 miles to the Sunrise Lakes Trailhead on the right, just west of Tenaya Lake.

Hiking to Clouds Rest is as much of an epic journey as climbing Half Dome, but with far fewer people elbowing you along the way. With a 2,300-foot climb and 14 miles to cover, the trail is not for casual hikers. The path as-

FEELING THE ALTITUDE?

Many hikers experience a shortness of breath when hiking only a few thousand feet higher than the elevation at which they live. If you live on the California coast, you may notice slightly labored breathing while hiking at an elevation as low as 4,000 feet (the exact elevation of Yosemite Valley). As you go higher, it may get worse, sometimes leading to headaches and nausea. It takes a full 72 hours to acclimate to major elevation changes, although most people feel better after 24 to 48 hours.

The best preparation for hiking at high elevation is to sleep at that elevation, or as close to it as possible, the night before. If you are planning a strenuous hike at 7,000 feet or above, spend a day or two beforehand taking easier hikes at the same elevation. Get plenty of rest and drink plenty of fluids. Lack of sleep and drinking alcohol can contribute to a susceptibility to "feeling the altitude."

Serious altitude sickness typically occurs above 10,000 feet. It is generally preventable by simply allowing enough time for acclimation. Staying fully hydrated and fueled with food will also help. If you start to feel ill (nausea, throwing up, severe headache), you are experiencing altitude sickness. Some people can get by with taking aspirin and trudging onward, but if you are seriously ill, the only cure is to descend as soon as possible.

cends steadily for the first four miles, then descends steeply for 0.5 mile, then climbs again, but more moderately. Keep the faith—the first 2.5 miles from the trailhead are the toughest. The final summit ascent is a little dicey for some hikers because of the breathtaking drop-offs into Tenaya Canyon, but as with other Yosemite peaks, watch your footing on the granite slabs and you'll be fine. Overall, this route is much safer than climbing Half Dome because the final ascent is far more gradual and there are no cables to maneuver.

The view from the top of Clouds Rest—of Tenaya Canyon, Half Dome, Yosemite Valley,

Tioga and Tuolumne

Tenaya Lake, the Clark Range, and various peaks and ridges—will knock your socks off. (Hope you brought along an extra pair.) If this long hike has made you hot and sweaty, you can stop at the Sunrise Lakes for a swim on the way back—the first lake is only 0.25 mile from the Clouds Rest/Sunrise Trail junction.

Sunrise Lakes

- Distance: 7.5 miles round-trip
- Duration: 4 hours
- Rating: Moderate
- Elevation Change: 1,000 feet
- Trailhead: Sunrise Lakes
- Directions: From the Big Oak Flat entrance station on Highway 120, drive southeast 7.7 miles to Crane Flat, then turn left to stay on Highway 120. Drive 30.3 miles to the Sunrise Lakes Trailhead on the right, just west of Tenaya Lake.

With all the hikers heading to Clouds Rest, combined with all the day hikers and backpackers heading to the Sunrise Lakes, the Sunrise Trailhead can look like a mall parking lot on a Saturday. But don't be scared off; the Sunrise Lakes are a great destination, especially if you're lucky enough to visit during the week or off-season. Much of the reason for its popularity is that in only 1,000 feet of elevation gain the trail shows off a lot of beautiful scenery, including great views of Clouds Rest at your back as you hike the final stretch to the lakes.

Follow the trail as it climbs steeply above the edge of Tenaya Canyon. At 2.5 miles, turn left at the sign for Sunrise High Sierra Camp. In about 10 minutes of easy walking, Lower Sunrise Lake shows up on the right, and the other lakes are shortly beyond it on the left. The upper lake is the largest and by far the most popular; lots of people swim and picnic here on warm summer days.

Tenaya Lake

- Distance: 2.0 miles round-trip
- Duration: 1 hour
- Rating: Easy
- Elevation Change: None
- Trailhead: Tenaya Lake
- Directions: From the Big Oak Flat entrance station on Highway 120, drive southeast 7.7 miles to Crane Flat, then turn left to stay on Highway 120. Drive 31.7 miles to the eastern Tenaya Lake picnic area (another Tenaya Lake picnic area lies 0.5 mile west). The trail leads from the parking lot.

Many park visitors drive east down Tioga Road in a big rush to get to Tuolumne Meadows, but when they see giant Tenaya Lake right along the road, they stop short in their tire tracks. Luckily the 150-acre, sapphire-blue lake has a parking lot and picnic area at its east end where you can leave your car and take a stroll down to the lake's edge. While most people stop at Tenaya Lake's white-sand beach to watch the rock climbers on nearby Polly Dome, you can leave the crowds behind and stroll to the south side of the beach. There, pick up the trail that leads along the south side of Tenaya Lake, far from the road on the north side. Wander along the lakeshore, stopping to have a seat on a boulder wherever you please. When you reach the lake's west end, the trail continues but the water views end, so just turn around and walk back. This is a perfectly easy hike alongside one of the most beautiful lakes in Yosemite.

Cathedral Lakes

- Distance: 7.4 miles round-trip
- Duration: 4 hours
- Rating: Strenuous
- Elevation Change: 1,000 feet
- Trailhead: Cathedral Lakes
- Directions: From the Big Oak Flat entrance station on Highway 120, drive southeast 7.7 miles to Crane Flat, then turn left to stay on Highway 120. Drive 37.4 miles to the Cathedral Lakes Trailhead on the right, by Tuolumne Meadows. Park your car in the pullouts on either side of the road; there is no formal parking lot.

The Cathedral Lakes are a tremendously popular and relatively easy backpacking destination in Yosemite, but it's such a short hike to reach them that they also make a great day trip. Located on a 0.5-mile spur off the John Muir Trail, the lakes are within a classic glacial cirque, tucked in below 10,840-foot Cathedral Peak. This is as scenic a spot as you'll find anywhere in Yosemite.

From the trail's start at Tioga Road you hike 3.2 miles on the John Muir Trail with a 1,000-foot elevation gain. Much of the trail is shaded by lodgepole pines, but when the path breaks out of the trees, views of surrounding peaks (especially distinctive Cathedral Peak, which looks remarkably different from every angle) keep you oohing and ahhing the whole way. At 3.2 miles, turn right on the Cathedral Lake spur to reach the lower, larger lake in 0.5 mile. You'll follow the lake's inlet stream through a gorgeous meadow to the water's edge, then start snapping photographs like mad. To reach the upper lake, retrace your steps to the John Muir Trail and continue another 0.5 mile. The fishing is usually better in the upper lake, and the scenery is equally sublime.

Lower Gaylor Lake

- Distance: 8.0 miles round-trip
- Duration: 4 hours
- Rating: Moderate
- Elevation Change: 800 feet
- Trailhead: Tuolumne Lodge/John Muir Trail
- Directions: From the Big Oak Flat entrance station on Highway 120, drive southeast 7.7 miles to Crane Flat, then turn left to stay on Highway 120. Drive 39.5 miles to the Tuolumne Lodge and Wilderness Permits turnoff on the right. Turn right and drive 0.5 mile. Park in the lot on the left signed for Dog Lake and John Muir Trail. The trail begins across the road from the parking lot. Additional parking is available in the Wilderness Permits parking lot.

This mellow, pretty hike starts on the John Muir Trail near Tuolumne Lodge, then heads east along the south side of the Dana Fork of the Tuolumne River. After two miles the trail crosses the river and Tioga Road and heads up-

hill for two miles to Lower Gaylor Lake, elevation 10,049 feet. The lake is deep turquoise and hemmed in by granite. From its edge you gain wide vistas of the peaks around Tuolumne Meadows—high-country beauty at its finest. Elevation at the trailhead is 9,250 feet; the total gain is about 800 feet to Lower Gaylor Lake, a gentle climb the whole way.

The Lower Gaylor Lake hike is one of the quieter trails in the Tuolumne Meadows area, so if you're looking for solitude, it's a good bet. Most visitors hike to the Middle and Upper Gaylor Lakes from the obvious trailhead at the Tioga Pass entrance station, but you can't reach the Lower Gaylor Lake from there, unless you travel cross-country.

Elizabeth Lake

- Distance: 4.5 miles round-trip
- Duration: 2 hours
- Rating: Easy to moderate
- Elevation Change: 850 feet
- Trailhead: Tuolumne Meadows Campground
- Directions: From the Big Oak Flat entrance station on Highway 120, drive southeast 7.7 miles to Crane Flat, then turn left to stay on Highway 120. Drive 39 miles to Tuolumne Meadows Campground. Turn right and follow the signs through the main camp to the group camp. The trail begins across from the group camp restrooms near group site B49.

Starting at the trailhead elevation of 8,600 feet, you have a mere 850-foot elevation gain over 2.25 miles to get to lovely Elizabeth Lake, set in a basin at the foot of distinctive Unicorn Peak. It's a day hike that is attainable for almost anybody, and you can bet that all the campers at Tuolumne Meadows Campground make the trip at some point during their vacations.

For non-campers, the trailhead is a bit tricky to find—it's tucked into the back of Tuolumne Meadows Campground, across from the group camp restrooms. Once you locate it, be prepared to climb steeply for the first mile, then breathe easier when the trail levels out. Fortunately the route is mostly shaded by a dense grove of lodgepole pines.

Upon reaching its shore, you'll see that Elizabeth Lake is a gorgeous body of alpine water. Some visitors swim or fish here; others try to climb Unicorn Peak (10,900 feet); but most are happy to sit near the lake's edge and admire the views of the sculpted peak and its neighbors in the Cathedral Range.

Lyell Canyon

• Distance: 6.0 miles round-trip
• Duration: 3 hours
• Rating: Easy
• Elevation Change: 200 feet
• Trailhead: Tuolumne Lodge/John Muir Trail
• Directions: From the Big Oak Flat entrance station on Highway 120, drive southeast 7.7 miles to Crane Flat, then turn left to stay on Highway 120. Drive 39.5 miles to the Tuolumne Lodge and Wilderness Permits turnoff on the right. Turn right and drive 0.4 mile toward Tuolumne Lodge. Park in the lot on the left signed for Dog Lake and John Muir Trail. The trail begins across the road from the parking lot. Additional parking is available in the Wilderness Permits parking lot.

This hike is one of the easiest in the Yosemite high country, and since it starts out beautiful and stays that way, you can walk the trail for as long or as short as you like. The total distance is eight miles one way as the Pacific Crest Trail/John Muir Trail parallels the Lyell Fork of the Tuolumne River. But most people just head out for a couple miles, often carrying their fishing rods or picnic supplies, then turn back.

To reach the Lyell Fork you must first cross the Dana Fork on a footbridge less than 0.5 mile from the parking lot. In another 0.5 mile, you cross the Lyell Fork on a second footbridge, then head left along the river's south side. A third bridge takes you across Rafferty Creek and into Lyell Canyon. If you enjoy gazing at gorgeous meadows and a meandering river, this is your hike. Anglers enjoy this area because small rainbow trout are plentiful. A bonus is that there are backpacking sites three to four miles out on the trail, so if you get a wilderness permit you can linger for a few days in paradise.

Glen Aulin and Tuolumne Falls

• Distance: 9.2 miles round-trip
• Duration: 4–5 hours
• Rating: Moderate
• Elevation Change: 400 feet
• Trailhead: Glen Aulin/Soda Springs
• Directions: From the Big Oak Flat entrance station on Highway 120, drive southeast 7.7 miles to Crane Flat, then turn left to stay on Highway 120. Drive 39 miles to the Lembert Dome/Soda Springs/Dog Lake/Glen Aulin Trailhead on the left. Begin hiking on the western edge of the parking lot at a gated dirt road signed Soda Springs, 0.5 mile.

Tuolumne Falls is one of the prettiest waterfalls in Yosemite (a park that has a lot to offer in the waterfall department), and reaching it requires only a 4.5-mile one-way walk with a 400-foot elevation loss on the way in. The climb back out is nothing to worry about, with most of the ascent in the first mile as you head up and over the various cascades of Tuolumne Falls on granite stairsteps.

Every step of this hike is lovely. Start by following the dirt road from the Lembert Dome parking lot toward Soda Spring. When you near Parson's Lodge, veer right on the signed trail to Glen Aulin. You'll walk through forest,

WHEN LIGHTNING STRIKES

If you see or hear a thunderstorm approaching, avoid exposed ridges and peaks. This may be disheartening advice when you're only a mile from the summit of Clouds Rest or Mount Hoffman, but follow it anyway. If you're already on a mountaintop when a thunderstorm is threatening, stay out of enclosed places such as rock caves or recesses. Confined areas can be deadly in lightning storms. Do not lean against rock slopes or trees; try to keep a few feet of airspace around you. Squat low on your boot soles, or sit on your day pack, jacket, or anything that will insulate you in case lightning strikes the ground.

then move closer to the Tuolumne River and gain inspiring views of Cathedral and Unicorn Peaks and Fairview Dome. From here on out you're never far from the river's edge.

After three miles you'll cross the Tuolumne River on a footbridge and in another 0.25 mile you see the first stunning drop of Tuolumne Falls, a 100-foot churning freefall. The trail keeps descending past more cascades to the base of the falls, where a footbridge leads back across the river to Glen Aulin High Sierra Camp. The final cataract of Tuolumne Falls, just before Glen Aulin, is known as White Cascade. Pick a spot around the edge of its large pool and have a seat to enjoy the show.

🅜 Lembert Dome

- Distance: 2.8 miles round-trip
- Duration: 2 hours
- Rating: Moderate
- Elevation Change: 850 feet
- Trailhead: Lembert Dome/Dog Lake
- Directions: From the Big Oak Flat entrance station on Highway 120, drive southeast 7.7 miles to Crane Flat, then turn left to stay on Highway 120. Drive 39 miles to the Lembert Dome/Soda Springs/Dog Lake/Glen Aulin Trailhead on the left. The trail begins near the restrooms.

Lembert Dome is a roche moutonnée, which is a French geologic term that means it looks something like a sheep. You may not see the resemblance, but you will feel like a mountain goat when you climb to the dome's lofty summit at 9,450 feet. From the parking area at Lembert Dome's base, you may see rock climbers practicing their stuff on the steep side of the dome, but the hikers' trail curves around to the more gently sloped back side. You can walk right up the granite—no ropes necessary. The Dog Lake and Lembert Dome Trail steeply winds its way uphill to the dome's north side; from there, pick any route along the granite that looks manageable. When you reach the top of the dome, you'll discover that the view from its highest point—of Tuolumne Meadows and surrounding peaks and domes—is well worth the effort.

Dog Lake

- Distance: 3.4 miles round-trip
- Duration: 2 hours
- Rating: Moderate
- Elevation Change: 650 feet
- Trailhead: Lembert Dome/Dog Lake
- Directions: From the Big Oak Flat entrance station on Highway 120, drive southeast 7.7 miles to Crane Flat, then turn left to stay on Highway 120. Drive 39 miles to the Lembert Dome/Soda Springs/Dog Lake/Glen Aulin Trailhead on the left. The trail begins near the restrooms.

Dog Lake is an easy-to-reach destination from Tuolumne Meadows, a perfect place for a family to spend an afternoon in the high country. The hike begins near the base of Lembert Dome, then heads through a gorgeous meadow with open views of Cathedral and Unicorn Peaks. The trail traverses a granite slab, then splits off from the path to Lembert Dome and starts to climb quite steeply through a lodgepole pine and fir forest. When you reach an intersection with the Young Lakes Trail you're only 0.25 mile from Dog Lake.

The lake is a delight. Set at 9,170 feet in elevation, it is wide, shallow, and deep blue. The colorful peaks to the east are Mount Dana and Mount Gibbs. You can hike around Dog Lake's perimeter if you please, go for a swim in late summer, or just sit by its peaceful shore and relax.

Mono Pass and/Spillway Lake

- Distance: 8.4–11.6 miles round-trip
- Duration: 5–6 hours
- Rating: Moderate
- Elevation Change: 900 feet
- Trailhead: Mono Pass
- Directions: From the Big Oak Flat entrance station on Highway 120, drive southeast 7.7 miles to Crane Flat, then turn left to stay on Highway 120. Drive 44.5 miles to the Mono Pass Trailhead on the right near road marker T-37 (1.3 miles west of Tioga Pass Entrance Station).

With an elevation gain of only 900 feet spread out over four miles, you'll hardly even notice you're climbing on the route to Mono Pass. That's if you're acclimated, of course, because you start out at 9,700 feet, where the air is mighty thin.

The Mono Pass Trail leads through barren, high-elevation lodgepole pine forests and meadows, then crosses the Dana Fork of the Tuolumne River, which is an easy boulder-hop by midsummer. (Earlier in the season you may need to find a log to cross.) As you proceed, you'll gain great views of Mount Gibbs, Mount Dana, and the Kuna Crest. At a trail junction at 2.0 miles, bear left and start to climb more noticeably. When you reach the Mono Pass sign at 3.8 miles, take the right spur trail (unsigned). It leads 0.3 mile to a cluster of four 19th-century mining cabins, which have been beautifully restored. You can explore the buildings and the mine ruins in this area and consider the hard life of those who lived and worked here.

Back on the main trail, continue another 0.5 mile past the sign marking Mono Pass for the best views of the trip. From a granite promontory above a water-filled tarn, you can see far down Bloody Canyon to Mono Lake and the surrounding desert.

Another option on the Mono Pass Trail is to take the right fork at 2.0 miles and head for Spillway Lake, a wide, shallow lake only 1.6 miles from this junction. You'll have more solitude along this pathway and a pleasant walk alongside Parker Pass Creek and its adjoining meadow. Views of the Kuna Crest are spectacular.

Middle and Upper Gaylor Lakes

- Distance: 4.0 miles round-trip
- Duration: 2 hours
- Rating: Moderate
- Elevation Change: 1,100 feet
- Trailhead: Gaylor Lakes/Tioga Pass entrance station
- Directions: From the Big Oak Flat entrance station on Highway 120, drive southeast 7.7 miles to Crane Flat, then turn left to stay on Highway 120. Drive 46 miles to the Gaylor Lakes parking lot just west of the Tioga Pass Entrance Station on the north side of the road.

The trail to Middle and Upper Gaylor Lakes offers world-class High Sierra scenery. This area is as stark, and as beautiful, as it gets. Starting a few yards from the Tioga Pass entrance station at nearly 10,000 feet, the trail climbs a steep ridge and then drops down to Middle Gaylor Lake. Although it's only one mile of ascent, it's a high-elevation butt-kicker that makes many hikers beg for mercy. Total elevation gain is just shy of 1,000 feet, but it's worth every step.

From the middle lake you can follow the creek gently uphill to the east to reach smaller Upper Gaylor Lake in another mile. Take the trail around its north side and uphill for a few hundred yards to the site of the Great Sierra Mine, where you'll find the remains of an old stone cabin. The Great Sierra Mine turned out to be not so great—no silver ore was ever refined, and the mine was abandoned. All that remains is this hauntingly beautiful glacial scenery.

Mount Dana

- Distance: 6.0 miles round-trip
- Duration: 4 hours
- Rating: Very strenuous
- Elevation Change: 3,100 feet
- Trailhead: Tioga Pass entrance station
- Directions: See Middle and Upper Gaylor Lakes above.

Mount Dana is a grueling hike. Yet many hikers make the trip every summer, perhaps as some sort of rite of passage to affirm that the long winter has truly ended in the high country. The path to the 13,053-foot summit requires a 3,100-foot elevation gain condensed into a mere three miles. To make matters more difficult, there is no maintained trail, only a series of informal-use trails created by the hearty Yosemite visitors who make this trek.

To join their ranks, leave your car at the Gaylor Lakes Trailhead by the Tioga Pass entrance station, then hike southeast on the unsigned but obvious trail to Mount Dana. The path begins with a pleasant ramble through Dana Meadows, then enters a dense lodgepole pine forest. Soon the grade becomes more intense, and in short order you've climbed above

WILDERNESS PERMITS

A wilderness permit is required year-round for any overnight stay in the backcountry areas of Yosemite. You do not need a permit for day hikes. Due to the number of people who wish to enter Yosemite's backcountry, quotas are in effect for the number of permits granted at all wilderness trailheads from mid-May to mid-September.

You can reserve a wilderness permit in advance for $5 per person. (The permit itself is free; the fee is for making the reservation.) If you show up in Yosemite without a permit reservation, you will have very limited choices as to where you can backpack, because most of the popular trailheads' quotas will be filled. Without a reservation, your best bet is to show up at one of the wilderness permit offices (Big Oak Flat Information Station, Tuolumne Meadows Wilderness Center, Yosemite Valley Wilderness Center, Wawona Information Station, or Hetch Hetchy Entrance Station) in the first hour it is open for the day, and see what is available. If you can be flexible about your destination, and/or if you are willing to wait 24 hours before leaving, you should be able to plan a backpacking trip that suits you. Phone 209/372-0308 or 209/372-0740 to find out the current hours of operation for the wilderness permit offices. In winter, only the Valley, Wawona, and Big Oak Flat offices are open, plus an additional office at Badger Pass Ski Area.

If you need to spend a night in the park before setting off on your permitted backpacking trip, a few backpacker's campsites are available at the Valley's North Pines Campground, at Tuolumne Meadows Campground, and at Hetch Hetchy. Campers who wish to stay in these sites may do so for only one night before or after their backpacking trip, and they must have their wilderness permit in hand. The sites are walk-in only, and only backpacking-type equipment may be brought in.

To learn more about the permit system and backpacking in Yosemite's wilderness, visit www.nps.gov/yose/wilderness. This site offers a complete list of trail descriptions, general wilderness information, and current regulations. Wilderness permit reservations are available from 2 to 24 weeks in advance for the quota season from mid-May to mid-September and are available online at the website above. Reservations may also be made by phoning 209/372-0740, weekdays 9 A.M.–4 P.M.—but this line is often busy. You can also mail your request to: Wilderness Permit Reservations, P.O. Box 545, Yosemite, CA 95389. Include a check payable to the Yosemite Association for your reservation fee ($5 per person) or a valid credit card number and expiration date.

Reserved wilderness permits must be picked up in person no earlier than the day before your reserved trip start date.

One more thing: If you think you can sneak off into Yosemite's backcountry without a wilderness permit and not get caught, think again. Especially in the summer months, rangers regularly patrol Yosemite's wilderness areas and check that backpackers are carrying permits.

11,000 feet. The path keeps ascending until the 11,600-foot mark, where a trail cairn marks a large plateau. If you're still feeling comfortable with the high altitude, continue onward and upward. In the final mile you must gain 1,500 feet, and it's slow going. Somehow, with what may seem like your last breath, you finally reach the summit. As you gasp for air, you are witness to one of the finest views in the Sierra. Your field of vision encompasses Mono Lake, Ellery and Saddlebag Lakes, Tuolumne Meadows, Lembert Dome, and an untold wealth of high peaks. Bring a map and identify all you can survey, or forget the map and just take in the majesty of it all.

A few tips for making the ascent safely: First,

wait until August to make the trip, as Mount Dana is snow-covered long into the summer. Second, get an early start in the morning so you have no chance of encountering afternoon thunderstorms. Third, carry (and drink) as much water as you can. Fourth, wear good sunglasses and sun protection at this high elevation. And lastly, pace yourself to give your body a chance to adjust to the 13,000-foot altitude.

BACKPACKING

Some of the most popular backpacking destinations on Tioga Pass Road are detailed in the day hiking section above: Cathedral Lakes, Sunrise Lakes, and Lyell Canyon. Because these areas are close enough to the road to be reachable by day hikers, they don't make ideal backpacking trips for those seeking solitude. Too many hikers line the trails and crowd the lakeshores, and during the day, you won't have any solitude at your camp. Nonetheless, because these trails are relatively short and easy, and because they lead to beautiful destinations, they are still favored by backpackers. Permits to camp along these trails are extremely difficult to come by, especially on weekends. It would be wise to save a trip to these high-profile destinations for a weekday in September or early October, when the crowds have thinned.

The following are four somewhat lower-profile backpacking trails that lead from Tioga Pass Road or Tuolumne Meadows, where you'll have a greater chance of a true backpacking experience, far from the madding crowd. Remember, though, this is Yosemite. These destinations are still popular, and you won't go without seeing other people.

Remember that if you plan to spend the night in Yosemite's wilderness, you must have a permit. Also, be sure to take adequate bear precautions. If you are visiting destinations higher than 9,600 feet, you must carry a bear canister.

Ten Lakes and Grant Lakes

• Distance: 12.8 miles round-trip

• Rating: Strenuous
• Trailhead: From the Big Oak Flat entrance station on Highway 120, drive southeast 7.7 miles to Crane Flat, then turn left to stay on Highway 120. Drive 19.4 miles to the Yosemite Creek and Ten Lakes Trailhead parking area on the south side of the road. The trail begins on the north side of the road.

The Ten Lakes area is a spectacularly beautiful wilderness destination, so reserve your wilderness permit early. Also, be prepared to do some serious climbing—this isn't a trail for the timid. But the rewards are great, because after a half day of hiking you'll be setting up camp at one of nearly a dozen sparkling, rockbound lakes.

From the Ten Lakes Trailhead, elevation 7,500 feet, the path ascends steadily for the first four miles. There's only one brutally steep stretch, which comes between miles four and five after a pretty stroll around Half Moon Meadow. A series of tight switchbacks pull you through a nasty 800-foot elevation gain to the top of a ridge and the Ten Lakes/Grant Lakes junction.

There you make a choice. Turn right to reach Grant Lakes and head mostly downhill for a mile; or, to reach Ten Lakes, continue straight, soon heading steeply downhill for 1.4 miles. The Grant Lakes offer a little more solitude, while the two larger of the Ten Lakes have the best campsites, with many trees along their shorelines offering protection from the wind.

Whether you go to Ten Lakes or Grant Lakes, don't miss taking a side trip to the rocky overlook above the Ten Lakes basin. It's only 0.5 mile from the Ten Lakes/Grant Lakes junction; continue straight for Ten Lakes, then take the unsigned fork to the left and head for the highest point. Four of the Ten Lakes are visible from this promontory, as well as a section of the Grand Canyon of the Tuolumne.

Waterwheel Falls and Beyond

• Distance: 16.0–28.0 miles
• Rating: Moderate
• Trailhead: From the Big Oak Flat entrance station on Highway 120, drive southeast 7.7

HIGH SIERRA CAMPS

Among people who love to hike but hate to carry a heavy backpack, the Yosemite High Sierra Camps are legendary. The five "camps" are spaced 5.7 to 10 miles apart along a loop trail that begins at Tuolumne Meadows. With nothing on your back but a light day pack with water, snacks, a change of clothes, sheets, and a towel, you can hike through the high country for nearly a week. Along the way, you eat first-rate meals, enjoy hot showers, and sleep in a comfortable bed in a tent cabin each night.

Not everybody does the whole loop and stays at all five camps. In fact, unless you plan a year in advance, it's virtually impossible to do so. Reservations for the High Sierra Camps are taken on a lottery basis each autumn, and only a lucky few win the lottery.

Still, many people manage to get reservations for an out-and-back trip to one or more of the camps. Even those who wait until the last minute have a fair chance because there are always cancellations. The key is to call the High Sierra Camp desk on a regular basis; availability changes by the minute. Another option for High Sierra Camp wannabes is to sign up for organized four- and seven-day trips led by National Park Service rangers; these cost more but include a naturalist guide for your trip. Organized horseback trips are also available.

If you aren't traveling the entire loop, the one-way hikes to the camps are as follows: Glen Aulin at 7,800 feet is five miles from the Lembert Dome Trailhead. May Lake at 9,300 feet is one mile from the May Lake Trailhead. Sunrise Camp at 9,400 feet is five miles from the Sunrise Trailhead. Vogelsang Camp at 10,300

feet is seven miles from the Tuolumne Meadows Trailhead. Merced Lake Camp at 7,200 feet is the only one that's a bit far to reach if you're not traveling from another camp on the loop; it's 15 miles from Tuolumne Meadows or 13 miles from Yosemite Valley.

The arrangement is basically the same at all five camps, although each has a different number of tent cabins so the size of the crowd will vary. Merced Lake Camp is the largest with a 60-person occupancy; the others fit 30–40 guests at a time. Dinner and breakfast are served in a main dining tent; box lunches can be purchased to go. Generally, the camps are very social: Meals are served family-style, and the tent cabins are spaced within a few feet of each other, so you'll get to know your neighbors.

One critical rule at the High Sierra Camps is that overnight accommodations are "dormitory style," which means that men and women are housed in separate tents, four people to a tent. The camp staff tries to keep families together, but if your significant other happens to be of the opposite sex, you might have to wave goodbye to him or her at night. Exceptions are made when a camp isn't full or if a camp has smaller, two-person tent cabins available.

To obtain a spot at Yosemite's High Sierra Camps, you must submit an application between October 15 and November 30 for the following summer, or hope for a last-minute cancellation. Fees are $112 per night and include meals. Contact Yosemite High Sierra Camps at 559/253-5674 or www.yosemitepark. com for more information.

miles to Crane Flat, then turn left to stay on Highway 120. Drive 39 miles to the Lembert Dome/Soda Springs/Dog Lake/Glen Aulin Trailhead on the left. Begin hiking on the western edge of the parking lot at a gated dirt road signed Soda Springs, 0.5 mile.

This hike could be called the Epic Waterfall Trip. If you hike the entire route, you'll see so many waterfalls and so much water along the

way that you'll have enough memories to get you through a 10-year drought.

You must arrange for a wilderness permit in advance or reserve a stay at the Glen Aulin High Sierra Camp. If you desire, you can continue your trip beyond Waterwheel Falls; many backpackers make this a one-way trip with a shuttle vehicle waiting for them at White Wolf, 28 miles away. Beyond Waterwheel Falls you'll have a lot less company.

The trail follows the Tuolumne River to Tuolumne Falls and Glen Aulin Camp, alternating between stretches of stunning flower- and aspen-lined meadows and stark granite slabs. Waterwheel Falls is only three miles from the camp, and two other major cascades, California and LeConte, are found along the way. Waterwheel is Yosemite's most unusual-looking waterfall. Its churning water dips into deep holes in the granite riverbed, then shoots out with such velocity that it doubles back on itself. When the river level is high, the resemblance to a waterwheel is obvious.

Backpackers who continue onward will keep following the path of the Tuolumne River. The second night of the trip is usually spent at Pate Valley, and then with a fresh head of steam you climb up a long series of switchbacks and eventually make your way to Harden Lake and then White Wolf. You may be able to get a shuttle bus here instead of leaving a car; check with the wilderness office about the current status of the bus system on Tioga Road.

Vogelsang Loop

- Distance: 19.0 miles round-trip
- Rating: Strenuous
- Trailhead: From the Big Oak Flat entrance station on Highway 120, drive southeast 7.7 miles to Crane Flat, then turn left to stay on Highway 120. Drive 39.5 miles to the Tuolumne Lodge and Wilderness Permits turnoff on the right. Turn right and drive 0.4 mile toward Tuolumne Lodge. Park in the lot on the left signed for Dog Lake and John Muir Trail. The trail begins across the road from the parking lot. Additional parking is available in the Wilderness Permits parking lot.

Although this loop is popular with hikers staying at the Vogelsang High Sierra Camp, backpackers who plan early can get a wilderness permit for their own self-designed trip. The traditional route is to head out on the western side of the loop along Rafferty Creek, then take a short spur and spend the night at Vogelsang Lake, which is without question the most visually dramatic spot on this trip. The lake is flanked by Fletcher Peak, a steep and rugged wall of glacier-carved granite. Few trees can grow in this sparse, high-alpine environment. If you're lucky, you can even score a spot at the dinner table at Vogelsang High Sierra Camp. They usually have a few extra spaces for backpackers, so bring your wallet.

The next day you rejoin the loop and continue eastward to Evelyn Lake, another favorite camping spot. When it's time to return, hike down to Lyell Fork, a 2,000-foot descent that takes a few hours, then meet up with the John Muir Trail and follow it north through lush, green Lyell Canyon, back to the trailhead at Tuolumne Meadows.

Young Lakes Loop

- Distance: 12.5 miles round-trip
- Rating: Moderate
- Trailhead: From the Big Oak Flat entrance station on Highway 120, drive southeast 7.7 miles to Crane Flat, then turn left to stay on Highway 120. Drive 39 miles to the Lembert Dome/Soda Springs/Dog Lake/Glen Aulin Trailhead on the left. Begin hiking on the western edge of the parking lot at a gated dirt road signed Soda Springs, 0.5 mile.

Starting from the Lembert Dome parking lot, the Young Lakes Loop is a classic Yosemite trip that works equally well as a short backpacking trip or a long day hike. The destination is a series of lakes set in a deep and wide glacial cirque at 9,900 feet. Because the mileage is short, this is a great trip for a weekend getaway.

The trip starts with a walk down the wide dirt road that leads to Soda Springs. Pick up the trail near Parson's Lodge that leads to Glen Aulin and follow it through lodgepole pines for 1.8 miles until you see the right turnoff for Young Lakes. Follow the Young Lakes Trail for three more miles, climbing steadily. At five miles out you'll see the return leg of your loop leading off to the right (signed for Dog Lake).

Continue straight for another 1.5 miles to Lower Young Lake, where you have a stunning view of Mount Conness and Ragged Peak. Two more lakes are accessible within a mile to the

Upper Young Lake, nestled at the base of Ragged Peak, is the highest and loveliest of the three Young Lakes.

east. You'll probably want to make camp at the lower lakes, but don't miss a hike to the third, uppermost lake, the most visually stunning of them all.

When you're ready to head home, retrace your steps to the junction and take the eastern (left) fork, returning via Dog Lake and Lembert Dome. Be forewarned: if you loop back this way, it won't be an all-downhill cruise, but the scenery makes the additional climbing worthwhile.

BIKING

Biking is generally not permitted on any trail in Yosemite, but there are a few exceptions to the rule. One of those is the six-mile section of the **old Big Oak Flat Road** that passes through the Tuolumne Grove of Giant Sequoias. Bikes are permitted because the road/trail is paved, not dirt. You don't want to ride this old road in the summer, however, because there are simply too many hikers using the route, especially in the first mile to the big trees. On the other hand, during a quiet autumn day this one-way, down-

hill route is very pleasant. The trail's terminus is at Hodgdon Meadow Campground, where a friend could pick you up. Ambitious cyclists can make a loop out of the trip by riding back to the Tuolumne Grove parking lot on Highway 120 (a 15-mile round-trip). Those who just want a little exercise could start at Hodgdon Meadow, ride uphill to the Tuolumne Grove, then turn around and ride back whenever the crowds get too thick.

Almost every day of summer you will see cyclists on road and mountain bikes tackling **Tioga Pass** itself. This 9,945-foot pass is not for the faint of heart. The downhill from Yosemite to Lee Vining is far more terrifying than the uphill is difficult. It can be very hard to control your bike on the steep descent, especially if the wind is blowing through the pass. This fact, combined with the number of cars driving on the route, makes this a very daring ride for experienced cyclists only.

Visitors looking for bike rentals will have to rent them at Curry Village in Yosemite Valley. There is nowhere in Tuolumne Meadows to rent bikes.

ROCK CLIMBING

The same climbing school that offers classes in the Valley, **Yosemite Mountaineering School and Guide Service** (209/372-8344), has a center at the Tuolumne Meadows Gas Station. It conducts seminars and classes for beginning, intermediate, and advanced climbers in the Tioga Pass Road area June–Sept. Classes meet daily and equipment rentals are available. Private guided climbs are available for up to three people.

The preponderance of granite domes in the stretch of highway from Tenaya Lake to the Tuolumne Meadows area makes this region a playground for rock climbers. Two of the best places for watching climbers in action are at **Polly Dome,** directly across the highway from Tenaya Lake, and at **Lembert Dome,** on the east end of Tuolumne Meadows. Two other popular domes for rock climbing in this area are Fairview Dome and Medlicott Dome, both just off Highway 120 near Tenaya Lake.

FISHING

Tioga Road is well known for its easy access to alpine lakes. At one time, most of these lakes were regularly planted with trout. The National Park Service stopped all fish stocking of park lakes in 1991 (stream stocking had been ended long before), and slowly, most of the fish have died out. If a lake did not have the proper conditions to allow the planted fish to reproduce, the last planted fish would live out their lifespans and that would be the end of the story. Some of the region's most famous bodies of water, like Tenaya Lake, are completely barren (although you may still see unknowing anglers dropping a line in along its shores).

Some Yosemite lakes did have the right conditions for reproduction, however. The **Ten Lakes,** a popular backpacking trip or long day hike off Tioga Road, have self-sustaining populations of brook and rainbow trout. The three **Young Lakes,** another favorite backpacking destination, contain fair numbers of brook trout. **May Lake,** the site of a busy High Si-

erra Camp and an easy one-mile hike from the trailhead parking area, has a small population of brook trout. **Upper Cathedral Lake, Elizabeth Lake,** and the **Sunrise Lakes** are all easily reached day hiking destinations that support fair numbers of brook trout. The creeks near these lakes also are laden with fish; in fact, you might have better luck in the creeks.

More stream-fishing opportunities exist in the South Fork of the **Tuolumne River,** which runs parallel to Tioga Road. There are plenty of places to pull off the road and try your luck at catching the small brook trout that reside there. At the Yosemite Creek Campground or nearby Yosemite Creek Picnic Area, you can try for rainbow, brown, and brook trout in the creek (rainbows are most plentiful). An informal-use trail leads out of camp both upstream and downstream. On the east side of Tuolumne Meadows, many anglers try their luck in both the Dana Fork and the Lyell Fork of the Tuolumne River.

HORSEBACK RIDING

Is the thin air at high elevation bothering your lungs? That's no reason not to see the high country. **Tuolumne Meadows Stables** offers horseback rides all summer long. Two-hour and four-hour rides depart daily ($40–55); the four-hour trip usually heads to Tuolumne Falls. All-day rides to Waterwheel Falls or Young Lakes can be arranged ($80). For half-day and all-day rides, saddlebags are provided, in which you can store your picnic lunch, water, a camera, a jacket, and maybe a bag of carrots for your trusty steed. Pack trips are also available. Children must be at least seven years old and 44 inches tall. The maximum a rider may weigh is 225 pounds. Helmets are required for all riders and are available free of charge. Phone 209/372-8427 for reservations.

WINTER SPORTS

Tioga Pass Road may be closed in the winter, but it's still a prime destination for cross-country skiers. The road is plowed up to Crane Flat,

Tioga and Tuolumne

usually about 100 yards past the parking area for the Tuolumne Grove of Giant Sequoias. The gentle grade of Tioga Pass Road in these first few miles makes great skiing for beginners to intermediates.

The trails to the **Merced Grove** and **Tuolumne Grove** would offer good cross-country skiing, but most often these paths are used by snowshoers and sometimes even people wearing regular snow boots, so the trails tend to be too chopped up for skiing. Snowshoers, however, will thoroughly enjoy the short treks to the two sequoia groves—it's a special treat to see the big trees crowned with a mantle of snow.

Crane Flat Campground is the site of the park's only official "snow play" area. The camp access road is plowed up to a point where there's a parking area and restrooms. There is no real sledding hill, but this is a good place to bring the kids to make snowballs or tool around on their sleds. Crane Flat is also the start of several cross-country skiing loops, as well as the popular trek up the snow-covered road to Crane Flat Fire Lookout Tower (3 miles round-trip by ski or snowshoe). The Crane Flat gas station (at Crane Flat off Highway 120, summer hours 8 A.M.–8 P.M., shorter winter hours) sells a winter ski trail map for $0.50. It also sells sleds and rents snowshoes.

Highly experienced cross-country skiers head to the **Tuolumne Meadows** region—but they have to ski all the way there, since the road is not plowed. Some follow trails from Yosemite Valley; others head in from U.S. 395. With a wilderness permit, skiers can camp and ski in and around Tuolumne Meadows for up to two weeks.

ENTERTAINMENT AND EVENTS

Ranger Talks and Walks

Rangers lead walks to the Tuolumne Grove of Giant Sequoias daily in the summer and on weekends in the fall. On Saturdays in summer, a ranger-led hike begins at the Big Oak Flat Information Station. In Tuolumne Meadows, rangers lead walks to the top of Lembert Dome and Pothole Dome, and along the Tuolumne River. Check the free Yosemite newspaper for scheduled walks and times, or ask for a schedule at the Tuolumne Meadows Visitor Center.

Campfire Programs

Crane Flat and Tuolumne Meadows Campgrounds have one-hour evening campfire programs designed for families, usually starting at 7 P.M. Program topics vary, but often include singing and storytelling. Star programs are held later in the evening (8:30 P.M.) on clear nights only at Tuolumne Meadows Campground. Bring something to sit on and dress warmly.

Parson's Lodge

During the summer, interpretive programs are held several times a week at Parson's Lodge in Tuolumne Meadows. The Tuolumne Meadows Visitor Center has details on scheduled events.

Tioga and Tuolumne

Hetch Hetchy

Most everybody in California has visited Yosemite Valley at one time or another, but substantially fewer people have visited Hetch Hetchy Valley, Yosemite's "twin" in the northern section of the park. Of the five park entrance stations, Hetch Hetchy gets the fewest number of cars passing through day after day.

Hetch Hetchy Valley was flooded in 1923 to create a water supply for the city of San Francisco. It was the tragic end of a long fight for naturalist John Muir, who tried in vain to save Hetch Hetchy from the big city politicians. When people see pictures of what Hetch Hetchy looked like before it was dammed and

flooded to provide water for San Francisco, they are struck by how much it resembles today's Yosemite Valley. Photos show the stark, pristine granite of Kolana Rock and Hetch Hetchy Dome jutting upward from the valley floor, waterfalls dropping hundreds of feet from hanging valley s like rivers falling from the sky, and lush, flower-filled meadows lining the edge of the meandering Tuolumne River. You can't help but wonder, what on earth were those politicians thinking?

But here's the great truth: Despite human's best efforts to destroy it, Hetch Hetchy remains beautiful. Without question the valley has lost

© ANN MARIE BROWN

Must-Sees

M O'Shaughnessy Dam: A remarkable feat of engineering, the 85-foot-high dam that forms Hetch Hetchy Reservoir took almost seven years to build. It was another 14 years until the infrastructure was completed to carry Hetch Hetchy's water to the city of San Francisco, a distance of 156 miles. See the dam in spring when its overflow valves are spraying thousands of gallons of

© ANN MARIE BROWN

hikers on a bridge below Wapama Fall

water into the free-flowing stretch of the Tuolumne River (page 91).

M Tueeulala and Wapama Falls: In spring and early summer, these two spectacular waterfalls drop more than 1,000 feet to the lakeshore at Hetch Hetchy. At full flow, both falls are visible from O'Shaughnessy Dam, but to see them up close, take a 4.8-mile round-trip hike along the reservoir's northern edge and enjoy a fabulous wildflower display along the way (page 93).

M Carlon Falls: A favorite swimming hole for more than 100 years, the pools below Carlon Falls make a fine destination for a short hike on a hot summer day. Plenty of people never make it as far as the falls; they just pick an inviting spot along the river near the trail's start at Carlon Day-Use Area (page 96).

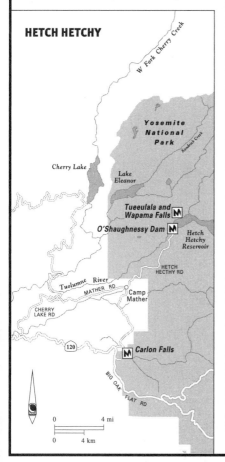

HETCH HETCHY

W Fork Cherry Creek

Yosemite National Park

Kendrick Creek

Cherry Lake

Lake Eleanor

Tueeulala and Wapama Falls **M**

O'Shaughnessy Dam **M**

Hetch Hetchy Reservoir

HETCH HETCHY RD

Tuolumne River

MATHER RD

Camp Mather

CHERRY LAKE RD

120

M Carlon Falls

BIG OAK FLAT RD

0   4 mi

0   4 km

M Hetch Hetchy

an irreplaceable amount of its original splendor. But when you hike along the shoreline of 360-foot-deep Hetch Hetchy Reservoir and observe the higher sections of granite and waterfalls that tower imposingly above the waterline, you get the sense that Nature has ceased crying over Hetch Hetchy. Instead, she has done what she does best—heal, beautify, and make the most of what is. Wildflowers blossom in the understory of massive ponderosa pines and incense-cedars. Birds and other wildlife make their homes along the edges of the deep blue reservoir. Hetch Hetchy's waterfalls still flow with exuberance, and its granite towers still stand guard over the valley.

Casual day-trip visitors can make the winding, 18-mile drive to Hetch Hetchy from Big Oak Flat, walk along the top of O'Shaughnessy Dam, and get a good look at the area's cliffs and waterfalls. Those who are in the mood for a short, level hike can walk the path to the base of impressive Wapama Fall. A longer day hike or a backpacking trip can be made to the far end of the reservoir and Rancheria Falls, or to many other worthwhile destinations in this remote region of Yosemite.

Exploring Hetch Hetchy

WEATHER AND SEASONS

Hetch Hetchy is best visited in springtime, when its waterfalls are flowing at their fullest and temperatures are still mild and cool. Summer can be quite hot, with temperatures frequently reaching 90°F to 100°F. Autumn is another good time to visit Hetch Hetchy, when temperatures drop to a more comfortable level. The region's deciduous trees put on a lovely fall color show, but the valley's waterfalls run dry by midsummer. Snowfall will sometimes, but not always, close the road to Hetch Hetchy in the winter.

SERVICES

When driving to Hetch Hetchy, you'll need to be completely self-reliant. The nearest gas pump is found at Yosemite Lakes (209/962-0110) or in the park at Crane Flat. Evergreen Lodge (33160 Evergreen Rd., 209/379-2606) has a small store and restaurant. Camp Mather (35250 Mather Rd., 209/379-2284) has a small camping supply store with a few grocery items. Once you drive past Camp Mather no supplies are available for the final nine miles to Hetch Hetchy. The nearest ATM is at the Yosemite Lakes store on Highway 120. There is no visitor center in this region of Yosemite, but the ranger working at the Mather entrance kiosk will happily answer any questions.

DRIVING TOUR

Hetchy Hetchy Reservoir is a 40-mile drive from Yosemite Valley via Highway 120 and the Evergreen and Hetch Hetchy Roads. In winter, these two roads are sometimes closed. Because the road is narrow and winding, vehicles longer than 25 feet are prohibited at all times. It's best to prepare for a trip to Hetch Hetchy by having everything you might need or want already in your car. Opportunities for food and supplies are limited once you leave Highway 120.

Starting from the Big Oak Flat Entrance to Yosemite, head west on Highway 120 for one mile, then turn right on Evergreen Road. Seven miles down this road is the Evergreen Lodge, a cabin resort with a good restaurant and store. A half mile farther is Camp Mather, a camp run by the city of San Francisco for its employees and their families. Bear right on Hetch Hetchy Road at Camp Mather, and in 1.5 miles you will pass through the Hetch Hetchy Entrance Station to Yosemite. Get any information you might need here; this is probably your last chance to see a park ranger.

The Hetch Hetchy Road continues for another 7.5 winding miles to O'Shaughnessy Dam. This road was the route of the Hetch Hetchy Railroad, which carried men, machinery, and materials to the dam's construction site. At several points in the road you will gain some long-

RESTORE HETCH HETCHY

Since the waters first rose up the granite walls of Hetch Hetchy Valley in 1923, a debate over the possibility of draining and restoring the valley has repeatedly surfaced. In the 1950s, David Brower, a highly influential conservationist and longtime president of the Sierra Club, produced a film about the reservoir that called for the removal of the dam and restoration of the valley. In 1970, only a few years after San Francisco voters approved a $115 million bond measure to expand the Hetch Hetchy water delivery system, the Sierra Club Board of Directors recommended a removal, rather than an expensive restoration or reconstruction, of both O'Shaughnessy Dam on Hetch Hetchy Reservoir and Eleanor Dam on Lake Eleanor.

Although it was 60 years too late for Hetch Hetchy, in 1985 U.S. Representative Rick Lehman steered legislation through Congress that prohibited the construction of any more dams in Yosemite or any other national parks. In 1987, President Ronald Reagan's Interior Secretary, Donald Hodel, proposed that the city of San Francisco undertake a feasibility study to see if the dam could be removed and the valley restored. His proposal generated a lot of heated discussion, then was quickly forgotten. Legislative funding to study Hetch Hetchy's restoration was defeated in committee.

Then suddenly, in 2000, bumper stickers on cars throughout California were seen bearing the message Restore Hetch Hetchy. This marketing effort was made by a nonprofit organization called Restore Hetch Hetchy, which was loosely culled from the Sierra Club and several other environmental groups. Their timing was apt: In 2002, a $1.6 billion bond measure was scheduled to appear on the San Francisco ballot to finance an upgrade of the aging Hetch Hetchy water supply system, which serves more than two million Bay Area residents but is not considered to be seismically safe or reliable in the event of a natural disaster. The reservoir's miles of aqueduct cross several major earthquake faults.

In November 2002, the voters approved the bond, giving the go-ahead to raise money for repairing the water supply system. Will this put an end to the Restore Hetch Hetchy movement? Certainly the environmentalists are fighting an uphill battle. Restoring Hetch Hetchy, and compensating the city of San Francisco for the loss of water and power generation, would cost upwards of $900 million, by a very conservative estimate. The work would take decades, and some contend that the granite walls of Hetch Hetchy Valley will be forever stained by the watermark of the reservoir.

And yet, in this latest round of debate, the seed has been planted in the minds of millions of Californians. Restore Hetch Hetchy? It might still happen someday. For more information, visit the Restore Hetch Hetchy website at www.hetchhetchy.org.

distance peeks at the reservoir and its waterfalls. After parking at the dam, be sure to walk across its massive, 600-foot-long concrete surface and take a closer look at what humans, and Mother Nature, have created in Hetch Hetchy Valley.

SIGHTS
M O'Shaughnessy Dam
Built by the city of San Francisco during the years from 1914 to 1923 to provide power and water for its citizens, O'Shaughnessy Dam was a product of its time. Although the dam's construction was adamantly opposed by John Muir, the Sierra Club, Pacific Gas and Electric Company, and the cities of Turlock and Modesto— all for their own reasons—the dam came into existence because of a piece of Congressional legislation called the Raker Act, signed into law by President Woodrow Wilson. (Although some progressives claimed this was a noble victory because it would mandate the break-up of Pacific

JOHN MUIR: HETCH HETCHY'S DEFENDER

Naturalist, conservationist, geologist, botanist, prolific writer, mechanical genius, wilderness advocate, founder and first president of the Sierra Club—John Muir was all these things and more. To a greater degree than anyone else, Muir's name is forever linked to Yosemite National Park. His dedicated involvement with the creation and protection of Yosemite, as well as several other national parks including Grand Canyon, Sequoia and Kings Canyon, and Mount Rainier, have led him to be called "the father of our national park system."

Although Muir is widely known for his role in creating the formalized boundaries of Yosemite National Park—a protected area much larger than its original borders, which included only Yosemite Valley and the Mariposa Grove of Giant Sequoias—one of Muir's greatest battles took place over the damming of Hetch Hetchy Valley to create a water supply for the city of San Francisco. It was one of the few contests that Muir was unable to win.

Muir first visited Hetch Hetchy Valley in 1871, and two years later he wrote of its wonders in the *Boston Weekly Transcript* and *Overland Monthly*: "It is a Yosemite Valley in depth and width, and is over 20 miles in length, abounding in falls and cascades, and glacial rock forms," wrote Muir. "The view from my first standpoint is one of the grandest I have ever beheld."

Despite the fact that in landscape and natural features Hetch Hetchy was an almost exact twin to Yosemite Valley, and more importantly a designated area of a federally sanctioned park, the city of San Francisco proposed damming the valley to create a public water supply. The request was twice denied by Secretary of the Interior Ethan Hitchcock, first in 1903 and later in 1905. Muir was aghast at the threat to Hetch Hetchy, and beginning in 1901, he led the newly formed Sierra Club and a consortium of other organizations in a campaign to protect the valley. It was one of the first known efforts at what we today call "grassroots lobbying," in which individual citizens were urged to write letters and contact their elected officials to express their opinions on an issue.

Muir wrote in the January 1908 *Sierra Club Bulletin,* "Dam Hetch Hetchy! As well dam for water-tanks the people's cathedrals and churches, for no holier temple has ever been consecrated by the heart of man."

But with Congress's passage of the Raker Act in 1913, John Muir lost his battle. Within a decade Hetch Hetchy Valley was filled with water. To add insult to injury, much of the lumber used to build the dam—more than six million board feet—was cut from trees within the national park border.

For the future of the conservation movement, the contest over Hetch Hetchy was not a complete defeat. The loss of the beautiful valley ("a grand landscape garden, one of nature's rarest and precious mountain mansions," as Muir described it) served to awaken many Americans to the idea that our national parks should be sacrosanct—that once they have been established,

Gas and Electric Company's San Francisco energy monopoly by creating a municipal, public power source, this never came to fruition.) The prevailing political mood at the time, particularly at the federal level, could not allow that the preservation of a national park was more important than the twin themes of progress and development. And so the massive dam was built, Hetch Hetchy Valley was flooded, and the world will never again see the twin to Yosemite Valley in its pristine state.

Whatever else we may think or say about it, the dam is a remarkable feat of engineering. It took almost seven years to build, and another 14 years before the aqueduct lines were completed over the 156-mile course to San Francisco, which required building 37 miles of tunnels. The original cost of construction was more than $12 million—a fortune at the time. By 1934, when the reservoir's water finally flowed to San Francisco, the cost had risen to $100 million. But the building didn't stop. In 1938, the origi-

their natural resources should not be tampered with. Since that time, conservationists have followed Muir's example and stopped dams from being built in Grand Canyon National Park and Dinosaur National Monument.

What kind of a person would fight so passionately to preserve and protect the lands of Yosemite? Born in Scotland in 1838, John Muir was raised by a ruthlessly strict, religious extremist father, first in Scotland and then later in the wilds of Wisconsin, where the Muir family homesteaded. Muir, along with his seven brothers and sisters, worked 17 hours a day on their 80-acre farm. As a teenager he was facile with machines and began to experiment with various mechanical inventions, while simultaneously developing a keen interest in botany and geology.

When Muir reached college age, he attended the University of Wisconsin, then sought employment in factories in Canada and Indiana. While working at a sawmill, an accident left Muir temporarily blind. He was forced to spend long weeks in a dark room to recover his eyesight. During this trial, Muir made a decision to leave the mechanical world behind and devote the rest of his life to studying "the inventions of God."

When Muir's health returned, he set off on a 1,000-mile walk from Indiana to the Gulf of Mexico. From there, he planned to head to South America to search for the headwaters of the Amazon River. But a long and painful bout with malaria and typhoid in Florida convinced him to stay out of the tropics. He decided to travel to California instead, "to see its Yosemite and Big Trees and wonderful flora in general."

Muir arrived in San Francisco in April 1868, then made his way to Yosemite Valley. He spent a few weeks there and was suitably awed by its wonders, then headed down out of the mountains to the San Joaquin Valley to find work. He toiled as a shepherd for a year, and in the summer of 1869 he drove a flock of sheep from the San Joaquin Valley to the Tuolumne Meadows area of Yosemite. This adventure was perhaps the most significant of Muir's life and is detailed in his famous book *My First Summer in the Sierra*. It was during this season that Muir embarked on his long and profound love affair with Yosemite.

Muir died at the age of 76 on Christmas Eve, 1914, in a Los Angeles hospital. He had been visiting his daughter Helen and her family when a winter cold developed into pneumonia. Six of the books he wrote were published during his lifetime; five more were published after his death. Muir's name is immortalized on an Alaskan glacier (one of several he discovered), on a variety of California landmarks from mountain peaks to public schools, in a species of wildflower, and in an ancient redwood forest that is now a National Monument.

Muir's home in Martinez, California, which he shared with his wife, Louie Strentzel Muir, and two daughters, Wanda and Helen, from 1890 to his death, is preserved as a National Historic Monument (925/228-8860; www .nps.gov/jomu).

nal dam was added to, which raised its height by 85 feet. Currently, the dam holds back 360,000 acre-feet of water. At its greatest depth, the reservoir is 362 feet deep.

Tueeulala and Wapama Falls

In the spring and early summer months, two waterfalls are visible from O'Shaughnessy Dam: Tueeulala and Wapama. Both falls drop about 1,400 feet before they hit the waterline of Hetch Hetchy Reservoir, which means they were nearly 1,800 feet high before the great manmade flood. By July, wispy Tueeulala Fall usually runs dry, but Wapama keeps a fair flow going into August. In spring, Wapama Fall sometimes runs with such force that the National Park Service is forced to close the trail below it.

Hetch Hetchy

Recreation

HIKING

Lookout Point

- Distance: 2.8 miles round-trip
- Duration: 1.5 hours
- Rating: Easy
- Elevation Change: 600 feet
- Trailhead: Mather ranger station
- Directions: From Groveland, drive east on Highway 120 for 22.5 miles to the Evergreen Road turnoff signed for Hetch Hetchy Reservoir (one mile west of the Big Oak Flat Entrance to Yosemite). Drive north on Evergreen Road for 7.4 miles and turn right on Hetch Hetchy Road. Drive 1.5 miles to the entrance kiosk by the Mather ranger station; the trail begins 100 yards past the entrance kiosk, just beyond the ranger station on the right.

Check your calendar. Is it springtime? Then it's time to take the easy jaunt to Lookout Point, where you can admire Hetch Hetchy Reservoir and its waterfalls from an unusual perspective and count the plentiful wildflowers along the trail as you walk. The Lookout Point Trail begins by the Mather Ranger Station on Hetch Hetchy Road. Begin hiking at the trail sign for Cottonwood and Smith Meadows and Hetch Hetchy. Turn left at the first junction, then follow the trail as it roughly parallels Hetch Hetchy Road for 0.5 mile. The trail turns away from the road with a brief uphill stretch, then enters a level, forested area that was severely burned in the wildfires of 1996. This is where the flowers bloom profusely in springtime. Look for a trail junction at one mile out and bear left for Lookout Point, 0.3 mile away. The path gets rather faint in places, but rock cairns mark the way. Head for the highest point you see atop a granite knoll dotted with a few Jeffrey pines. You'll know you're at Lookout Point when you can see the west end of Hetch Hetchy Reservoir, including its immense dam, and two of Hetch Hetchy's beautiful waterfalls: Wapama and Tueeulala.

Tueeulala and Wapama Falls

- Distance: 4.8 miles round-trip
- Duration: 2.5–3 hours
- Rating: Easy
- Elevation Change: 350 feet
- Trailhead: O'Shaughnessy Dam
- Directions: From Groveland, drive east on Highway 120 for 22.5 miles to the Evergreen Road turnoff, signed for Hetch Hetchy Reservoir (one mile west of the Big Oak Flat Entrance to Yosemite). Drive north on Evergreen Road for 7.4 miles and turn right on Hetch Hetchy Road. Drive 9.0 miles to the dam and trailhead.

The trail to this spectacular early-season waterfall starts by crossing the giant O'Shaughnessy Dam, where you may pause

Sturdy steel footbridges cross over the base of Wapama Fall. In spring, the waterfall can flow with such fury that the park service has to close the trail below it.

RATTLESNAKES

Although they are occasionally spotted on the trails leading out of Yosemite Valley, rattlesnakes are quite rare in Yosemite National Park, with the exception of one large area—the Hetch Hetchy region. Throughout the state of California rattlesnakes are almost never seen above 6,500 feet in elevation and are seen only infrequently between 5,000 and 6,500 feet. Below 5,000 feet they are common. Rattlesnakes prefer low elevations and warm temperatures in the 70°F to 90°F range, which makes the arid climate of Hetch Hetchy an ideal habitat.

Rattlesnakes have the honor of being California's only poisonous species of snake. The species found in Hetch Hetchy and throughout the lower elevations of the western Sierra Nevada is the northern Pacific rattlesnake, a subspecies of the western rattlesnake. These members of the pit viper family have wide triangular heads, narrow necks, and rattles on their tails. They are brown with a series of darker brown patches down their backs, similar to the more common (and nonpoisonous) gopher snake.

Even though rattlesnakes are prevalent in the Hetch Hetchy region, most hikers never see one. Rattlesnakes are shy creatures who generally prefer to be left alone and will slither off at the vibration of your footsteps. If you should encounter a rattlesnake in Hetch Hetchy or elsewhere, the standard advice is to give it lots of room. Once cornered, a rattlesnake will hold its ground, so freeze or move back slowly so it can get away. Rattlesnakes almost always give fair warning before striking: They shake their tails to produce a rattling or buzzing noise. The sound is unmistakable, even if you've never heard it before.

Rattlesnakes often sun themselves in open areas—sometimes even in the middle of a trail. When you are hiking, watch where you are going so you don't accidentally step on one. (The snakes can blend in with the brown and tan colors of a trail and surrounding leaf litter.) Watch where you put your hands, especially if you are scrambling over rocks. Be particularly wary of rattlesnakes in the spring and early summer months; most bites occur then, when the snakes come out of their winter hibernation and are particularly active.

Although rattlesnake bites sting and are quite frightening, they are only rarely fatal. Rattlesnakes will sometimes strike without biting, and even when they do bite, their bites do not always release venom. If you should get bitten by a rattlesnake, snake bite kits (or venom extractors) are basically useless. Instead, your car key is your best first aid. Don't panic or run. Walk slowly back to your car, then drive yourself to the nearest hospital or call 911. Avoid fast or unnecessary movements, because this will help spread the venom through your circulatory system. The bitten area may start to swell, so remove any jewelry or constricting clothing from the area. Do not apply ice to the wound, and keep the bite area below the level of your heart. (Because most bites are on ankles or hands, this is usually easy.) Most importantly, stay calm and move slowly.

Hetch Hetchy

to curse the San Francisco politicians who believed that flooding Hetch Hetchy Valley was a good idea. After passing through a lighted, 500-foot-long tunnel, the trail opens out to a mixed forest along the edge of the deep blue lake. Wildflower displays are often excellent in late spring. In 1.5 miles you reach Tueeulala Fall, a delicate wisp of a freefall.

Less than a mile farther you reach powerful Wapama Fall on Falls Creek, a Bridalveil-like plume of whitewater that makes a dramatic plunge into the reservoir. Depending on how early in the year you visit, you may get soaking wet standing on the sturdy steel bridges that cross over Wapama Fall's coursing flow.

ⓜ Carlon Falls

- Distance: 4.0 miles round-trip
- Duration: 2 hours
- Rating: Easy
- Elevation Change: 350 feet
- Trailhead: Carlon Day-Use Area
- Directions: From Groveland, drive east on Highway 120 for 22.5 miles to the Evergreen Road turnoff, signed for Hetch Hetchy Reservoir (one mile west of the Big Oak Flat Entrance to Yosemite). Drive north on Evergreen Road for one mile to the far side of the bridge, just past Carlon Day-Use Area. Park in the pullout on the right. Begin hiking on the closed-off road, heading upstream.

Carlon Falls is not located in Hetch Hetchy Valley; its trailhead is found on the road to Hetch Hetchy (Evergreen Road). This means it gets missed not just by the large number of Yosemite visitors who never see Hetch Hetchy, but also by visitors who are heading so intently to Hetch Hetchy that they ignore everything along the way. This waterfall on the South Fork of the Tuolumne River shouldn't be passed by. It has two big factors going for it: (1) It's accessible by an easy, nearly level, pleasant hike; and (2) It's a river waterfall, so it has a dependable amount of flow even in autumn, when Hetch Hetchy's and Yosemite's waterfalls have all but gone dry.

Follow the obvious trail on the north side of the river from Carlon Day-Use Area (the trail on the south side is an unmaintained anglers' route). Although you begin your hike in Stanislaus National Forest, you will soon walk into Yosemite National Park. The trail passes through an impressive old-growth pine and fir forest, highlighted by wildflowers in the spring and colorful oak and dogwood leaves in the autumn. After two miles of riverside meandering, you'll reach 40-foot Carlon Falls, a lacy cascade that drops over a granite ledge in the river. The rocks below it make a fine picnic spot. The waterfall's namesakes are Dan and Donna Carlon, who operated the popular Carl Inn from 1916 to 1930 near what is now Carlon Day-Use Area.

Lake Eleanor

- Distance: 3.0 miles round-trip
- Duration: 1.5 hours
- Rating: Easy
- Elevation Change: 100 feet
- Trailhead: Cherry Lake
- Directions: From Groveland, drive east on Highway 120 for 14 miles toward Yosemite. Turn left on Cherry Lake Road and drive 24 miles to Cherry Lake's dam, then cross it and turn right on Road 1N14, a dirt road. Follow this road four miles to the gated Yosemite National Park boundary. Park and hike in to the lake. (You could also turn left after Cherry Lake's dam and drive to another trailhead for Lake Eleanor, although this one requires a longer hike to reach the lakeshore.)

Lake Eleanor is a second, less famous reservoir in the Hetch Hetchy region of Yosemite. Originally a naturally shallow glacial lake, Lake Eleanor was "improved" by the city of San Francisco by damming Eleanor Creek in 1928, five years before O'Shaughnessy Dam at Hetch Hetchy was completed. The dam raised the lake's water level 40 feet. Today it is the second largest lake in Yosemite after Hetch Hetchy. Its waters are not used by San Francisco as a drinking water supply but rather to generate power.

Set at elevation 4,657 feet, Lake Eleanor is popular with hikers who tote along a fishing rod while traversing the trail around the three-mile-long lake's edge. The access road to Lake Eleanor ends at a gate 0.25 mile before the lake, so you start your hike there, then take a mellow walk along the lake's south shore. Much of Lake Eleanor's western side is dotted with picturesque islands. A backcountry ranger station is on the southwest shore; it is usually staffed in the summer months.

It takes more than an hour's drive from Highway 120 to access Lake Eleanor, so people who come here to hike or fish often plan on spending the night. A first-come, first-served campground is located at nearby Cherry Lake. The road to Lake Eleanor is open only May 1–Sept. 15 (the road is usually closed beyond Cherry Lake's dam).

Preston Falls

- Distance: 8.8 miles round-trip
- Duration: 4 hours
- Rating: Moderate
- Elevation Change: 750 feet
- Trailhead: Early Intake/Kirkwood Powerhouse
- Directions: From Groveland drive east on Highway 120 for 14 miles toward Yosemite. Turn left on Cherry Lake Road and drive 8.5 miles to Early Intake, where you cross a bridge over the Tuolumne River. Turn right on the far side of the bridge and drive 0.8 mile to the trailhead parking area at the end of the road, just beyond Kirkwood Powerhouse.

Although some day hikers choose to suffer through the nearly intolerable grade of the Poopenaut Valley Trail to reach the swimming holes and fishing spots on the Tuolumne River's free-flowing stretch west of Hetch Hetchy Dam, a much more pleasant approach is on the Preston Flat Trail. The trailhead is off Cherry Lake Road in Stanislaus National Forest, outside Yosemite's border. The path travels 4.4 miles up the north side of the Tuolumne River Canyon on a moderately undulating grade. At its end is a photogenic vista of Preston Falls, a cascade formed where the Tuolumne River drops 15 feet over a granite ledge into a wide, clear pool. The cataract is just a half mile downstream of Yosemite's boundary line.

Compared to the Poopenaut Valley Trail, the Preston Flat Trail is by far the better choice for hikers who wish to reach the river. Hike it in spring, when the raging Tuolumne River provides the most exciting viewing. Those who wish to fish or swim should wait to visit until summer, when the river quiets down.

BACKPACKING

You're hungering for a Yosemite backpacking trip, but Tuolumne Meadows is knee-deep in melting snow. There's no better time than spring to hike along the northern edge of Hetch Hetchy Reservoir, elevation 3,796 feet, admiring three stunning waterfalls along the way: Tueeulala, Wapama, and Rancheria. An easy overnight backpacking trip leads to the eastern edge of the reservoir and **Rancheria Falls,** where the bears are some of the boldest in all of Yosemite. Bear canisters are not just a good idea here; they are required.

O'Shaugnessy Dam is the trailhead for Rancheria Falls. The trail to Rancheria Falls backpacker's camp is mostly level, with a total elevation gain of only 1,300 feet spread out over 6.5 miles. This makes it manageable even for most beginners. Fishing in the reservoir is fair to middling in spring and fall, but remember: swimming is not allowed in this public water supply.

More adventurous backpackers will continue past Rancheria to **Tiltill Valley** (three miles farther). **Vernon Lake** lies a half day's hike beyond (another 6.5 miles). The granite-backed lake is popular with those who tote along fishing gear in the hope of inviting a few rainbow trout to dinner. Good campsites can be found on Falls Creek (permits required) and also near the lake. Take this trip in the early season, however, because the route through Tiltill Valley is notoriously hot and dry in summer. You can easily turn this into a 27-mile loop by heading back via Beehive Meadow and Laurel Lake, then hiking south to Hetch Hetchy.

The same destinations can be reached via a shorter (and preferred by many) route. Take the **Beehive Trail** northward from the edge of Hetch Hetchy Reservoir, one mile from the trailhead at O'Shaughnessy Dam. The trail follows an old road through a series of switchbacks, climbing 1,200 feet over two miles to the canyon rim. The trail then departs from the road and meanders on a much easier grade through pine and incense-cedar forest. Beautiful **Laurel Lake** is eight miles from O'Shaughnessy Dam. The lake is surrounded by aspen groves, firs, and lodgepole pines, and its waters are a fair bet for rainbow trout fishing. Spend your weekend here or set out for even more scenic **Vernon Lake** the next day (four miles distant). Loop back via Tiltill Valley or retrace your steps.

Hetch Hetchy

BACKPACKER'S ESSENTIALS

Going backpacking in Hetch Hetchy or elsewhere in Yosemite? It's far too easy to head out on the trail and realize too late that you left a critical item at home. Use this handy checklist as a plan to help you pack, or tailor it to your own individual needs.

1. **Permit:** First and foremost in Yosemite, you need a wilderness permit. Reserve it in advance by visiting www.nps.gov/yose/wilderness or phoning 209/372-0740.

2. **Shelter:** Tent, rainfly, poles, and stakes, plus a ground tarp (a rain poncho can serve this purpose).

3. **Sleeping:** Sleeping bag, stuff sack, and sleeping pad.

4. **Food and Cooking:** In Hetch Hetchy, you must store your food (and any scented items) in a bear canister. This is not just a good idea—it's the law. Buy or rent one at the Hetch Hetchy entrance station or at other locations in Yosemite. To cook and eat, you'll need a camp stove and plenty of fuel, waterproof matches or a lighter, a set of lightweight pots and pans with lids, pot grips for handling hot pots, zip-top bags, aluminum foil, trash bags, lightweight cutlery and dishes, and a cup for drinking. Carry as much freeze-dried or lightweight food as you can (more than you think you'll need). Most important, don't forget a water bottle and filter or purifier.

5. **Clothing:** A good basic packing list includes: underwear, socks, T-shirts, shorts or convertible pants, synthetic or fleece shirt or sweater, windproof and waterproof jacket and pants, gloves, hat (both a warm wool hat and a wide-brim hat for sun protection), sunglasses, rain poncho, gaiters, hiking boots, and camp shoes.

6. **Toiletries:** You can go without a lot in the backcountry, but you don't want to go without sunscreen and sun-protecting lip balm, insect repellent, toothbrush and toothpaste, and maybe a comb or hair bands. Some backpackers bring toilet paper; if you do, remember that you must pack it out. (Minimalists use large leaves instead.) A small plastic trowel is useful for burying human waste.

7. **First Aid:** A basic kit should include an emergency space blanket made of Mylar film, tweezers, sterile gauze pads, adhesive medical tape, adhesive bandages in assorted sizes, an ace bandage, aspirin or ibuprofen, moleskin for blisters, antibiotic ointment, and any prescription medications you might need.

8. **Other Critical Stuff:** Two or more flashlights and extra batteries, compass, small signal mirror, appropriate maps, hiking poles, whistle, 50-foot nylon cord, candles, extra matches, repair kit and/or sewing kit, safety pins, and a Swiss Army–style pocket knife.

9. **Fun Stuff:** Camera and film, extra camera battery, binoculars, fishing gear and license, pen and pencil, playing cards, star chart, and nature identification guides for birds, flowers, trees, etc.

10. **What to Put It All In:** A backpack, of course. And you might also want to carry a smaller day pack for day hiking.

A short but steep Hetch Hetchy backpacking trail is **Poopenaut Valley Trail,** which provides fast access to a beautiful stretch of the Tuolumne River. It's a merciless downhill jaunt of 1.3 miles and 1,200 feet of elevation loss to a flat river stretch west of O'Shaughnessy Dam. If you like being close to a fast and free river, you'll love the camping spots here. Fishing and swimming are excellent, but be wary of rattlesnakes, especially in spring. Because the trail's so short, you might expect it to be crawling with day hikers, but they are noticeably absent except on occasional weekends. Nobody enjoys the return trip uphill, which, although brief, is the worst grade in all of Yosemite. Start early in the morning and make sure you've eaten everything in your pack. The trailhead is at a minuscule parking lot off Hetch Hetchy Road, 3.9 miles from the Mather Ranger Station.

An alternative to Poopenaut Valley Trail is

the **Preston Flat Trail.** This trail heads to a stretch of river just west of Poopenaut Valley. Many good camping spots are found along the trail, as well as fishing and swimming opportunities. The trail is located in Stanislaus National Forest, just outside of Yosemite, so check with the Groveland ranger station for current backpacking regulations (209/962-7825). If you plan to use a camp stove or make a campfire, you'll need to get a free campfire permit.

Another popular backpacking route begins near Cherry Lake in Stanislaus National Forest and then heads into the Hetch Hetchy region of Yosemite for an overnight stay at **Kibbie Lake.** The trailhead is at the end of the road about five miles beyond Cherry Lake's dam. (Follow Cherry Lake Road 24 miles north from Highway 120, cross the dam, then turn left on Road 1N45Y and follow it to its end.) Hike the Kibbie Ridge Trail 1.2 miles to the Kibbie Lake Trail, then go right and head for the lake in another 2.7 miles. The route leads through lodgepole pine forest to the granite-bound lake at elevation 6,800 feet. The lake is fairly shallow and supports a good population of rainbow trout. The four-mile hike to Kibbie Lake makes a very short, rewarding backpacking trip that is suitable for most beginners.

If summit vistas strike your fancy, head for the top of **Smith Peak,** elevation 7,751 feet. The trail begins by the Mather Ranger Station (follow the directions to Lookout Point in the Hiking section). Follow the Lookout Point Trail for 1.2 miles, then cut off on the trail to Smith Meadow. You'll pass Base Line Camp Road, then climb up along Cottonwood Creek to Cottonwood Meadow, soon followed by Smith Meadow. A trail comes in on the right beyond Smith Meadow; this is another popular route to Smith Peak leading from White Wolf Lodge and Campground off Tioga Road. Campsites are found near this junction of trails. Get a good night's rest before bagging Smith Peak the next morning. (You've hiked six miles thus far; it's only two more to the summit.) The peak is covered with pockmarked granite boulders and offers a panoramic view of Hetch Hetchy Reservoir and the Grand Canyon of the Tuolumne River.

RAFTING

Just a few miles to the west of Hetch Hetchy Reservoir lies a spectacular river canyon known to rafters as a whitewater jewel. Several commercial outfitters run trips down the **Tuolumne River Canyon** west of Hetch Hetchy in the summer months. Access to this designated Wild and Scenic stretch of river is a few miles off Highway 120 between Groveland and the Big Oak Flat Entrance. The rafting put-in point is just north of Buck Meadows, the take-out is at Wards Ferry just east of Don Pedro Reservoir. Rafters usually meet at La Casa Loma River Store on Ferretti Road off Highway 120 outside Groveland.

Water flow on this section of the Tuolumne is dependent on releases from Hetch Hetchy. When the river flow is high, this is a very advanced and exciting run of river in a remote canyon filled with birds and other wildlife. Several local outfitters offer two- and three-day trips on the river. For more information, contact Zephyr Whitewater (800/431-3636, www.zrafting.com), ARTA River Trips (800/323-2782, www.arta.org), Whitewater Voyages (800/488-7238, whitewatervoyages.com), or OARS Inc. (800/346-6277, www.oars.com).

FISHING

The Tuolumne River is a well-loved trout stream, and some of its best fishing prospects are found in the northwest stretch of Yosemite in and around the Hetch Hetchy region. For good angling only a short drive from Highway 120, head for the **Middle Fork of the Tuolumne River,** which is well stocked with pan-sized rainbow trout. A popular access point is the Middle Fork Day-Use Area off Evergreen Road, one mile west of the Big Oak Flat Entrance and on the road to Hetch Hetchy. If you seek more of a challenge, the main branch of the Tuolumne River is a favorite of more seasoned anglers, who ply its waters for trophy-sized native trout.

Many park visitors don't realize that fishing is permitted in **Hetch Hetchy Reservoir** itself.

The lake has brook trout, rainbow trout, and some large brown trout, but because anglers are permitted only to fish from shore, prospects are not great. The warm summer weather makes the fish go deep, and since anglers cannot launch boats into the lake, they have little chance of getting close to the fish. Still, when people catch trout in Hetch Hetchy (usually while standing on the shoreline using spinners; no live bait is allowed), the fish are large. Fishing is best in spring and fall.

Those looking for more of a sure thing don't bother with the reservoir but instead head for the west side of O'Shaughnessy Dam and the free-flowing stretch of the Tuolumne River. Hiking the short Poopenaut Valley Trail is one way to get to the river, but it's too steep for all but the most ambitious anglers. Many prefer the mellower **Preston Flat Trail** off Cherry Lake Road.

If you're willing to take a backpacking trip from Hetch Hetchy, you will find plentiful fish in Laurel Lake and Lake Vernon. Both lakes have self-sustaining populations of rainbow trout, although both lakes are fished heavily. The stretch of **Falls Creek** near Lake Vernon is popular with fly fishers.

People who just want to fish, not hike, should drive to **Lake Eleanor,** another big reservoir within Yosemite's borders, located just northwest of Hetch Hetchy. Rainbow trout and bluegill are the usual catch. Accessing Lake Eleanor is easiest via Cherry Lake Road off Highway 120, 14 miles east of Groveland. The road to the lake is open only May 1–Sept. 15. You must walk the final 0.25 mile to the lake. Most anglers who make this long 28-mile drive also plan to fish at larger and more popular **Cherry Lake,** located four miles west of Lake Eleanor. Cherry Lake is just outside of the Yosemite National Park boundary in Stanislaus National Forest, so in addition to excellent fishing for rainbow, brook, and brown trout, it features several amenities you won't find at Lake Eleanor: a boat launch, a designated swim area, and a Forest Service–operated campground. The lake is stocked regularly, so it offers much more reliable fishing than Lake Eleanor.

HORSEBACK RIDING

The closest place to rent horses near Hetch Hetchy is at **Mather Saddle and Pack Station** at Camp Mather (209/379-2334). Hourly, half-day, and all-day rides are available. Possibilities include a cowboy breakfast ride and a sunset ride. Another pack station is located at Cherry Lake in Stanislaus National Forest. **Cherry Valley Pack Station** (209/962-5671) leads horseback trips into the Hetch Hetchy region of Yosemite.

Hetch Hetchy

The Eastern Sierra

Less visited but equally spectacular to the high country of Yosemite National Park is the land that lies just east of Tioga Pass along the corridor of U.S. 395. Known in generic terms as the Eastern Sierra, this region includes two major mountain resorts, Mammoth Lakes and June Lake, plus a host of unusual features and destinations, including Bodie State Historic Park, a historic gold rush ghost town, and Mono Lake, a 700,000-year-old saline lake.

The Eastern Sierra also includes another unit of the National Park system—Devils Postpile National Monument—plus a wealth of natural resources ideal for outdoor recreationists: mountain slopes for skiers and snowboarders, miles of trails for hikers and equestrians, crystal-clear streams and rivers for anglers, and alpine lakes backed by granite cliffs for photographers and scenery lovers.

Much of this land was once a part of Yosemite National Park. In 1890, when the region surrounding Yosemite Valley was designated by Congress as national parkland, the boundary lines included a large area southeast of today's Yosemite—a wide swath of the Minarets and Ritter Range, and the land that is now

Must-Sees

M **Mono Lake:** This enormous saline lake, as large as a small sea, is one of the oldest lakes in North America at approximately 700,000 years old. With about 60 square miles of surface area, the lake has two large islands, Paoha and Negit. To see it close-up, take a hike on the Mark Twain Scenic Tufa Trail or go for a guided canoe tour with the Mono Lake Committee (page 104).

Devils Postpile

M **Bodie State Historic Park:** The largest unrestored ghost town in the American West, the 1870s Gold Rush settlement of Bodie is remarkably well preserved. That's partly because it is located far out in the desert hills north of Mono Lake, where the air is dependably dry, even in the snowy winter months. Take a walk around the old buildings and let your imagination travel back in time (page 104).

M **Bennettville:** Don't miss the easy hike to Bennettville, the site of a 19th-century silver mining settlement at 10,000 feet in elevation. A couple of buildings and mine ruins remain from Bennettville's heyday in the 1880s (page 106).

M **Mammoth Lakes Basin:** Five scenic, high alpine lakes are found in the Mammoth Lakes Basin, all accessible by car. Dozens more are within easy hiking distance. Hikers, campers, and anglers will be in their element here (page 116).

M **Devils Postpile:** A bus ride from Mammoth Mountain Ski Area will take you to Devils Postpile National Monument, a small but remarkably scenic national park along the banks of the San Joaquin River. The undisputed highlight is the park's namesake, the Devils Postpile, a fascinating collection of columnar basalt "posts" remaining from an ancient lava flow (page 118).

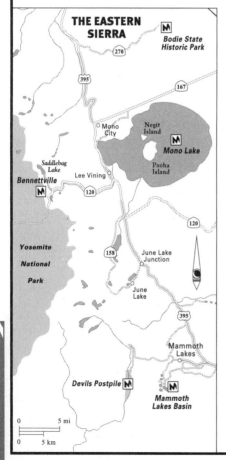

THE EASTERN SIERRA

The Eastern Sierra

Devils Postpile National Monument. But pressures from mining and timber interests were so strong that, in 1905, more than 500 square miles of land on the east side of the Sierra Nevada Mountains were removed from national park protection. The miners may have gotten their way, but it didn't work to their advantage. Despite a massive effort at prospecting for gold and silver in the Eastern Sierra, hardly any was ever found.

Exploring the Eastern Sierra

WEATHER AND SEASONS

Most of the Eastern Sierra is blanketed in a thick layer of snow from November until May. However, because winter recreation is so popular in this area, most roads stay plowed and open year round, except for portions of the June Lake Loop and Highway 120 from Lee Vining into Yosemite. From Memorial Day until Labor Day, count on mild days and cool nights at the mostly high elevations of the Eastern Sierra. It is rare for summer daytime temperatures to reach above 85°F, but nights will often drop down close to freezing. September and October daytime and nighttime temperatures can be considerably cooler, and frost is common on fall evenings.

DRIVING TOUR

Yosemite visitors who drive east out of Tioga Pass make a precipitous descent over 13 miles from the Yosemite entrance station at 9,945 feet in elevation to the valley floor at U.S. 395 at 6,800 feet. Waiting at the bottom of this spine-tingling drive is the small town of Lee Vining, the gateway to the Eastern Sierra. From here, a driving tour is best split into two parts taking place over two days, with one tour leading north to Bodie State Historic Park and another leading south to Mammoth Lakes.

For the northward tour, stop in Lee Vining and pick up snacks and drinks at one of the local stores, then drive two miles north to the **Mono Basin Scenic Area Visitor Center** turnoff on the right. Here you can obtain all kinds of information about the region, and enjoy a wide vista of Mono Lake from the visitor center's high vantage point.

After a visit, return to U.S. 395 and head north. If you are fortunate enough to be traveling during September or October, turn west at Lundy Lake Road seven miles north of Lee Vining and drive through groves of bright yellow quaking aspens to the large, narrow lake. Or continue northward for 11 more miles, driving over Conway Summit to the right turnoff for **Bodie State Historic Park.** Turn east here and drive 13 slow miles to this still-standing ghost town. The last few miles are gravel.

For the southward tour, begin at the junction of U.S. 395 and Highway 120 at Lee Vining and drive south five miles to the left (east) turnoff for **Mono Lake Tufa State Reserve** (Highway 120 East). Turn east and drive 4.6 miles, then turn left and drive one mile to the Mono Lake Tufa State Reserve parking area. Here you can walk the level, one-mile Mark Twain Scenic Tufa Trail to see the tufa spires at the edge of ancient Mono Lake.

Then backtrack to U.S. 395 and turn right (north) for 0.5 mile to the north end of the **June Lake Loop** (Highway 158). Turn left (west) here and drive the length of the loop, passing four lovely lakes—Grant, Silver, Gull, and June—all of which are set under the imposing granite cliffs of 10,909-foot Carson Peak. Supplies are available at resorts and stores along the loop and in the main village area of June Lake.

Where the June Lake Loop returns to U.S. 395, head south for 15 miles to the turnoff for Mammoth Lakes (Highway 203). Turn right here and head into the town of Mammoth Lakes, where supplies are available. Then continue beyond the town (for a total of four miles from U.S. 395) to a stoplight and junction at Lake Mary Road. Here, go straight on Lake

Mary Road for a scenic tour of the **Mammoth Lakes Basin** and its five sparkling lakes, or turn right to stay on Highway 203/Minaret Road for a five-mile drive to the Mammoth Mountain Ski Area. Just beyond it lies Minaret Overlook and the shuttle stop for **Devils Postpile National Monument.** Between the hours of 7 A.M. and 7 P.M., all visitors must ride a shuttle bus into Devils Postpile. If you choose to board a bus into the monument, you'll be granted many options for short hikes and sightseeing. If you don't have the few hours necessary for Devils Postpile, make a quick stop at **Minaret Overlook** and take in a memorable vista of the sawtoothed peaks of the Minaret Range. Sunset-watching at this drive-to overlook is a deservedly popular activity in Mammoth Lakes.

Lee Vining, Mono Lake, and North

VISITORS CENTERS

Two visitor centers serve the Lee Vining and Mono Lake area: the Mono Basin Scenic Area Visitor Center perched high above Mono Lake (760/647-3044, www.r5.fs.fed.us/inyo, daily 9 A.M.–4 P.M., closed in winter), and the Mono Lake Committee's Visitor Center (also the Lee Vining Chamber of Commerce) in downtown Lee Vining (760/647-6595, daily 9 A.M.–5 P.M.). The former is the best source for recreation information; the latter has a wonderful stock of hard-to-find books about the human and natural history of the Eastern Sierra. Be sure to watch the informative video about Mono Lake at the Mono Basin Scenic Area Visitor Center.

SIGHTS

Ⓜ Mono Lake

You see it as you drive east out of Tioga Pass from Yosemite—an enormous lake, as wide as a small sea and dotted with two massive islands. That's Mono Lake, a saline body of water that is one of the oldest lakes in North America. No trip to the Eastern Sierra is complete without a walk to the edge of this mighty, ancient lake. To see it up close, take a walk on the Mono Lake Scenic Tufa Trail at Mono Lake State Reserve. (Drive five miles south on U.S. 395 from Lee Vining, then turn east on Highway 120 and drive 4.6 miles to the left turnoff for the reserve.) The half-mile trail leads to the edge of the lake, passing its trademark tufa formations along the way. Interpretive signs explain the natural history of the lake, and what humans have done to alter it.

Ⓜ Bodie State Historic Park

One of the most popular tourist attractions in the Eastern Sierra is located way out in the middle of nowhere. Bodie, the largest unrestored ghost town in the American West, sprawls across a windswept valley in the hills north of Mono Lake. The state-run park is a genuine 1870s gold-mining town, devoid of the scourge of tourist shops and high-priced entrance fees that travelers find at many other California ghost towns.

The town's history is similar to that of many other gold rush towns throughout the Sierra Nevada, except that everything that happened here took place on a larger, more exaggerated scale. Gold was discovered in Bodie in 1859. The town saw its heyday in the 1870s, when it boasted more than 30 operating mines, 65 saloons and dance halls, three breweries, and a population of more than 10,000 people. Partly because of its remote location far from law-abiding civilization (the area around Bodie was then, and still is now, an extremely desolate region southeast of Bridgeport), the town developed a reputation for having more drinking, gambling, and shooting than any other mining town. Robberies, stage holdups, and street fights took place in the course of a normal week. Killings occurred frequently; death was too often the answer to any disagreement.

© ANN MARIE BROWN

The tufa spires at Mono Lake are created when underwater springs containing calcium are released from the lake bottom and combine with the lake's saline water.

Like most mining towns, Bodie eventually suffered a complete decline and all its residents moved elsewhere. Oddly, they seemed to have departed in a hurry. The townspeople left the store shelves stocked and writing on the school's blackboard.

With some minimal help from California State Parks, Bodie's buildings have withstood the test of time. The town is maintained in a state of "arrested decay," which means the powers-that-be don't fix up the structures, but they don't let them fall down, either. Visitors can walk around the streets of town, peek in the windows of buildings, and imagine what life was like in another era. A museum is open daily during summer, but there are no food services, gas stations, or services of any kind in the park.

To get to Bodie, from Lee Vining drive 18 miles north on U.S. 395 and turn east on Highway 270. It's 13 miles to the ghost town (the last few miles are gravel).

Aspen Groves

If you are fortunate enough to visit the East-ern Sierra during September or October, you are in for a visual treat. Mountain canyons and lakeshores are transformed by blazing shows of autumn color, thanks to the quaking aspens and cottonwoods. The best fall color viewing is generally found in Lee Vining Canyon, just below Tioga Pass; in Lundy Canyon, seven miles north of Lee Vining; and along the June Lake Loop (Highway 158). Don't forget your camera.

HIKING

An amazing wealth of hiking trails is found in the region just east of Yosemite's Tioga Pass Entrance Station. With few exceptions, these trails feature scenic beauty that rivals anything you'll find in Yosemite, but they are usually much less crowded than park trails. The following are some of the best trail choices (listed in order of their proximity to the Tioga Pass Entrance Station). For more information on these or any other hikes in the area, contact the Mono Basin Scenic Area Visitor Center at 760/647-3044.

The Eastern Sierra

SALT WATER AND TUFA SPIRES: MONO LAKE'S EXTRAORDINARY WORLD

You have probably heard of Mono Lake, but until you've seen it, it's hard to imagine. A majestic body of water covering about 60 square miles—looking like a small sea in this mountainous landscape—Mono Lake is three times as salty as the ocean and 80 times as alkaline. It's set in the middle of the high desert, just east of the Sierra crest at Yosemite National Park. Its wide expanse fills the landscape to just west of the Nevada state border.

Among its other charms, Mono Lake is one of the oldest lakes in America, at more than 700,000 years. The lake has no natural outlet, only inlet streams. As a result, over the course of the lake's long life, salts and minerals have washed into its waters from Eastern Sierra streams and never left. Freshwater constantly evaporates from the big lake, leaving the salts and minerals behind and creating the strange chemical makeup of the water. If you swim in Mono Lake, you will be nearly buoyant.

The most apparent wildlife at Mono Lake is the birds—many thousands of them. The lake is a major stopover for migratory species passing over the desert lands to the east, and it's also a huge breeding area for California gulls. In fact, 85 percent of the gulls that live on the California coast are born here at Mono Lake. The lake's population of tiny brine shrimp feeds the gulls, and also the loons, grebes, pintails, and vast array of other migratory birds that visit. From April to November, visitors can easily spot thick masses of brine shrimp clustered near the lake surface.

Two obvious features of Mono Lake are its huge, bald islands, **Paoha** and **Negit.** These islands have figured prominently in the recent history of Mono Lake. Since 1941, four streams that fed Mono Lake were diverted into the California Aqueduct to provide water for Los Angeles. The lake started to shrink rapidly, losing an average of 18 inches per year. As the water level dropped, a land bridge formed that reached to the islands. Coyotes and other predators were given access to the gulls' nesting area, devastating the bird populations. The result was a long conservation battle over Mono Lake, which continues to this day. Now the state's Water Resources Board must regulate the level of Mono Lake so that its natural resources remain protected. The lake level has been kept stable for the past decade, although it is still not at the level it once was.

The best introduction to Mono Lake is a walk on the short trail at the **Mono Lake**

Ⓜ Bennettville

- Distance: 2.6 miles round-trip
- Duration: 1 hour
- Rating: Easy
- Elevation Change: 500 feet
- Trailhead: Junction Campground
- Directions: From the Tioga Pass entrance to Yosemite, drive east on Highway 120 for two miles to the left turnoff for Saddlebag Lake. Turn left and then left again immediately to enter Junction Campground. The trail begins at the campground entrance.

This first-class high-country hike is suitable for even the most novice hikers and is sure to spark your imagination. The remote high-country region of Bennettville was the site of a 19th-century silver mining community. Although the town thrived only from 1882 to 1884, it was the primary reason for the construction of the Tioga Pass Road from the west. The original road, called the Great Sierra Wagon Road, was built by the Great Sierra Consolidated Silver Company in anticipation of the riches they would make from the mines at Bennettville and nearby. Ultimately, no valuable minerals were ever extracted, and the company went broke in record time.

Tufa State Reserve. The trail is named for Mark Twain, who visited the lake in 1863 and wrote extensively about it in his book *Roughing It*. Twain was fascinated by the coral-like structures found near the edges of the lake, called tufa. These off-white mineral formations are created when underwater springs containing calcium are released from the lake bottom and combine with the lake's saline water. This process forms calcium carbonate, the chemical expression for tufa.

The tufa formations grow upright, swelling into odd vertical shapes up to six feet high as spring water pushes upward inside them. The tufas only stop growing when exposed to air, which in effect ruins the chemistry experiment. Although tufas are found at various points along Mono Lake's 16,000 acres of lakeshore, the best examples of them are seen along Mono Lake's south shore. Visitors who take a level and easy stroll on the **Mark Twain Scenic Tufa Trail** will pass some high-and-dry inland tufas on the path to the lakeshore, then skirt the edge of the lake and its miniature islands of tufa. When you touch the tufa, you'll find it feels surprisingly hard, almost like concrete, although it appears brittle to the eye.

Another great way to see Mono Lake is to make a stop at the **Mono Basin Scenic Area Visitor Center.** The center is perched on a hill high above Mono Lake, with benches outside that afford a delightful view (760/647-3044). Or, to see Mono Lake close-up, take a canoe tour. This program, organized by the Mono Lake Committee, is offered every Saturday and Sunday in summer. Canoes, life jackets, and paddles are provided; no experience is necessary. Trips usually last about one hour and leave at 8, 9:30, and 11 A.M. For information and reservations, contact the Mono Lake Committee Visitor Center at 760/647-6595.

Framed by snow-capped mountains on one side and sagebrush plains on the other, Mono Lake is also remarkably photogenic. Almost every evening of summer, photographers line up along the lake's edges in the hope of capturing the perfect sunset image.

No matter how you view it—on foot, from the visitor center, through a camera lens, or on top of a canoe gliding along its surface—Mono Lake is unlike anything else you'll find in California. A visit to this huge turquoise lake leaves you with a strong appreciation for what Mark Twain called "one of the strangest freaks of nature to be found in any land."

A mostly level trail leads to the two buildings that remain from Bennettville's heyday: the assay office and barn/bunkhouse. An open mine tunnel lined with railcar tracks can also be seen, as well as some rusting mining equipment. Much of the machinery and supplies for this mine was hauled here from the May Lundy Mine over Dore Pass. Men and animals carried several tons of equipment on their backs and on sleds, sometimes through driving snowstorms in the middle of winter at this 10,000-foot elevation.

You can extend this hike by following the trail 0.5 mile uphill from the mine buildings to small Shell Lake, or proceed onward past another small pothole lake to Fantail Lake and another mine site, 0.5 mile farther.

Gardisky Lake

- Distance: 2.0 miles round-trip
- Duration: 1.5 hours
- Rating: Moderate
- Elevation Change: 800 feet
- Trailhead: Gardisky Lake
- Directions: From the Tioga Pass entrance to Yosemite, drive east on Highway 120 for two miles to the left turnoff for Saddlebag Lake. Turn left and drive 1.3 miles north on Saddlebag Lake

Road; the parking area is on the left side of the road and the trail is on the right.

A short but fairly difficult trail leads to lovely Gardisky Lake. The one-mile trail goes straight up, gaining 800 feet in too little distance, with not nearly enough switchbacks. To make matters more difficult, the trailhead is set at 10,000 feet, which means you will want to be acclimated to the high elevation before you pant your way up this kind of grade. The trip offers many rewards, though, such as fewer people than at nearby Saddlebag Lake and a stellar high-alpine setting. Once you gain the ridgetop, you have a nearly level 0.25-mile stroll through a fragile alpine meadow to reach the lake, a shallow body of water. It's not the lake itself that is the highlight of this trail; it's the beauty and delicacy of the total landscape at this high elevation. That 11,500-foot mountain you see as you climb (ahead and to your right) is Tioga Peak; some hikers choose to ascend to its summit from Gardisky Lake. White Mountain and Mount Conness are also prominent, both over 12,000 feet.

Saddlebag Lake and 20 Lakes Basin

- Distance: 8.4 miles round-trip
- Duration: 4 hours
- Rating: Moderate
- Elevation Change: 800 feet
- Trailhead: Saddlebag Lake
- Directions: From the Tioga Pass entrance to Yosemite, drive east on Highway 120 for two miles to the left turnoff for Saddlebag Lake. Turn left and drive 2.7 miles north on Saddlebag Lake Road to the trailhead parking area.

Starting from the resort buildings at the south end of 10,087-foot Saddlebag Lake, you can design a wonderfully scenic hiking trip into the 20 Lakes Basin of any length that suits your time and energy. A benefit of hiking here is that you can cut off some miles by taking the boat taxi across the lake, rather than hiking along its lakeshore. A one-way ride on the boat taxi will cut 1.5 miles off your mileage; a round-trip cuts off three miles. Unfortunately, this

high-country region is so beautiful, so easy to access, and so close to Yosemite that on summer weekends, it can be as crowded as the most popular trails in the park. A great time to hike here is a few weeks after Labor Day, when the vacation crowds have dispersed.

To hike alongside Saddlebag Lake instead of riding in the boat taxi, follow the trail on either the lake's east or west side. The east-side trail is more scenic; the west-side trail is shorter. If you just want to make a short 3.6-mile loop, hike out on one trail and back on the other, but be sure to take the short left spur at Saddlebag's northwest edge to **Greenstone Lake,** which is backed by photogenic North Peak. If you want to hike farther, you can continue past Greenstone Lake to **Wasco Lake** and then on to deep, stark **Steelhead Lake** (three miles out if you start on the west side trail). Several more lakes lie beyond, including **Shamrock, Helen,** and **Odell.** If you hike the entire loop and visit all six lakes that lie immediately beyond Saddlebag, you'll have an 8.4-mile day (or a 5.4-mile day, if you take the boat taxi round-trip). No matter how far you go, you'll be awed by the incredible high-country scenery—a blend of blue sky, granite, water, and hardy whitebark pines.

Slate Creek Trail to Green Treble Lake

- Distance: 4.5 miles round-trip
- Duration: 2 hours
- Rating: Easy
- Elevation Change: 500 feet
- Trailhead: Sawmill Campground
- Directions: From the Tioga Pass entrance to Yosemite, drive east on Highway 120 for two miles to the left turnoff for Saddlebag Lake. Turn left and drive 1.5 miles north on Saddlebag Lake Road to Sawmill Campground's parking area on the left.

One of the most beautiful and serene campgrounds in the High Sierra, Sawmill Walk-in Camp is accessed by a quarter-mile walk from its parking area. The trail continues through and past the campground's widely spaced sites into Hall Research Natural Area, a specially protected region of Inyo National Forest that is open to day-hikers only (no backpacking). The trail leads one mile to Timberline Station, an old research station built in 1929. From here you can ford Slate Creek and hike another mile to Green Treble Lake at the headwaters of Slate Creek. Where two forks of the creek join, about 0.5 mile beyond Timberline Station, follow the south fork (left) another 0.5 mile to Green Treble Lake. This is a remarkably level hike at 10,000-plus feet in elevation—pristine high country that is only accessible a few months each year.

Gibbs Lake

- Distance: 5.4 miles round-trip
- Duration: 2.5 hours
- Rating: Moderate
- Elevation Change: 1,500 feet
- Trailhead: Horse Meadow
- Directions: From Lee Vining, drive 1.8 miles south on U.S. 395 and turn west on Forest Road 1N16 (look for the sign indicating Horse Meadow). Drive 3.4 miles to the trailhead at the end of the road. Note: Forest Road 1N16 requires a vehicle with high clearance.

This relatively short hike leads to scenic Gibbs Lake, elevation 9,530 feet. The trail starts at Upper Horse Meadow, elevation 8,000 feet, and climbs up Gibbs Canyon. Unfortunately the first stretch goes straight uphill on an old dirt road with nary a switchback. Once you get through that grunt of an ascent, the rest of the route is on a much mellower grade as it travels alongside Gibbs Creek. The trail ends at Gibbs Lake, a lovely glacial cirque backed by bare granite and fronted by conifers. Are you feeling ambitious? If you study the lake's back wall for a few minutes, it will soon become obvious that there is another, higher lake in this drainage. If you are sure-footed and have plenty of energy, you can pick out your route and go visit that lake. Although Gibbs Lake is pretty, the higher Kidney Lake (10,388 feet) is a stunner. It will take you about 40 minutes of challenging cross-country scrambling to get from Gibbs to Kidney; you'll gain almost 900 feet

in less than a mile. Just pick your route carefully and go slow. Kidney Lake is indeed kidney-shaped, and it is flanked by Mount Dana (13,057 feet) on one side and Mount Gibbs (12,773 feet) on the other.

Lake Canyon and May Lundy Mine

- Distance: 7.0 miles round-trip
- Duration: 3.5 hours
- Rating: Moderate
- Elevation Change: 1,000 feet
- Trailhead: Lundy Lake's dam
- Directions: From Lee Vining, drive north on U.S. 395 for seven miles to Lundy Lake Road. Turn west on Lundy Lake Road and drive five miles to Lundy Lake's dam. Turn left and drive 0.25 mile to a locked gate and trailhead.

Lundy Lake is the start of a terrific day hike to Lake Canyon and May Lundy Mine. The mine was worked continuously for two decades starting in 1878, producing a total of about $2 million in gold. The surrounding community of Lundy grew to support 500 people, despite severe winters and deadly avalanches. Besides mining, a primary activity here was the operation of three sawmills along Lundy Creek, used to supply timber to the nearby bustling gold rush town of Bodie.

The hike to the May Lundy Mine is a fairly steep 3.5 miles one-way, climbing above Lundy Lake on the old mine road, built in 1881. The road/trail passes Blue Lake and Crystal Lake, where old mining relics can be found. (Crystal Lake is 0.3 mile off the trail via a left fork.) Continue on the main trail and you'll see the mine remains—old railcar tracks, tailings, and a closed-off mine shaft. Just beyond is Oneida Lake, whose waters were used to run the stamp mill for the mine. Even without the fascinating traces of history, this is an extraordinarily beautiful place. You'll want to linger a while at sparkling Oneida Lake.

Lundy Canyon

- Distance: 4.4–10.0 miles round-trip
- Duration: 2–5 hours

The Eastern Sierra

- Rating: Moderate
- Elevation Change: 400–1,500 feet
- Trailhead: Lundy Lake
- Directions: From Lee Vining, drive north on U.S. 395 for seven miles to Lundy Lake Road. Turn west on Lundy Lake Road and drive five miles to Lundy Lake. Continue past the lake for two more miles (unpaved) to the end of the road and the trailhead.

The Lundy Canyon Trail is the back door into the 20 Lakes Basin, a well-traveled area of the Hoover Wilderness most commonly accessed from Saddlebag Lake off Highway 120. This is your passport into the sculpted-granite high country, complete with half a dozen gemlike lakes. The trail rises gently along Mill Creek, passing several beaver ponds, a dilapidated miner's cabin, and two small but boisterous waterfalls (Lower and Upper Lundy Falls) as it heads into the Hoover Wilderness. Most visitors hike to the first or second falls, enjoying the gorgeous Eastern Sierra scenery with a relatively mellow walk, then hike back out. Those who continue find that the trail, which climbed gently but steadily for the first 2.2 miles, suddenly reaches what appears to be the back of the canyon. But look straight up the canyon wall to your left—that's where the path continues, although it isn't much of a path. An unmaintained, marginally switchbacked route leads 0.8 mile upward over a frighteningly steep wall of shale. Anyone afraid of heights (or not in great shape) should turn back here. If you continue, use great caution; one slip and you could take a nasty fall. When you finally make it up the slope, you come out to a beautiful high mountain meadow and a junction near the austere shores of Lake Helen, elevation 10,100 feet (3.3 miles from your start). By going right, you can take a lesser-traveled trail to Shamrock and Steelhead Lakes. Shamrock is 0.3 mile farther and dotted with many islands; Steelhead is another 0.5 mile beyond and framed by 12,242-foot North Peak towering above.

The main trail goes left to Odell Lake (3.6 miles from your start). From Odell Lake, you could continue on to Hummingbird Lake, then to the north shore of Saddlebag Lake. If you can arrange a car shuttle at Saddlebag Lake, you can extend your trip into a one-way hike of seven miles, and that would save you the harrowing trip back down that shale-covered slope.

Note that one of the best times to visit here is in October, when Lundy Canyon's stands of quaking aspen turn bright gold and seem to dance in the breeze. This is one of the best places to admire fall colors in the Eastern Sierra. July is another first-rate time to visit; the canyon's wildflower displays are remarkable.

Virginia Lakes Trail

- Distance: 6.2–10.2 miles round-trip
- Duration: 3–5 hours
- Rating: Moderate
- Elevation Change: 1,600 feet
- Trailhead: Big Virginia Lake
- Directions: From Lee Vining, drive 12 miles north on U.S. 395 to Conway Summit. Turn west on Virginia Lakes Road and drive 6.5 miles to the trailhead at the Big Virginia Lake day-use area.

By following the Virginia Lakes Trail, you can easily hike to a series of high alpine lakes—eight are found within a two-mile radius. The trailhead is at 9,500 feet, and from there you hike west past Blue Lake to Cooney Lake and on to Frog Lakes (a very easy 1.4 miles), then start climbing seriously, continuing almost 1.8 more miles to 11,110-foot Burro Pass. The landscape here is windswept, barren, and beautiful—a mix of rock, occasional whitebark pines, and high alpine wildflowers. Many hikers take a look at the scene from the pass, then retreat to one of the aforementioned lakes to spend the afternoon, making a 6.2-mile day. If you continue beyond the pass, you curve downhill through dozens of switchbacks for 1.4 miles, then climb gently 0.5 mile west to Summit Lake at 10,203 feet in elevation, on the northeast boundary of Yosemite National Park. Summit Lake is set between Camiaca Peak (11,739 feet) to the north and Excelsior Mountain (12,446 feet) to the south. This is the logical place for backpackers to make camp, and for day-trippers to turn around for a 10.2-mile day.

Green Creek Trail to East, West, and Green Lakes

- Distance: 8.6 miles round-trip
- Duration: 5 hours
- Rating: Moderate to strenuous
- Elevation Change: 1,800 feet
- Trailhead: Green Creek
- Directions: From Bridgeport, drive south on U.S. 395 for 4.5 miles to Green Creek Road (dirt). Turn west and drive 8.2 miles to the signed trailhead parking area shortly before Green Creek Campground.

Like Lundy Canyon to the south, this canyon is a prime area for summer wildflowers and autumn aspen colors. Green Creek played a critical role in the development of the gold rush town of Bodie. It was the site of a power plant that generated electricity that was then transported via power lines to Bodie over a distance of 13 miles—a revolutionary feat in 1892.

It's only five miles round-trip on the Green Creek Trail to Green Lake, but you can hike farther for an 8.6-mile round-trip that includes larger East Lake as well. Or take a 1.5-mile spur off the main trail for a memorably steep jaunt to West Lake. The trail climbs moderately through groves of aspens, passing tumbling cascades as it closely parallels the West Fork of Green Creek. The turnoff for West Lake is on the right at 2.4 miles. Green Lake is straight ahead in about 150 yards, and East Lake is to the left, another 1.8 miles away and 500 feet higher. All three lakes are sparkling, rockbound gems, so you can't go wrong here no matter which one you choose to visit.

BIKING

Just 11 miles east of the Tioga Pass Entrance to Yosemite lies a U.S. Forest Service–sanctioned trail built just for fat-tire lovers. The **Moraines and Meadows Loop** starts in an area burned by the Azusa Wildfire in 1999, but the route quickly leaves the blackened terrain

and enters a world of alpine meadows and glacial moraines. The trail provides wide looks at giant-sized Mono Lake and neighboring Mono Craters, plus a visit to Upper and Lower Horse Meadows. A predominant manmade feature is also visible: the Los Angeles Aqueduct.

Several other trails in this region of Inyo National Forest are also open to mountain bikers. The best source of information is the Mono Basin Scenic Area Visitor Center off U.S. 395 just north of Lee Vining (760/647-3044).

A great event for road cyclists every autumn is the **High Sierra Fall Century,** a 100-mile ride that takes place on a course just east of Tioga Pass, roughly from Bishop to Mono Lake. Short courses of 30 or 45 miles are also offered; the event usually takes place in mid-September. Visit www.fallcentury.org for details.

FISHING

Some of the best fishing in California is found in the lakes and streams of the Eastern Sierra. A highlight is **Saddlebag Lake,** the highest California lake you can drive to, at elevation 10,087 feet. A resort, lunch counter, and boat rentals are available on its south shore each summer. The resort operates a water taxi that transports anglers to the far side of the lake, where they can disembark to hike and fish in the 20 Lakes Basin. Or you can rent a boat, or fish from Saddlebag's lakeshore, for golden, brook, or rainbow trout. Saddlebag Lake is located 2.5 miles north on Saddlebag Lake Road, which is off Highway 120 just east of Tioga Pass Resort.

Tioga and Ellery Lakes, both within four miles of the Tioga Pass Entrance Station and right along Highway 120, are popular with shore fishers and also anglers using float tubes. Both brook and rainbow trout are caught at the two lakes.

Lee Vining Creek parallels Highway 120 in the stretch from Tioga Pass to U.S. 395. An access road runs between U.S. 395 and the stream, allowing entrance to a series of campgrounds. The creek is an excellent place for fly-fishing or bait fishing. The town of Lee Vining has shops with bait, tackle, and plenty of free fishing advice.

TROUT OF THE EASTERN SIERRA

Trout fishing in the Eastern Sierra is some of the best to be found in the state of California. Regularly stocked streams and lakes tucked into mountain canyons on the west side of U.S. 395 provide dependably good fishing. East of U.S. 395, fly fishers can test dry-fly and nymphing skills for wild trout on classic spring creek sections of the Owens River and Hot Creek.

When fishing in the lakes and streams of the Eastern Sierra, expect to catch one of five trout species. The most common is the colorful **rainbow trout,** distinguished by its signature pink or rose stripe on its side and black spots on its olive-colored back. Despite these fairly distinct markings, this species can fool anglers by taking on a wide variety of shapes, colors, and sizes, which vary according to the conditions found in the water in which it lives.

The second most common trout species, and the most common in high alpine lakes, is the **brook trout.** These trout are not native to California and were first planted here in the 1870s. The "brookie" is considered by many the best-tasting trout, and it is generally quite easy to catch. The fish are dark gray or olive, with many large yellowish spots and a few small red spots. Their bellies are white except during spawning, when the males develop a bright reddish-orange color on their undersides. Brook trout are the smallest of the five Eastern Sierra trout; adults are typically only 9–11 inches, whereas other trout species grow to 14 inches and larger.

The **brown trout** is also nonnative to California, although it has been planted here since the late 1800s. The species comes from Europe and is common in Germany and Scotland. True to their name, brown trout are brown on top with olive-colored sides, usually dotted with large dark brown spots and small red spots. The brown trout can tolerate higher water temperatures than other trout.

Two other species of trout are caught in the Eastern Sierra, although more rarely than the others. The **golden trout** is a close cousin to the rainbow trout and is even more colorful. With a bright golden yellow color on its sides and lower parts, its identity is unmistakable. It has gray and red patches along its lateral line and a bright red belly. The golden trout is California's official state fish, although its numbers have dwindled significantly throughout the state. It is native only in Kern County in the southern portion of the Sierra Nevada. Golden trout often breed with rainbow trout, creating a hybrid species.

The **cutthroat trout,** with its olive and rust-colored body painted with black spots and a distinctive slash of red on both sides of its throat, is found only in limited areas of the Eastern Sierra: in June Lake, the Upper Owens River, Crowley Lake (south of Mammoth Lakes), Topaz Lake, and the Walker River (north of Bridgeport).

Remember to always check with local fish and tackle stores or marinas for updates on fishing regulations. What is legal at one spot in the Eastern Sierra may not be legal at another.

Twelve miles north of Lee Vining, along Lundy Lake Road, is large **Lundy Lake,** where brown and rainbow trout are regularly planted by the Department of Fish and Game. Lundy Lake Resort rents boats with or without motors, and plenty of anglers fish from shore, too. Mill Creek, the stream that feeds Lundy Lake, is also stocked. Anglers who hike into Lundy Canyon can catch brook and rainbow trout.

A few miles farther north on U.S. 395 is Virginia Lakes Road and three lakes: **Little Virginia, Big Virginia,** and **Trumbull Lakes.** All three are planted weekly with rainbow trout. If you want to catch only the big ones, trophy fish are stocked on a monthly basis. The three lakes, plus seven others in the surrounding basin, also contain populations of eastern brook and German brown trout. It's a regular fish-o-rama.

HORSEBACK RIDING

The **Virginia Lakes Pack Outfit** (760/937-0326, www.virginialakes.com) is near the end of Virginia Lakes Road, 12 miles north of Lee

Vining and six miles west of U.S. 395. It specializes in multi-day pack trips into the Hoover Wilderness but also offers fly-fishing trips and two-hour, four-hour, and all-day rides.

WINTER SPORTS

The Eastern Sierra's large and popular ski resorts are located farther south at June Lake and Mammoth Lakes, but the Lee Vining area has its own claim to fame in the winter sports category. It may not be the type of sport that appeals to those who ride the gondola wearing the latest ski fashions, but the skiing just outside of Tioga Pass is world-class. There are no lift lines, lift tickets, or even lifts. The centerpiece of the area is **Tioga Pass Resort,** a private lodge located two miles east of Yosemite's boundary. "TPR," as it is known, sets the standard for a winter skiing destination. The slopes around the resort are a cross-country skier's paradise. Most years, both deep powder and spring corn snow are in plentiful supply. The road to the resort isn't plowed; you have to ski in six miles to reach it. Guests stay in heated cabins, then get together in the main lodge for meals, which are included in the price. For more information, phone 209/372-4471 or visit www.tiogapassresort.com.

June Lake

VISITOR CENTER

The small town of June Lake doesn't have its own visitor center. The nearest visitor centers are in Lee Vining. However, a number of the cabin resorts stationed along the June Lake Loop (Highway 158) are excellent sources of information. Best bets for local knowledge, especially outdoor recreation information, are the Double Eagle Resort (760/648-7004) and Silver Lake Resort (760/648-7525).

HIKING

Several excellent day hiking trails can be accessed from points on, or near, the June Lake Loop.

Bloody Canyon Trail

• Distance: 8.2 miles round-trip
• Duration: 4 hours
• Rating: Strenuous
• Elevation Change: 1,800 feet
• Trailhead: Walker Lake
• Directions: From Lee Vining, drive five miles south on U.S. 395 to the north end of the June Lake Loop (Highway 158). Turn right and drive 1.3 miles on Highway 158, then turn right on a dirt road signed for Parker and Walker Lakes. Drive 0.5 mile to a junction, turn right, then drive another 0.5 mile and turn right again. Continue 2.9 miles to the trailhead.

The historic Bloody Canyon Trail leads to Lower Sardine Lake in 3.8 punishing miles, and then beyond it to Mono Pass in Yosemite National Park. This was the route of Chief Tenaya and his tribe in their flight from the U.S. Army in 1852. The trail was commonly used by the Indians of the Mono Basin to visit the Indians of the Yosemite high country. The first mile to Walker Lake gains 600 feet and is very steep; the next three miles gain an additional 1,200 feet, so this hike isn't for the aerobically challenged. As you near Lower Sardine Lake, a beautiful waterfall (the lake's outlet stream) will help to spur you on. When you reach the high-elevation lake, you'll find it is surrounded by rocky cliffs on one side and offers great views of the Mono Basin to the east. The lake is cradled in a high glacial bowl at 9,888 feet in elevation. Backpackers can continue hiking up and over Mono Pass and into Yosemite National Park's remote backcountry.

Parker Lake Trail

• Distance: 3.8 miles round-trip
• Duration: 2 hours
• Rating: Easy to moderate
• Elevation Change: 500 feet

The Eastern Sierra

An easy hike from the June Lake Loop, Parker Lake is backed by 12,861-foot Parker Peak.

- Trailhead: Parker Lake
- Directions: From Lee Vining, drive five miles south on U.S. 395 to the north end of the June Lake Loop (Highway 158). Turn right and drive 1.3 miles on Highway 158, then turn right on a dirt road signed for Parker and Walker Lakes. Drive 2.4 miles to the Parker Lake Trailhead at the end of the road.

This mellow trek is suitable for families and anyone seeking an easy walk to a beautiful lake. From the trailhead, the path follows Parker Creek upstream first rather steeply and then much more gently before arriving at Parker Lake at 8,318 feet. As you ascend, the landscape transitions from sagebrush plains into a mixed forest alongside Parker Creek, complete with quaking aspens and mammoth-sized Jeffrey pines. Parker Lake is a deep blue beauty backed by 12,861-foot Parker Peak—a great place to have a picnic or just sit and enjoy the scenery. On the way back downhill you'll enjoy wide views of Mono Lake.

Rush Creek Trail
- Distance: 4.6–14.0 miles round-trip
- Duration: 2–7 hours
- Rating: Moderate to strenuous
- Elevation Change: 1,300 feet to Agnew Lake or 2,200 feet to Waugh Lake
- Trailhead: Rush Creek
- Directions: From Lee Vining, drive about 11 miles south on U.S. 395 to June Lake Junction. Turn right on Highway 158/June Lake Road and drive seven miles to the Rush Creek Trailhead, across the road from Silver Lake Campground.

The most well-known trail in the June Lake area is the Rush Creek Trail. Although it is most heavily used by backpackers and horse packers, day hikers can follow it upstream along Rush Creek to Agnew Lake, 2.3 miles from the start. Or you can turn right at a junction just before Agnew Lake and hike to Gem Lake, one mile farther. Backpackers and very ambitious day hikers usually continue to Waugh Lake, seven miles from the start, or beyond it to the headwaters of Rush Creek. Any or all of these destinations are well worth the effort required; the lakes are startling in their austere granite beauty.

Yost Lake
- Distance: 9.4 miles round-trip
- Duration: 4.5 hours
- Rating: Moderate
- Elevation Change: 1,200 feet
- Trailhead: Yost Meadows
- Directions: From Lee Vining, drive about 11 miles south on U.S. 395 to June Lake Junction. Go right on Highway 158/June Lake Road and drive two miles to the town of June Lake. The trailhead is on the west (left), across the road from the fire station.

Yost Lake is a small glacial lake hidden at 9,000 feet on the slopes of June Mountain. Many people visit the June Lakes area for years without even knowing it exists. From the trailhead (7,800 feet), Yost Meadows Trail rises very steeply in the first mile, climbing 800 feet—a real butt-kicker. That discourages many from going farther—after all, it is 4.7 miles to the lake. But after that first grunt of a climb, the trail gets much easier, contouring across the mountain slopes. It rises gradually to the headwaters of Yost Creek and then drops into the small basin that guards the lake.

A shorter option is to begin at the Yost Creek/Fern Lake Trailhead, making it a much shorter, 4.8-mile round-trip. It is just as pretty but has a more difficult grade. This trailhead is located three miles west of the town of June Lake on the west (left) side of June Lake Road, past the ski resort.

BIKING

The **Panorama Mountain Trail,** a mountain bike route sanctioned by the Forest Service, consists of three consecutive loops on jeep roads and graded dirt roads that lead through sagebrush and Jeffrey pines. Small brown Forest Service signs guide you along the route, as do a few prominent landmarks: U.S. 395, which is visible every time you climb a bit; the Mono Craters, a chain of barren-looking volcanic vents poking up from the surrounding sagebrush plains; and the Aeolian Buttes, where the most recent volcanic activity in this area occurred perhaps only 600 years ago. The third of the three loops circles the buttes and will take you up high enough to get surprising views of Mono Lake and its neighboring craters to the northeast, plus the snow-capped, granite mountains of the Eastern Sierra to the west. It's startling to see this juxtaposition of glacier-carved mountains and volcanic vents and tablelands—all in one glance.

The trailhead for this ride is found off U.S. 395, 150 yards north of June Lake Junction. Turn east on Forest Service Road 1S35 and drive 100 yards to the signed trailhead.

For road bikers, pedaling the **June Lake Loop** is an obvious choice. Of course, the "Loop" is not really a loop at all, but more like a horseshoe shape on Highway 158 that is made into a loop by connecting with U.S. 395. While this may be fine for car drivers, it's not ideal for cyclists, who do better by riding out and back on Highway 158, rather than completing a loop on the busy U.S. highway.

Start anywhere you like along Highway 158 and you'll be treated to some of the finest scenery in the Eastern Sierra. You'll witness imposing granite peaks, the dancing leaves of aspen groves, and four sparkling, bright blue lakes. Because the route has many places to stop for supplies or breaks, this ride is well within the abilities of most cyclists. Traffic is as you might expect: heavier on summer weekends, lighter the rest of the time.

On the north end of the "Loop," a good turnaround point is the Mono Craters Viewpoint; it's 1.2 miles from the road's end at U.S. 395. At the viewpoint, you get a good look at the barren, pumice-covered volcanic cones called Mono Craters, which were created by a series of volcanic eruptions as recently as 600 years ago.

FISHING

All four drive-to lakes along the **June Lake Loop** (Gull, June, Silver, and Grant) are planted with rainbow, brook, and brown trout. Boats can be rented at the various resorts and marinas along the lakeshores. Anglers on foot often head for Rush Creek, particularly the section between Silver Lake and Gull Lake.

If you'd like to learn how to fly-fish, or just brush up on your skills, the **Double Eagle Resort** at June Lake (760/648-7004) offers lessons daily in summer. Full guide service is available, plus a fly-fishing shop. There's even a fly-fishing pond just for kids.

Just southeast of June Lake is **Alpers Owens River Ranch** (760/648-7334), where Tim Alpers raises world-class trophy trout. Alpers trout, known for their size, beauty, and feisty nature, are planted in many waters of the Eastern Sierra, including the trophy ponds of several resorts. In addition to Owens River access, the ranch has cabins for rent and a four-acre trophy trout pond. Make a reservation to fish the pond, then bring your float tube for your private three-hour time slot.

HORSEBACK RIDING

Frontier Pack Train at Silver Lake (in June Lake, 760/648-7701, www.frontierpacktrain.com, summers only) leads one-hour to all-day trail rides ($25–85), following the Rush Creek Trail alongside the gurgling waters of Rush Creek. Trips can be as short as one hour or as long as several days. If you'd like to live the life of a cowboy or cowgirl for a few days, you can join in the horse drives each spring and fall, when the pack station's 100 horses are transferred from their summer home in June Lake to their winter pastures in Round Valley, and then back again.

WINTER SPORTS

In winter, 2,500 vertical feet of skiing is available on **June Mountain** (800/626-6684, www.june mountain.com). Unlike the larger and more famous ski resort at Mammoth Mountain in Mammoth Lakes, the June Lake Ski Resort caters to families and more casual skiers. Many snowboarders insist that the boarding is better here than at Mammoth. One thing is certain: The lines at the chairlifts are shorter, and the lift tickets are cheaper. The two ski resorts have such a different ambience that it's surprising they are owned by the same company.

If you'd prefer a nonvertical and completely free-of-charge adventure, strap on a pair of snowshoes or cross-country skis and explore the closed-in-winter section of the June Lake Loop.

Mammoth Lakes

Famous for its ski resort at Mammoth Mountain, the town of Mammoth Lakes has become a year-round vacation destination. Spring, summer, and fall activities include hiking, lake and stream fishing, mountain biking, and horseback riding. Winter activities have expanded from the obvious (skiing and snowboarding) to the more esoteric: dog sledding, bobsledding, sleigh rides, and the like. Truly there is an activity for everyone in and around Mammoth Lakes.

VISITOR CENTER

The Mammoth Visitor Center and Forest Service Ranger Station (760/924-5500, www.r5.fs.fed.us/inyo, daily 8 A.M.–5 P.M.) is on the north side of Highway 203 as you drive into Mammoth Lakes from U.S. 395 (across from McDonald's). The staff can provide you with information on lodging, restaurants, camping, and recreational activities. A small bookstore sells maps and guidebooks.

SIGHTS

M Mammoth Lakes Basin

The scenic, lake-filled basin just east of the town of Mammoth Lakes is what gives this region its name. The five drive-to lakes in Mammoth Lakes Basin—Mary, Twin, George, Mamie, and Horseshoe—offer a wealth of opportunities for anglers and scenery admirers. Additionally, the lands surrounding the lakes are laced with hiking trails and campgrounds. To reach the Mammoth Lakes Basin, head east on Lake Mary Road from the junction of Lake Mary Road and Highway 203/Minaret Road in Mammoth Lakes. It takes only 20 minutes to drive around the five lakes, but it's unlikely you'll want to leave that soon. Bring a picnic lunch and stay a while. If you are interested in gold rush history, take the short walk to see the preserved buildings and equipment from the Mammoth Consolidated Gold Mine, found near the trailhead parking area at Coldwater Creek Campground.

Hot Creek Geologic Site

This popular spot just three miles south of Mammoth Lakes is a family-oriented hot springs, where hot water bubbles up from the middle of much cooler Hot Creek. At the parking lot are changing rooms and restrooms for bathers and interpretive signs that explain what makes this stretch of water bubble and boil. A short but steep paved trail leads down to the creek and hot springs, but

THE VOLCANIC MARVELS OF DEVILS POSTPILE

Few U.S. national parks are designated with monikers as colorful, or as intriguing, as Devils Postpile National Monument. First-time visitors all want to know: What the heck is the Devils Postpile? In brief, the Postpile is a formation of towering volcanic rock posts, or columns, made from lava that was forced upward from the earth's core. At the base of the standing 30-foot columns is a huge pile of rubble—the crumbled remains of those that have collapsed.

The Devils Postpile is proof positive that the Mammoth Lakes area is volcano country. Less than 100,000 years ago, lava filled the San Joaquin River valley more than 400 feet deep. As the lava began to cool from the air flow on top, it also cooled simultaneously from the hard granite bedrock below. This caused the lava to harden and crack into tall, narrow pieces, forming nearly perfect columns or posts. Although there are other examples of lava columns found throughout the world (the closest example is at Columns of the Giants on Highway 108 in Sonora Pass, north of Yosemite), the Devils Postpile is considered the finest example of lava columns in the world. The columns here are more regular in size and shape, and more distinctively hexagonal, than anywhere else.

You will notice, however, that although many of the lava columns are almost perfectly straight, others curve like tall candles that have been left out in the sun. This curvature was caused by the varying rates at which the massive lava flow cooled. If you take either of the side trails to the top of the Postpile, you can stand on the columns and marvel at the fact that so many are nearly the same height. Under your feet, the tops of the columns look like honeycomb, or tiles that have been laid side by side.

A trip to Devils Postpile National Monument is not complete without a visit to Rainbow Falls on the San Joaquin River. The falls can be accessed by a one-mile trail from Reds Meadow Pack Station, or by taking a longer trail from the Devils Postpile Ranger Station, passing the Devils Postpile along the way. Rainbow Falls, besides being an extraordinarily beautiful river waterfall, is another geologic wonder. The fall drops over volcanic rock of a different type than the basalt of Devils Postpile. The waterfall's cliff is rhyodacite, which forms an extremely hard horizontal layer at the waterfall's lip. This keeps the San Joaquin River from eroding the waterfall and eventually beveling it off. Rainbow Falls can expect to hold on to its impressive height of 101 feet for a long, long time.

True to its name, Rainbow Falls does have a rainbow that dances through the mist near its base. The rainbow is best seen at midday, when direct light rays are passing through the water droplets that plummet over the falls.

even from above you can see the bright aqua pools with thick flows of steam venting upward. Change into your bathing suit and go for a dip, but remember to obey all posted signs and fences that indicate areas to avoid. People have been badly burned by venturing into unsafe areas along the creek. Watch children carefully, too. To reach the geologic site, take U.S. 395 2.8 miles south of the Mammoth Lakes/Highway 203 turnoff. Turn left (east) on Hot Creek Hatchery Road and drive three miles to the parking lot.

Inyo Craters

The Inyo Craters are part of a chain of craters and other volcanic formations that reaches from Mammoth to Mono Lake. Evidence of Mammoth's fiery past, the craters are the remains of a volcanic explosion of steam that happened only 600 years ago. At that time the mountain was a smoldering volcano. Melted snow found its way inside, and when the cold water hit hot magma, an explosion occurred. The walk to the craters is a 0.25-mile uphill trek through a lovely open forest of red fir and Jeffrey pine.

The Eastern Sierra

In each of the two Inyo Craters lies a tiny pond that fills with the collected drops of melting snow each spring, then dries up during summer. To reach the trailhead for Inyo Craters, turn right (north) on Highway 203/Minaret Road at its junction with Lake Mary Road in downtown Mammoth Lakes. Drive 1.2 miles to the right turnoff for the Mammoth Lakes Scenic Loop. Turn right and drive 2.7 miles to the sign for Inyo Craters on the left side of the road. Turn left (west) and follow this dirt road 1.3 miles to the parking area.

M Devils Postpile

Devils Postpile National Monument features two geologic marvels: the Devils Postpile itself—an amazing collection of columnar basalt "posts" remaining from an ancient lava flow—and 101-foot Rainbow Falls, one of the Sierra's most beautiful waterfalls. Seeing the Postpile requires a 0.3-mile walk from the ranger station at the monument. Visitors can turn back here or continue onward for a total four-mile round-trip to Rainbow Falls, or divide the trip into two shorter walks by starting at two different trailheads. A shorter trail to Rainbow Falls begins near Reds Meadow Pack Station at the end of Devils Postpile Road.

Devils Postpile is generally open from June to October. All visitors arriving between 7 A.M. and 7 P.M. are required to ride a shuttle bus into the monument. The bus ride is free with the purchase of an access pass, which is $7 per adult and $4 for children ages 3 to 15. Once you're in the park, you can ride the free shuttle buses from one trailhead to another. Passes may be purchased at the Mammoth Mountain Shuttle Bus Terminal (near the ski area) or at Minaret Station (at the entrance to the monument). If you are camping in the Devils Postpile area, you are permitted to drive your own car instead of taking the shuttle, but each passenger in the car must purchase an access pass.

From the town of Mammoth Lakes, drive four miles west on Highway 203, then turn right on Minaret Road (still Highway 203). Drive 4.5 miles to the Devils Postpile entrance kiosk, by Mammoth Mountain Ski Area.

HIKING

Just minutes from downtown Mammoth Lakes, hikers can find dozens of hiking trails leading to alpine lakes and flower-filled meadows. The number of short, rewarding day hikes in the Mammoth Lakes Basin alone is remarkable.

Barrett and TJ Lakes

- Distance: 1.0 mile round-trip
- Duration: 30–40 minutes
- Rating: Easy
- Elevation Change: 500 feet
- Trailhead: Lake George
- Directions: From the Mammoth Lakes junction on U.S. 395, turn west on Highway 203 and drive four miles through the town of Mammoth Lakes to the junction of Minaret Road/Highway 203 and Lake Mary Road. Continue straight on Lake Mary Road and drive four miles to a junction for Lake George. Turn left here, drive 0.3 mile, then turn right and drive 0.3 mile to Lake George. The trailhead is located near the campground.

Campers at Lake George, and Mammoth visitors who just want a short and easy day hike, will be pleased to find that this "no-sweat" trail provides access to hidden Barrett and TJ Lakes. The trail starts on the northeast shore of Lake George, which in itself is a gorgeous spot, follows the lakeshore for about 100 yards, then climbs alongside a small stream to little Barrett Lake. The tiny lake is framed by Red Mountain in the background. Hey, this was so easy, you might as well continue another 0.25 mile to TJ Lake, the more scenic of the two lakes. The distinctive granite fin of Crystal Crag (10,377 feet) towers above TJ Lake's basin, adding drama to the scene. In addition to the pretty but popular lakes, this trail shows off some lovely mountain meadows, gilded with colorful penstemon, shooting stars, and paintbrush in midsummer.

Crystal Lake and Mammoth Crest

- Distance: 3.8–7.8 miles round-trip
- Duration: 2–4 hours

- Rating: Easy to moderate
- Elevation Change: 700–1,400 feet
- Trailhead: Lake George
- Directions: From the Mammoth Lakes junction on U.S. 395, turn west on Highway 203 and drive four miles through the town of Mammoth Lakes to the junction of Minaret Road/Highway 203 and Lake Mary Road. Continue straight on Lake Mary Road and drive four miles to a junction for Lake George. Turn left, drive 0.3 mile, then turn right and drive 0.3 mile to Lake George. The trailhead is on the right, near some cabins.

If you think Lake George is gorgeous, wait until you see Crystal Lake, located southwest of George Lake in a bowl scoured by glaciers and tucked into a hollow below 10,377-foot Crystal Crag. The trail to reach it has a 700-foot elevation gain and is pleasantly shaded by a hearty hemlock, pine, and fir forest. The path begins near the cabins at Woods Lodge but rises quickly above them. Many hikers huff and puff as they climb this ridge, but the view of the Mammoth Lakes Basin makes it all worthwhile. You gain a bird's-eye look at the basin's four major lakes: George, Mary, Mamie, and Twin. At a junction at one mile, go left and descend to Crystal Lake. The lake is a true jewel, highlighted by permanent snowfields that line its granite backdrop. You aren't likely to find much solitude here, since the lake is so easy to reach, but the scenery more than makes up for it.

If you want to turn this into a longer hike, you can take the other trail at the fork and head for Mammoth Crest at 10,400 feet two miles farther. The trail gains another 700 feet as it leaves the forest and enters a stark, volcanic landscape peppered with whitebark pines. The expansive view from the high point on the crest includes the Mammoth Lakes Basin, the San Joaquin River, the Minaret Range, and Mammoth Mountain. If this hike hasn't taken your breath away, the vista will.

Emerald Lake and Sky Meadows

- Distance: 4.0 miles round-trip
- Duration: 2 hours

- Rating: Easy to moderate
- Elevation Change: 500 feet
- Trailhead: Coldwater Campground
- Directions: From the Mammoth Lakes junction on U.S. 395, turn west on Highway 203 and drive four miles through the town of Mammoth Lakes to the junction of Minaret Road/Highway 203 and Lake Mary Road. Continue straight on Lake Mary Road and drive 3.5 miles to a fork just before Lake Mary; turn left and drive 0.6 mile to the Coldwater Campground turnoff on the left. Turn left and drive 0.5 mile through the camp to the trailhead at the first parking lot.

This is one of the Eastern Sierra's premier wildflower trails, and it's easy enough for children to hike. The trail starts just south of Lake Mary, at the end of the Coldwater Campground road. The hike is short and direct, climbing straight to Emerald Lake on an easy grade. Picnickers are often found seated among the rocks by the water's edge, although by mid-summer the tiny lake dwindles to something that more closely resembles a pond. No matter, the lake is not the star of the show here—the flowers are. The trail skirts the east shore of Emerald Lake and continues along its inlet stream. Three brief climbs lead you past Gentian Meadow to the southeast edge of Sky Meadows, which is filled with wildflowers throughout the summer. Beyond the meadows, permanent snowfields decorate the granite cliffs of Mammoth Crest. Among the wide variety of flower species to be seen and admired, one standout is the tall orange tiger lily, a flower showy enough to be in a florist's shop.

Duck Pass Trail to Duck Lake

- Distance: 10.0 miles round-trip
- Duration: 5 hours
- Rating: Moderate
- Elevation Change: 1,900 feet
- Trailhead: Coldwater Campground
- Directions: From the Mammoth Lakes junction on U.S. 395, turn west on Highway 203 and drive four miles through the town of Mammoth Lakes to the junction of Minaret

Road/Highway 203 and Lake Mary Road. Continue straight on Lake Mary Road and drive 3.5 miles to a fork just before Lake Mary; turn left and drive 0.6 mile to the Coldwater Campground turnoff on the left. Turn left and drive 0.5 mile through the camp to the trailhead at the farthest parking lot.

The Duck Pass Trail offers myriad options for day hikers and backpackers alike. How far you hike on the Duck Pass Trail is up to you, but if you have the energy and time, head out for five miles to Duck Lake, elevation 10,450 feet. If a 10-mile round-trip sounds too ambitious, you can stop at one of the other lakes found along the way—Arrowhead Lake at 1.3 miles out, Skelton Lake at 2.0 miles, or Barney Lake at 3.0 miles. If you head all the way to Duck Lake, you'll climb 1,600 feet to the top of Duck Pass. Just beyond the pass the trail drops 300 feet to reach Duck Lake, one of the largest natural lakes in the Eastern Sierra. Most of the climbing is in the stretch from Barney Lake to the pass, as the trail switchbacks up a talus-covered slope. Day hikers can make their way from Duck Lake on a faint path to Pika Lake, visible in the distance about a half mile away.

Red Cones Loop

- Distance: 6.7 miles round-trip
- Duration: 3.5 hours
- Rating: Moderate
- Elevation Change: 800 feet
- Trailhead: Horseshoe Lake
- Directions: From the Mammoth Lakes junction on U.S. 395, turn west on Highway 203 and drive four miles through the town of Mammoth Lakes to the junction of Minaret Road/Highway 203 and Lake Mary Road. Continue straight on Lake Mary Road and drive 4.8 miles to the road's end at Horseshoe Lake. The trailhead is on the northwest side of the lake, signed for Mammoth Pass.

Horseshoe Lake, elevation 8,900 feet, lies at the end of the Mammoth Lakes road and has an excellent trailhead that makes for a great day hike. Don't be put off by the dead trees

and the barren look of Horseshoe Lake's shoreline. A small area by the lake has been affected by carbon dioxide gas venting up through the soil—the result of localized seismic activity—but you leave this strange ghost forest quickly. Set out from the northwest side of the lake, ascend the slope, and take the left fork for McLeod Lake. In just under two miles you'll reach the start of the loop. Go right to reach Crater Meadow, a beautiful little spot set just below Red Cones, and then circle around to Upper Crater Meadow. Either meadow makes a fine destination.

Devils Postpile and Rainbow Falls

- Distance: 5.0 miles round-trip
- Duration: 2.5 hours
- Rating: Easy to moderate
- Elevation Change: 500 feet
- Trailhead: Devils Postpile Ranger Station
- Directions: From the Mammoth Lakes junction on U.S. 395, turn west on Highway 203 and drive four miles through the town of Mammoth Lakes to Minaret Road (still Highway 203). Turn right and drive 4.5 miles to the shuttle bus terminal (adjacent to the Mammoth Mountain Ski Area). Purchase an access pass and board a shuttle bus here. Disembark at the Devils Postpile Ranger Station.

The first time you lay eyes on 101-foot Rainbow Falls, this tall, wide, and forceful waterfall comes as an awesome surprise. Most first-time visitors see it before or after a trip to the Devils Postpile, a fascinating collection of volcanic rock columns and rubble left from a lava flow nearly 100,000 years ago.

Start at the ranger station and hike to the Devils Postpile lava columns in only 0.5 mile. Stop and gape at this geologic wonder, and perhaps take the short but steep side trip to the top of the columns, then continue downhill to Rainbow Falls at 2.5 miles. In order to see the rainbow that gives the waterfall its name, you must show up in late morning or at midday. The rainbow is the result of a prism effect from sun rays refracting through the falling water. Two overlook areas across from the waterfall's brink give you an excellent view, but you can hike down a series of stairsteps to the waterfall's base for an even better vantage point.

Shadow Lake

- Distance: 7.6 miles round-trip
- Duration: 4 hours
- Rating: Moderate
- Elevation Change: 1,900 feet
- Trailhead: Agnew Meadows
- Directions: From the Mammoth Lakes junction on U.S. 395, turn west on Highway 203 and drive four miles through the town of Mammoth Lakes to Minaret Road (still Highway 203). Turn right and drive 4.5 miles to the shuttle bus terminal (adjacent to the Mammoth Mountain Ski Area). Purchase an access pass and board a shuttle bus here. Disembark at Agnew Meadows.

Those seeking a longer trek in Devils Postpile National Monument should make the trip to Shadow Lake from the trailhead at Agnew Meadows. The 7.6-mile round-trip starts out quite mellow as it wanders through the wild-flowers at Agnew Meadows, then follows the River Trail along the Middle Fork of the San Joaquin River. Just beyond shallow Olaine Lake at two miles lies a junction, where you go left for Shadow Lake. Cross a bridge and prepare to climb. A long series of steep, shadeless switchbacks ensues as you ascend alongside a narrow creek gorge. Fortunately the view looking down the San Joaquin River canyon becomes ever more grand as you rise upward. At last you reach the waterfall on Shadow Lake's outlet stream and climb the final stretch to the lake. Its backdrop is like something you've seen on postcards of the Sierra, with the Minarets, Mount Ritter, and Mount Banner towering above the lake. Pick a spot along the 8,737-foot lakeshore and drink in the view.

BIKING

Mammoth Lakes is a mecca for mountain biking. The best-known trails are found at **Mammoth Mountain Bike Park** (800/MAMMOTH or 800/626-6684, www.mammothmountain.com), the summertime persona of

Mammoth Mountain Ski Area becomes Mammoth Mountain Bike Park in the summer, with more than 70 miles of single-track trails.

Mammoth Mountain Ski Area. The park is famous for its occasional pro races, when all the big-name mountain bikers show up. Most of the time, though, it's just regular vacationers cruising around the more than 70 miles of single-track trails, which run the full spectrum from easy to extremely difficult. You and your bike can ride the Panorama Gondola to the 11,053-foot summit of Mammoth Mountain, then race all the way back downhill. Bike rentals are available if you didn't bring your own.

If you'd rather ride farther from the crowds, you can check out a wealth of trails on Inyo National Forest lands. The **Inyo Craters Loop** is a popular 10-mile mountain-biking loop on mostly dirt and gravel roads, suitable for strong beginners and intermediates.

Mountain bikers seeking challenging single-track should try out the 5.5-mile **Mountain View Trail,** which runs from Minaret Vista near the Mammoth Mountain Ski Area to the Earthquake Fault access road off Highway 203 (Minaret Road). You can retrace your tire treads for the route home, or loop back on the paved Minaret Road.

Beginning mountain bikers can ride the five-mile **Shady Rest Loop** at Shady Rest Park near the entrance to the town of Mammoth Lakes, or put together a combined dirt and paved loop from Mammoth Creek Park by starting out on its paved bike trail. More advanced riders can start at Shady Rest Park and ride the **Knolls Loop,** which branches off the Shady Rest Loop.

Road bikers seeking a challenge will want to try out the demanding ride from Mammoth Mountain Ski Area to Reds Meadow at **Devils Postpile National Monument.** The road into the monument is quite narrow and has a 1,500-foot elevation change (down on the way in, up on the way back, with 1,000 feet of change concentrated in a 2.5-mile stretch). Incredibly scenic throughout its entire length, the 20-mile round-trip offers a major bonus for cyclists: In summer, a mandatory shuttle bus system operates during daylight hours, so the amount of traffic on the Devils Postpile road is severely restricted. This makes cycling here surprisingly safe, considering the popularity of this park.

If you prefer to do more cruising and less hard climbing on your road bike, take an easy spin around the **Mammoth Lakes Basin.** By starting at Twin Lakes, you can ride a nearly level 12-mile loop around the five lakes.

ROCK CLIMBING

The Eastern Sierra, especially the region between Mammoth Lakes and Bishop, 30 miles south, has no shortage of rocks to climb on. The **Sierra Mountain Center** (760/873-8526, www.sierramountaincenter.com) is a large guide service that can set you up on a rock climbing or mountaineering adventure. In the town of Mammoth Lakes, **Mammoth Mountaineering Supply** (760/934-4191) and **Kittredge Sports** (760/934-7566, www.kittredgesports.com) are good sources for climbing equipment and local knowledge.

FISHING

Of the five lakes found in the Mammoth Lakes Basin, four of them are the happy hunting ground of anglers: Mary, Twin, George, and Mamie. (Horseshoe Lake, the fifth of the lot, is considered barren.) These four lakes are regularly planted with catchable rainbow trout. Occasional brown trout and brook trout are also caught. You can rent boats on **Lake Mary** or Twin Lakes (760/934-7295).

Experienced fly fishers head for the Middle Fork of the San Joaquin River in Devils Postpile National Monument. They also flock to **Hot Creek,** a few miles southeast of Mammoth Lakes on the opposite side of U.S. 395. Hot Creek originates as an underground creek, formed from a combination of 11 different springs. It bubbles forth from a fissure in volcanic rock, then runs down a narrow gorge, creating excellent habitat for wildlife, including wild rainbow and brown trout. How big are the fish? The standard trout is at least 12 inches; fish in excess of 20 inches are not unusual. This is a remarkable, world-class fishing stream.

A good source for Mammoth Lakes fly-fishing information, as well as lessons and rentals, is **The Trout Fly** at the junction of Main Street and Old Mammoth Road (760/934-2517, www.thetroutfly.com). Another good fishing source in town is **The Troutfitter** (760/924-3676, www.thetroutfitter.com).

Just a few miles south of Mammoth Lakes is **Convict Lake,** a large drive-up lake with a cabin resort and campground near its edges. This big lake is filled with planted rainbow trout, but has developed a reputation for hoarding some big brown trout. **Convict Lake Resort** (760/934-3800 or 800/992-2260) rents motor boats, pontoon boats, rowboats, and canoes, and sells bait and tackle.

HORSEBACK RIDING

Mammoth Lakes Pack Outfit (888/475-8747 or 760/934-2434, www.mammothpack.com) is located in Mammoth Lakes Basin. Guided horseback rides are available daily, as well as four- to six-day horseback vacations and customized wilderness pack trips. You can even join in the spring and fall horse drives, when the pack outfit's herd of horses and mules are moved between their winter pasture near Independence and their summer home in Mammoth Lakes Basin, and then back again.

Reds Meadow Resort and Pack Station (760/934-2345 or 800/292-7758, www.redsmeadowpackstation.com), on the border of Devils Postpile National Monument, offers two-hour, half-day, and full-day horseback rides. It also runs a dizzying array of multi-day trips into the wilderness.

Convict Lake Pack Station at Convict Lake (760/934-3800, www.convictlakeresort.com), a few miles south of Mammoth, leads guided horseback rides along the lakeshore and longer rides into the John Muir Wilderness.

WINTER SPORTS

Mammoth Mountain Ski Area (1 Minaret Rd., Mammoth Lakes, 800/MAMMOTH or 800/626-6684, www.mammothmountain .com) is considered one of the finest ski resorts in all of California. The resort has a lot to brag about: 3,500 acres, 3,100 vertical feet, an average 385 inches of snow, and 300 days of sunshine each year. The ski season begins in early November (the resort makes snow if needed, but it's not usually required) and runs until June or July. The 11,053-foot summit of Mammoth Mountain is easily accessible via a glass-paneled gondola, and a passel of chairlifts are always in motion up and down the slopes.

The same company that runs Mammoth Mountain also manages a cross-country ski resort at **Tamarack Lodge** on Twin Lakes in the Mammoth Lakes Basin (760/934-2442, www.tamaracklodge.com). Here, in the lands surrounding this historic lodge, more than 45 kilometers of groomed track are open to cross-country skiers and snowshoers. The resort has cabins for rent in the winter and offers equipment rentals and instructions. Clinics, races, and nature tours are offered on the weekends.

If you want to try out other winter sports, **DJ's Snowmobile Adventures** (760/955-4480, www.snowmobilemammoth.com), near Mammoth Mountain, leads one-hour and all-day snowmobile tours through the lands of Inyo National Forest.

Lodging

Most Yosemite travelers want to stay overnight inside the park boundary, and ideally within Yosemite Valley. If you are the kind of person who can plan far in advance—as much as a year in advance for some lodgings—this is easily achieved. If you're not, you should plan on visiting only in the off-season or plan on sleeping outside the park. On peak summer weekends, last-minute lodgings even outside of Yosemite can be difficult to obtain.

However, if you're willing to be flexible, and you don't need to stay at the Ritz, you can usually find a place to spend the night within an hour's drive of one of the park's entry points, even on holiday weekends. The good news is that areas outside of the park offer many of the same good things as the park itself, including spectacular scenery and plentiful recreation opportunities, so you're likely to enjoy yourself no matter where you end up. And remember, too, driving long distances is simply part of the deal in Yosemite—after all, the park is nearly the size of the state of Rhode Island.

Yosemite's Best

Look for **N** to find the best lodging.

N White Wolf Lodge: Book a stay in one of the four quaint wooden cabins at White Wolf and you have hit the Yosemite lodging jackpot. If those cabins are full, the tent cabins are a good second choice, but you'll have to live without a private bathroom and most other luxuries. Still, you couldn't be in a better spot for exploring the high country (page 128).

N Wawona Hotel: Far from the madness of Yosemite Valley, the historic Wawona Hotel with its wide veranda and vintage ambience is a good choice for Yosemite travelers entering the park from the south (page 130).

N Ahwahnee Hotel: Room prices start at nearly $400 per night here, so a reservation at the Ahwahnee is a hefty indulgence. Still, this National Historic Landmark hotel is a Yosemite classic. Try to sleep here at least one night of your life (page 131).

N Yosemite View Lodge: Set alongside the Merced River only two miles from Yosemite's Arch Rock entrance, Yosemite View Lodge can brag of having three key features: location, location, location. For the best experience, reserve a room with a fireplace and river view (page 142).

N Château du Sureau: It's a gross understatement to say you wouldn't expect to find a hotel like this in the Sierra foothills. Praised by just about every major travel magazine and guide-

© ANN MARIE BROWN

White Wolf Lodge

book, the Château du Sureau takes European luxury to a new level. Rates are similar to what you would pay at the Ahwahnee, but you'll be even more spoiled here (page 150).

N Tioga Pass Resort: Situated along Tioga Pass Road just two miles from Yosemite's eastern entrance, "TPR" boasts an elevation of nearly 10,000 feet. For a quintessential Yosemite high-country experience, book a stay in one of the log cabins (page 154).

Inside Yosemite

Of the seven lodgings available inside the park boundaries, four are in Yosemite Valley—the marvelous but pricey Ahwahnee Hotel, the midpriced Yosemite Lodge, and the budget-priced Curry Village and Housekeeping Camp. The two rustic park lodgings located in Yosemite's high country on Tioga Pass Road—White Wolf Lodge and Tuolumne Lodge—are open only June–September. The grand Wawona Hotel in the southern part of the park is open daily in summer but weekends only in winter.

Reservations for these seven accommodations are made at one central place: **DNC Parks and Resorts at Yosemite,** 9001 Village Drive, Yosemite, CA 95389, 559/252-4848 or 559/253-5676, or www.yosemitepark.com. The reservations phone line is open weekdays 7 A.M.–7 P.M., weekends 8 A.M.–5 P.M. Note that room rates are not guaranteed, even if

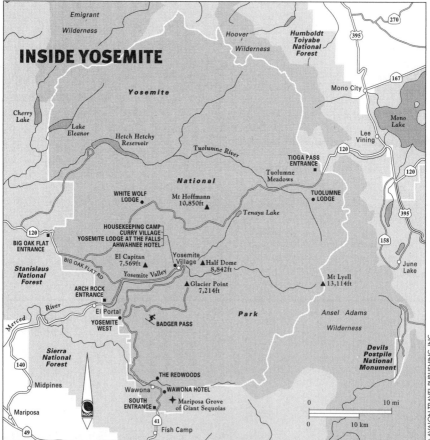

© AVALON TRAVEL PUBLISHING, INC.

you pre-pay when making your reservation. If the park's lodging rates increase between the time you make your reservation and the time you visit, you will be required to pay the additional amount.

For reservations at park lodgings May–Sept., it is wise to make reservations up to a year in advance. Cancellations do happen, so if you strike out, keep calling back. During the rest of the year, it is not difficult to get a room, even in Yosemite Valley, particularly midweek. A few days' notice should be all you need, except during holidays.

Two additional lodgings are located on private land holdings within the national park: The Redwoods at Wawona and Yosemite West. These are not on the central reservation system and, as such, are much easier to reserve.

If you want to stay in park lodgings and save money, you should visit Yosemite during what is called "value season," Nov.–March, excluding major holidays. Value-season rates, as much as 40 percent lower than regular rates, can be obtained at Curry Village, Yosemite Lodge, and the Wawona Hotel. Note that the "major holiday" exclusion knocks out a fair number of winter days: the four-day Thanksgiving weekend, the last two weeks of December, the three-day weekend surrounding Martin Luther King Jr. Day in January, and the week during which President's Day falls in February.

$50–100
Housekeeping Camp

From the outside, Housekeeping Camp looks a lot like a crowded inner-city slum in a developing country. Nonetheless, many repeat visitors to Yosemite Valley are devotees of Housekeeping Camp, for two main reasons: location and value. The 266 duplex units are all the same—a strange hybrid between a cabin and a campsite. Each unit consists of one room that will sleep up to six people in two bunk beds and a double bed ("cot" is a more accurate description). The "room" has a concrete floor, three concrete walls, and a curtain for a fourth wall. A canvas awning covers the roof and extends over

a patio, which also serves as the cooking and dining area. The patio has a small table with a light and electric outlet where you can set up your camp stove and electric coffeemaker. A fire grill is provided, so with a small stack of chopped wood you can blacken all the marshmallows you want.

Unlike at nearby Curry Village, you can park your car right beside your Housekeeping Camp unit. All units are located near a popular sandy beach on the Merced River, and many have views of Yosemite Falls or Half Dome. Unfortunately, they are also located on the busy road to Curry Village and the Pines campgrounds. Earplugs are a wise investment, especially for sleeping. And don't count on much privacy.

The overall experience at Housekeeping Camp is only a very small step up from camping. An advantage is that you don't need any equipment to stay here; you can rent bed linens, blankets, pillows, camp stoves, chairs, cots, and cribs. Or save a few bucks and bring this stuff from home.

Showers and restrooms are located in communal buildings nearby. A laundry and small grocery store are on the premises. Food storage rules are in effect; to keep the bears away, you'll have to stow everything after you finish cooking. Bear boxes are provided.

Housekeeping Camp is open April–Oct. only; rates are $68 per night. To reserve, phone 559/252-4848 or 559/253-5676 or visit www.yosemitepark.com.

Curry Village

Many visitors have a love-hate relationship with Curry Village. On the one hand, they love Curry Village because it's centrally located and it comes with all the amenities: lodging, food, parking, bus shuttles, stores, etc. On the other hand, they hate Curry Village because it embodies the worst of Yosemite Valley on its most hectic summer days: too many people, too crowded, too noisy.

That said, make sure you know what you are signing up for when you book a stay here. In the off-season (or even in summer if you plan way in advance), you could be fortunate enough to rent one of Curry Village's 180 private, cozy, wooden cabins ($89–135). If you were born under a lucky star, you might even get one of the cabins with a private bath, or one of the 19 lodge rooms with a private bath ($112), which will save you a hike to the restroom in the middle of the night.

But most of the time, and for the vast majority of visitors, the only cabins available at Curry Village are the 427 tent cabins ($69). What you should know about these cabins is that they are made of canvas and they are placed about nine inches apart. This is convenient if you want to stay up late and learn a new language from the bevy of international visitors. It's inconvenient if you enjoy sleeping. Seasoned Curry Village veterans travel with earplugs.

The tent cabins have electric lights, and some are heated. Other than that, don't expect much more than a couple beds with linens and a small dresser, a few posters for art, and a bedside lantern. New bedspreads made to look and feel like sleeping bags, added in 2004, have given the cabins a cozier feel. Bathrooms and showers are a short walk away; soap and towels are provided. There are no phones or televisions in any of the units.

If you stay in the tent cabins, you have to put up with a few inconveniences: First, you won't be able to drive right up to your lodging. You'll park in a central lot and then carry your suitcases for a few hundred feet. Also, bears are a major problem in and around Curry Village, so you won't be able to keep anything scented (food, toothpaste, sunscreen, cosmetics) in either your cabin or your car. Bearproof lockers are provided and must be used. Rangers strictly enforce the bearproofing rules.

Despite these minor hassles, families with kids tend to be pretty happy here. Not only is Curry Village the cheapest lodging in the park, it also has many "extras" on the grounds: cafeteria, pizza and beer joint, coffee and ice cream place, grocery store, camping and outdoor equipment shop, outdoor swimming pool with lifeguards, amphitheater with nightly programs, post office, and bicycle and raft rent-als. You can walk to Mirror Lake, Happy Isles, and Vernal and Nevada Falls from your cabin door. There's even an ice-skating rink in the winter months.

Curry Village is open year-round. To reserve a stay, phone 559/252-4848 or 559/253-5676 or visit www.yosemitepark.com.

White Wolf Lodge

The first time you glimpse the cabins at White Wolf, you sense the realization of your Yosemite lodging dreams. Set at the sweet high-country elevation of 8,000 feet, the white wooden cabins are trimmed in hunter green, with Adirondack chairs lined up on the porches to face a wildflower-filled meadow. If you think that it doesn't get any better than this, you're exactly right.

Except you might be wrong too. The trick is that not every White Wolf cabin is one of those quaint *Sunset* magazine–style jobs; only four cabins fit that bill. Right behind them are two dozen typical Yosemite tent cabins—large, off-white tents on raised wooden platforms, almost bare inside except for a wood-burning stove, candles for lighting, and a couple of beds.

The wooden cabins ($105) have their own bathrooms, propane heat, daily maid service, and electricity (generated only during certain hours of the day). The tent cabins ($75) have none of the above. Guess which ones are harder to come by?

Regardless of which cabin you reserve, everything about a stay at White Wolf is easy. An excellent restaurant on the premises serves breakfast and dinner and makes box lunches to go. A small store sells snacks, drinks, and a few minimal supplies. A couple of hiking trails begin practically at your doorstep, and a multitude of trails on Tioga Road are just a few miles away. Yosemite Valley is a one-hour drive.

So how do you get one of those white-and-green cabins? Plan on reserving at least a year in advance. Rub your rabbit's foot, then pick up the phone and call 559/252-4848 or 559/253-5676 or visit www.yosemitepark.com. The lodge is open from mid-June through early September.

Tuolumne Lodge

Tuolumne Lodge has the same upsides as the nearby tent cabin resort at White Wolf. The upsides: A chance to stay in convenient lodging right in the midst of Yosemite's best day hiking, fishing, and scenery-watching country, with easy access to hearty meals and necessary supplies.

It also has the same downsides as White Wolf: The tent cabins ($75) are a bit dreary (canvas tents on raised wooden platforms with nothing but beds, candles, and a wood-burning stove). And they are packed in so tightly that you can hear your neighbors talking, coughing, and snoring at night. The complex at Tuolumne Lodge includes a whopping 59 tent cabins—it's a small tent cabin city. Each one can accommodate four people, although two people are more comfortable.

Of course, few who stay here ever complain. The upsides simply far outweigh the downsides. Guests come to be within one mile of Tuolumne Meadows and not for any other reason. The cabins are one mile down an access

© ANN MARIE BROWN

The tent cabins at Tuolumne Lodge are barebones on the inside, but after all, you don't stay here so you can stay indoors.

road directly across from Lembert Dome and the Soda Springs trailhead, and within a stone's throw of the John Muir Trail and Pacific Crest Trail. Tioga Pass itself, and all the hiking and fishing options on its east side, is only six miles away. Trail choices are virtually unlimited.

After exploring the high country all day, you'll sit down to a hearty dinner at the Tuolumne Meadows Lodge dining tent alongside the Tuolumne River. The food is excellent and prices are reasonable, especially considering the spectacular setting. The lodge is open from mid-June through mid-September. Reserve by phoning 559/252-4848 or 559/253-5676 or visit www.yosemitepark.com.

$100–200

Yosemite Lodge at the Falls

In 2004, Yosemite Lodge got a face-lift and an extension to its name—it's now Yosemite Lodge at the Falls. Basically, it's still the same place, but with new carpets, drapes, mattresses, paint and a more marketable title. Whether or not that justifies the accompanying raise in room rates is subject to debate. The lodge is comfortable, clean, and nothing fancy—kind of like the Best Western of Yosemite. Its major selling point is an ideal location in Yosemite Valley, directly across from Yosemite Falls. In fact, a couple of rooms have a first-rate view of the falls. You can sit outside on your balcony, drink your coffee, and study the incredible flow of white water pouring down. Unfortunately, you can't make a reservation for any particular room. Your place is assigned to you when you arrive, so you only get the waterfall-view rooms by sheer good fortune. Still, most of the rooms have decent views of woods or meadows.

You do get to choose between two types of rooms: lodge hotel rooms ($150–175) and standard hotel rooms ($120–140). In both cases, the word "hotel" is a euphemism. Despite their name, these rooms are more motel-style than lodge- or hotel-style. Yosemite Lodge's 245 rooms are arranged in several small buildings, with interior hallways that look rather drearily like college dorm halls, but the rooms themselves are nice. The higher-priced rooms are larger and airier and come with either a patio or a balcony. The standard rooms are, well, standard. All have private bathrooms and telephones, and since the 2004 remodeling project, 19-inch television sets. If you need to stay connected to the Internet, wireless hot spots are found at several locations around the lodge (but you'll have to pay a flat daily rate to connect). And if you left your laptop at home, you can still check your email, surf the Web, or download digital pictures via two public Internet kiosks available in six different languages (cost is $.25 per minute).

Besides location, one of the best things about a stay at Yosemite Lodge is its convenience. Three restaurants and a cocktail lounge, a swimming pool, bike rentals, a grocery store, and evening slide shows are all part of the deal. Many of the park's most popular tours depart from the lodge. The trailhead for Yosemite Falls is right across the street. To reserve a stay here, phone 559/252-4848 or 559/253-5676 or visit www.yosemitepark.com.

M Wawona Hotel

The white-and-green Victorian main building of the Wawona Hotel creates an elegant impression to visitors driving by on Highway 41. It has a Southern appeal, with a wide verandah out front and porch chairs scattered about its green lawns.

Considered one of California's oldest mountain hotels (one of its cottages was built in 1876; the main hotel was added three years later), the Wawona is a great place to stay if you enjoy historic buildings and don't need the amenities of the Ritz. The hotel has a vintage quality, and it's not just due to the preponderance of brass doorknobs, crown moldings, Victorian wallpaper, and steam radiators. The building itself is a National Historic Landmark. The room furnishings include wicker chairs, brass beds, and some antique furniture—even a few clawfoot tubs. You won't find TVs or telephones here. A 2005 renovation includes a new foundation for the aging structure, as well as new furnishings for the rooms.

A major advantage to staying at the Wawona

is the peace and quiet. You're far from the hustle and bustle of the Valley, which is an hour's drive away. Yet the hotel is very convenient to the many trailheads and the spectacular vista point on Glacier Point Road, a half hour away. The Mariposa Grove of Sequoias and the trailhead for Chilnualna Falls are minutes away, as is the Pioneer Yosemite History Center in Wawona.

The hotel is open year-round, but only on weekends in winter. The rooms are generally small but comfortable. Those in the main building are not quite as nice as those in various buildings around the grounds. Of 150 rooms, only 50 have private baths, and these fall into the higher end of the $120–175 fee range. The lower-priced rooms share communal bath and shower facilities, which are surprisingly comfortable and private. Bathrobes are provided in rooms without baths for late-night trips.

The Wawona's dining room is dependably good, and eating there feels like an "experience." The restaurant is not particularly formal, but it has the same grand, vintage feel as the rest of the hotel, with high ceilings and big windows overlooking a green lawn.

Most other standard hotel services are found at the Wawona Hotel, including a swimming pool and two tennis courts. A piano player entertains in the main lobby every evening. This is fortunate because the dining room doesn't take reservations unless your party is larger than eight, so most small groups end up waiting for a table.

One more note about the Wawona, and it's a big plus for some park visitors and an eyesore for others: the Yosemite nine-hole golf course is just across the road. A golf course in a national park? Yes, odd as it seems. At least it's historic—it was built in 1917.

To reserve a room at the Wawona, phone 559/252-4848 or 559/253-5676 or visit www.yosemitepark.com. To speak to someone at the Wawona Hotel front desk, phone 209/375-1218.

Yosemite West

Yosemite National Park is packed with people every day all summer long, but over at Yosemite

West you can hear a pin drop on your cabin's deck. A 30-year-old subdivision that consists of a collection of private homes, Yosemite West is located on a hillside right across from Chinquapin junction, the meeting place of Highway 41 and Glacier Point Road. The neighborhood is a "private inholding" within the federal park boundary. Some year-round residents live here, but more than 140 homes in the neighborhood are vacation rentals.

The rental homes at Yosemite West are on the upscale, modern side. They vary in size from two to six bedrooms, and most come with extras like a hot tub, barbecue, pool table, or home entertainment center. Most have fireplaces; free firewood is provided. The homes' lot sizes are fairly large, so you probably won't hear or see much of your neighbors. This place is for those who want peace, quiet, and seclusion.

Although many park travelers book a stay at Yosemite West in the summer, a cabin here is also an ideal choice for a winter trip, because it's the closest lodging to the downhill runs at Badger Pass (a 20-minute drive).

Several companies, as well as private individuals, rent homes or bed-and-breakfast-style rooms in Yosemite West. This is a bonus for vacationers; if you strike out for reservations with one company, phone another. Fees range $125–700 per night, depending on size of accommodations. Off-season rates are available midweek Sept.–April, excluding holidays. Contact one of the following companies for reservations in Yosemite West: Yosemite West Lodging, 559/642-2211 or www.yosemitewestreservations.com; Yosemite's Scenic Wonders, 800/296-7364, 888/967-3648, or www.scenicwonders.com; Yosemite's Four Seasons, 209/372-9000, 800/669-9300, or www.yosemitelodging.com; The Falcon's Nest, 209/372-8517, www.yosemitewest.com; or Yosemite Peregrine Bed and Breakfast, 209/372-8517, 800/396-3639, or www.yosemiteperegrine.com.

The Redwoods

The Wawona area of Yosemite is like the poor cousin of Yosemite West up the road. Like Yosemite West, it's a private inholding within the national park, where anyone can own (or rent) a home. But unlike at Yosemite West, the homes in the Wawona area are densely clustered on small lots. Many of the houses are truly "cabins"—meaning they're on the rustic side.

However, being the poor cousin isn't necessarily a bad thing. The Wawona cabins, collectively known as The Redwoods Vacation Home Rentals, are a real bargain. For not much more than $100, two people can rent a small cabin complete with linens, cookware, dishes, barbecue, and firewood. Larger houses that can accommodate a whole family or large group are also available. Every home is privately owned and reflects the owner's personal tastes and requirements, so you should be able to find one that suits you, too.

To make it easy, The Redwoods has arranged its 130 vacation rentals into categories. Category "C" rentals are the smallest and cheapest, and have the fewest amenities (no fireplace, for example). Category "U" cabins are the priciest; they may have as many as six bedrooms, plus frills like satellite TV, a dishwasher, or a gas grill. Every kind of cabin in between falls into four additional categories. Fees are $189–600 per night in summer and $143–430 per night in winter, depending on the size and category of the rental. There is a three-night minimum stay in summer and on holidays, and a two-night minimum stay in the off-season. To reserve, phone 209/375-6666 or visit www.redwoodsinyosemite.com.

$200 AND UP
Ahwahnee Hotel

If a wad of bills is burning a hole in your pocket, book a stay at the Ahwahnee. If your budget runs more to cheeseburgers than caviar, at least pay a visit to the Ahwahnee's public rooms. The old stone lodge is a classic, with fireplaces so large you could hold a tea party inside them.

Built in 1927, the Ahwahnee Hotel is a National Historic Landmark. Stained glass and wrought-iron chandeliers are a given. The public areas of the hotel are decorated with Native

American motifs and Miwok basketry. Turkish Kilim rugs serve as wall hangings. Six historic paintings, created when the hotel opened, depict Yosemite's waterfalls and sequoias. The elegant dining room is a perfect setting for the hotel's annual Bracebridge Dinner, a recreation of a 17th-century English Christmas feast. Equally popular events are the Chefs' Holidays and Vintners' Holidays, held at the Ahwahnee on several weekends Nov.–Feb., during which the culinary elite from across California strut their stuff. An annual New Year's Eve dinner and dance is another sell-out.

Some say the rooms at the Ahwahnee are overrated and overpriced. True, they are small, in typical 1920s fashion. But the views from the windows of the rooms often override any shortcomings in square footage or decor. One side of the hotel faces Glacier Point and Half Dome. The other side faces Yosemite Falls. The higher the room, the better the view, so be sure to request a spot on the fourth, fifth, or sixth floor. If you have an unlimited budget, reserve one of the handful of ultra-pricey two-room suites on the top floor. If that's not an option, go for one of the 24 cottages in the forest behind the hotel. The suites have the best views, but the cottages have the most privacy and some have fireplaces. All of them cost a bundle ($379–1,189 per night), but you will feel pampered. Even in the hotel's 99 "ordinary" rooms, expect plenty of small luxuries: terrycloth bathrobes, plush towels, valet parking, bell service, turn-down service, mini-

refrigerators, and televisions. If a TV insults your national park sensibilities, ask the management to remove it and they will do so graciously. For Ahwahnee guests who can't live without Internet access, wireless hotspots are available throughout the hotel.

A $2.25 million remodel completed in 2004 resulted in new carpeting, mattresses, down bedding, window treatments, furniture, and even coffeemakers in the hotel's rooms. A 2005 restyling of the Ahwahnee's cottages includes new tile and shower fixtures.

On warm summer days, you'll want to hang out by the Ahwahnee's small, heated swimming pool or have lunch on the terrace and enjoy the Valley scenery. In winter, relax with a book in the Great Lounge, where afternoon tea is served at 5 P.M. daily. Watch the flames flicker in the hotel's many fireplaces, or gaze at snowflakes falling or deer grazing on the meadow outside.

Knowing that Queen Elizabeth slept here, as well as John F. Kennedy, Ronald Reagan, and Winston Churchill, it probably won't surprise you that the hotel is full service. In addition to its world-class restaurant, the Ahwahnee also has gift shops, a cocktail lounge, tennis court, and tour desk. Anything you might need or want that you can't find here is available nearby at Yosemite Village.

To reserve, phone 559/252-4848 or 559/253-5676 or visit www.yosemitepark.com. And make sure you book early. Even with its high prices, the Ahwahnee is often full.

West of the Park: Highway 120

Visitors approaching Yosemite from Sacramento, San Francisco, and Northern California often use the Highway 120 approach through Groveland. Founded in 1849, Groveland was a rough-and-ready gold mining town. Until 1875 it was known as Garrote, which translates loosely as "hanging." The town was infamous for its swift and gruesome manner of carrying out Wild West justice, although whether this was more in reputation than in fact remains unknown.

Groveland experienced a major boom beginning in 1914 with the building of the nearby Hetch Hetchy dam, when the town served as headquarters for more than a decade's worth of construction efforts. Today Groveland offers the convenience of shops, gas stations, and restaurants for Yosemite travelers. The town provides a convenient place to stay if you are visiting Tioga Pass Road, Tuolumne Meadows, or the Hetch Hetchy area of Yosemite. A stay in Groveland puts you 25 miles (about 45 minutes) from the Big Oak Flat entrance; a stay in Buck Meadows cuts 12 miles off that distance. Groveland is a bit far from Yosemite Valley—about a 75-minute drive—but still doable for a day trip.

The lodgings listed below are arranged within each price category according to their proximity to Yosemite's Big Oak Flat entrance. The first listing in each category is the closest to the park.

$50–100

Yosemite Lakes

Run by the Thousand Trails/NACO camping organization, Yosemite Lakes (31191 Hardin Flat Rd., Groveland, 209/962-0121 or 800/533-1001, www.1000trails.com) offers a wide variety of accommodations, including a bunk-style hostel, cabins, and yurts. Thousand Trails/NACO members have a sweet deal here; they stay for a 20 percent discount off the regular prices.

If you aren't a member, the 12-room hostel provides a place to lay your head for $60–80 (a shared bathroom is down the hall). The 10

bunkhouse cabins are rustic wood-frame units with beds that sleep four ($70–90); a shared bathroom is a short walk from the cabins. The yurts are the most luxurious option: They are circular, tent-like structures with a skylight and windows and are equipped with full kitchens and bathrooms ($130–160). They even have air-conditioning, heating, and satellite TV. Ten yurts are clustered together in "Yurt Village," each one surrounded by a fair-sized lawn. A dozen more, priced a bit higher, are down by the river. Barbecues and picnic tables are set outside each yurt. A cafe and grocery store are part of the Yosemite Lakes complex.

Most people who stay at Yosemite Lakes are there because it's only a five-mile drive into Yosemite National Park. But if you choose to hang around your lodging for the day, you'll find that recreation opportunities abound even closer. The South Fork of the Tuolumne River runs right through Yosemite Lakes' property. Kayaks, inner tubes, fishing poles, and gold pans are available for rent. Horseback riding is popular from mid-May–mid-Sept.; stables are located on the grounds.

© ANN MARIE BROWN

The yurts at Yosemite Lakes offer a surprising amount of luxuries, from stereos to air conditioning to rugs on the floor.

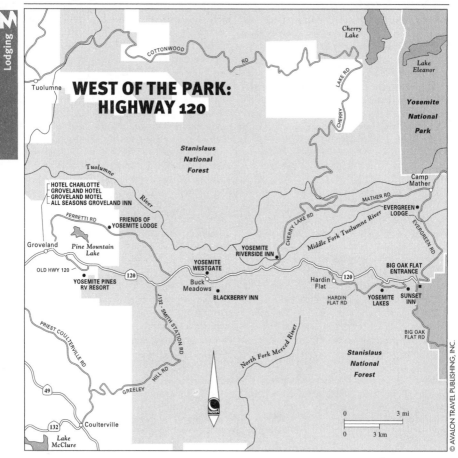

WEST OF THE PARK: HIGHWAY 120

© AVALON TRAVEL PUBLISHING, INC.

Yosemite Pines RV Resort

Despite its name, this is more of a campground than a resort. Still, Yosemite Pines (20450 Old Hwy. 120, Groveland, 209/962-7690 or 800/368-5386, www.yosemitepines.com) has cabins and yurts for rent, which will appeal to the non-camping crowd. Some cabins have fully furnished kitchens and bathrooms; others are "sleeping cabins" with nothing but beds inside. A communal restroom is a short distance away. These are truly budget accommodations—the standard cabins start at $89 and the sleeping cabins and yurts start at $49. Families will find plenty to do here to keep the kiddies occupied: there's a petting zoo, pony

rides, hayrides, gold panning, a gold mine tour, and campfire storytelling. Yosemite Pines even offers a free shuttle to the nearby swimming hole at Rainbow Pool. It's a 22-mile drive to the Big Oak Flat Yosemite entrance.

Groveland Motel

Don't confuse the Groveland Motel with the Groveland Hotel. The more expensive Groveland Hotel is all about Victorian charm. The Groveland Motel (18933 Hwy. 120, Groveland, 209/962-7865 or 888/849-3529, www.grovelandmotel.net) is all about economy and convenience. It boasts the widest range of accommodations of any place in town, but, despite the name, none of the accommodations are motel rooms. Instead, they are side-by-side cabins (with shared walls), mobile homes, and teepees. You read that right. If you've never stayed in a teepee before, think "tall, wide, conical tent" and you have the idea. The canvas structures are large enough so that you can stand up in them and even walk around a bit. They have concrete foundations and electric lights (Native Americans never had this kind of luxury). Beds and linens are provided; bathrooms and shower buildings are a short walk away. The teepees sleep two to four people for $36–50 per night. A central barbecue and picnic area allow you the opportunity to cook your own dinner.

The side-by-side cabins have queen beds, bathrooms with showers, cable TV, and air-conditioning. They run $79–99 per night and sleep two to six people. The air-conditioning is fortunate, because the cabins are set close to the road and you'll want to close your windows to minimize the noise. The mobile homes have queen or full beds, bathrooms, refrigerators, microwaves, TVs, and air-conditioning; they sleep 6–20 people. They range $79–259 per night. A few recreational vehicles are also for rent, although you don't get to drive them anywhere, just sleep in them. They have the same amenities as the mobile homes but are smaller. Two to four people can stay in one for $65–85 per night.

The motel and teepees are situated on the eastern edge of the town of Groveland, right across from a grocery store, deli, and restaurant. All the town's restaurants are a five-minute walk away. A kids' playground and community park are across the street.

$100–200

Sunset Inn

For an unusual and secluded stay in a mountain setting nearly a stone's throw from Yosemite, book one of the three Craftsman-style cabins at Sunset Inn (33569 Hardin Flat Rd., Groveland, 888/962-4360 or 209/962-4360, www.sunsetinnusa.com). Located off the main highway, the cabins are set on a lush meadow surrounded by huge pine trees. If it's a hot summer day in Groveland, it will be much more comfortable here—you're at 4,500 feet elevation, the same as the Big Oak Flat entrance to Yosemite, which is a mere two miles away. Two of the cabins are perfectly sized for couples, with queen-size beds, fully equipped kitchens, private bathrooms, and wood-burning stoves. The "family cabin" has two separate bedrooms and can accommodate up to five people. The cabin interiors have been recently remodeled and are cozy and comfortable. Rates are $120–150 per night for two people or $170–200 per night for the family cabin.

Evergreen Lodge

Nine miles from the Big Oak Flat entrance and about halfway up the road to Hetch Hetchy, Evergreen Lodge (33160 Evergreen Rd., Groveland, 209/379-2606 or 800/935-6343, www.evergreenlodge.com) is a convenient place to stay for visiting either Yosemite's high country or Hetch Hetchy's spectacular waterfilled valley. You can spend a comfortable night in your cabin, then get up early and head to the trailhead at Hetch Hetchy's impressive dam, or drive into the main part of the park and cruise over to Tuolumne Meadows and Tioga Pass.

If you've stayed at Evergreen Lodge in the past, you'll be surprised at the changes that have taken place here. In 2004, the lodge went through a major expansion. The original 12 one- and two-bedroom cabins, which date back to the 1920s, now sit side-by-side with 52 brand-new cabins. In addition to all the new buildings, there is a first-class restaurant serving three meals a day, and now the lodge offers tons of organized activities: nature hikes, full moon hikes, campfire talks, and the like, most of which are free to guests. With everything going on here, this is an ideal place for families and groups to stay. Rates are $99–259 per night.

Yosemite Riverside Inn

Less than one mile off Highway 120 and only a 10-mile drive to the Big Oak Flat entrance,

Yosemite Riverside Inn (11399 Cherry Lake Rd., Groveland, 209/962-7408 or 800/626-7408, www.yosemiteriversideinn.com) enjoys a park-like setting overlooking the Tuolumne River. There's nothing fancy about the place—it's more "fishing camp" than luxury accommodation—but for many Yosemite travelers, it is sufficient.

The inn has standard motel rooms ($115–135), river-view log cabins ($125–155), and a suite with a balcony overlooking the Middle Fork of the Tuolumne River ($185–235). The cabins have kitchenettes with microwaves; the motel rooms have satellite TV. A free continental breakfast is served each day May–September. The inn is popular with trout anglers, because you can catch fish a few steps from your door. The Middle Fork of the Tuolumne River is well stocked with pan-sized rainbow trout. If you seek more of a challenge, the main branch of the Tuolumne is only minutes away, where seasoned anglers catch trophy-sized native trout. The inn also sees its share of rafters in the late spring and summer months, as several commercial outfitters enter the river a short distance away.

Yosemite Westgate

It's surprising how many visitors pass this motel by, since it's clean, serviceable, affordable, quiet, and within 30 minutes of the Big Oak Flat entrance to Yosemite. The Yosemite Westgate (7633 Hwy. 120, Buck Meadows, 209/962-5281 or 800/253-9673, www.innsight.com—click on "properties") is a standard two-story motel that's a safe, dependable bet. All the usual amenities are available: cable TV, phone, in-room coffee, and an outdoor swimming pool and spa. In addition to 44 standard motel rooms with queen-size beds, 10 "family-style" rooms have limited cooking facilities—refrigerator and microwave—and a small dining area. Two kids under 12 stay free with two adults. Summer rates are $109–198, but they drop way down in winter—as low as $59 per night. If you're hungry, the 49er Restaurant is right next door.

Blackberry Inn

This casually elegant bed-and-breakfast offers the perfect respite for nature lovers. Set on five acres of oaks, pines, cedars, and meadows, the Blackberry Inn (7567 Hamilton Station Loop, Buck Meadows, 209/962-4663 or 888/867-5001, www.blackberry-inn.com) is home to hummingbirds, deer, rabbits, and quail, as well as weary Yosemite travelers. The two-story farmhouse, built in 1992, is warm and inviting, with high ceilings, big windows, and a wraparound porch. Two spacious guest rooms on the second floor have king-size feather beds, fireplaces, and private baths; the downstairs guest room has a queen-size feather bed and private bath. A large common room filled with books and chocolate chip cookies baked fresh daily complete the picture. The innkeepers are extremely knowledgeable about Yosemite and the surrounding area and will gladly help visitors plan their trip. The inn is only 13 miles (15–20 minutes) from the Big Oak Flat entrance to Yosemite. Room rates are $145–175 April–Oct., less in winter, and include a full, two-course breakfast.

Friends of Yosemite Park Lodge

This small, intimate bed-and-breakfast is located 20 miles from the Big Oak Flat entrance to Yosemite, and offers three spacious guest rooms plus a private cottage for families or small groups traveling together. Friends of Yosemite Park Lodge (13349 Clements Rd., Groveland, 866/410-4545 or 209/962-4544, www.friendsofyosemitepark.com) is operated as a membership lodging, so in addition to the room rate, guests pay an additional $10 per year membership fee. The grounds and building are beautifully maintained, and the guest rooms ($169–189) are tastefully furnished with queen beds and private baths. A hearty breakfast is included in the price. The 1,100-square-foot cottage has two bedrooms and additional sleeping space for up to eight people ($275–300). Rates go down in winter.

Hotel Charlotte

The 10 rooms at the Hotel Charlotte (18736 Hwy. 120, Groveland, 209/962-6455 or

800/961-7799, www.hotelcharlotte.com) are located upstairs above the hotel's lobby and excellent restaurant. Recently remodeled, the rooms provide all the basics for a good night's sleep without a lot of unneeded frills. Most have queen-size beds; a few have twin beds or double beds. Small groups and families will appreciate the adjoining rooms connected by a shared bathroom. Room rates are a bargain by Yosemite standards ($96–169, less in winter), and a breakfast buffet is included in the price. Guests appreciate the convenience of being right in the middle of Groveland and having a hotel with a good restaurant to return to after a day in Yosemite.

If you are wondering about its name, the hotel was built by Charlotte DeFerreri, an ambitious young immigrant from Italy, in 1918. Her inn provided a home for the workers who were building the Hetch Hetchy dam. Charlotte was well known as a gracious hostess and an excellent cook, and it is rumored that her ghost still roams the Hotel Charlotte's halls today. But even though this is a historic building in a historic town, the Hotel Charlotte is thoroughly modern—wireless Internet access is available throughout the building.

Groveland Hotel

This hotel is one of the grande dames of the Gold Country. Built during the Gold Rush era, the Groveland Hotel (18767 Hwy. 120, Groveland, 209/962-4000 or 800/273-3314, www.groveland.com) was revered in those days as "The Best House on the Hill." The original 1849 adobe was reconstructed and added on to in 1914, when it was needed to house the big shots who were planning and building Hetch Hetchy Dam. Some of the original Gold Rush features remain, like the central staircase, casement windows, and wraparound veranda. They sit side-by-side with Queen Anne architecture of the early 20th century, plus even more modern additions.

The historic hotel was headed for demolition in the late 1980s until it was rescued by the current owner, Peggy Mosley, who treated it to a multimillion-dollar face-lift. Today it attracts visitors from all over the world and

has become something of a destination in its own right. *Country Inns* magazine rated it one of the top 10 inns in the United States. *Sunset* magazine ranked it one of the West's best inns. Its 17 rooms and suites are tastefully decorated, if you don't mind a bit of frilliness—floral-patterned fabrics and wallpaper are a common theme. Down comforters, European armoires, antique chests, and well-dressed beds are standard issue, and thick, fluffy bathrobes are provided for all guests. The Lillie Langtry honeymoon suite is quite popular, with its 1900 brass bed and fireplace. The Tony Smith room is the most masculine, with a carved maple bed and marble-topped nightstand. A favorite of many guests is Lyle's Room, which is reputedly home to Lyle, the hotel's resident ghost.

In addition to all of this, the Groveland Hotel's dining room serves truly exceptional food. It's a popular spot for weddings. The hotel is not stuffy at all; it even has a few charming quirks, like the fact that owner Peggy went to high school with Elvis Presley, so she holds an Elvis Birthday Celebration every January. Guests wear poodle skirts and saddle shoes, and Peggy cooks up her Southern family recipes of barbecue pork and coleslaw. Year-round, Peggy's dog Rusty can usually be found holding court in the hotel's saloon.

The Big Oak Flat entrance to Yosemite is 40 minutes from the Groveland Hotel, but a stay here is so special that nobody minds the drive. Book summer reservations in advance; this is a popular place. Rates run $135–195 for rooms and $210–275 for suites, which have spa tubs and fireplaces. A substantial breakfast buffet is included in the price. Wireless Internet access is available throughout the hotel.

All Seasons Groveland Inn

This is the most creative lodging in all of Groveland. The owners possess exquisite taste and have transformed the rooms of this old Victorian into works of art—literally. Murals are painted on the walls at the All Seasons Groveland Inn (18656 Hwy. 120, Groveland, 209/962-0232 or 800/595-9993, www.allseasonsgrovelandinn.com).

For $130–180 a night, you can choose from five themed rooms, each with private bath, and some with a whirlpool tub and fireplace. Clouds Rest has a mural of rainbows bursting out of clouds behind the headboard of the bed. A door opens to a private deck with a telescope. Emerald Pool features a mural of the famous wide, colorful stretch in the Merced River above Vernal Fall. A steam room enhances the bathroom.

Eagles Tower has a private deck and telescope, a mural of seven eagles and Half Dome, and a skylight over the whirlpool tub. The best of the lot may be Yosemite Falls, which has a slate waterfall and a wall-length mural of the tallest waterfall in North America.

You might expect to find a place like this in the Napa wine country or the Gold Country near Tahoe, but in Groveland, it comes as a pleasant surprise. The inn is in the center of town, so all shops and restaurants are a short walk away. From December 1 to May 1, excluding holidays, you can take advantage of a 40 percent discount on the rates.

West of the Park: Highway 140

Visitors approaching Yosemite from San Jose, the Central Coast, or the San Joaquin Valley frequently use the Highway 140 approach through Merced and Mariposa, especially if they are heading for Yosemite Valley. Mariposa, the county seat of the county by the same name, is a small town at the junction of Highway 140 and Highway 49, comprising a six-block-long main street lined with small shops and restaurants. A side street leads up the hill to the county courthouse, the oldest one still in use west of the Mississippi River. Many other historic buildings are found in the downtown area. The town has several bed-and-breakfasts, inns, and motels, some on the main drag and some spread around the surrounding countryside.

A stay in Mariposa puts you 30 miles from the Arch Rock entrance to Yosemite, or 44 miles from Yosemite Valley. A stay in Midpines will cut eight miles off those totals. Keep in mind that Highway 140 is a mountain road, not a superhighway, so you won't drive much faster than 45 miles per hour. Plan on an hour's drive to Yosemite Valley, but what a scenic drive it is—following Highway 140 alongside the Merced River, a federally designated Wild and Scenic River. If you can reserve a place to stay in El Portal, you are only a handful of miles from the Arch Rock entrance, which is 14 miles from Yosemite Valley.

For information on local bed-and-breakfasts, you can try the Yosemite-Mariposa Bed and Breakfast Association, 209/742-7666; www.yosemitebnbs.com.

The lodgings listed below are arranged within each price category according to their proximity to Yosemite's Arch Rock entrance. The first listing in each category is the closest to the park.

$50–100
Yosemite Redbud Lodge

If mining history interests you, stay at the Yosemite Redbud Lodge (9486 Hwy. 140, El Portal, 888/742-4371, www.yosemite-motels.com), located at the 1850s site of Savage's Trading Post. Here trader James Savage ran a mining outpost at the confluence of the South Fork and Main Fork of the Merced River, serving the miners who worked throughout these canyons. Savage was later famous for leading the Mariposa Battalion into Yosemite Valley to round up all the Indians who lived there. Although Savage's men failed at their task, they went down in the history books as the first white men to see the Valley.

This small lodge has only eight rooms in aging wooden buildings, each with air-conditioning and refrigerator ($100). A few rooms are suites, which include fireplaces, kitchenettes, and small decks overlooking the river ($350). After a buyout in 2005, the Yosemite Redbud was completely remodeled and

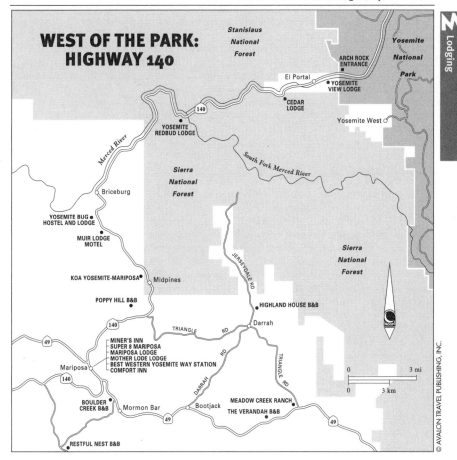

© AVALON TRAVEL PUBLISHING, INC.

upgraded by the same corporation that manages nearby Cedar Lodge and Yosemite View Lodge. When the rooms are re-opened for business in summer 2006, they will surely be a lot more upscale than they used to be. Expect the prices to go up substantially, too.

If you are here during the March–May wildflower season, don't miss a short hike on Hites Cove Trail, which begins right by the lodge. The flower display is possibly the best in the Sierra foothills, and the views of the river are inspiring as well. The trail ends at the site of Hites Cove Mine, which produced $3 million in gold in its day.

In addition to all this history, Redbud Lodge offers a big advantage over other nearby lodgings: it's only 10 miles from the Arch Rock gate to Yosemite.

Yosemite Bug Hostel and Lodge

The quirky name of this establishment tells you something about its fun-loving feel. For the young and young-at-heart, the Yosemite Bug (6979 Hwy. 140, Midpines, 209/966-6666, www.yosemitebug.com) is an inexpensive, rustic resort that provides the antithesis of the impersonal chain-motel experience. The atmosphere is very social and friendly, both for the staff and guests. This complex of buildings was once a dorm camp that catered to youth and work project groups before it opened in its present incarnation in 1996.

The range of available accommodations runs the gamut: modern cabins with private baths, lodge rooms with shared baths, tent cabins, hostel-style dormitories, and even campsites. Rates are $55–115 for rooms and cabins. Tent cabins are $30–50. Hostel rooms are only $20, but you'll share a large bunk-style room with 6–12 people. In keeping with the "young at heart" theme, the Yosemite Bug is all about outdoor recreation. Staff members can fill you in on everything you want to know about the area's hiking, mountain biking, rafting, and rock climbing opportunities. Yosemite Bug added a health spa in 2005, complete with redwood hot tubs and a massage room.

You won't have to go far to find food if you stay at the Bug. Its cafe, the Recovery Bistro, serves breakfast, lunch, and dinner and is well known locally for its delicious food. It's also the central hangout spot at the resort, with a wood-burning stove, comfortable couches, games, books, and musical instruments. The Bug is 22 miles from the Arch Rock entrance to Yosemite, or 9.5 miles east of Mariposa on Highway 140.

Muir Lodge Motel

Okay, so it's a little run-down. It has a right to be—the Muir Lodge (6833 Hwy. 140, Midpines, 209/966-2468) is Yosemite's economy motel. "Economy" really means something here: Summer rates are a meager $55 per night; winter rates are a few bucks cheaper. If you want the propane heat turned on in your room, you pay an extra $5. A maximum of three people are permitted per room. Not surprisingly, the rooms are basic affairs, but they do have TVs. As long as you aren't expecting much, you'll do fine here. Muir Lodge is five miles east of Mariposa and 22 miles west of the Arch Rock entrance.

KOA Yosemite-Mariposa

You can say what you want about a place that spells "cabin" with a K, but the KOA Yosemite-Mariposa is a godsend for thrifty Yosemite travelers. Located in the town of Midpines, the KOA (6323 Hwy. 140, Midpines, 209/966-2201 or 800/562-9391, www.yosemitekoa.com) has 12 "Kamping Kabins" that serve as a home away from home for $55–62 a night, based on double occupancy. The cabins are close quarters for two adults but will accommodate four if need be. Children under eight stay free.

Note that the KOA property is basically a campground, with plenty of RVs and tents, but its dozen cabins are private, cozy, and soundproof (as long as the windows are closed). The cabins are the same as what you'll find at many KOAs across America: one-room log buildings, with two working windows and a locking front door. Inside are a log-frame double bed and twin bunk beds, complete with mattresses but not bedding (bring your own). A central restroom and shower are a short distance away. Each cabin has electric lights and a small heater, plus a front porch with a swing wide enough for two. There's a barbecue grill and picnic table right outside your door.

The KOA also has two "Kamping Lodges" that can accommodate up to six people. These are larger, more luxurious cabins with a separate bedroom and bathroom, plus a living and dining area with a full kitchen. The lodges rent for $150–170 per night—a great bargain for a family. The campground property has a swimming pool, a fishpond, a real train caboose with video games inside, a TV lounge with Yosemite videos, and a small store. The owners, who took over in March 2000, make a concerted effort to keep the place clean, safe, and friendly.

Miner's Inn

The Miner's Inn (5181 Hwy. 49, Mariposa, 209/742-7777 or 888/646-2244, www.yosemite-rooms.com) is best described as a low-budget chain motel with a Western theme, but if you need a place to sleep in Mariposa, it serves that purpose just fine. Standard rooms go for $75. The most expensive of the 76 rooms include king beds, spa tubs, balconies, and propane fireplaces ($125 summer, $89 winter).

Televisions, telephones, and air-conditioning are supplied in all rooms. The inn complex has a restaurant, lounge, and swimming pool; a fair-sized shopping center is right next door. It's located at the junction of Highway 140 and Highway 49.

Super 8 Mariposa

What's the difference between a Motel 6 and a Super 8? Not much. This Super 8 (5059 Hwy. 140, Mariposa, 209/966-4288 or 800/800-8000) took over the location of the old Holiday Inn in Mariposa. The motel offers about what you'd expect from a budget chain motel: clean, air-conditioned rooms, cable TV, and a complimentary continental breakfast laced with white flour and sugar. Everything in the town of Mariposa is within walking distance. Summer rates are $70–110; winter rates are $50–80.

Mariposa Lodge

The 45 rooms at Mariposa Lodge (5052 Hwy. 140, Mariposa, 209/966-3607 or 800/966-8819, www.mariposalodge.com) are the nicest place to stay in downtown Mariposa. They are AAA-approved and come with everything that all the neighboring chain motels offer: HBO, refrigerators, phones, in-room coffee, outdoor pool, and spa. The difference is that Mariposa Lodge has been family-owned and -operated for more than 30 years, so visitors find more warmth and personality here. The gardens and courtyards, for example, are clearly cared for by someone who loves flowers. Strategically placed gazebos and patios, secluded from the highway, provide benches and seating areas from which you can enjoy the warm summer evenings in Mariposa. Rooms are clean, modern, and comfortable. Rates are $99 in summer and $79 in winter. Children eight and under stay free.

Mother Lode Lodge

In the budget category, the Mother Lode Lodge (5051 Hwy. 140, Mariposa, 209/966-2521 or 800/398-9770, www.motherlodelodge.com) does the trick. Its 14 rooms cost a mere $78 per night, $10 less in the winter. The no-frills rooms have one or two queen-size beds, a small

desk, and TV. On hot summer evenings in Mariposa, you can swim in the outdoor pool. The lodge is right in the downtown area, so you can walk to restaurants and shops.

Best Western Yosemite Way Station

What you get at the Best Western Yosemite Way Station (4999 Hwy. 140, Mariposa, 209/966-7545 or 888/742-4371, www.yosemite-motels.com) is the typical Best Western experience—clean but boring. You can count on certain classic BW elements: a coffeemaker in your room, phone, cable TV, HBO, and a complimentary continental breakfast that will spike your blood sugar. Still, you are only one block from downtown Mariposa, so you can wander around, explore the local shops, and dine at the local restaurants. The 78 rooms here are an affordable $60–90 per night year-round. After a day in the park, you can come back to the Best Western and relax in its outdoor pool and spa.

Comfort Inn

The Mariposa Comfort Inn (4994 Bullion St., Mariposa, 209/966-4344, www.comfortinn.com) offers all the standard chain amenities: phone, cable TV, HBO, outdoor pool and spa, family suites, and wheelchair-accessible rooms. Personality? No. A place to sleep within an hour of Yosemite? Yes. The Comfort Inn is located a short distance off the highway, so it's a little quieter than many of Mariposa's motels on the main drag. Its 61 rooms go for $90 in summer and $60 in winter.

Restful Nest Bed and Breakfast

Located six miles outside of Mariposa, Restful Nest (4274 Buckeye Creek Rd., Mariposa, 209/742-7127 or 800/664-7127, www.restfulnest.com) is a bit of a drive, but if you like peace and quiet, it's worth it. The bed-and-breakfast has three rooms that rent for $95 per night, plus one guesthouse for $125. The one-bedroom guesthouse (it can sleep up to four people) is a private gem, with a separate living room and bathroom and a wood-burning stove. All rooms have air-conditioning for the summer, a necessity in the warm foothills. The innkeepers make breakfast into a big production, with freshly baked brioche and other breads, homemade sausages, fruit, and fresh jams and preserves. One of the owners is French, so Parisians can speak their own language here, if they wish. Restful Nest is set on 11 acres of oaks and grasslands, with amenities including a swimming pool, hot tub, catch-and-release fishing pond, barbecue pit, and picnic area. Plan on a little over an hour to get to Yosemite Valley.

$100–200

Yosemite View Lodge

This is as close as you can get to Yosemite National Park's west side and Yosemite Valley without being in the park. The lodge is set right on the Merced River, only two miles from Yosemite's Arch Rock entrance, and about 20 minutes from Yosemite Valley. Managed by the same company that handles nearby Cedar Lodge and several other local accommodations, Yosemite View Lodge (11136 Hwy. 140, El Portal, 209/379-2681 or 888/742-4371, www.yosemite-motels.com) has 278 rooms, including some family units with kitchenettes, all with cable TV and HBO. Many of the rooms have fireplaces and spa tubs; the most desirable ones have balconies or patios with riverfront views ($125–175; winter rates drop below $100). The entire lodge was thoroughly renovated in 1995, so everything looks new and modern. The complex has one indoor and two outdoor pools, five spas, a cocktail lounge, and two restaurants—a pizza parlor and a more formal dining room. The Gateway Visitor Center, operated by a private group called Yosemite Guides (www.yosemiteguides.com), is also located at the lodge. The visitor center was developed by the El Portal community and features local artwork and exhibits on river habitat, geology, and native plants.

Cedar Lodge

Only eight miles to the El Portal entrance to Yosemite, Cedar Lodge (9966 Hwy. 140, El Portal, 209/379-2612 or 888/742-4371, www.yosemite-motels.com) has a choice of room types, including a master suite that sleeps 14 and has

its own private outdoor pool, family units with kitchenettes, honeymoon suites, and regular rooms sized for one or two people. The best bet here is one of the deluxe rooms with a king-size four-poster bed. Rates are $110–199 in summer and drop down Nov.–March. With 211 rooms, the lodge is large enough to have all the amenities of a major hotel: phone, cable TV, HBO, indoor and outdoor swimming pools, cocktail lounge, conference room, two restaurants, and a gift shop. It doesn't offer much in the way of personality, but it is convenient.

Cedar Lodge's best selling point, at least in summer, is its private beach access to the Merced River. It's a haven for swimmers and bathers on warm days, and a great place to watch river rafters in the early summer.

Poppy Hill Bed and Breakfast

Time it right and you'll stay here in springtime, when the poppies are in full bloom along the hillsides surrounding this bed-and-breakfast. Poppy Hill (5218 Crystal Aire Dr., Mariposa, 209/742-6273 or 800/587-6779, www.poppyhill.com) is a lovingly restored country home decorated with impeccable taste, inside and out. Three rooms have queen-size beds and private bath and are priced at $110–125, which includes a gourmet breakfast prepared by innkeeper Mary Ellen Kirn. (You will remember the taste of her puffed apple pancakes long after your visit.) All the rooms are lovely, but a favorite is the Poppy Room; it is filled with antiques, including an old spinning wheel, and has a private sitting room overlooking the garden. Mary Ellen keeps a refrigerator stocked with complimentary soft drinks, and guests can use the hot tub on the patio.

Highland House Bed and Breakfast

There aren't too many bed-and-breakfasts where your horse can travel with you, but Old Paint and Mr. Ed are welcome at Highland House (3125 Wild Dove Ln., Mariposa, 209/966-3737, www.highlandhousebandb.com). Three stalls are available for visiting horses, and three rooms are available for visiting humans ($95–135). The Forest Retreat room has a mahogany four-poster bed and fireplace, plus a private bath with a two-person shower and soaking tub. Spring Creek has two rocking chairs and a king or two twin beds. Morning Dove is a smaller, dormer-style room and the least expensive of the lot. All three rooms have down comforters and pillows, fine linens, and soft robes. Breakfast is a highlight here and usually includes freshly baked breads and/or gourmet pancakes. Note that the inn is located about six miles off Highway 140, so this will add some time to your drive to Yosemite.

Boulder Creek Bed and Breakfast

Only three rooms ($110) are available at this European chalet-style bed-and-breakfast two miles from downtown Mariposa, but that is part of its charm. Boulder Creek Bed and Breakfast (4572 Ben Hur Rd., Mariposa, 209/742-7729 or 800/768-4752, http://mariposa.yosemite.net/ bcreek) enjoys a serene location right alongside a gurgling creek on three acres of oak, pine, and cedar forest. Floor-to-ceiling windows in the living and dining area provide lovely views; deer are frequently seen ambling through the nearby meadows. The innkeeper is a former chef from Germany who serves a delightful sit-down breakfast on fine china each morning. If you enjoy the B&B experience, this place does it well. And if you speak German, you'll be in good company here.

The Verandah Bed and Breakfast

If you are the kind of person who enjoys sitting in a wicker chair on a wraparound porch with a glass of lemonade in hand, you'll love The Verandah Bed and Breakfast (5086 Tip Top Rd., Mariposa, 209/742-5086 or 800/754-0372, www.theverandahbnb.com). This antique-laden country farmhouse is as charming as can be, complete with clawfoot tubs in the bathrooms, down comforters on the beds, and herb and vegetable gardens outside. The owners have been exploring Yosemite for more than 30 years, so they will be more than happy to help you plan your trip. Room rates are $110–125 per night, including a full breakfast for two people.

Meadow Creek Ranch

The most popular accommodation at Meadow Creek Ranch (2669 Triangle Rd., Mariposa, 209/966-3843 or 800/853-2037, www.meadowcreekranchbnb.com) is, believe it or not, the chicken coop. The owners of this 1858 stagecoach stop converted the coop into a charming guest cottage, complete with an Austrian carved wood canopy bed, a clawfoot tub, wicker furniture, and a gas fireplace. Meadow Creek Ranch also rents out the Garden Gate Room, furnished with antiques and accessed via a private garden patio entrance. The room has a carved oak queen-size bed, plus a twin bed tucked into an alcove, which works well if you are traveling with a child. The ranch is situated on seven acres, so there is plenty of room to roam. Rates are $110–120 per night.

South of the Park: Highway 41

Visitors approaching Yosemite from Los Angeles, the Central Coast, and southern California most often use the Highway 41 approach to the park through Fresno and Oakhurst. Oakhurst is the last "big town" before Yosemite's south entrance and the most developed of any of the towns near Yosemite's borders. You can buy pretty much anything in Oakhurst, from hardware to hiking boots to a fancy dinner.

This town of 15,000 inhabitants has several bed-and-breakfasts, inns, motels, and even a spectacular château. A stay in Oakhurst puts you 15 miles from the southern entrance to Yosemite, and about 45 miles from Yosemite Valley. Bass Lake, a popular fishing and waterskiing destination, is just five miles from Oakhurst and offers lodging possibilities. Both Oakhurst and Bass Lake lodgings are convenient for visitors who want to spend most of their Yosemite vacation in the south part of the park. If you plan to spend a lot of time in Yosemite Valley, understand that it will take you about 90 minutes to drive there.

Lodging

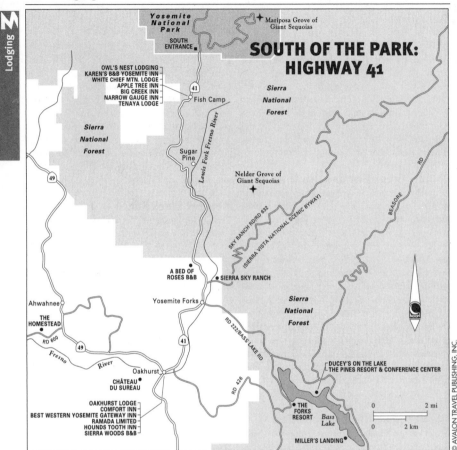

SOUTH OF THE PARK: HIGHWAY 41

© AVALON TRAVEL PUBLISHING, INC.

North of Oakhurst is the tiny town of Fish Camp, an old logging town that today consists of only a couple of small stores and a few private homes. On its outskirts are two large resorts and multiple smaller lodgings, including several bed-and-breakfasts. At Fish Camp, you are less than five miles from Yosemite's southern entrance, and right next door to the Yosemite Mountain Sugar Pine Railroad, a popular destination especially for families.

The lodgings listed below are arranged within each price category according to their proximity to Yosemite's south entrance. The first listing in each category is the closest to the park.

$50–100
White Chief Mountain Lodge

The great unsung lodging option in Fish Camp is just two miles from Yosemite's southern entrance. Situated 300 yards off the main highway, White Chief Mountain Lodge (7776 White Chief Mountain Rd., Fish Camp, 559/683-5444) goes unnoticed by the vast majority of visitors. It is a comfortable, semi-rustic, motel-style lodge run by some very nice folks. Room rates are determined by the number of people, which seems fair enough: $72 for one person, $77 for two, $88 for three, and so on.

Larger units are available for $165. The owners of White Chief don't bother with a fancy website or creative marketing techniques; they just rent out their small, no-nonsense, 1950s-era rooms to happy, bargain-hunting visitors who generally return year after year. A restaurant and bar are on the premises, open for dinner only. The lodge is open only April–October.

Oakhurst Lodge

A dependable bet in the town of Oakhurst, the Oakhurst Lodge (40302 Hwy. 41, Oakhurst, 559/683-4417 or 800/655-6343, www.oklodge.com) has 60 rooms with all the touches you'd expect from a modest chain motel (queen beds, cable TV, HBO, in-room coffee, swimming pool, guest laundry), except this isn't a chain. The owners actually care that you have a good experience on your vacation. The rooms won't win any prizes for interior decorating (they were built in the 1970s and remodeled in 1995), but summer rates are a modest $70–100 per night. Winter rates are a steal at $55 per night. It's a 15-mile drive to Yosemite's south gate.

Comfort Inn

If you want the convenience of staying in the middle of a decent-sized town, where you'll find large grocery store chains, sporting goods stores, a couple dozen restaurants, and even a McDonald's, Oakhurst's Comfort Inn (40489 Hwy. 41, Oakhurst, 559/683-8282 or 800/321-5261, www.yosemite-motels.com) will fit the bill. Its 110 rooms and three two-room suites have phones, refrigerators, and cable TV with HBO. A complimentary continental breakfast is served each morning in the guest lobby. At the end of the day, you can splash around in the outdoor pool or sit back and relax in the spa. Rates are $90–125 per night in summer, less in winter. Two Chinese restaurants are right next door, just in case you get a craving for won ton soup.

Ramada Limited

At the base of the hill on Highway 41 just as you come into Oakhurst, the Ramada (48800 Royal Oaks Dr., Oakhurst, 559/658-5500 or 800/658-2888) is a safe bet for no-nonsense lodging. Clean and well maintained, the facility is designated as "Tour Group Friendly," and in fact there are usually a few large buses parked in the lot. Summer rates are $99 per night, but winter rates drop as low as $39. The usual chain-motel services are provided: HBO and cable, continental breakfast, and in-room coffee. A swimming pool, spa, and laundry are available. If you strike out here, try the **Shilo Inn Yosemite/Oakhurst** (40644 Hwy. 41, Oakhurst, 559/683-3555 or 800/222-2244, www.shiloinns.com), which is of the same ilk.

Miller's Landing

Bass Lake has so much development around its edges that it can seem like a small city. With several campgrounds, restaurants, and resorts, plus numerous places to rent boats or buy fishing equipment, the lakeshore is more like a vacation town than a peaceful mountain retreat.

That's why a stay at Miller's Landing (37976 Road 222, Wishon, 559/642-3633, www.millerslanding.com) is so refreshing. Set at the southern edge of the lake, Miller's Landing has easy access to Bass Lake's commercial services but is far removed from the hubbub of the Pines Village area. The resort is self-contained—it has cabins, a restaurant, and its own marina with boat rentals (patio boats, ski boats, Waverunners, fishing boats, kayaks, and canoes).

The 13 cabins at Miller's Landing run the gamut from bare-bones to elaborate. The most deluxe cabins sleep eight; they have two bedrooms, two baths, satellite television, and a full-size kitchen with all the accoutrements ($140–190). For the budget-minded, cabins 3 through 6 are two-bedroom rustic cabins with a full kitchen ($40–50). Restrooms and showers are a short walk away, and you must bring your own linens, bedding, dishes, and pots and pans. A picnic table and fire ring are right outside your door. Cabin 2 is equally minimalist, but even smaller and less expensive.

It will take you about 45 minutes to reach Yosemite's south gate from Miller's Landing, but if you want to divide your vacation time between Yosemite and Bass Lake, this location works well.

$100–200

Owl's Nest Lodging

Some people are well suited for the jobs they do, and that's certainly true for Bob and Barbara Taylor. The couple runs Owl's Nest Cabins (1237 Hwy. 41, Fish Camp, 559/683-3484, www.owlsnestlodging.com), and they love living in Fish Camp and having visitors stay at their three cabins, just across the street from their house. The cabins are all completely different; one is a small upstairs unit above a utility room, another is a large chalet for a family, and the third is a rounded A-frame, sized just right for two people. Fees are $100–150 per night for two people, plus $20 for each additional person (up to six). All units have fully furnished kitchens, plus a barbecue grill outside, and each has a TV and VCR with a stock of videotapes about Yosemite.

The Taylors will happily supply guests with information about what to do and see in Yosemite (two miles north) and Sierra National Forest (all around to the south and east). Big Creek runs behind the Taylors' main house, and visitors can fish in it or just stand by and admire its coursing flow.

Apple Tree Inn

One of the nicest places to stay in Fish Camp is the Apple Tree Inn (1110 Hwy. 41, Fish Camp, 559/683-5111 or 888/683-5111, www.appletreeinn-yosemite.com). Set on seven pine-covered acres, the inn enjoys a prime location right off Highway 41, just two miles from Yosemite's southern gate. In addition, it is only a half mile from the depot for the Yosemite Mountain Sugar Pine Railroad, a popular draw for railroad buffs and families.

The inn's 53 duplex- and triplex-style cottages, plus one stand-alone unit, are new-looking and prettily decorated in Laura Ashley fabrics; all come with convenient amenities like hair dryers and coffeemakers. Ceiling fans, wicker chairs, and floral patterns are a recurring theme. Each unit has a gas fireplace and patio or balcony. The resort has an indoor swimming pool, hot tub, and racquetball court.

A complimentary continental breakfast is served each morning at the Apple Tree's dining room, and a short footpath leads to the restaurants at neighboring Tenaya Lodge. Fees are $125–180 per night midweek September through mid-May, and $159–229 per night the rest of the year and on weekends and holidays.

Big Creek Inn

On the upscale side for a bed-and-breakfast, the Big Creek Inn (1221 Hwy. 41, Fish Camp, 559/641-2828, www.bigcreekinn.com) is a place that caters to adult guests who can appreciate some of the finer elements of a quality inn: a modern, beautifully appointed dining room, spa services available in the privacy of your own room, and a sitting room with a state-of-the-art robotic telescope for gazing at the galaxies. Three rooms are available in the inn's sprawling, 5,000-square-foot building, priced at $149–209 per night in summer, less in winter. A group of eight can rent the entire second floor for $450–590 per night. Rooms have king or queen beds, fireplaces, and private balconies. Add to this the sight and sound of tumbling Big Creek and you have a very special bed-and-breakfast experience, just two miles from Yosemite's south entrance.

Narrow Gauge Inn

In addition to a very fine restaurant, the Narrow Gauge Inn (48571 Hwy. 41, Fish Camp, 559/683-7720 or 888/644-9050, www.narrowgaugeinn.com) has 25 romantic rooms situated on a steep hillside lined with incense-cedars, oaks, and pines. And it's just four miles from the southern entrance to Yosemite. The inn gets its name from the neighboring Yosemite Mountain Sugar Pine Railroad, which offers scenic train rides aboard a restored late-1800s steam locomotive. All of the Narrow Gauge Inn's rooms have balconies or decks, although some are private and some shared, with lovely views of the forest and surrounding mountains. (You pay more for a private deck.) Standard room rates are $129–179 in summer and drop as low as $79 in winter. The large Mission Suite includes two bathrooms (one with clawfoot tub) for $259 in summer. A continental breakfast is included in the price of all rooms. Everything is well done here, from the room furnishings to the restaurant menu to the lovely grounds. If you're looking for a reasonably priced, romantic getaway spot near Yosemite, it doesn't get nicer than this.

A Bed of Roses Bed and Breakfast

Located just 10 miles from Yosemite's South Entrance, in between Oakhurst and Fish Camp, is this newly opened, pet-friendly bed-and-breakfast. A Bed of Roses (43547 Whispering Pines Drive, Oakhurst, 559/642-6975 or 877/624-7673, www.abedofrosesbandb.com) has five rooms and some colorful, quirky touches, like its petting zoo. Each room has a private bath and king or queen bed. A few of the rooms have whirlpool bathtubs. A big breakfast is served each morning; chocolate chip cookies are available 24 hours a day. Rates are $98–150 per night.

Hounds Tooth Inn

This inn's location might discourage potential guests—it's a hop, skip, and a jump to busy Highway 41 in Oakhurst. But the Hounds Tooth Inn (42071 Hwy. 41, Oakhurst, 559/642-6600 or 888/642-6610, www.hounds toothinn.com) does an excellent job of concealing its roadside location: It's set below the highway and out of its sight line, and the inn's three-acre grounds are beautifully landscaped with walkways, trees, and foliage. Accommodations include 12 guest rooms and a separate 850-square-foot cottage. The guest rooms ($95–150) come with a variety of amenities, including spas and fireplaces, and are decorated in nouveau Victorian style. Each has its own outside entrance. The cottage ($225) features a large suite with a king-size bed, spa, fireplace, and kitchenette, plus its own private patio with a garden and mini-waterfall. It is

frequently used for honeymoons but can also house a small family. The kitchenette is a bit of a disappointment for people who like to cook, but because the town of Oakhurst is a mere two minutes away, you won't starve. A complimentary breakfast and afternoon tea, wine, and cookies are served each day in the common area.

Sierra Woods Bed and Breakfast

For bed-and-breakfast types, Sierra Woods (49522 Road 426, Oakhurst, 559/642-6248, www.sierrawoodsbandb.com) offers a variety of intimate lodgings on five acres of oaks and pines bordering China Creek. Although the inn is within walking distance of downtown Oakhurst, it is far from the bustle and traffic noise. Guests enter their rooms through a lofty garden atrium, where breakfast is served each morning. The large rooms come with private or shared bath and king, queen, or two double beds. A suite with a fireplace is also available. For families, a separate cottage can be rented, with two bedrooms, kitchen, bath, laundry, and wood-burning stove. Rooms are $105–115; the suite and the cottage are $180. All guests have access to an outdoor pool and spa. This B&B was previously known as China Creek, but it has new owners and a new name.

Sierra Sky Ranch

More than 125 years old, Sierra Sky Ranch (50552 Road 632, Oakhurst, 559/683-8040, www.sierratel.com/skyranch) is an unusual lodging where you can experience a touch of the old West. The ranch was built in 1875 and renovated in 1946, and its 25 rooms are clean, comfortable, and charming. Room rates are $109–139; children under 12 stay free. There are no phones or TVs in the rooms, though there's a large-screen TV in a common area. The ranch is set on 14 acres of foothill country, with Lewis Creek flowing right by the property—a big draw for anglers, because it is stocked with rainbow trout. The ranch has a steakhouse, saloon, and swimming pool, and the entire facility is sometimes rented for weddings and corporate retreats. The ranch is five miles off Highway 41 and a 10-mile drive to Yosemite's south gate.

Best Western Yosemite Gateway Inn

This particular Best Western (40530 Hwy. 41, Oakhurst, 559/683-2378 or 800/545-5462, www.yosemitegatewayinn.com) has a little more kitsch than most, including a 25-foot Statue of Liberty flanked by the American and California flags, plus an indoor pool and spa backed by a small, fenced-off waterfall and a hand-painted mural of Yosemite's Vernal Fall. The Viewpoint Restaurant and Lounge is on the premises and offers all the charm of your average Denny's. Still, the 123 guest rooms are pleasant enough, and, this being a Best Western, you can count on certain things: air-conditioning, direct-dial phones, cable TV, HBO, a small exercise room, and very bland color-coordinated bedspreads, wall coverings, and window treatments. Some two-room suites are available for groups of up to six people. Rates run $92–146 in summer, $49–92 in winter.

The Pines Resort and Conference Center

Located right in the center of busy Pines Village on Bass Lake, The Pines Resort (54432 Road 432, Bass Lake, 800/350-7463, www.basslake.com) offers visitors 84 two-story chalets with kitchens, fireplaces, and private decks. The chalets are modern in style; they were built in 1978 and renovated in 1997. This is more like staying in a townhouse or a condo than in a mountain cabin, but it's convenient if you want to be near Bass Lake. The resort also has tennis and basketball courts, a swimming pool, two hot tubs, a children's playground, and boat rentals. A restaurant, bar, and grill are on the premises. Plan on a 14-mile drive to the southern gate of Yosemite. Rates are $159–369.

The Forks Resort

A stay at Bass Lake fits the bill for anybody who likes boating or fishing. The Forks Resort (39150 Road 222, Bass Lake, 559/642-3737, www.theforksresort.com) is one of the old-style resorts on Bass Lake; it's been owned and operated by the same family for three generations. Set right on the lakeshore, the resort has cabins of varying sizes, a general store, its own dock with boat rentals (patio boats, motorboats, rowboats, and canoes), and a cafe.

The 20 one- and two-bedroom cabins at The Forks Resort are unremarkable, but they make the perfect base camp for a combined Yosemite/Bass Lake vacation. Only a handful have lake views, but all are right across the road from the water's edge. Each cabin has a fully equipped kitchen, plus a porch with a barbecue grill so you can cook up all the fish you catch. The one-bedroom cabins have two double beds; you can squeeze in four people. The two-bedroom cabins can accommodate as many as six people; in addition to the extra space, you also get a fireplace and a microwave. Cabin rates run $95–190 per night.

The Forks Resort is a family-oriented place, and it's reinforced by a "no party" policy. That keeps the ambience quiet and peaceful even though this is a very busy and popular resort. You won't be awakened at 2 A.M. by a bunch of drunkards next door.

The Homestead

Cindy Brooks and Larry Ends are the perfect people to run a resort for outdoor enthusiasts, because they are outdoor lovers themselves. In 1992, they left their desk jobs and big-city life in Los Angeles and moved to Ahwahnee to open The Homestead (41110 Road 600, Ahwahnee, 559/683-0495 or 800/483-0495, www.homesteadcottages.com), an oak-dotted resort on 160 acres.

The Homestead's five one-bedroom cottages are modern in style and beautifully appointed. Their interiors are lined with saltillo tiles, warm pine wood, and simple but tasteful furnishings. Each cottage, including an above-the-barn stargazing loft, has a fully equipped kitchen and a fireplace for cool nights. They also have air-conditioning, a real bonus in the summer at this 2,000-foot elevation. Fees are $145–219 per night for two adults, with a two-night minimum stay on weekends. A new cot-

Lodging

The five cabins at The Homestead are spaced comfortably far apart on an oak-dotted hillside and are close to Bass Lake and southern Yosemite.

tage for families and small groups was added in 2004—the "Ranch House" houses up to six guests at $374 per night. The drive to Yosemite's south gate will take just under an hour.

$200 AND UP

Tenaya Lodge at Yosemite

There is nothing not to like about Tenaya Lodge (1122 Hwy. 41, Fish Camp, 559/683-6555 or 888/514-2167, www.tenayalodge.com), unless you have an allergic reaction to well-run resort-style accommodations. The huge, 244-room lodge seems a bit out of place in the small town of Fish Camp, but it has created a world unto itself. Since it opened in 1990, it has won the AAA Four Diamond award each year. The guest rooms look and feel like those of a modern mountain lodge, with earth-toned, Native American patterns and art. All of the standard room luxuries are found here, including a mini-fridge honor bar and in-room safe for your diamond tiara.

The resort sits on 35 acres and comes complete with indoor and outdoor pools, a fitness center, and spa services. Because this is a resort, not a simple inn or lodge, organized activities are plentiful. If you want someone else to plan your entire visit to Yosemite and the surrounding region, you can get that here. Families will find a variety of programs for kids, including gold panning, fishing, biking, and hiking. With all this, you can expect the rates to be fairly high, and they are: $265–319 in summer, $159–229 in winter.

In 2005, Tenaya Lodge was taken over by Delaware North Companies, which manages all the lodgings within Yosemite National Park. So far, there hasn't been much change at the lodge, but it will be interesting to see what the new managers have in store for the place.

Ducey's on the Lake

On the shores of Bass Lake and only 14 miles from the southern entrance to Yosemite, Ducey's (54432 Road 432, Bass Lake, 800/350-7463) romantic lakeview rooms may make it difficult to get out of bed and head for the park. Ducey's looks a bit like a 1990s version of the Ahwahnee Hotel, with its wood and stone exterior and exposed pine beams. Everything is modern here, though. The lodge has 20 rooms and suites, each with private bath, fireplace, television, telephones—the works. Some rooms have tubs designed for two, which is one reason this place is known for romance. Another reason is its two luxury honeymoon suites, Bridalveil and Rudi's Retreat, which run $350 a night in summer. Get a room on the second floor for more privacy; the first-floor rooms all share a common deck. Most rooms cost $265 per night April–Oct.; winter rates are much lower. If you're looking for something less expensive, the jointly managed Pines Resort should do the trick.

M Château du Sureau

Château du Sureau (48688 Victoria Lane, Oakhurst, 559/683-6860, www.chateausureau.com) is so remarkable that it has been praised by just about every major travel magazine. Dreamed up by Erna Kubin-Clanin, an Austrian woman with amazing talent and a taste for perfectionism, it is best described as an elegant, castle-like inn.

Imagine a classic French château and you have captured the idea here: featherbeds, goosedown comforters, Oriental carpets, trompe l'oeil frescoes, Parisian balconies, Italian linens, a grand piano, and a wealth of antiques.

No expense has been spared in decorating this 9,000-square-foot manse.

The Château has 10 guest rooms, each with fireplace and private bath, plus a separate two-bedroom villa. The least expensive of the guest rooms goes for $350 per night; the most expensive will run you $550 (but hey, breakfast is included). The villa comes stocked with china and crystal in the kitchen, a 24-hour personal butler, a supply of your favorite vintage wines, and the use of a complimentary, fully insured Jeep Cherokee for the duration of your stay—all for a mere $2,800 per night. An overnight at Château du Sureau makes staying at a suite in the Ahwahnee seem like pinching pennies.

Is it worth the money? Since it opened in 1991, the Château has earned the Mobil Five Star and AAA Five Diamond awards. It's definitely worth it.

Don't miss the three-foot-tall chess pieces arranged on a giant game board in the manicured garden. Play a little bocce ball or make a wish on one of the stone fountains while you're outside. All this and you're only 16 miles from the southern entrance to Yosemite.

If you have enough dough to spend a few nights here, you should certainly eat at the adjacent restaurant, Erna's Elderberry House, which is also run by Kubin-Clanin. It is equally divine and equally expensive.

East of the Park: U.S. 395

Visitors coming from Tahoe, Nevada, or points east commonly use the Highway 120/Tioga Pass approach to Yosemite from U.S. 395. Some Southern California travelers also choose the U.S. 395 corridor for their northward trek. For anyone accessing Yosemite in this manner, Lee Vining is the last "town" before the climb to the pass and the national park entrance; it makes a convenient stop for travelers.

The town was named for Leroy Vining, a prospector who established a camp here in 1852. An overnight stay in Lee Vining puts you 13 miles from the Tioga Pass entrance to Yosemite, and those miles cover one of the most

spectacular drives in the West—climbing up through the granite walls of Lee Vining Canyon to 9,945-foot Tioga Pass. This is a drive for savoring. It's a much longer drive to Yosemite Valley—figure on two hours—but scenic all the way.

Lee Vining also has its own major attraction—the 700,000-year-old Mono Lake, with its strange tufa spires and saline waters. It is one of the greatest bird-watching spots in the entire Sierra.

To the north of Lee Vining is a lonely corridor of U.S. 395 heading north toward Bridgeport. A few lodgings are found along, or a few miles off, this route, set in spectacular mountain scenery. Bodie State Historic Park, the largest "unrestored" ghost town in the American West and a popular destination for travelers, is found in this region.

Fifteen miles south of Lee Vining lies the popular winter and summer resort town of June Lake. This area includes four large drive-to lakes set off a looping highway and provides options for lodgings at classic mountain cabin resorts, as well as spectacular fishing and hiking. If you're willing to drive 45 minutes to reach the Tioga Pass entrance to Yosemite, June Lake could be an ideal spot to make your base camp for your Yosemite vacation. Yosemite Valley would be too far for a day trip (2.5 hours each way), but much of Yosemite's high country is within an hour's drive.

The lodgings listed below are arranged within each price category according to their proximity to Yosemite's Tioga Pass entrance. The first listing in each category is the closest to the park.

$50–100

Best Western Lake View Lodge

The lake referred to in this motel's name is spectacular Mono Lake, one of the oldest lakes in North America and without question the most surreal looking. It's a strangely beautiful body of salty water, almost as big as a sea. Unfortunately, you can't see it from most of the rooms at the Best Western Lake View Lodge (30 U.S. 395, Lee Vining, 760/647-6543 or 800/528-1234, www.bwlakeviewlodge.com). A few rooms are located on the lake side of the highway, with a fair-to-decent perspective on the water, but most are not. If you really want a view, you are much better off checking in elsewhere.

Instead of lake views, the Best Western offers what all Best Westerns offer: a clean, comfortable room with a dependable level of quality and service. Room rates are $90–155 in summer. They drop as low as $59 in the winter, when Highway 120 into Yosemite is closed and Lee Vining becomes a frozen ghost town.

April–Oct., the lodge owners also operate neighboring Lake View Cottages, plus a tent campground and RV park. The cottages run $85–170 per night and have one to three bedrooms, a full kitchen, and dining area. Their decor is straight out of the 1950s, but they are a practical option for families. A three-night minimum stay is required.

El Mono Motel

The unofficial motto at El Mono Motel (51 U.S. 395, Lee Vining, 760/647-6310, www.elmonomotel.com) is "We do funky very well." With room rates of only $60–78 for one person or $82–92 for two, you might expect shabby furnishings at this built-in-1927 relic, but the rooms are cheerful and decidedly unboring. Warmed by steam heat from an antique boiler, each room is painted in a variety of pleasant colors, and most are furnished with at least one piece of willow furniture. The original glass is still in many of the windows. Rooms are available with private or shared baths. A bonus is that the owner operates Latte Da Coffee Café in the front of the motel, so you can wander out in your slippers in the morning and get a cappuccino.

Murphey's Motel

There isn't much that's fancy about the little town of Lee Vining, the eastern gateway to Yosemite. There isn't much that's fancy about Murphey's Motel (51493 U.S. 395, Lee Vining, 760/647-6316 or 800/334-6316, www.murpheysyosemite.com), either, but the price is reasonable ($78–108 in summer, $53 in winter). The motel caters to ice climbers in the winter months; in the summer it welcomes the usual cabal of Yosemite tourists and U.S. 395 travelers. The AAA-approved rooms are clean, pleasant, and non-noteworthy. All rooms have in-room coffee, phones, and TVs with cable, so you can catch up on all the latest pro wrestling. Everything in Lee Vining is within walking distance. You'll have your pick of a half dozen restaurants, burger joints, and coffee shops. Spectacular Mono Lake is only a stone's throw away—a must-see on your Yosemite vacation.

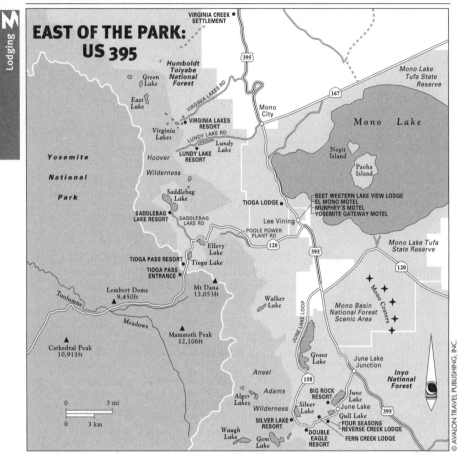

Tioga Lodge

This historic lodge is right smack on U.S. 395. Although you might think the road noise would deter from the lodge's desirability, the effect is greatly mitigated because its roadside setting allows open vistas of Mono Lake. Tioga Lodge's cabins (54411 U.S. 395, two miles north of Lee Vining, 760/647-6423 or 888/647-6423, www.tiogalodge.com) have a clear view of that spectacular 60,000-acre saltwater oddity, with its coral-like tufa spires and strange volcanic islands.

The lodge opened in 2000, but several of its buildings were transported here in the 1880s.

They came from the nearby gold mining town of Bodie, now a state historic park. Present owners Walter and Lou Vint restored the original buildings and added new ones. The one- and two-bedroom cabins are furnished with late-1800s antiques and pine log furniture. No two accommodations are alike; each has its own personality that reflects the Mono Basin area's history. A favorite is the Joseph Walker Mountain Man room, with its handmade pine log bed and a wall-mounted elk head and rifle. Rates are $60–110 per night in summer. The lodge has its own restaurant, which serves surprisingly gourmet food for breakfast and dinner.

Besides visiting Yosemite, the most obvious attraction, of course, is Mono Lake. Tioga Lodge is just two miles north of the Mono Basin Scenic Area Visitor Center, where you can learn everything about the 700,000-year-old water body.

Lundy Lake Resort

Lundy Lake Resort (Lundy Lake Road, five miles west of U.S. 395 and seven miles north of Lee Vining, 626/309-0415) is the opposite of fancy or showy. If you spend much time thinking about what clothes to wear or what kind of car to drive, you won't like it here. The resort's cabins are bare-bones and rustic, although they do come furnished with linens, bedding, and cooking utensils. Electricity comes from a generator, so forget your hair dryer or espresso maker. They won't work very well.

The resort and its six cabins are set at the west end of Lundy Lake. At elevation 7,800 feet, the big lake is one mile in length and has 100 surface acres, with a Southern California Edison dam at one end. Boats with motors are for rent and fishing is quite popular here. Hiking trails lead from the lake's dam. The scenery is classic Eastern Sierra: tall pines, quaking aspens, and breathtaking granite mountains. If you can time your stay properly, two natural events should not be missed at Lundy Lake Resort: the riotous wildflower bloom in Lundy Canyon, which usually occurs around July, and the colorful autumn aspen show in October. Cabin rental fees are $60–100 per night for two people, plus $5 for each additional person, with a three-night minimum stay required June 15–Sept. 15. The resort is open late April–Nov. 1.

Fern Creek Lodge

All of the cabin resorts in June Lake are clean, serviceable, and well situated for recreation enthusiasts. But some simply have more character than others, and Fern Creek Lodge (4628 Hwy. 158, June Lake, 760/648-7722 or 800/621-9146, www.ferncreeklodge.com) falls in that category. Maybe it's because the lodge has been around since 1927, or maybe it's because each of its 10 cabins and four apartment-style units is completely different in style and appearance. There's just something about this resort that makes it cozy and appealing.

The cutest cabin is the green-and-white Old Schoolhouse, a tiny little house for two people only. It's at the back of the property, farthest from the road. Dutch Lady and Heart Tree are the largest cabins; they're both two-story units with four bedrooms, two bathrooms, and a sundeck around the front. Fees are $70 per night for the one-bedroom cabins, $125–150 per night for the two-bedroom cabins, and $235 per night for the four-bedroom cabins, which can accommodate up to 14 people.

A common hot tub is set in the middle of the cabins; guests take turns using it. A barbecue area and fish-cleaning facilities are available. All cabins have fully equipped kitchens, but if you don't feel like cooking, several restaurants are nearby.

Virginia Creek Settlement

If you want to visit the ghost town at Bodie, there's no better place to stay than Virginia Creek Settlement (U.S. 395, 20 miles north of Lee Vining, 760/932-7780, www.virginiacrk-settlement.com). This is especially true if you have kids with you, or kids-at-heart. Not only is Virginia Creek Settlement the closest lodging to Bodie State Historic Park, but it's also designed to get you in the Old West spirit.

The place looks like a movie set. It has six cabins, which are actually large converted sheds with clever false fronts, crafted to look like the buildings of an Old West town. Each represents a different "enterprise," including Cooper's Freight and Mercantile Company, Assay and Land Office, and Anthony Agony M.D. Three covered wagons (also for rent) complete the scene. If you want to stay in something more conventional, the resort has motel rooms and tent sites, but why spoil the ghost town mood?

Inside, the cabins and covered wagons are one single room with beds. You must remember to bring your own linens or sleeping bags. A communal restroom and showers are a few feet away. Sure, this is a little like roughing it, but it only costs $24 per night. Larger cabins cost $116–126 per night. Motel rooms are $62–80. Meals are available at the resort's historic dining room; the menu is a mix of Italian and American, including pizza and wine. Order something Italian and pretend you're in a spaghetti Western.

Know that it will take you about 45 minutes to reach the Tioga Pass entrance to Yosemite from here, but if you want to see both Bodie and Yosemite in one trip, this place makes a good base camp.

$100–200
M Tioga Pass Resort

You can forget about staying at Tioga Pass Resort (Hwy. 120, two miles east of Tioga Pass, 209/372-4471, www.tiogapassresort.com) in the summer unless you're one of those people who can plan far in advance. This resort is heavily booked for two big reasons: it's perfectly situated next to Yosemite's high country, and it has a loyal clientele of folks who come back year after year.

The resort is situated on Tioga Road, just two miles from Yosemite's eastern entrance, at the mighty elevation of 9,600 feet. In summer, the resort's store, cafe, and outdoor espresso cart are popular stops for visitors driving in and out of the park.

But only a lucky few stay in the cabins. Many are booked a full year in advance. The 10 one- and two-bedroom cabins ($140–210 per night) are quaint and rustic, built of logs and painted brown with yellow and green trim. They are set quite close to the road and resort parking lot, but fortunately a stream runs between them, keeping unwanted noise to a minimum. You can cook in your cabin if you wish, but it's hard to justify when Tioga Pass Resort's cafe makes such great food. Four motel rooms are also available ($100–120 per night).

In winter, Tioga Pass Resort transforms into a cozy ski lodge. Most years, both deep powder and spring corn snow are in plentiful supply. The road to the resort isn't plowed in winter; you have to ski in six miles. Consequently, winter reservations are easier to come by. Guests stay in heated cabins, then get together in the main lodge for meals, which are included in the price. Rates are $150 per person per night, less midweek.

Yosemite Gateway Motel

Sure, the small rooms are a bit worn at the Yosemite Gateway Motel (51340 U.S. 395, Lee Vining, 760/647-6467 or 800/282-3929, www.yosemitegatewaymotel.com), but each one has a framed vista of Mono Lake—a fairly wide, expansive view, not a tiny, peek-a-boo view that makes you long for more. All rooms also have coffeemakers and cable TV. Furnishings are unremarkable but adequate, and all of downtown Lee Vining is a few footsteps away. Rates are $109–179 in summer, $79–139 in autumn, and as low as $49 in winter.

Virginia Lakes Resort

"Watch your step; sea level is 9,770 feet down," notes the sign above the door at Virginia Lakes Resort (Virginia Lakes Road, six miles west of U.S. 395 and 12 miles north of Lee Vining, 760/647-6484, www.virginialakesresort.com). The resort is set on Little Virginia Lake, which is right next to Big Virginia Lake and within a half-mile drive of Trumbull Lake. Behind the lakes rise a few magnificent Sierra summits: Dunderberg Peak, Mount Olsen, Virginia Peak, and Black Mountain.

This is a classic mountain lodge resort, at the end of a six-mile drive from the main highway. Although plenty of people go fishing while they are here, this isn't a fish camp. Virginia Lakes Resort caters to a somewhat upscale crowd, with tidy cabins and newer furnishings. It's not Ritz-Carlton quality here, more like Best Western, but the place is clean, attractive, and appealing. In addition to its cabins, Virginia Lake Resort has a store, a cafe (open for breakfast and lunch only), and rowboat rentals. Bring plenty of cash or traveler's checks with you; the resort doesn't accept credit cards.

Nine of the 19 cabins have lake views; the other 10 are on Virginia Creek. For the best experience, make sure you request a cabin with a fireplace and a deck overlooking the lake. All cabins have fully stocked kitchens. Not surpris-

ingly, the resort is wildly popular, so its cabins are usually rented by the week only June 15– Labor Day ($500–1,700 per week, depending on the number of people and size of cabin). The rest of the season, which usually means early June and September, there is a three-night minimum stay and fees are $77–252 per night.

Big Rock Resort

The cabins at Big Rock Resort (1 Big Rock Road, June Lake, 760/648-7717 or 800/769-9831, www.bigrockresort.net) are perched alongside big, blue June Lake, giving summer visitors easy access to excellent trout fishing, sailing, and boating. The resort provides motorboat and paddleboat rentals, or cabin guests can bring their own boat and launch it free.

The eight one- to three-bedroom cabins at Big Rock Resort are nothing out of the ordinary, but they have fully equipped kitchens and everything you need for your June Lake/Yosemite vacation. Fees run $135–235 per night, depending on cabin size. Reduced rates are available in September, October, and May, excluding holidays. Some of the cabins are duplexes, so make sure you request a single unit if you don't want to share exterior walls. Plan on a 45-minute drive to reach the Tioga Pass entrance to Yosemite.

Four Seasons

If the idea of looking out your cabin's floor-to-ceiling windows at 10,909-foot Carson Peak appeals to you, you'll enjoy staying at the Four Seasons (Hwy. 158, five miles west of U.S. 395, June Lake, 760/648-7476, www.junelake.com/lodging/foursns). The resort's A-frame chalets are just off the main highway at the base of Carson Peak. From the front, they don't look like much. The six chalets are packed in like sardines (they're almost touching each other). But once you're inside, you remember why you came here: the view of Carson Peak's snow-covered granite is truly stunning.

Each chalet is identical: 800 square feet in size, with an enclosed master bedroom plus a loft bedroom that overlooks the living room. The living room has the giant windows with the view. If you want an even better view, go sit outside on your chalet's sundeck. In summer, you can flip hamburgers while you gaze at the scenery; the chalets have gas barbecues. If you prefer to cook indoors, the kitchens are fully stocked with everything you need except food. Fees are $119 for two people plus $20 for each additional person (maximum is seven). Rates are slightly higher in August and during summer and winter holidays. A three-night minimum stay is required. Yosemite's Tioga Pass entrance is a 45-minute drive.

Reverse Creek Lodge

"Our family welcomes yours" is the motto at Reverse Creek Lodge (Hwy. 158, 4.5 miles west of U.S. 395, June Lake, 760/648-7535 or 800/762-6440, www.reversecreeklodge.com). The Reverse Creek family is David and Denise Naaden and their 12 children, whom they call their "cleaning crew." With that many kids, the place ought to be clean as a whistle, and sure enough, it is.

The Naadens took over the lodge and its cabins and A-frame chalets in 1995. The rustic cabins are set in the pines along Reversed Creek, but the modern A-frame chalets are the more popular rentals. Down the street about 100 yards from the rest of the resort, the chalets are perched above Reversed Creek in a cluster of pines. Some have a fair view of 10,909-foot Carson Peak, a mammoth granite landmark in June Lake. They are a bit cramped—each one only a few feet from the next.

Like the cabins, the A-frames have fully stocked kitchens, cable TV, VCRs, gas fireplaces, gas barbecues, and all the other amenities of home. For big groups, the resort has a "private residence cabin" with four bedrooms and two full baths. Fees are $75–120 per night for the cabins, $140 per night for the chalets, and $285 per night for the four-bedroom house.

Silver Lake Resort

Most people agree that 110-acre Silver Lake is the prettiest of the four lakes on the June Lake Loop, which is a major reason that Silver Lake

The Double Eagle Resort boasts June Lake's most luxurious cabins, set under the imposing shadow of Carson Peak.

Resort (Hwy. 158, 7.5 miles west of U.S. 395, June Lake, 760/648-7525, www.silverlakeresort.net) is so popular. The resort is a full-service operation with a general store, cabins, cafe, RV park, and boat rentals. It was established in 1916, which makes it the oldest resort in the eastern Sierra.

The 17 cabins of varying sizes are rustic-looking on the outside, but clean and well cared for. Many have been redone on the inside, with new curtains and bedding. All have fully equipped kitchens, but none have telephones, and only a few have televisions. The cabins are set amid a grove of aspens, giving the illusion of seclusion even though they are grouped close together. All cabins are only a stone's throw from the lake; a few have lake views. Most resort guests take advantage of fishing on Silver Lake; motorboats and canoes are for rent by the hour or the day. Rates are $95–235 per night, depending on cabin size. The resort is open June–Oct., weather permitting.

$200 AND UP

Double Eagle Resort

Having just opened in 1999, Double Eagle Resort (5587 Hwy. 158, June Lake, 760/648-7004, www.doubleeagleresort.com) has quickly established itself as one of the best lodging destinations in the East Sierra. If you like the idea of an upscale version of a mountain lodge and cabin resort, Double Eagle does it well.

Double Eagle's 14 cabins ($258–319 per night) are two-bedroom models with fully equipped kitchens and fireplaces. They are tastefully decorated and large enough to fit four to six people. All the extra amenities are provided: microwave oven, barbecue, TV/VCR, phones, and the like.

Additionally, the resort includes the Creek-side Spa and Fitness Center, which has a 60-foot indoor pool and hot tub and all kinds of fitness equipment and classes. A full-service salon is on-site for guests who want to get their nails or hair done or have a facial treatment or massage. Delicious meals can be had at the resort's Eagle's Landing Restaurant.

So when you've finally finished your pedicure, aromatherapy massage, tai chi class, and gourmet lunch, what's next? Head outside and try out the resort's trophy trout pond, which is stocked with trout up to 18 pounds. What, you don't know how to fly-fish? No matter, they offer lessons daily. There's even a fly-fishing pond just for kids. Full guide service is available, plus a fly-fishing shop. With all this going on, you might just forget that you came here so you could see Yosemite.

Camping

Many visitors consider camping out an integral part of the national park experience. If you come to a national park for nature, they reason, why spend the night walled off from it? One look at some of the park's campgrounds on a Saturday night will tell you why: Because camping in Yosemite can sometimes be more like waging battle than communing with nature.

But not always. With some careful forethought and planning, you can secure a spot in or near the park and have the camping vacation of your dreams. First, if you call the park reservations office (800/436-7275, or 301/722-1257 if you are outside the United States) or visit its website (http://reservations.nps.gov) up to five months in advance, you can reserve a site at one of three reservable campgrounds in Yosemite Valley or one of four reservable campgrounds elsewhere in the park.

The reservation system works like this: Reservations are available in blocks of one month at a time, up to five months in advance, on the 15th of each month. Nearly all reservations for the months of May through September are filled on the first day they become available. In other words, you need to act on January 15 if you want a reservation for May 15–June 14. You need to act on February 15 if you want a reservation for June 15–July 14. And so on. Both the telephone and the online reservation systems are open 7 A.M.–7 P.M. Pacific standard time. If you wait until the 16th of the month to

Yosemite's Best

⏹ **Bridalveil Creek:** This camp is close to Glacier Point Road's many great day hiking trails. An unexpected luxury is that the bathrooms have flush toilets (page 163).

⏹ **White Wolf:** A summertime favorite, this campground at 8,000 feet in elevation along Tioga Pass Road is available on a first-come, first-served basis. Sites are tucked in among rocky boulders and in a forest of lodgepole pines (page 166).

⏹ **Summerdale:** Popular with anglers because of its setting along Big Creek, this convenient campground is only a mile from the southern entrance to Yosemite (page 176).

⏹ **Ellery Lake:** Campers and RVers who desire a campsite within a few yards of a 10,000-foot alpine lake will be very happy here. All of the Tioga Pass area, plus the Eastern Sierra, is at your doorstep (page 179).

⏹ **Sawmill Walk-In:** Every site here has a drop-dead gorgeous view of High Sierra scenery, and each is strategically placed with plenty of room around it. The catch? You have to hike in about 100–200 yards from your car (page 179).

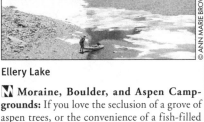

© ANN MARIE BROWN

Ellery Lake

⏹ **Moraine, Boulder, and Aspen Campgrounds:** If you love the seclusion of a grove of aspen trees, or the convenience of a fish-filled stream just a few feet from your tent, this is your spot (page 180).

try to make reservations, you'll probably be out of luck, although cancellations do occasionally become available.

Once you're armed with a reservation for a given campground, it's wise to show up there right around check-out time (or maybe an hour or so before), so you can have your pick of available sites as campers vacate their spots. Checkout/check-in in Yosemite Valley is 10 A.M.; for the rest of the park's campgrounds it is noon. If you wait to arrive until evening, you'll end up with the worst site in the campground—the one that nobody else chose. With your reservation, you are guaranteed a site, but you are not guaranteed a good site.

And although having reservations for a Yosemite campsite is your best bet (and for Yosemite Valley in the summer, it's imperative), even campers without reservations have an excellent chance of camping in the park—as long as they don't wait to look for a site until 6 P.M. on Saturday evening. One campground in Yosemite Valley, one on Glacier Point Road, and four on Tioga Pass Road are first-come, first-served throughout the summer. As long as you show up early in the day, you'll probably find a site somewhere. And if you aren't happy with any of the offerings at these six campgrounds, you can always head east through Tioga Pass to the first-come, first-served Mono County and Inyo National Forest campgrounds just a few miles outside of the park.

Camping

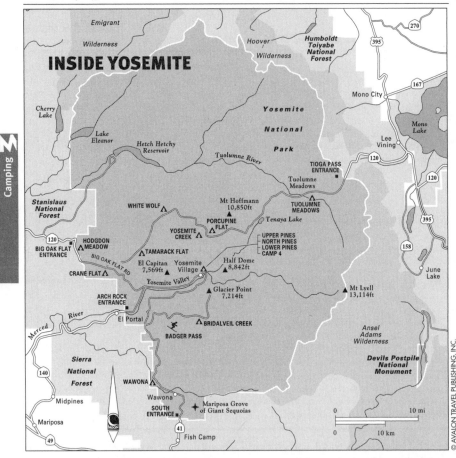

Inside Yosemite

YOSEMITE VALLEY

If you have your heart set on camping in Yo-semite Valley, you better be one of those people who can plan far in advance. Either that or you should be one of those people who relishes camping in the middle of winter, which is the only time you can get away with not having an advance reservation for a Valley campsite. Simply put, these sites are at a premium. For the summer vacation season, every reservable site in Yosemite Valley is usually taken as soon as it shows up on the reservation system (five months in advance).

With all these hoops to jump through, you'd think that the campgrounds in Yosemite Valley would be fabulous. Truth is, they're not. Sure, they have all the amenities we've come to expect from campgrounds: picnic tables, drinking water, fire rings, and even that great unheralded luxury, flush toilets. But if you think camping should feel like a real "nature

YOSEMITE CAMPGROUND RULES

With all the people who want to camp in Yosemite, there just have to be a few rules to keep things orderly. If you follow the guidelines below, you *and* your neighbors will be happy campers.

- Only six people and two vehicles are allowed at each campsite.
- You must keep your food properly stored from bears 24 hours a day. Store all food in the bearproof container provided at your campsite. Do not store food, or anything with a scent, in your car.
- You may sleep in your vehicle only in designated campsites. Visitors caught sleeping in their cars outside of a campground will be asked to move, regardless of time of night, and may also be cited.
- Quiet hours are 10 P.M.–6 A.M.
- RV generators may be used sparingly 7 A.M.–7 P.M.
- Check-in and check-out is at noon (except for Yosemite Valley; see below).
- You may gather wood for campground fires anywhere in the park except for Yosemite Valley, the park's three sequoia groves (Mariposa, Merced, and Tuolumne), and in areas above 9,600 feet in elevation. Conifer cones are never permitted as fuel for fires; they are needed in the forest for regeneration of trees.
- The backpackers' campsites at the Valley's North Pines Campground, at Tuolumne Meadows Campground, and at Hetch Hetchy are designated for those beginning or ending a wilderness trip. Campers who wish to stay in these sites may do so for only one night before or after their backpacking trip, and they must have their wilderness permit in hand. The sites are walk-in only, and only backpacking equipment may be brought in.

Campground Rules Specific to Yosemite Valley

The regulations are a little more strict at Yosemite Valley's campgrounds:

- From May 1 through Oct. 15, campground fires are allowed only 5–10 P.M. Gas stoves may be used at any time.
- Firewood and kindling (including pine cones and needles) may not be gathered in the Valley. You can purchase campfire wood from the stores in Yosemite Village and Curry Village.
- Between May and September, you may camp for only seven days in Yosemite Valley. The rest of the year, there is a 14-day stay limit.
- Check-in and check-out is at 10 A.M.

experience," you've come to the wrong place. The Valley's campsites are so close together that you'll feel like your neighbors are sharing your vacation with you. You'll hear the sound of cars driving around the campgrounds and nearby roads all night.

And you'll spend a fair portion of your camping time engaged in the business of "taking bear precautions." This means, first and foremost, that you do not store any food, or any item with a scent (including cosmetics, sunscreen, lip balm, toothpaste, and insect repellent) in your car or tent. Everything with a scent gets placed in your campsite's "bear box," including your cooler filled with food and ice. Most bear boxes are 33 inches deep, 45 inches wide, and 18 inches high, so make sure you don't have more stuff than will cram into that space. When you pull out food from the bear box to cook it, you must keep it within sight at all times. You shouldn't turn your back for a moment on a frozen chicken or some raw corn on the cob.

Thus, the preparation of every meal involves numerous trips back and forth to the bear box. While this may seem amusing at first, it quickly becomes downright tiresome. If you slack in your duties, you risk having a bear steal all your food in the brief time it takes to say, "Look, a bear is stealing all our food." You also risk receiving a citation from a ranger.

With all that said, there is still a big reason why Yosemite Valley's campsites are booked all summer long. This is Yosemite Valley—one of the most scenic places on earth. If you can put up with some inconveniences, and you don't mind the crowds and lack of privacy, you will find yourself in an ideal location for exploring the Valley. In fact, there's a good chance you won't need your car at all once you're here. Most everything is within walking distance of Valley campgrounds, and free shuttle buses are available.

Upper Pines, North Pines, and Lower Pines

Of the three central Yosemite Valley camps, collectively known as "the Pines," only Upper Pines is open year-round; the other two are open April–Sept. or October. Upper Pines has 238 sites, North Pines has 81 sites, and Lower Pines has 60 sites. Which camp is best? All three are pretty similar, although North Pines has a slightly nicer setting with some sites right alongside the Merced River. All Pines camps offer easy access for hiking to Mirror Lake, Vernal and Nevada Falls, Half Dome, and the Valley's other highlights. Pine trees keep most of the packed-together sites shaded, which is a real bonus in summer but a major negative in the winter, when you can freeze your buns off if you're in a tent instead of a heated RV. Even if there isn't snow, Upper Pines is often covered in ice Nov.–February. The sun never hits it.

In summer, there is no guarantee of sleep in the three Pines campgrounds. It seems that during every hour of the night, someone is driving around, your neighbor is snoring like a locomotive, a bear is wreaking havoc somewhere in the campground, or a car alarm is going off. Asthmatics should be forewarned that during dinner hours, Yosemite Valley can become quite smoky from the campfires of nearly 400 campers at the combined Pines Campgrounds.

The camps have drinking water, flush toilets, picnic tables, and fire grills. All sites will

One of the greatest appeals at one of the Pines Campgrounds is easy access to the sandy beaches on the Merced River.

accommodate tents or RVs up to 40 feet long. The fee is $18 per night. To reserve a site, phone 800/436-7275, or 301/722-1257 if you are outside the United States; or visit http://reservations.nps.gov. The Pines camps are located midway between Yosemite Village and Curry Village in Yosemite Valley.

Camp 4

Quite different in ambience from the three other Valley Campgrounds, Camp 4 was set aside to provide an inexpensive place for the Valley's rock climbers to stay (climbers are notorious for having empty wallets). If you think the three Pines Campgrounds are crowded, wait till you see Camp 4. The 35 sites are packed in so tightly that each site is virtually indistinguishable from the next. Unlike the three Pines Campgrounds, no reservations are taken for Camp 4. When you arrive, you are assigned a site if one is available. If you don't have six people in your group, you will share your site with another group. The result is a very communal environment that appeals to some campers but not to others. (You know who you are.) Don't plan on sleeping much. This is a party place.

Campers must walk in to Camp 4; all cars are left about 100 to 200 feet away in a large parking lot. You won't have an SUV fender parked next to your tent, and you won't have to listen to anybody's RV generator. The camp is equipped with drinking water, flush toilets, picnic tables, and fire grills. Best of all, Camp 4 is a bargain: sites cost only $5 per person per night. If you want to hike to the top of Upper Yosemite Fall, you couldn't be better situated. The trail begins right at Camp 4.

WAWONA AND GLACIER POINT

Campground choices are not plentiful in the southern part of the park. If you don't have a reservation at Wawona Campground, you can take a chance at getting a site at first-come, first-served Bridalveil Creek. If it's late in the day in the summer, you are probably out of luck and would do better heading south, out of the park, to find a campsite. The kiosk at the park's south entrance usually has updated status on which park campgrounds are full, so you can check there before making the 24-mile drive up to Bridalveil Creek Camp.

Bridalveil Creek

There's only one campground up on Glacier Point Road, and Bridalveil Creek is it. If you want to camp close to Glacier Point's great day hiking trails, or be able to enjoy sunsets from the world-famous overlooks at Glacier Point or Sentinel Dome without facing a long drive afterward, this camp is where you want to be. The trick is that you have to get here early to secure a site; no reservations are accepted. Generally the camp fills early, especially on weekends. Many would-be campers who get turned away in Yosemite Valley wind up here looking for a site.

A total of 110 sites are available that can accommodate tents or RVs up to 35 feet long. Because the elevation here is 7,200 feet, the camp is only open from June or July to mid-September (the official starting date depends on when Glacier Point Road opens). Although many of the sites are quite densely packed in, in typical Yosemite fashion, there are a few winners located on the outside of the loops. If you score one of these outer, private sites, you're in heaven. Bridalveil Creek runs right through the camp, and the meadows alongside it produce a wonderful wildflower display in July.

A trail to Ostrander Lake leaves right from the campground; the 13-mile round-trip is a wonderful, though long, day hike. Swimming in the lake is popular on warm summer days. Yosemite Valley is a 45-minute drive. If you want to visit Tuolumne Meadows, you're about two hours away.

Of all the camps in Yosemite, this is the one where you want to be the most self-contained—in other words, bring everything you need. If you forgot the hamburger patties, it's a long drive out to the nearest store. There is a snack shop on Glacier Point in the summer months, but it's only open 9 A.M.–4 P.M. and has a very limited menu.

Camping

The camp has drinking water, flush toilets, picnic tables, and fire grills. The fee is $12 per night. Two group sites for groups of 13–30 people ($40 fee per night) and a horse camp ($25 fee per night) are also available. Reservations are required for the group sites (800/436-7275 or 301/722-1257 if you are outside the United States, http://reservations.nps.gov). Located eight miles east of Highway 41 on Glacier Point Road or 24.5 miles from the park's southern entrance.

Wawona

Some park visitors like Wawona Campground because of its setting on the South Fork Merced River. They rhapsodize about the joys of relaxing in a camp chair, sniffing the scent of their camp dinner cooking as the lyrical South Fork Merced rolls by. Other park visitors regard this 93-site campground with disdain because it is set in an open flat right alongside Highway 41, so campers never get a break from the sight and sound of cars cruising past, nor do they get any shade or much privacy.

If you get a reservation here, you can settle this dispute for yourself. Whether you will see the glass half full or half empty depends on how lucky you are. If fortune is smiling on you, you'll obtain one of the sites that are right on the river. Four walk-in tent sites are prime riverfront property and even offer some privacy. If you're unlucky, you'll get one of the sites farther from the river, in full view of the road, and with no screening around it.

The camp is open year-round; Oct.–April, reservations are not taken (except for at the group camp)—it's first-come, first-served. RVers are particularly fond of this campground because it is easy-in, easy-out. The camp offers drinking water, flush toilets, picnic tables, and fire grills. All sites will accommodate tents or RVs up to 40 feet long. The fee is $18 per night May–Sept., $12 per night Oct.–April. A group site for groups of 13–30 people ($40 fee per night) and a horse camp ($25 fee per night) are also available. To reserve a site, phone 800/436-7275 or 301/722-1257 if you are outside the United States, http://reservations.nps.gov.

Wawona Campground is one mile north of Wawona, or seven miles north of the park's southern entrance.

TIOGA PASS AND TUOLUMNE MEADOWS

For people who simply can't stand to plan ahead, the best bet for last-minute camping in Yosemite is on Tioga Road. Not in Tuolumne Meadows, mind you. That particular campground is nearly as popular, and hard to reserve, as the camps in Yosemite Valley. But at several other camps just off Tioga Road/Highway 120, you'll be able to drive right in and find a decent campsite on most days of the summer. That's because sites at several camps (Tamarack Flat, White Wolf, Yosemite Creek, Porcupine Flat) are not reservable; they operate on a first-come, first-served basis.

Don't be too relaxed about finding a site, however. If it's a Saturday, you'd be well advised to start your search early in the day, not at 7 P.M. If it's a holiday weekend, start looking on Friday. The concessions you must make to stay in these nonreservable campgrounds are relatively small: They don't have flush toilets, and some don't have running water. (The camps that do have these luxuries cost more than the camps without them, so you save money by roughing it.)

For camps without running water, it's wise to bring along the biggest bottles of water you can buy. You'll need them for drinking, cooking, washing up, and brushing your teeth. You never realize how much water you use in the normal course of a day until you can't get to a faucet.

Also, bear precautions are in effect at all high-country campgrounds, just like in Yosemite Valley. Use the bear box in your campsite to store any item that has a scent, or even looks like food, and you will be rewarded by having a car that remains in one piece.

Hodgdon Meadow

This is the first campground you reach after entering the park on Highway 120 at the Big Oak

WHERE CAN I TAKE A SHOWER?

Camping is great. But camping is also a bit, well, unclean. Sure, you can go for a while with your hair unwashed and dirt behind your ears, but after a few days, you may find yourself longing for a shower.

Many first-time Yosemite campers are surprised to find that, unlike at California state park campgrounds, national park campgrounds do not have showers. But there's no need to throw in the towel. You can get a shower in Yosemite Valley for $2 at Curry Village (year-round) or Housekeeping Camp (April–Oct.). Curry Village's showers are open 24 hours a day. Housekeeping Camp's showers are open 7 A.M.–2 P.M. and 3:30–10 P.M. The $2 fee includes use of a towel and soap.

If you're camping in the high country on Tioga Road, Tuolumne Meadows Lodge and White Wolf Lodge offer $2 showers noon–3 P.M. for nonguests. If you drive east through Tioga Pass, you can purchase showers at Mono Vista RV Park ($2 for five minutes) at the north end of Lee Vining on U.S. 395 (760/647-6401).

13–30 people are reservable for $40 per night; the group sites are open April–Oct. only. (Remember that if you are traveling with a large group in separate cars, each car has to pay the $20 park entrance fee. Suddenly the $40 group campsite can become pretty pricey.) The camp has drinking water, flush toilets, picnic tables, and fire grills. The camp is 0.25 mile down a side road located 100 feet past the Big Oak Flat entrance station.

Crane Flat

This is the second campground you reach after entering the park on Highway 120 at the Big Oak Flat entrance station. Reservations are required when the camp is open, generally June–September. Families usually enjoy this campground; the evening ranger programs are excellent. Crane Flat's 166 sites make it a guarantee that your kids will get to mingle with plenty of other young campers.

Crane Flat's location is ideal for visiting both Yosemite Valley and the trailheads along Tioga Pass; each are about 30 minutes away. The camp is only a few minutes from easy hiking in two giant sequoia groves: Tuolumne and Merced. The camp elevation is 6,200 feet, which is why it's open only June–Sept., and even then there's usually a chill in the air in the evenings and mornings.

The sites are spread out over five loops, and there is plenty of room for RVs up to 35 feet long. A few winners are found among a host of not-so-desirable sites, namely the even-numbered sites ranging 214–228 and 502–522, which have the most space and the fewest neighbors.

The camp has drinking water, flush toilets, picnic tables, and fire grills. The fee is $18 per night. To reserve a site, phone 800/436-7275 or 301/722-1257 if you are outside the United States, http://reservations.nps.gov. The camp is 10 miles east of the Big Oak Flat entrance station on the south side of Highway 120, just west of the Crane Flat junction and gas station.

Tamarack Flat

If you are driving in to Yosemite from the west side, this is the first campground you'll

Flat entrance station. Reservations are required May–Sept. for the camp's 105 sites; the rest of the year, it's first-come, first-served. RVs up to 35 feet long are permitted. The elevation is 4,900 feet, which means warm summer nights. The main attractions on Tioga Road and in Yosemite Valley are about 45 minutes away.

The biggest advantage to staying here is that you've made it past the entrance station and you're in the park. Don't expect peace and quiet. The sites are packed in tightly. On most summer nights, newcomers just arriving in the park from heaven-knows-where drive around the camp hoping to find an open space. They don't find one, but they keep driving in circles anyway, shining their headlights in your tent. After September, however, this can be a very pleasant campground.

The fee is $18 per night May–Sept. and $12 the rest of the year. Four group sites for

find on Highway 120 that doesn't take reservations. The camp's remote flavor is owed to the fact that it is three miles off Highway 120 on a rough paved road, which gets rougher as you go.

The camp's access road is part of the old Big Oak Flat Road. The road is gated off beyond the camp, but you can ride your bike on the paved portion of it or hike it for 16 miles to Yosemite Valley. Some people hike this road for 6.4 miles to the Foresta junction with the "new" Big Oak Flat Road, then have someone pick them up there. If you want to head for other trailheads, you are less than an hour's drive from Yosemite Valley and about 40 minutes from Tuolumne Meadows.

The camp has 52 sites, which are not located on a loop but rather on a series of one-way spurs. It can accommodate RVs up to 24 feet long, although few RV drivers will enjoy the access road or the dirt roads in between the campsites. Many of the sites are quite private due to the large amount of space around them and the number of big boulders and lodgepole pine trees. The camp's elevation is 6,300 feet; you drive downhill from Highway 120 to get here. That makes this one of the warmer camps at night on the Tioga Road.

Because there isn't any visible presence of "authority" at this camp as there is at Yosemite's more developed camps, some campers get a little rowdy here. Don't expect that your neighbors will necessarily follow the "quiet time at 10 P.M." rule. You might get lucky and have pleasant, quiet neighbors; you might not.

Tamarack Flat is open June–Sept. and costs a mere $8 per night because of the lack of drinking water, so bring your own. The camp has vault toilets, picnic tables, and fire grills. The access road to Tamarack Flat is 3.7 miles east of Crane Flat on Highway 120. Turn right and drive 2.9 miles to the camp.

White Wolf

This 74-site campground is a favorite of many who come to Yosemite year after year. Reservations are not accepted; it's first-come, first-served, and you have a decent chance at a site

on most nights except Saturday and possibly Friday. Because the camp access road is only one mile long and smoothly paved, it's easy enough to cruise in and look for a spot. If you strike out, just head for one of the other camps on Tioga Road.

The camp has a pleasant setting at 8,000 feet in elevation amid a forest of lodgepole pines. Some sites are tucked in among rocky boulders and others are on the outside of the loop among the trees, so you can achieve a modicum of privacy. In general, though, the sites are packed in too densely for this small area. Small RVs (less than 27 feet) can fit in here.

Besides its location, White Wolf is popular because it has all the advantages of a fully developed car campground, including flush toilets. An even greater luxury is the proximity of White Wolf Lodge (about 100 yards from the camp), where you can enjoy delicious homemade meals if you don't feel like blackening another hot dog. The lodge also has a small store that sells drinks and snacks. The fee to camp at White Wolf, including all these extravagances, is only $12 per night. A trail to Harden Lake leads right from the camp; many other trails are close by. The camp is open June–Sept., weather permitting. It has drinking water, flush toilets, picnic tables, and fire grills. It's 14 miles east of Crane Flat on Highway 120. Turn left at the White Wolf sign and drive one mile to the campground.

Yosemite Creek

Another one of the no-reservations camps on Tioga Road, Yosemite Creek is similar to Tamarack Flat in that it is located a good distance off the highway. In fact, it's even farther than Tamarack Flat—the access road is a whopping 4.7 miles that takes a tedious 20 minutes to drive. For decades, this road has been littered with potholes. Will the Park Service ever repair it? Probably not. It's one of those roads that never should have been paved in the first place; it would hold up better through Yosemite's harsh winters if it were a graded dirt road.

The long drive gives the camp a remote feel (much more so than any other camp in Yosemite) and discourages people from cruising in just to look around. But if you're the kind of camper who likes to drive in and out of camp several times a day, this pothole-ridden access road will make you crazy.

On the plus side, the camp road is not suitable for RVs over 24 feet, so tent campers can enjoy being alone among their ilk. All of the trailheads on Tioga Road are accessible in less than an hour's drive. An advantage here is that the sites aren't set on a loop; rather, they are spread out in a line, which limits the number of neighbors you can have.

All in all, this 75-site camp is a good option for people who prefer a more primitive camping experience. Like nearby Tamarack Flat, Yosemite Creek tends to attract campers who want to do their own thing. Hopefully their "thing" doesn't include partying all night, but you never know.

The elevation is 7,700 feet, so it can be chilly at night. The fee is only $8 per night because you don't have the luxury of flush toilets or drinking water (so pack bottled water). The camp has vault toilets, picnic tables, and fire grills. It's located 14.3 miles east of Crane Flat on Highway 120 (.25 mile past the turnoff for White Wolf Camp). Turn right at the Yosemite Creek Campground sign and drive 4.7 miles to the campground. Summers only.

Porcupine Flat

The easternmost of the first-come, first-served camps on Tioga Road, Porcupine Flat has 52 sites for tents or RVs up to 35 feet long. The camp is located right off Highway 120 (within a stone's throw), but if you head for some of the sites on the far north end, you can get away from most of the road noise. The sites become larger and more private the farther back into the campground you go. This camp is generally more popular with tent campers than RV campers; its road is mostly dirt and many sites aren't large enough for RVs.

Set at 8,100 feet, Porcupine Flat has an ideal location close to Tuolumne Meadows and Tioga Pass. All of the trailheads of Yosemite's high country are close by, plus the many attrac-

tions just outside of the park boundary, east of Tioga Pass. Because of the high elevation, the camp is open only July–September.

The camp has vault toilets, picnic tables, and fire grills. Bring your own drinking water. No reservations; the fee is $8 per night. The camp is located 23.7 miles east of Crane Flat on the north side of Highway 120.

Tuolumne Meadows

This is Yosemite's largest camp, with a whopping 304 sites. The camper-density level is high, to say the least. Everybody wants to camp here for three reasons: location, location, location. You are right across the road from Tuolumne Meadows. You could spend a week camping, hiking, and fishing around here and never once drive your car. Many trailheads are within walking distance of the camp, as is the Tuolumne River. A decent grocery store and the Tuolumne Meadows Grill are right next door, so if you forget to bring food, it's no problem.

Half of the sites can be reserved in advance; the other half are first-come, first-served. This system results in a line-up of hopeful campers every morning outside the Tuolumne Meadows Reservations Office, praying that they'll score a site. If they get there early, they have a decent chance on weekdays. Weekends are tough.

Elevation is 8,600 feet at Tuolumne Meadows, with the fresh, cool air of the high country. The high elevation means this campground is only open July–Sept. each year.

Considering its massive size, the camp has many sites that have a lot going for them. A dense forest of lodgepole pines lends some sites a modicum of seclusion. One of the camp's loops has a number of riverside sites. Others have an A-plus view of Lembert Dome. Nonetheless, it is an unalterable law of nature that 304 separate groups of campers can never be quiet at the same time. Camping here can feel like camping in the city. If you need to get some solid sleep so you can wake up the next morning and climb Cathedral Peak, pack along earplugs for sure.

Tuolumne Meadows Camp has drinking water, flush toilets, picnic tables, and fire

Camping

grills. Sites will accommodate tents or RVs up to 35 feet long. The fee is $18 per night. Seven group sites are also available for groups of 13–30 people ($40 per night). A horse camp is available for $25 per night. To reserve a site, phone 800/436-7275, or 301/722-1257 if you are outside the United States), or visit http://reservations.nps.gov. The camp is 39 miles east of Crane Flat on the south side of Highway 120, just past the Tuolumne Meadows Grill and Store.

West of the Park: Highway 120

On Highway 120 east of Groveland you'll find several camps operated by the Groveland Ranger District of Stanislaus National Forest (209/962-7825). In addition, several privately operated campgrounds are found here, including a few good camps for RVs.

One bugaboo for site-seekers to watch out for: many guidebooks mention a series of three camps along the Tuolumne River called Lumsden, Lumsden Bridge, and South Fork. Although it appears from the map that these camps are five miles off Highway 120, their access road is dirt and gravel, extremely steep and narrow, and very dangerous to drive, especially at night. One wrong move and your car plunges hundreds of feet into the Tuolumne River. Do not attempt this road unless you have a high-clearance vehicle and you're in the mood for adventure. And know that if you plan to drive in to Yosemite in the morning, you'll spend at least 20 minutes crawling back out the camp access road, then another 30 minutes on the highway. This is an awful lot of trouble to go to for a campsite.

The campgrounds listed below are open in summer only and are arranged here according to their proximity to Yosemite's Big Oak Flat entrance on Highway 120. The first listing is the closest to the park.

GROVELAND AND VICINITY

Yosemite Lakes

You don't have to be a member of the Thousand Trails/NACO club to camp at Yosemite Lakes (3119 Hardin Flat Rd., Groveland, 209/962-0121 or 800/533-1001, www.1000trails.com), although this is a rarity in this nationwide chain of campgrounds. The camp opened its doors to the general public because of its unbelievably fortunate location just five miles from the Big Oak Flat entrance. Not surprisingly, it gets a lot of overflow traffic when the park's campgrounds are full.

The campground is really a small city, with 254 full-hookup RV sites and 130 tent sites, plus rental trailers, cabins, yurts, and just about every other kind of lodging. The South Fork of the Tuolumne River runs through the preserve and is ideal for swimming, fishing, and even trying your luck at panning for gold. You can participate in all kinds of organized activities here, if you wish: horseback riding, kids' activities, kayak rentals, mini-golf, volleyball, and so forth. The best aspect of all this development is that the camp store is open until midnight on summer nights. Tent sites are $21; full-hookup RV sites are $28. If you are a member of Thousand Trails/NACO, you'll save 20 percent on your overnight fees. Located 18 miles east of Groveland or five miles west of the Big Oak Flat entrance; turn south off Highway 120 at Hardin Flat Road.

Dimond O

A medium-sized campground that is meticulously managed by a concessionaire for the U.S. Forest Service, Dimond O (34660 Evergreen Rd., Groveland) is a short and easy drive off Highway 120. It's just far enough so that it is peaceful and quiet amid the incense-cedars and ponderosa pines, but still only 10 minutes from Yosemite's Big Oak Flat entrance. This camp also makes a convenient choice if you plan to visit Hetch Hetchy (10.5 miles away), or if you want to fish in the Middle Fork of the Tuolumne River. A day-use area for the river is only 0.5 mile from the camp. Those who prefer a sense of certainty will like that

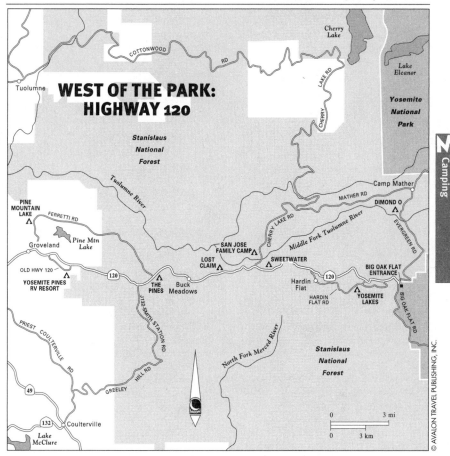

WEST OF THE PARK: HIGHWAY 120

Tuolumne

COTTONWOOD RD

Cherry Lake

Lake Eleanor

Stanislaus National Forest

LAKE RD

CHERRY

Yosemite National Park

Tuolumne River

Camp Mather

MATHER RD

DIMOND O

PINE MOUNTAIN LAKE

FERRETTI RD

Pine Mtn Lake

Groveland

CHERRY LAKE RD

Middle Fork Tuolumne River

EVERGREEN RD

SAN JOSE FAMILY CAMP

LOST CLAIM

SWEETWATER

BIG OAK FLAT ENTRANCE

OLD HWY 120

YOSEMITE PINES RV RESORT

120

THE PINES

Buck Meadows

J-132-SMITH STATION RD

Hardin Flat

120

HARDIN FLAT RD

YOSEMITE LAKES

BIG OAK FLAT RD

PRIEST COULTERVILLE RD

HILL RD

North Fork Merced River

Stanislaus National Forest

49

GREELEY RD

132

Coulterville

Lake McClure

0   3 mi

0   3 km

© AVALON TRAVEL PUBLISHING, INC.

Camping

Dimond O's sites are reservable May–September. Small trailers and RVs are fine here. The 38-site camp has drinking water, picnic tables, fire grills, and vault toilets. The fee is $16 per night; reserve in advance by phoning 877/444-6777, or visit www.reserveusa.com. Located 5.6 miles north of Highway 120 on Evergreen Road. The Evergreen Road turnoff is 25 miles east of Groveland or one mile west of the Big Oak Flat entrance.

Sweetwater

It isn't easy to get a site here on summer weekends, since this clean and pleasant campground is less than 10 miles from the Big Oak Flat entrance and directly on Highway 120. Still, if you don't have reservations anywhere, give this one a try. The 13 sites are set in an open, sparse pine forest, so you won't get much screening between sites, although the tall trees provide some shade. The best and most private site is number 3. Overall, this camp's location is excellent, and the restrooms are usually clean. One disadvantage is that the camp usually closes by mid-September, even though Highway 120 stays open through Tioga Pass for at least another month. This makes very little sense, since the camp is set at 3,000 feet in elevation and there is no

RVS IN YOSEMITE

You've got your rig and you're ready to roll. But when you get to Yosemite, you can't find a suitable place to camp to save your life. A vacation that is supposed to be made easier by having a self-contained vehicle suddenly turns out a whole lot harder than you planned. Here are a few guidelines for camping with your RV in Yosemite:

- All Yosemite campgrounds have RV sites except for Camp 4 in the Valley, and Tamarack Flat and Yosemite Creek on Tioga Road.
- There are no RV hookups at any campground in Yosemite.
- RVs over 40 feet long are not permitted in Yosemite Valley.
- RVs over 35 feet long are not permitted in other areas of the park.
- Generator use is permitted only between 7 A.M. and 7 P.M.
- RV dump stations are found at Upper Pines Campground, Wawona Campground, and Tuolumne Meadows Campground.

Many RVers find they have an easier time staying outside of the park in private campgrounds that are designed for big rigs. Try one of these:

Yosemite Lakes, 18 miles east of Groveland off Highway 120

Yosemite Pines RV Resort, three miles east of Groveland off Highway 120

Pine Mountain Lake Campground, 2.5 miles off Highway 120 in Groveland

Indian Flat RV Park, off Highway 140 in El Portal

KOA Yosemite-Mariposa, 6.5 miles east of Mariposa off Highway 140

High Sierra RV and Mobile Park, off Highway 41 in Oakhurst

Mono Vista RV Park, off U.S. 395 in Lee Vining

danger of pipes freezing. The camp has drinking water, picnic tables, fire grills, and vault toilets. The fee is $15 per night; no reservations are taken. Located on the north side of Highway 120, 15 miles east of Groveland or nine miles west of the Big Oak Flat entrance. For information, contact Stanislaus National Forest at 209/962-7825.

San Jose Family Camp

Located right next to the Yosemite Riverside Inn, the San Jose Family Camp (11401 Cherry Lake Rd., Groveland, 209/962-7277 or 408/277-4666) is a good choice for—you guessed it—families. The surprising part is that you don't have to live or work in San Jose, California, to be able to camp here, even though the camp is run by San Jose Parks and Recreation. San Jose residents get a discount on the fees, however. This is an organized camp that provides tent cabins for all guests—you aren't allowed to set up your own gear. The tent cabins have steel bed frames with mattresses, a wooden bookcase, and a small table with two benches. Rates at the camp are per-person and include lodging, three meals per day, and a variety of organized activities. Typically the camp is open from mid-June to late August for individual campers (before and after that period, it is available for rent to large groups). Rates are $45–60 for adults, and $25–45 for children aged 6–15. You must make reservations in advance to stay here.

Lost Claim

Lost Claim Camp is quite similar in appearance to nearby Sweetwater Camp, although a bit smaller and more protected from the sight and sound of Highway 120. With only 10 sites, you'll be quite lucky if you get a spot here on summer weekends. Tall pine trees and manzanita provide some shade and screening for the sites.

Unfortunately, like the other National Forest camps in this area, Lost Claim is shut down by mid-September each year, even though Yosemite's high country is open for another month. The camp has drinking water, picnic tables, fire grills, and vault toilets. The fee is $12 per night; no reservations. Located on the north side of Highway 120, 12 miles east of Groveland or 12 miles west of the Big Oak Flat entrance. (It's less than a mile west of the Rim of the World Vista Point.) For information, contact Stanislaus National Forest at 209/962-7825.

The Pines

This Stanislaus National Forest campground works on several counts: It's just off Highway 120, only 15 miles from the Big Oak Flat entrance to Yosemite. It's located behind the Forest Service ranger station, where you can get all the information you need for exploring the surrounding area. Its 12 sites are level and roomy enough; even small RVs can find a spot in here. And it's open year-round. But the Pines Campground doesn't work on a few counts: The sites are spaced much too close together and do not have enough foliage around them to provide privacy. Most are open and fully exposed to the sun, so don't expect the ice to hold up in your cooler in summer. Don't plan on sleeping late in your tent, either—you'll get baked.

Still, if you are driving into the park late at night and you just need a spot to lay your head, this camp will do the trick. The camp has drinking water, picnic tables, fire grills, and vault toilets. The fee is $12 per night; no reservations. A 40-person group site is a short distance from the individual sites; reserve the group site by phoning 877/444-6777, or visit www.reserveusa.com. Located on the south side of Highway 120, 7.5 miles east of Groveland or 15 miles west of the Big Oak Flat entrance station. Turn right at the Ranger Station sign and drive 0.5 mile to the campground. (Another road enters this camp one mile farther east on Highway 120.) For information, contact Stanislaus National Forest at 209/962-7825.

Yosemite Pines RV Resort

RVers are going to like the fact that Yosemite Pines RV Resort (20450 Old Highway 120, 209/962-7690 or 800/368-5386, www.yosemitepines.com) has hookups—something you won't find in the park itself. Dusty hikers are going to like the fact that this resort has showers. With 216 sites ($17–32), this place feels more like a small city than a campground. It comes complete with a mini-market, pool, laundry, clubhouse, and cabin and RV rentals. Kids will have plenty of fun here: there's a petting zoo, pony rides, hay rides, gold panning, a gold mine tour, and campfire storytelling. Yosemite Pines even offers a free shuttle bus to local attractions. It's a 22-mile drive to the Big Oak Flat Yosemite entrance. You'll find "old" Highway 120 two miles east of Groveland off "new" Highway 120.

Pine Mountain Lake Campground

This campground (13500 Rocky Point Drive, off Ferretti Road, Groveland, 209/962-8615, www.pinemountainlake.com) is little known except by people who know someone who lives in the Pine Mountain Lake development. It's only a couple miles from Highway 120 in Groveland and makes an easy, dependable layover on your way into the park. The camp is open all year, and you can even get a reservation in advance if you wish by phone or online. The 49 sites are spaced far enough apart in a pleasant pine, oak, cedar, and manzanita forest. Showers are available for $5. It's clean, safe, and, most important, you can almost always find a site. Hookups and a dump station are available for RVs.

The camp has drinking water, picnic tables, fire grills, and flush toilets. The fee is $15 for tents and $25 for RVs. From Highway 120, turn left on Ferretti Road, drive 2.5 miles to Rocky Point Drive, turn left and enter the camp.

West of the Park: Highway 140

On Highway 140 in the 30-mile stretch before the park entrance, public campground pickings are slim: a couple of Forest Service camps and a small cluster of BLM camps located on the Merced River. Fortunately, free enterprise comes to the rescue with a handful of privately operated camps and RV parks that can save the weary traveler from a long night in the car.

The campgrounds listed below are arranged according to their proximity to Yosemite's Arch

Rock entrance on Highway 140. The first listing is the closest to the park.

EL PORTAL
Dirt Flat and Dry Gulch

These two small campgrounds have less than a half-dozen sites each, but what sweet sites they are—set alongside the north bank of the Merced River just a few miles from the Arch Rock

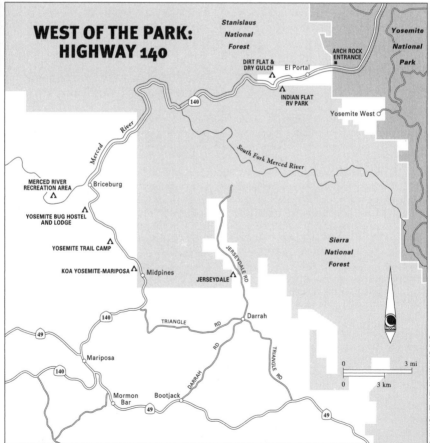

WEST OF THE PARK: HIGHWAY 140

entrance to Yosemite. Many Yosemite-bound drivers cruising down Highway 140 see the campsites on the far side of the river but have no idea how to get to them. The only way is to cross over the river on the Foresta Bridge, then backtrack (head west) on Incline Road. The two separate camps are located just off an old stretch of the Yosemite Railroad Grade. You park your car in a central parking lot, then walk a few hundred feet to your chosen site. The camps have picnic tables, fire grills, and vault toilets. Bring your own drinking water. The fee is $17 per night; reserve by phoning 877/444-6777 or visit www.reserveusa.com. To reach the camps, turn left (north) on Foresta Road off Highway 140 in El Portal, near Redbud Picnic Area. Cross the river bridge, then turn left (west) and drive 1.4 miles to the camps, which are 0.2 mile apart.

Indian Flat RV Park

Location is everything, and Indian Flat RV Park (9988 Highway 140 in El Portal, 100 yards east of Cedar Lodge, 209/379-2339) has it. Located eight miles from the Arch Rock entrance to Yosemite, this is the closest private campground to Yosemite Valley. You can pull out of Indian Flat in the morning and be gazing at Half Dome a half hour later. The RV park has full water and electric hookups (these are also the closest hookups to Yosemite Valley), tent sites, group sites for large groups, and even some low-budget cabin rentals if you forgot your tent. It would be wise to make a reservation if you plan to stay here in the busy summer months. The camp has 40 sites in the $30–35 range. Even the tent sites are $20–30, but what you are paying for is location.

MIDPINES AND VICINITY

Merced River Recreation Area

Yosemite travelers either know about these three Bureau of Land Management–run campgrounds (209/966-3192) along the Merced River, or they don't. Most don't, because they aren't located right along Highway 140; they are on the north side of the river and can only be accessed by a side road and an old suspen-

sion bridge. The bridge is behind the Briceburg Visitor Center, a fairly prominent structure on a mostly desolate stretch of the highway. Understand that while these campgrounds are unknown to most Yosemite travelers, they are very well known to river rafters, many of whom use Railroad Flat as a take-out point. If you are visiting during the main part of the Merced rafting season (May–July), your chance of getting one of the 30 tent or RV sites here is slim. As soon as the river level drops, usually by late July, your chances improve greatly.

This is a lovely area along the river, with plentiful opportunities for hiking and fishing, but it gets terribly hot in summer. Also, if you are driving in late at night and are unfamiliar with the camp access road, exercise great caution. The dirt road is narrow and drops off steeply into the Merced River. Fortunately it's an old railroad grade, so it's pretty smooth and fairly level. The three camps, **McCabe Flat, Willow Placer,** and **Railroad Flat,** are each about one mile apart (the first camp is 2.5 miles from the Briceburg Visitor Center; the last camp is almost five miles from it). The camp has picnic tables, fire grills, and vault toilets. Bring your own drinking water. $10 fee; no reservations. Located 12 miles east of Mariposa off Highway 140. Turn left at the visitor center, cross the suspension bridge, then turn left and drive 2.5 miles to the first camp.

Yosemite Bug Hostel and Lodge

Amid a wide array of other possible lodgings, the Yosemite Bug Hostel (6979 Hwy. 140, 9.5 miles east of Mariposa, 209/966-6666 or 866/826-7108, www.yosemitebug.com) has pleasant, forested tent sites for $17 per night for two people. If you like a predominantly younger crowd, you'll enjoy this place. The cafe serves surprisingly good food three meals a day, and the staff is very knowledgeable about recreation options inside and outside Yosemite. Expect a drive of about 45 minutes into Yosemite Valley.

Yosemite Trail Camp

Located in Midpines, 24 miles from Yosemite's El Portal entrance, Yosemite Trail Camp

(6617 Hwy. 140, eight miles east of Mariposa, 209/966-6444; www.yosemitetrailcamp.com) is a private campground with tent cabins already set up, and tent sites where you can erect your own tent. The camp caters mostly to groups—church retreats, scouting activities, and the like—but is happy to house individuals, too. The tent cabins are just like the ones in Yosemite—white canvas structures with a wood floor and cots. Rates are $25 for two people in a tent cabin or $20 for a tent site for two. Groups are charged $10 per person. If you drive in to Mariposa late at night, check the registration sign at the main building. If a group hasn't taken over the whole place, there will be a sign informing you that tent cabins with a green flag are empty, and you can put your payment in the night drop slot. Now that's easy. Or, to ensure yourself a space, phone ahead for reservations.

KOA Yosemite-Mariposa

It's true that if you've seen one KOA, you've seen them all. Still, this is a particularly clean and well-managed KOA (6323 Hwy. 140, 6.5 miles east of Mariposa, 209/966-2201 or 800/562-9391). The RV parking lot is filled up with the shiny white "vacations on wheels" all summer long, with RVers happy to find full water and electric hookups. Tent campers won't enjoy that the sites cost $28 and are spaced close together and within inches of the KOA's driveway, but if you're desperate for a spot on your way into the park, you'll probably keep your complaints to yourself. Also, due to possible fire danger, you can't light a campfire in this campground, although charcoal barbecues are permitted. Full-hookup RV sites are $38–42. Like most KOAs, this one has a full range of amenities: restrooms with hot showers, laundry, swimming pool, fish pond, real train caboose with video games inside, TV lounge with Yosemite videos, and a small store. It's a 25-mile drive to the Arch Rock entrance, so figure on a full hour to reach Yosemite Valley.

Jerseydale

If there is a "secret" campground within an hour of Yosemite Valley, Jerseydale (off Jerseydale Road in Midpines, 559/877-2218 for the Sierra National Forest) is it. The camp is nine miles off Highway 41 near Mariposa, and if you didn't know it was here, you'd never go looking for it. For people driving in to Yosemite on Highway 140 late at night, this camp can be a lifesaver. You can almost always find a spot, even on holiday weekends. The camp is small and pleasant, with eight sites tucked into a tall pine forest. It has everything a camper needs: drinking water, picnic tables, fire grills, and vault toilets. And it has one thing a camper really appreciates: no fee. Located on Jerseydale Road near its junction with Triangle Road. From Mariposa, drive five miles northeast on Highway 140 to Triangle Road. Turn right and drive six miles to Darrah and Jerseydale Road. Turn left and drive three miles to the camp on the left.

South of the Park: Highway 41

On the south side of the park, you'll find several Forest Service campgrounds in Sierra National Forest (North Fork Ranger Station, 559/877-2218). These provide great options for campers driving into the park from Fresno and Los Angeles. Some of the camps require a drive of up to 12 miles from the main highway, but your reward for this effort is a peaceful campsite in a beautiful setting. If you are planning to center your vacation on activities in Yosemite Valley,

you will face a drive of 90 minutes one-way from the most distant of these camps. However, if you are planning your Yosemite vacation around the southern section of the park (Wawona, the Mariposa Grove, and the hiking trails on Glacier Point Road) you'll be conveniently situated.

The campgrounds listed below are arranged according to their proximity to Yosemite's south entrance on Highway 41. The first listing is the closest to the park.

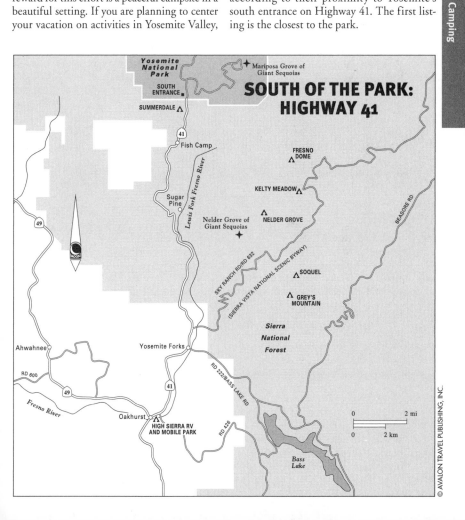

Camping

FISH CAMP

🆅 Summerdale

This campground might as well be in Yosemite—it's that close to the park border. Located within a mile of the park's southern entrance, it is just as popular as the campgrounds within the park. Sites are reservable on the Forest Service reservation system, and you'll definitely need a reservation in the summer months, except midweek. The 30-site camp is set at 5,000 feet in elevation on Big Creek. Many campers spend summer afternoons cooling off in the stream's deep, clear swimming holes. Fishing is good, too, but it gets better the farther you go from camp. Although the camp is a bit close to the busy highway, and road noise can be noticeable, nobody who scores a spot here ever complains. The camp has drinking water, picnic tables, fire grills, and vault toilets. The fee is $17 per night; reserve by phoning 877/444-6777 or visit www.reserveusa.com. Located one mile north of Fish Camp on the west side of Highway 41.

OAKHURST

High Sierra RV and Mobile Park

The High Sierra RV Park (40389 Hwy. 41, Oakhurst, 559/683-7662, www.highsierra rv.com) isn't located in the High Sierra; it's in downtown Oakhurst, about a block from the highway at an elevation of 4,000 feet. But never mind. It's only 16 highway miles to Yosemite's southern gates, and rates are a reasonable $18–28 for tent and RV sites (full hookups available), most which are packed together like sardines. A small stream runs through the property, although it goes dry by mid-July. If you want to visit Bass Lake, it's only eight miles away. All the usual amenities of a well-equipped RV park are offered here: restrooms, showers, laundry, phone hookups, cable TV, picnic tables, and an RV dump. Campers in tents will not be happy here, but RVers will find everything they need.

SIERRA NATIONAL FOREST

Nelder Grove

If you're a fan of giant sequoias, you've come to the right campground. At this camp, you can put up your tent right next to one of several giant sequoia stumps left from an old logging operation, then take a hike through the nearby Nelder Grove of Sequoias (where fortunately the trees are whole, not stumps) on the Shadow of the Giants Trail. The camp is pleasant, shaded, peaceful, and, best of all, free. Its 10 sites have picnic tables, fire grills, and vault toilets. Bring your own drinking water. To reach the camp, go six miles east on Sky Ranch Road (Road 632, which becomes Road 6S10), off Highway 41 five miles north of Oakhurst. Turn left at the sign for Nelder Grove, then follow the signs for two miles to the camp. For information, call the Sierra National Forest at 559/877-2218.

Soquel

This is one of the few reservable campgrounds in this semi-remote region of Sierra National Forest south of Yosemite. The 11 sites have most of the basics: picnic tables, fire grills, and vault toilets. You must bring your own drinking water. The fee is $13–26 per night; reserve by phoning 877/444-6777 or visit www.reserveusa.com. To reach the camp, go seven miles east on Sky Ranch Road (Road 632, which becomes Road 6S10), off Highway 41 five miles north of Oakhurst. Turn right on Road 6S40 and drive one mile to the camp.

Grey's Mountain

It's a nine-mile drive from Highway 41 to this campground, some of it on a rough dirt road, but the reward for this trek is one of 20 campsites near a wonderful swimming hole on Willow Creek. The fee is $14–26 per night. Grey's Mountain Campground is lined with firs and incense-cedars. It has picnic tables, fire grills, and vault toilets, but no water, so bring your own. To reach the camp, go seven miles east on Sky Ranch Road (Road 632, which becomes Road 6S10), off

Highway 41 five miles north of Oakhurst. Turn right on Road 6S40, signed for Soquel Campground, then drive two miles to Grey's Mountain Campground. For information, call the Sierra National Forest at 559/877-2218.

Kelty Meadow

If you're traveling with your horse, there's room for both of you at Kelty Meadow Campground. Make a reservation at one of 10 sites and you'll wind up with the double-wide kind, big enough for you and your horse trailer. Kelty Creek flows right by the campground, which is a great bonus for anglers. The fee is $13–28 per night; reserve by phoning 877/444-6777 or visit www.reserveusa.com. To reach the camp, go 10 miles east on Sky Ranch Road, (Road 632, which becomes Road 6S10), off Highway 41 five miles north of Oakhurst.

Fresno Dome

This lovely campground comes with a bonus: It's only 2.5 miles from the trailhead for the easy, scenic hike to the top of Fresno Dome. Its 12 sites have picnic tables, fire grills, and vault toilets. You must bring your own drinking water. The fee is $13–28 per night. It will take you a while to drive from this camp back to the highway and up to Yosemite, but the surrounding area is so pretty you probably won't mind. To reach the camp, go 11 miles east on Sky Ranch Road (Road 632, which becomes Road 6S10), off Highway 41 five miles north of Oakhurst. Take the left fork signed for Fresno Dome Campground and drive 1.5 miles to the camp. If you don't like the choices at Fresno Dome Campground, you can always continue another mile to Little Sandy Campground, which offers similar amenities. For information, call the Sierra National Forest at 559/877-2218.

East of the Park: U.S. 395

On the east side of the park, several Forest Service campgrounds in Inyo National Forest (760/647-3044, www.r5.fs.fed.us/inyo) are within a few miles of the Tioga Pass entrance to Yosemite. Most are first-come, first-served; no reservations are taken. Mono County Public Works Department (760/932-5440) operates a campground in Lundy Canyon, just north of Lee Vining.

Whereas the National Park Service shuts down the park's four campgrounds on Tioga Road by mid-September, the National Forest and Mono County camps stay open through October. Since Tioga Road is usually open until November 1, visitors get an entire extra month to camp and play in Yosemite's high country.

The campgrounds listed below are arranged according to their proximity to Yosemite's Tioga Pass entrance on Highway 120. The first listing is the closest to the park.

INYO NATIONAL FOREST

Tioga Lake

The sight of granite-lined Tioga Lake is a real stunner for drivers coming through Tioga Pass.

Managed by the U.S. Forest Service, the high mountain lake is regularly stocked with rainbow trout by the Department of Fish and Game; it provides a good place to fish from shore or from a float tube. The lake and its small campground are plainly obvious from Highway 120, as visitors drive to and from Yosemite through Tioga Pass. The campground here at 9,700 feet leaves a little to be desired, however: It is 100 percent visible from the road, and none of the sites have much, if any, protection from the wind that frequently whips off the surface of the lake. Of the camp's 14 sites, you don't want to get stuck with number 3. It is set just below a curve in Highway 120, and if some idiot decides to throw something out the window as he drives by, you'll get hit on the head. (Think it won't happen? It already has.) On the other hand, sites 13 and 14 are the most coveted of the lot, because they are right on scenic Tioga Lake's edge. Highway or no highway, this is some world-class scenery. The camp has drinking water, picnic tables, fire grills, and vault toilets. The fee is $15 per night; no reservations. Located on Highway 120, 1.2 miles east of the

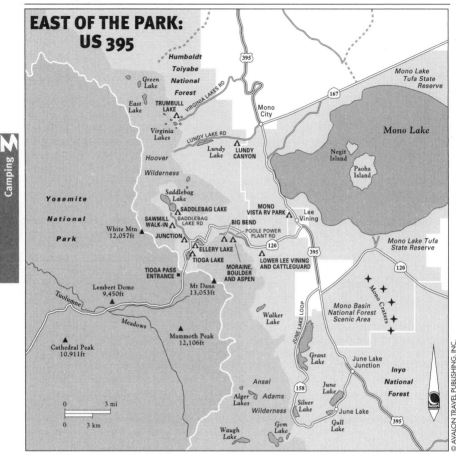

EAST OF THE PARK: US 395

Tioga Pass entrance station and 11 miles west of U.S. 395. For information, contact Inyo National Forest at 760/647-3044.

Junction

Junction Campground is a stone's throw from Tioga Pass Resort and just 2.5 miles east of Tioga Pass. It's located near the junction of Saddlebag Lake Road and Highway 120, 2.5 miles east of the Tioga Pass entrance station and 10 miles west of U.S. 395. For proximity to Yosemite—and to Saddlebag Lake, Tioga Lake, Ellery Lake, and all the recreation opportunities of Lee Vining Canyon—it doesn't

get much better than this. A trail to the historic mining settlement of Bennettville leads right from camp. Sites 12 and 13 are the best of the lot, but anything from number 6 on up is pretty good. The camp is first-come, first-served, and because of its proximity to Yosemite, it is filled almost all summer long. One advantage to staying here instead of at the other nearby Forest Service camps is that you can walk over to Tioga Pass Resort for meals if you don't feel like cooking. The camp has picnic tables, fire grills, and vault toilets. Bring your own water. The fee is $9 per night; no reservations. Located 50 yards north on Saddlebag

Lake Road off Highway 120, 2.5 miles east of the Tioga Pass entrance station and 10 miles west of U.S. 395. For information, contact Inyo National Forest at 760/647-3044.

Ellery Lake

Ellery Lake is a gorgeous blue, granite-lined gem of a lake just three miles west of the Yosemite border, at an elevation of 9,600 feet. Surrounded by jagged granite peaks, it provides excellent fishing and bird-watching opportunities and is managed by the same Forest Service concessionaire as nearby Tioga Lake. Its 14 campsites are filled up almost all the time. Most people think they get a look at the whole campground as they cruise past on the road, but in fact they don't. The best sites (numbers 9–14) are set off from the main cluster of sites by a 100-yard access road, which places them in a spot not easily seen from the highway. Lucky campers who snare these sites are insulated from the road noise. Site number 13 even has a view of the lake. The camp is first-come, first-served, but unless you happen to pull in just as someone else is leaving, it's nearly impossible to get a site

here until after mid-September, when the summer vacation crowds disperse. It has drinking water, picnic tables, fire grills, and vault toilets. RVers will like that the parking slips are paved. The fee is $15 per night; no reservations. Located on Highway 120, three miles east of the Tioga Pass entrance station and 9.5 miles west of U.S. 395. For information, contact Inyo National Forest at 760/647-3044.

Sawmill Walk-In

The camping gods are smiling down on you if you manage to get a spot at Sawmill Walk-In Camp, the most beautiful campground in or near Yosemite. The camp is unusual in every way: It is a walk-in camp, which means you park your car in a central parking lot and then walk about 100 to 200 yards to your campsite. You can't see the cars from the campground, so once you're at your site, the setting seems very much like what you would get while backpacking. The 10 sites are spaced remarkably far apart—as much as 50 yards or so—so camping here is a more private experience than traditional car camping. You aren't

Camping

© ANN MARIE BROWN

Lakeside campsites are a rare commodity, but you'll find a few of them at Ellery Lake and Tioga Lake, just outside Tioga Pass.

forced to listen to other campers' conversations or noisy snoring. And every campsite has a drop-dead gorgeous view of the High Sierra countryside—mountain peaks, a subalpine meadow with a stream running through it, scattered stands of conifers, and the like. If there is camping in heaven, this is what it looks like. The camp has picnic tables, fire grills, and vault toilets. Bring your own water. The fee is $9 per night; no reservations. Located 1.5 miles north on Saddlebag Lake Road off Highway 120, 2.5 miles east of the Tioga Pass entrance station and 10 miles west of U.S. 395. For information, contact Inyo National Forest at 760/647-3044.

Saddlebag Lake

Saddlebag Lake is the highest lake you can drive to in California, at 10,087 feet in elevation, in a stark landscape high above the tree line. A major entrance point for the Hoover Wilderness that leads into the spectacular 20 Lakes Basin, it is a favorite spot of both hikers and anglers. With all that, it's only slightly more than five miles outside Yosemite's borders, sealing its fate as a well-known and popular destination all summer long. The lake has two separate campgrounds—one called Saddlebag Lake for individuals and families and one called Trailhead for large groups of up to 25 people. The two camps are spaced far enough apart so that if there is a Boy Scout troop at Trailhead, you won't feel like you're a part of their campout. Both camps are less than a 100-yard walk to the lakeshore. Sites 16 and 18 of the regular camp have a view to die for, perched high above Saddlebag Lake, with an unobstructed vista. The camp is usually open June–mid-October. It has drinking water, picnic tables, fire grills, and vault toilets. The fee is $15 per night; reservations are taken for the Trailhead group camp only; phone 877/444-6777 or visit www.reserveusa.com. Located 2.8 miles north on Saddlebag Lake Road off Highway 120, 2.5 miles east of the Tioga Pass entrance station and 10 miles west of U.S. 395. For information, contact Inyo National Forest at 760/647-3044.

▶ Moraine, Boulder, and Aspen Campgrounds

These three campgrounds are located side by side along Poole Power Plant Road, just off Highway 120 in Lee Vining Canyon, nine miles from Yosemite. When you take the turnoff, the sign points you left to Moraine and right to Boulder and Aspen campgrounds. Take your pick of these three camps at 7,500 feet in elevation; they're all good, they cost the same, and all three usually have a couple of sites open, even on summer weekends (no reservations are taken). For years, these camps were run rather informally by Mono County, but as of 2005 their management has been transferred to the U.S. Forest Service. This has led to better services at the campground and a higher fee of $14 per night.

Moraine and Boulder are the closest to the turnoff—useful if it's late at night and you just want to land a spot. Aspen is a 1.5-mile drive down Poole Power Plant Road; it may be the prettiest of the camps, but it's a close call. It does have the advantage of a drinking water faucet located at the entrance to the camp; the other two camps have no drinking water. Many of the sites at the three camps are quite primitive, with only a rock fire ring and picnic table. (But since the Forest Service has just taken over the place, this may change.) For now, you may want to bring your own grill to set on top of the fire for cooking.

Not all sites are equal, even within each campground. A good number are true fantasy sites located right on Lee Vining Creek, with complete privacy thanks to aspens and foliage, great views of nearby granite peaks, and the pleasant sight and sound of the creek flowing right by your tent. (The creek is a fine spot to try your luck fishing.) Other sites would be best described as a makeshift fire ring on the edge of a dirt parking lot. But never mind. At least you found a peaceful place to sleep, and you're only a couple minutes from Yosemite. The camps have picnic tables, fire rings, and vault toilets. Aspen Campground has a water faucet; for Moraine and Boulder Camps, bring your own drinking water. Located on Poole

Power Plant Road off Highway 120, nine miles east of the Tioga Pass entrance station and 3.5 miles west of U.S. 395. For information, contact Inyo National Forest at 760/647-3044.

Big Bend

Big Bend Campground is exactly the same as, and simultaneously completely different from, its neighboring campgrounds in Lee Vining Canyon. The setting makes it the same: It is tucked into an aspen and Jeffrey pine forest along beautiful Lee Vining Creek and nestled in the heart of Tioga Pass, with granite walls towering thousands of feet overhead. But while the other nearby camps are on the primitive side, Big Bend is deluxe. That is either a minus or a plus, depending on your point of view. On the one hand, RVs have a much easier time of it here because the sites are paved and comparatively easy to pull in and out of. The vault toilets are kept spic and span and are even lit up at night. But, since this camp is run like a business, the 17 sites are too close together. Still, nobody seems to mind. The scenery is lovely, the creek fishing is excellent, and Yosemite is close at hand. Site number 17 is a favorite; it's the only one that doesn't have any direct neighbors. The camp has drinking water, picnic tables, fire grills, and vault toilets. The fee is $15 per night; no reservations. Located on Poole Power Plant Road off Highway 120, nine miles east of the Tioga Pass entrance station and 3.5 miles west of U.S. 395. Drive 2.5 miles west on Poole Power Plant Road to the camp. For information, contact Inyo National Forest at 760/647-3044.

Lower Lee Vining and Cattleguard Campgrounds

Two more in the series of campgrounds located in Lee Vining Canyon, these two camps are separate from the three on Poole Power Plant Road. Each has its own entrance from Highway 120, a quarter mile apart. The camps have much in common with their cousins up the road but have fewer sites. Sites 1 and 2 in Cattleguard Camp are away from the creek and out in the open in the sagebrush plains, which pro-

vides a stunning open view of Tioga Pass but little or no protection from the wind. A couple of huge Jeffrey pines provide a little shade. These are good bets if you are pulling in late at night and don't care about trying to cook a meal or have a campfire. If you do want to cook, bring your own grill to set on the rock fire ring or learn how to prepare dinner on a stick. Lower Lee Vining Camp's best sites are numbers 11–13; they are right on the stream. Ditto for sites 8–10 in Cattleguard. The camps have picnic tables, fire rings, and vault toilets. Bring your own drinking water. The fee is $14 per night. No reservations. Cattleguard Camp is located 9.5 miles east of the Tioga Pass entrance station and three miles west of U.S. 395. Lower Lee Vining Camp is located 0.3 miles east of Cattleguard. For information, contact Inyo National Forest at 760/647-3044.

LEE VINING AND VICINITY

Mono Vista RV Park

If you've been hiking for days and you desperately need a shower, you'll kiss the ground at Mono Vista RV Park. Located on the north end of Lee Vining, this private, clean, and pleasant campground has full hookups for RVs ($22–28), grassy tent sites ($15), and—the best part—hot showers for a mere $2. Buy your shower tokens at the office (each one is good for five minutes; buy two if you're really dirty). A laundry and dump station are also available. The camp is right by the highway and close to town, so although it isn't optimal for scenery, it's very convenient. The Tioga Pass entrance station is a 14-mile drive. The camp has picnic tables, fire grills, and flush toilets. Reserve a site if you wish by phoning ahead (760/647-6401), or just pull in and take your chances. Located on the north end of Lee Vining on U.S. 395, one mile north of the Hwy. 120 junction.

Lundy Canyon Campground

Lundy Canyon Campground is a favorite among fishermen and people who like peace and quiet. The camp is set in a dense grove of aspens, and

Camping

you haven't lived until you've seen these trees decorated in their autumnal colors. Camping here in late September or October can seem like paradise. Choose between sites right along the stream and others in a mixed aspen and Jeffrey pine forest. Because this camp is located a few miles north of the town of Lee Vining, it gets missed by the vast majority of Yosemite visitors. You can almost always find a spot here. Lundy Lake is a couple of miles up the road. A small store is found there, as well as boat rentals, cabins, and trailheads for hiking.

Although they look terribly tempting, the first 10 "sites" in Lundy Camp are signed as day use only, so keep pushing back into the canyon until you reach the overnight sites. The 54 sites have picnic tables, fire rings (some sites have grills, some only rock rings), and vault toilets. Bring your own drinking water. The fee is $8 per night; cash only—no checks accepted. No reservations. Located 2.7 miles west on Lundy Canyon Road, seven miles north of Lee Vining on U.S. 395. For more information, contact Mono County Department of Public Works at 760/932-5440.

Trumbull Lake Campground

This may be too far for most Yosemite visitors to go to find a good campground, but then again, for what it has to offer, maybe not. An efficiently managed and well-run campground right on Trumbull Lake and a short distance from the two Virginia Lakes, Trumbull Lake Campground is ideal for people who like to fish. It's also ideal for those who like high mountain scenery—the camp is set at 9,500 feet, in a fairly dense lodgepole pine forest. A nearby trailhead leads into the Hoover Wilderness.

The 45-site camp is a 20-minute drive from Lee Vining if you need supplies. If you're lucky, the little store at neighboring Virginia Lakes Resort might just have what you need. The small café gives you an option for breakfast or lunch if you don't feel like firing up your camp stove. It will take about 45 minutes to make the 29-mile drive to Yosemite's Tioga Pass entrance. A big selling point here is that sites are reservable in advance from July through the first week in September.

The camp has drinking water, picnic tables, fire grills, and vault toilets. The fee is $13 per night; reserve in advance by phoning 877/444-6777 or visit www.reserveusa.com. Located 5.9 miles west on Virginia Lakes Road, 12 miles north of Lee Vining on U.S. 395.

Dining

California is known as a state with a taste for good food. From the beachside fish taco stand in L.A. to the Napa wine country château serving haute cuisine, Californians have developed a passion for eating fresh, creative food and are proud of it. This makes the experience of dining in Yosemite National Park that much harder to swallow.

It's not that there isn't good food in the park; it's just that you have to pay a lot to get it. If you can afford to eat at the Ahwahnee, you can be assured that your palate will be tempted, teased, and pleased. If you can afford to eat only at Curry Village, you can be sure your belly will be full—but that's all. Fortunately, a few of the park's other dining establishments (the Wawona Hotel, the Yosemite Lodge Mountain Room) find a balance somewhere between the two extremes, but they don't come

at a bargain. Bring your checkbook, or maybe your personal banker, if you plan to eat many quality meals in the park.

On the other hand, the gateway towns just outside the park's borders offer some pleasant surprises in the realm of good food. Towns as small as Lee Vining and Fish Camp, where you might expect to find nothing better than an average burger joint, provide a selection of top-notch dining opportunities well worth the short drive out of the park. These restaurants are listed according to their proximity to Yosemite's Big Oak Flat, Arch Rock, South, or Tioga Pass entrances. In each instance, the first listing is the closest to the park.

One caveat: Restaurant hours vary not just seasonally but also at the whim of the establishment, so call ahead if you have your heart set on eating at any one place.

Yosemite's Best

N Ahwahnee Dining Room: The 37-foot-high ceilings at the Ahwahnee create an aptly grand setting for the restaurant's elegant food and first-rate service. Dinner costs a small fortune; breakfast and lunch are more affordable (page 186).

N Yosemite Lodge's Mountain Room Restaurant: The Mountain Room keeps getting better year after year. If you are craving a solid, square meal after a long hike, this is your best bet in Yosemite Valley, unless you have an excess wad of bills to burn at the Ahwahnee (page 187).

N Wawona Hotel Dining Room: The menu and food are dependably good at the Wawona, and everything tastes better when you are seated in the hotel's large-windowed dining room. Check out the chandeliers made from the cones of sequoia trees (page 188).

N Tuolumne Meadows Grill: There's nothing fancy about the Tuolumne Meadows Grill, but if you don't mind standing in line to get a hamburger, it will be the best hamburger you've ever had. Ditto for the breakfasts, the veggie burgers, the soft-serve ice cream, and the chili. It's hard to know if it's really the food that's so good, or the Tuolumne Meadows scenery (page 189).

N White Wolf Lodge: Score a seat outside on the deck of the White Wolf Lodge restaurant and you can gaze at a pine-bordered meadow while you nosh on a hearty breakfast or dinner (page 190).

Ahwahnee Dining Room

N Tioga Gas Mart/Whoa Nellie Deli: No discussion of food in Yosemite would be complete without mentioning the food at the Tioga Gas Mart. The gas station isn't even in Yosemite, it's about 10 miles east of Tioga Pass, but you won't mind the drive. This is the place to be on Saturday night, or just about any time you are hungry. Grilled salmon salad or lobster tacquitos at a gas station in the mountains? You'll find them here (page 199).

Inside Yosemite

YOSEMITE VALLEY

Without fail, the busiest spots in Yosemite Valley are always the places that serve food. You'd think that people came to this national park just for the chance to eat. Or perhaps the lines at the Valley's dining establishments are just because Yosemite's sweet mountain air makes visitors hungry.

The Valley offers a wide range of food choices, and most are several steps up from blackened hot dogs and marshmallows at your Upper Pines campsite. There are four central areas of the Valley where you can find food: Yosemite Lodge, Yosemite Village, Curry Village, and the Ahwahnee Hotel. If you're visiting in the summer season, you'll find that most food places are open until 9 P.M. (the Ahwahnee serves food until 10 P.M.). This means if you're up at Glacier Point for sunset during the

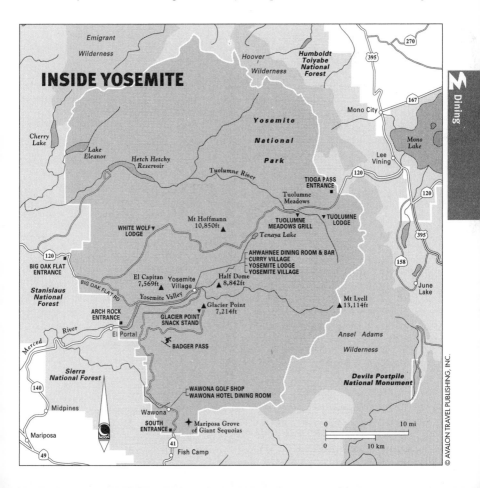

INSIDE YOSEMITE

Dining

© AVALON TRAVEL PUBLISHING, INC.

long days of July and August, you may have trouble getting back down to the Valley in time for dinner. Plan carefully. For current hours of operation of all the in-park restaurants listed below, phone 209/372-1001.

Ahwahnee Dining Room

If you like formality and have money to blow, don't hesitate for even a moment: Get a reservation for dinner at the Ahwahnee. Ties and jackets are apropos, although in recent years the Ahwahnee has slackened its dress code, allowing men entrance to the dining room *sans* coat and tie (collared shirts and long pants are still required; no jeans, tennis shoes, or T-shirts). Considering the high quality of the food and the accompanying astronomical prices, formal attire seems fitting here. If you're dying to eat at the Ahwahnee but you're not the dress-up type, show up for breakfast or lunch, when even shorts and hiking boots are not frowned upon in the grand Ahwahnee Dining Room.

Just how grand is the Ahwahnee? The dining room fills a space 130 feet long and has towering 37-foot-high ceilings. It contains dozens of wrought-iron chandeliers and enormous picture windows that look out on classic Valley scenery. Four hundred and fifty people can eat dinner under its open-beamed roof all at once, with plenty of room to spare. Bounded by massive timbered walls, the place looks downright medieval.

Best of all, the food tastes as good as the dining room looks. The menu changes constantly, but certain well-loved items show up frequently, like salmon Ahwahnee stuffed with Dungeness crab. In recent years the chef has placed a greater emphasis on organic and sustainably harvested ingredients, creating signature dishes such as pan-roasted line-caught halibut and grilled wild king salmon. Entrées are in the $25–50 range; appetizers are $12 and up. Lavish Sunday brunches are legendary ($35). Breakfast and lunch are not only the most casual meals of the day, they are also the most affordable ($13–18). Keep in mind that if you want to eat at the Ahwahnee at any meal other than breakfast, reservations are a must.

The Ahwahnee is open year-round; for reservations phone 209/372-1489.

Ahwahnee Bar

You can still eat at the Ahwahnee even if your budget won't stretch far enough for the Dining Room. The Ahwahnee Bar serves light lunch and dinner fare, cocktails, and a sampling of fine liquors year-round. If you're hungry or just curious, the Ahwahnee version of "light fare" includes items like smoked Sonoma duck Cae-

FINDING ESPRESSO IN YOSEMITE

I'm hooked, you're hooked—we're all hooked. It used to be that only visiting Europeans yearned for a morning sip of espresso or a flavorful cappuccino, but now almost every Yosemite visitor is a card-carrying Starbucks devotee. Let's face it, a couple of shots of the strong stuff first thing in the morning can really help you make those 100 switchbacks to Upper Yosemite Fall.

Where can you find a decent latte in the park?
• Degnan's Cafe in Yosemite Village
• The Coffee Corner in Curry Village
• The vending machines at the Big Oak Flat entrance (but it's not very good)
• The Wawona Hotel Dining Room
• The Ahwahnee Dining Room (but you can't afford it)

What about outside of the park?
• La Casa Loma River Store midway between Groveland and the Big Oak Flat entrance
• Pony Expresso in Mariposa
• Yosemite Coffee Roasting Company in Oakhurst
• Tioga Gas Mart in Lee Vining
• Tioga Pass Resort in Lee Vining (espresso cart is usually parked outside)
• Tioga Baking Company in Lee Vining
• Latte Da Coffee Cafe in Lee Vining

sar salad and French onion soup ($10–20). In the drink category, martinis are a specialty. In the evening at the Ahwahnee Bar, a pianist will tinkle the black and whites with graceful melodies while you and your loved one sip a glass of port and share a dessert. On summer days, the bar opens up to an outside deck near the Ahwahnee swimming pool. Put on your best sunglasses, order a salad and a tonic water, sit out on the deck, and pretend you're a movie star.

Yosemite Lodge's Mountain Room Restaurant

The Mountain Room (209/372-1281, open year-round, dinner only) is the fanciest of a handful of dining choices at Yosemite Lodge; it's a real sit-down dining room with classic entrées like steaks, seafood, and pasta dishes ($17–26). Try to get a table near the windows so you can enjoy the spectacular view. If you have dinner before dark, you can gaze up at Yosemite Falls while you eat. Diners show up wearing everything from high heels to hiking boots, so come as you are. Steaks are a popular item here, but several kinds of pasta, fish, and chicken are available also (try the mountain trout or tequila shrimp). Vegetarians can always find a pasta dish to suit their tastes. One of the most interesting food items is the bread sticks, which are shaped like elongated triangles. It's a wonder none of the waitstaff has ever had an eye poked out by one of them. Everything on the menu is à la carte, so if you order an appetizer, an entrée, and dessert, you can easily spend $100 for two people without even opening the wine list.

Yosemite Lodge's Food Court

If you have a lot of mouths to feed, and some of those mouths are of the age where they'll eat only macaroni and cheese, you might do well at the Food Court, a glorified cafeteria. You go through the lines, fill up your tray with your food choices, then pay the cashier and find a seat in the large dining room. Because almost everything is à la carte, you may get a small shock when you find out the combined total of the items on your tray. Dinner entrées like chicken with rice and vegetables, or spaghetti with meatballs, cost about $10. A soda will set you back $2. Dessert is another $4. Still, the Food Court is fast, it has a dependably large selection, and it's open for three meals a day. The guy who flips the pancakes here is a legend in his own time. The Food Court serves breakfast, lunch, and dinner year-round.

Yosemite Lodge's Garden Terrace

One more choice over at Yosemite Lodge is the Garden Terrace, situated in between the Mountain Room and the Food Court. Open in summer only, the Garden Terrace serves all-you-can-eat lunch and dinner buffets ($9–14), with soups, salads, baked goods, and carved meats.

Yosemite Lodge's Mountain Room Bar

If you just want a snack, and maybe a libation to go with it, try the Yosemite Lodge, which has a comfortable cocktail lounge with good seating, sports on TV, and a spacious bar. Those who don't imbibe can still order from the abbreviated menu, which includes a few sandwiches, shrimp cocktail, a cheese and fruit sampler, and chef's salad. Everything costs about $5–9. The Mountain Room Bar is open afternoon and evenings year-round.

Curry Village

Curry Village offers a variety of food options (it would be a stretch to call any of it "dining.") In the cheap-and-easy category, you can always get a burrito at the walk-up **Curry Taqueria** window (summer only), or a pizza at the **Pizza Patio**. Eat them at one of the picnic tables outside from noon to 11 P.M. Beer is served at the tavern with the unimaginative name **Curry Bar** right next door.

If you'd prefer to eat indoors, there's a cafeteria-style buffet at **Curry Pavilion** for breakfast ($10) and dinner ($12), but no lunch. The food is nothing to write home about, but there's a huge variety. It's all-you-can-eat, so come hungry if you want to get your money's worth. Breakfast is 7–10 A.M.; dinner is 5:30–9 P.M. in summer.

And for caffeine and sugar addicts, there's the **Coffee Corner** located right next to the Pavilion. Lattes, mochas, ice cream, and assorted pastries and snacks are available all day, 6 A.M.–10 P.M. in summer.

Note that before Memorial Day and after Labor Day the restaurants' hours usually decrease, and some of the restaurants close. For example, in the winter the Pavilion breakfast buffet is not usually served; instead, limited breakfast items are available at the Coffee Corner. The free Yosemite newspaper has all the latest details on opening and closing times for food establishments.

Yosemite Village

Degnan's Deli (open year-round, summer hours from 6 A.M.–7 P.M., $3–5) is a busy place at lunchtime. Sandwiches are the big sell here ($5–6)—the staff will make them to your specifications or you can choose from a premade selection. The deli also does good business in packaged salads, chips, snacks, and drinks, and a fair trade in bowls of soup and chili in winter. **Degnan's Cafe** used to be a fast and convenient place that served individual pizzas, hamburgers, and the like, but has recently been converted to an ice cream and coffee outfit open from spring to fall, much to the chagrin of longtime Yosemite visitors. It also has a few bakery items to go with your espresso and some meager lunch items. If you want real food you have to go upstairs to **The Loft** for pizza and salads, but it's only open in the summer noon–9 P.M. The Loft is an employee hangout in the winter months, which might be the reason for the pool tables that seem so grossly out of place in a national park. The pizza is good, though, and includes a variety of toppings from chicken and pesto to olives and pepperoni. You can wash it down with beer, wine, or sodas.

One more summer-only choice in the Village is **The Village Grill,** (open April–Oct., 11 A.M.–5 P.M., $5–9) which serves hamburgers, veggie burgers, fish sandwiches, and other fast food items. You can eat out on the deck.

WAWONA AND GLACIER POINT

Aside from the grocery store, there are only three places to find food in the southern area of the park, and two are open in summer only (Glacier Point Snack Stand and Wawona Golf Shop). If you strike out for food here, your best bet is to head south on Highway 41 to the town of Fish Camp (45 minutes from Glacier Point and 10 minutes from Wawona).

Wawona Hotel Dining Room

You might think you have to stay at the Wawona Hotel to have the chance to eat here, but this is not the case. Everybody is welcome. The only problem is that the food is dependably delicious, the restaurant is popular, and they don't take reservations unless your party is eight people or more (209/375-1425, open daily in summer, usually weekends only in winter). Waiting around for a dinner table is not so bad, however; the hotel lobby is always hopping with live piano music and guests making merry. Its walls are lined with wonderful, historic black-and-white photos of the Wawona area.

Typical dinner entrées at the Wawona Hotel Dining Room include roast duck, prime rib, and freshly caught trout ($13–20). Like so many places in and around Yosemite (although it's a mystery why), French onion soup is a popular item. You don't have to dress up for dinner here, although some people do.

Breakfast is served 7:30–10 A.M. (Sunday brunch is 10 A.M.–1:30 P.M.). Lunch is 11:30 A.M.–1:30 P.M., and dinner is 5:30–9 P.M. In the summer months, a barbecue is held on the lawn each Saturday evening, complete with corn on the cob, hamburgers, steak, potato salad, and plenty more good ol' American food.

Glacier Point Snack Stand

A hot dog never tastes so good as when you are standing on Glacier Point, looking out at Half Dome and all its granite neighbors. Yes, sir, this is one tasty hot dog. The baked potatoes hit the spot, too. Perhaps the biggest draw here, especially on warm summer days, is the wide selection of ice cream bars. Open 9 A.M.–4 P.M. daily in summer only.

Wawona Golf Shop

Snacks and sandwiches are available for the hungry golfer (or anybody else) who wanders into this area of the Wawona Hotel complex, called the Annex. While you're ordering some lunch, you can rent a set of clubs or ask the pro for advice on your swing. Open daily in summer only.

TIOGA PASS AND TUOLUMNE MEADOWS

There's nothing quite like high mountain air to work up an appetite. Fortunately, there are a couple good places on Tioga Road to replenish those calories lost to hiking and recreating.

Tuolumne Meadows Grill

When Tioga Road closes for the winter, seasoned Yosemite visitors dream of the day that Tuolumne Meadows will be free of snow and they can once again eat buckwheat pancakes from the Tuolumne Meadows Grill. This place really knows how to fill up a hiker's empty stomach. The Grill's breakfasts are highly acclaimed, particularly the pancakes and the biscuit sandwiches filled with egg, bacon or sausage, and cheese. For lunch, the Grill serves hamburgers, veggie burgers, chicken sandwiches, and fries. Everything is tasty and in the $5 range. Soft ice cream cones go over big on warm summer days.

The Grill is located in Tuolumne Meadows, right alongside the road. You can't miss it. Summer hours are approximately 8 A.M.–6 P.M., but this seems to vary somewhat according to the whim of whoever is working each day.

Tuolumne Lodge

A part of the Yosemite High Sierra Camp Loop, Tuolumne Lodge has a big white tent situated right on the Tuolumne River that serves as its dining room. The cheerful space (they've even put curtains on the tent's windows) is open to everyone, not just people staying at the lodge. You will need reservations for dinner, however, because it's a deservedly popular spot (209/372-

Dining

Get a reservation for dinner at White Wolf Lodge and enjoy a meal inside or out on the porch of this charming wooden building.

© ANN MARIE BROWN

8413, dinner 6–8 P.M., summer only). Typical entrées are $10–18 and usually include trout, chicken, steak, hamburgers, and a vegetarian dish. This is fun, communal-style dining, in which you're sure to get to know your neighbors at the table. Breakfast (hotcakes, French toast, or eggs and toast, for $5–7) is served 7–9 A.M. Takeout lunches are available, but you must place an order the night before.

White Wolf Lodge

Similar to the Tuolumne Meadows Lodge, White Wolf is a part of the High Sierra Camp Loop and its restaurant is open in summer to all. Breakfast is served 7:30–9:30 A.M. and dinner 6–8 P.M. Dinners include New York steak, fish of the day, chicken, a vegetarian entrée, and hamburgers. Prices are reasonable ($10–16 for entrées), the wine list is more extensive than you'd expect in the high country, and the setting can't be beat, whether you eat inside in the small and cozy dining room or outside on the deck. Dinner reservations are advised; phone 209/372-8416. A takeout lunch is available noon–2 P.M. Breakfast consists of made-to-order omelettes, blueberry pancakes, fried potatoes, and the like. White Wolf Lodge has been in operation every summer since 1927, so they know how to do things right.

West of the Park: Highway 120

GROVELAND AND VICINITY

Evergreen Lodge

Unless they happen to have booked a cabin there, most visitors to Yosemite don't even know the Evergreen Lodge (33160 Evergreen Rd., Groveland, 209/379-2606, entrées $15–28) exists, let alone realize that it has an outstanding restaurant on the premises, just nine miles off Highway 120 on the way to Hetch Hetchy. This newly expanded cabin resort doesn't look like the kind of place where you'd find a quality restaurant, but it is. The menu changes often, but frequent highlights include the roasted duck and seared ahi.

49er Restaurant at Yosemite Ridge Resort

One of the best things about the 49er Restaurant (7589 Hwy. 120, Buck Meadows, 209/962-6877) is its dependability: It's open seven days a week, 7 A.M.–9 P.M. May–Oct., somewhat shorter hours Nov.–April. Located right next door to the Yosemite Westgate Lodge in the tiny hamlet of Buck Meadows, the restaurant serves good old-fashioned American roadhouse food: New York steak, hamburgers with all the trimmings, hot dogs, french fries, spaghetti and meatballs, and so on.

Newly opened in 2005, the 49er is a godsend for hungry travelers leaving Yosemite. Just one caveat: Don't check your cholesterol level after you eat here.

La Casa Loma River Store

If you've already left Groveland and you're on your way into the park when the urge for espresso strikes, you're in luck: La Casa Loma (Hwy. 120 and east end of Ferretti Road, Buck Meadows) offers a caffeine fix 6 A.M.–6 P.M. April–September. The store/cafe is well known to river rafters, who meet at this spot on their way to adventures on the Wild and Scenic-designated Tuolumne River. A few sandwiches, breakfast items, and snacks are available, plus the latest word on how gnarly the rapids are.

PJ's Cafe and Pizzeria

The last food establishment as you drive east out of Groveland to Yosemite, PJ's Cafe (18986 Hwy. 120, Groveland, 209/962-7501) knows how to keep things simple. It doesn't accept credit cards. It doesn't serve fancy food. It is open a reliable seven days a week for breakfast, lunch, and dinner. Its dinner specials include comfort food like Yankee pot roast, country-fried steak, and fried chicken ($8). For lunch, order a tuna or chicken salad sandwich, cheeseburger, or turkey club ($5–8). For breakfast, all the standard egg dishes are available. There aren't any surprises here, and maybe that's why the locals like this place so much. After 4 P.M. each day, you can also order from the pizza menu.

Two Guys Pizza

Located just a short distance off Highway 120, Two Guys Pizza (18955 Ferretti Rd., Groveland, 209/962-4897) serves up a variety of pizzas and calzones, oven-baked subs, and appetizers like buffalo wings and salads. This is a good bet if you need to feed the whole family

without breaking the budget. Locals love this place but most tourists never find it, because it isn't located on the main drag in Groveland (turn north on Ferretti Road and drive about 200 yards).

The Groveland Hotel's Victorian Room

Delicious and well-prepared food is surprisingly affordable at the Groveland Hotel's Victorian Room (18767 Hwy. 120, Groveland, 209/962-4000). The small, semi-formal dining room is graced by outstanding California

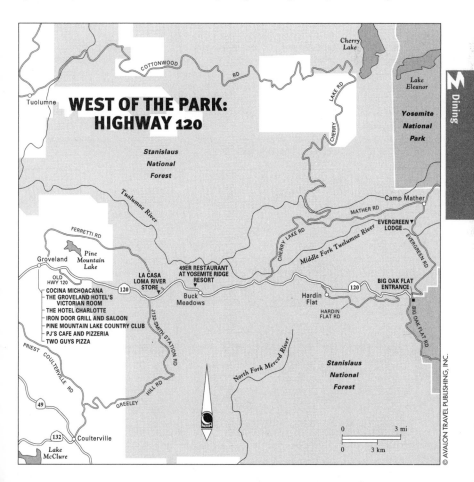

© AVALON TRAVEL PUBLISHING, INC.

Dining

cuisine. Although the ocean is a long way from Groveland, the hotel's crab cakes are out of this world. Ditto for the ahi tuna. The food is beautifully presented here—try the queen salad, which looks like a royal crown—and tasty to boot. This is the sort of food you might expect to find in San Francisco but wouldn't even hope for in Groveland. Entrées range $15–30. If a good pairing of food and wine matters to you, know that the Victorian Room was awarded the *Wine Spectator* Award of Excellence for its well-chosen wine list.

Iron Door Grill and Saloon

Next door to the Groveland Hotel is the infamous Iron Door Saloon (18761 Main St., Groveland, 209/962-6244, www.iron-door-saloon.com, open Sun.–Thurs. 11 A.M.–9 P.M., Fri.–Sat. until 10 P.M.), home of what is reputed to be the oldest saloon in California. (It opened its doors in 1850, but there is a bar in Bolinas, California, which may have been open longer. The debate rages on.) In addition to the hard stuff, the saloon offers up a long list of microbrews and selections from California foot-

hill wineries. Adjacent to the saloon is the Iron Door Grill, where you'll find delicious casual food, from salads to buffalo burgers to cheese steak sandwiches ($5–8). You don't have to sit in the bar to eat—a separate dining room is available, lined with black-and-white photographs of Groveland and the Hetch Hetchy area in the old days. Take the kids along and enjoy a treat from the next-door soda fountain—a sarsaparilla, hot fudge sundae, or old-fashioned malt.

The Hotel Charlotte

The locals cheered when new owners took over the Charlotte (18736 Hwy. 120, Groveland, 209/962-6455) in 2003 and re-opened its dining room after a long absence. The restaurant is homey and informal, befitting of the historic building it occupies. The food is dependably delicious—try the artichoke chicken or the shrimp scampi; both have legions of devoted fans. Hosts Lynn and Victor and their staff are as friendly and accommodating as you'll find anywhere. Entrées are in the $12–22 range.

© ANN MARIE BROWN

The Iron Door Saloon in Groveland, established in 1852, is reputed to be the oldest saloon in California.

Cocina Michoacana

If you're craving a little salsa on your way into Yosemite, Cocina Michoacana (18730 Hwy. 120, Groveland, 209/962-6651) will graciously provide it. The kitchen cooks up huevos rancheros, chorizo, and other specialties for breakfast ($5) and a wide variety of tamales, enchiladas, tacos, taquitos, and sopes for lunch and dinner ($7–10). The dining room is windowless and a bit dark, but the food is tasty. Chips and salsa are delivered to your table as soon as you sit down.

Pine Mountain Lake Country Club

Pine Mountain Lake is a resort community, complete with a golf course and lake, just 1.5 miles outside of Groveland. Residents enjoy all the amenities of a resort combined with close proximity to Yosemite. The Pine Mountain Lake Country Club (12765 Mueller Dr., 209/962-8638, www.pinemountainlake.com, entrées $15–20) is a safe bet for a typical country club dinner: prime rib, filet mignon, lobster tail, or trout amandine. Early-bird specials are available before 6 P.M. Buffets are frequent occurrences. Breakfast and lunch are an affordable $5–8 (Sat.–Sun. only). The dining room has a wide view of the golf course, which is quite scenic. Sit outside on the deck if the weather is nice. Open Wednesday through Sunday only, dinner is served 5 –8 P.M. and until 9 P.M. Fri.–Saturday.

West of the Park: Highway 140

EL PORTAL

Yosemite View Lodge Restaurants

This place can save you from going to bed without supper if you come back late from a hike in Yosemite Valley. Whereas the Valley's restaurants stop serving food at 9 P.M., Yosemite View Lodge's two restaurants, only two miles from the Arch Rock entrance (11136 Hwy. 140, El Portal, 209/379-2183), stay open until 10 P.M. in summer. The main dining room serves standard American dinners: chicken marsala, New York steak, broiled salmon, burgers, and vegetarian entrées ($13–18). Appetizers like calamari strips, potato skins, and buffalo wings ($5–8) are popular. For a more affordable way to fill your belly, try the pizza at the neighboring Little Bear's Pizza Restaurant. The main dining room also has a breakfast buffet 7–11 A.M. ($10), and box lunches are available. Carry them with you into the park.

Cedar Lodge Restaurants

The food here is nothing to get excited about. The hours, on the other hand, are worth singing a few praises over. Located eight miles from the Arch Rock entrance (9968 Hwy. 140, El Portal, 209/379-2316), Cedar Lodge has two restaurants—one is a Mexican diner with tostadas, burritos, enchiladas, and the like ($2–10), and the other is a traditional American dining room that serves pepper steak, prime rib, pork ribs, chicken breast, and trout ($17–20). A variety of pastas are a little more affordable, in the $13–15 range, and a children's menu is offered. But the really good news is that between the two restaurants, one is always open at every hour between 7 A.M. and 10 P.M., so you can get food whenever you want it. For night owls, the bar/lounge stays open until 1:30 A.M.

MIDPINES

Yosemite Bug Lodge Cafe

When you make the drive up the dirt road to the Yosemite Bug Hostel, it's hard to guess what to expect. The dusty path brings you to a parking lot below a cluster of buildings, and a short walk leads you to the registration building and the Recovery Cafe (6979 Hwy. 140, Midpines, 209/966-6666, open daily). Walk up to the kitchen counter, order your food, then settle in on the glassed-in deck to enjoy your meal, or have a seat in the college dorm–style lounge and read a book while you eat.

Dining

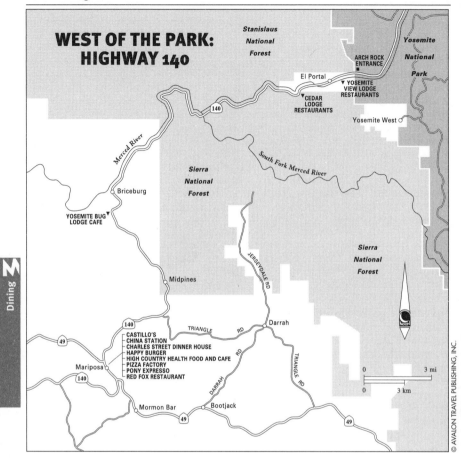

WEST OF THE PARK: HIGHWAY 140

Stanislaus National Forest

Yosemite National Park

ARCH ROCK ENTRANCE

El Portal

▼ YOSEMITE VIEW LODGE RESTAURANTS

▼ CEDAR LODGE RESTAURANTS

Yosemite West

140

Merced River

Briceburg

Sierra National Forest

South Fork Merced River

YOSEMITE BUG LODGE CAFE ▼

Midpines

JERSEYDALE RD

Sierra National Forest

MOON

140

TRIANGLE RD

Darrah

49

CASTILLO'S
CHINA STATION
CHARLES STREET DINNER HOUSE
HAPPY BURGER
HIGH COUNTRY HEALTH FOOD AND CAFE
PIZZA FACTORY
PONY EXPRESSO
RED FOX RESTAURANT

DARRAH RD

RD

TRIANGLE RD

Mariposa

140

0   3 mi

0   3 km

Mormon Bar

Bootjack

49

49

© AVALON TRAVEL PUBLISHING, INC.

Dining

The cafe is as casual as it gets. The menu is a mix of American and Mediterranean foods, with a variety of beers on tap and a selection of good wines. Breakfast (muesli, wheat pancakes, omelettes) runs $4–6 and is available 7–10 A.M.; lunch (a variety of sandwiches) is available until 3 P.M. and costs $6. Dinner is served 6–9 P.M. and features an ever-changing menu with entrées like steak, Caribbean stir-fry, roast pork, trout, and salmon ($9–13). Vegetarians always have plenty of choices here. Christmas and Thanksgiving feasts are a big event—reserve way in advance if you want to be a part of the fun.

MARIPOSA

High Country Health Food and Cafe

Mariposa is such an Old West–style meat-and-potatoes town that you wouldn't expect to find a health food store within the city limits. But High Country Health Food (49er Shopping Center, 5176 Hwy. 49 North, Mariposa, 209/966-5111) is doing a fine business in town. Its cafe, located next to its store, prepares a wide selection of sandwiches (both with meat and without), freshly made salads and quiches, and daily specials. Everything is in the $5–6 range. This is perfect "to go" food to take with you into Yosemite. Open Mon.–Sat. 9 A.M.–3 P.M.

Happy Burger

The local high school sports teams come to Happy Burger (5120 Hwy. 140, Mariposa, 209/966-2719) after every game, so that tells you what kind of place this is. The burger joint boasts "the Sierra's largest menu" and it may be true. Breakfast items are $2–5 and include that Mariposa favorite, biscuits and gravy. Burgers are $3–6, and they aren't just the usual beef kind—try an ostrich or buffalo burger. Add fries and an all-you-can-drink soda for another couple of bucks, and you can feed the whole family with a 20-dollar bill. Check out the ceiling while you eat—it is completely lined with record albums, most of which date to the groovy 1970s.

Red Fox Restaurant

From the outside, the Red Fox (5114 Hwy. 140, Mariposa, 209/966-7900) looks like little more than a modest diner, but the menu and meals may surprise you. The owner/chef presents savory dishes prepared from fresh ingredients and prides himself on being the first restaurateur to bring a variety of fresh seafood to Mariposa. Dinner entrées include Pacific salmon, rainbow trout, filet mignon, and meatloaf ($10–16). Lunch includes a Monte Cristo sandwich or linguini with portobello mushrooms ($8–11). Several good wines are available by the glass, including some local Gold Country vintages. The cheesecake is quite popular, and, again, it's not what you'd expect—a slice of traditional cheesecake is wrapped in a wonton and deep-fried until it gains a crispy, golden crust. There go the arteries.

Charles Street Dinner House

It's worth saving a couple hours on a trip into or out of Yosemite for dinner at the Charles Street Dinner House (5043 Hwy. 140, Mariposa, 209/966-2366, www.charlesstreetdinnerhouse.com, Wed.–Sat. 5 P.M. to closing). This restaurant serves a baked potato so big you will want to split it with a friend. It comes alongside a delicious range of hearty entrées, like breast of duck, pork loin, New Zealand rack of lamb, shrimp scampi, and brochette of beef ($13–20). The French onion soup is a winner ($5). Owner-chef Ed Uebner was previously the chef at Chicago's famous Drake Hotel. His wife and daughters run the cozy dining room, filled with antiques and mining relics, and create a friendly, comfortable atmosphere. Eating here feels a lot like having dinner at a friend's house (if your friend happened to live in the Old West). You even get to see the family's photographs on the restaurant walls. The *Fresno Bee* voted this restaurant the best dinner house in the Central Valley area.

Pony Expresso

Mariposa finally got an espresso joint in 2000, and a very charming one at that. Although short on floor space, Pony Expresso (5040 Hwy. 140, Mariposa, 209/966-5053) offers a wide variety of coffee drinks, smoothies, and flavored ices, plus soups and sandwiches. A few tables in the pleasant, sunlit building give you a place to read the newspaper while you drink your morning libation.

China Station

A little to-go Mandarin or Cantonese food could be just the thing to tide you over for the ride into Yosemite. China Station (5004 Hwy. 140, Mariposa, 209/966-3889) serves Mariposa's only Asian food, featuring a big menu filled with chow meins, fried rice, chop suey, and stir-fried meats and vegetables. The sizzling beef or chicken and the mu shu vegetables are good bets ($7–9). Unlike so many restaurants that come and go, China Station has been alive and well in Mariposa since 1985.

Pizza Factory

With all the tourist activity in Mariposa in the summer months, this pizza joint is always hopping. Families will like the fact that the whole gang can eat here for about $30. Pizza Factory (5005 Fifth St., Mariposa, 209/966-3112) offers everything you'd expect: pizza, calzone, pasta, salad bar, and sandwiches.

Dining

Castillo's

This popular Mexican restaurant (4995 Fifth St., Mariposa, 209/742-4413) is located one block off the main drag and is open for lunch and dinner only. Castillo's is designed for lingering, with a cheerful, comfortable din-ing room that has been open since 1955. The carne asada is revered throughout the foothills. Vegetarians will like the wide variety of burri-tos, tostadas, and tacos without meat. Service is speedy and friendly, and two can eat a big dinner here for about $20.

South of the Park: Highway 41

FISH CAMP

Sierra Restaurant and Jackalope's Bar and Grill

The resort at Tenaya Lodge has two restaurants for its patrons and anyone else cruising along Highway 41: Sierra Restaurant and Jackalope's Bar and Grill (1122 Hwy. 41, Fish Camp, 559/683-6555). The Sierra Restaurant is a for-mal affair with high-priced entrées ($20–25) like seared ahi tuna and lamb medallions. Jack-alope's Bar and Grill is a more affordable (and more laid-back) choice. You can sit outside on the deck and order soups, salads, burgers, and pasta dishes, all well prepared by a chef with a talent for presentation. Prices are surprisingly reasonable for this high-priced resort ($8–15). Jackalope's is open 7 A.M.–11 P.M. daily, and these extended hours can be a real lifesaver if you are returning late from a sunset hike on Glacier Point Road or the Valley.

Narrow Gauge Inn

Make a reservation before showing up at the Narrow Gauge Inn (48571 Hwy. 41, Fish Camp, 559/683-6446). Well-prepared din-ners and a warm, inviting dining room have earned this restaurant its popularity. The res-taurant looks like a cross between a church (complete with stained glass windows) and a historic hunting lodge (complete with trophy animal heads on the walls). A couple of stone fireplaces, antiques, white linens, and oil lamps complete the decor. The menu is on the upscale side, with a few unusual entrées such as filet of ostrich ($23) and venison steak ($30). The sal-ads are first-rate; if you order the "hearty" size ($18), it's enough for dinner. This isn't a place for penny-pinchers, but the food is very good. Adjacent to the dining room is the Buffalo Bar, decorated with an authentic birch bark canoe and old Yosemite memorabilia.

OAKHURST AND VICINITY

El Cid Mexican Cuisine

El Cid (41939 Hwy. 41, Oakhurst, 559/683-6668) is an old favorite in the Oakhurst restau-rant scene. If you're in the mood for Mexican food, take your pick from nearly 100 combina-tions and dinner plates. Just reading the menu will take up a good portion of your evening. El Cid's margaritas are coveted throughout the southern Yosemite region. If you're more in the mood for drinking coffee, breakfast is served all day.

Yosemite Forks Mountain House

More than a dozen kinds of hamburgers are served at Yosemite Forks Mountain House (Hwy. 41 at Bass Lake turnoff, Oakhurst, 559/683-5191). What kind? Ortega burger, blue cheese burger, chili burger… you get the idea. There's also a long list of breakfasts and a selection of steaks. This is "mountain food," as they say. The price range swings about as wide as the menu itself—expect to pay any-where from $5–7 for a burger to $11–20 for a dinner entrée.

Sierra Sky Ranch Restaurant

The atmosphere is casual at Sierra Sky Ranch (50552 Road 632, Oakhurst, 559/683-8040; www.sierratel.com/skyranch), the foothill scenery is bucolic, and the steaks and seafood entrées come in hearty portions suitable for a hungry cattle rancher. Entrées are in the $15–20 range and include the usual steakhouse fare: steaks of all cuts and sizes, seafood, and a couple of chicken and pasta dishes. This 125-year-old ranch rents guest rooms and runs a steakhouse and saloon, Wed.–Sat., April–Dec. When the ranch is filled with guests, the restaurant serves breakfast, too. Otherwise, they don't bother.

Yosemite Coffee Roasting Company

Nothing hits the spot before a long day of hiking better than a double shot of espresso.

Hit the Yosemite Coffee Roasting Company (40879 Hwy. 41, Oakhurst, 559/683-8815) on your way into the park and you'll be stronger, faster, and a whole lot more cheerful. In addition to an array of coffee drinks, this place also makes great breakfast burritos, bagels with scrambled eggs, and lunch sandwiches. Everything is under $7.

Katie's Country Kitchen

Nothing fancy to be found here at the locals' favorite breakfast spot—just good, hearty food. Katie's (40470 Hwy. 41, Oakhurst, 559/683-

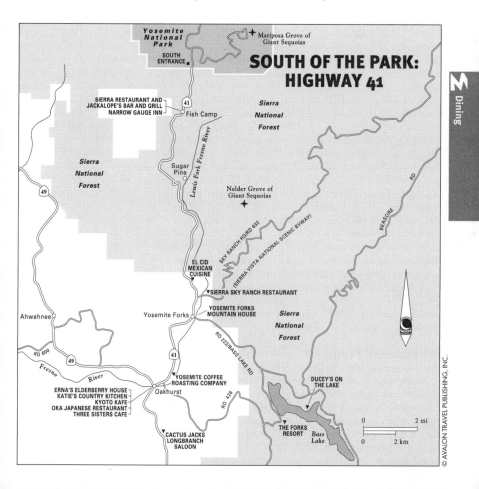

© AVALON TRAVEL PUBLISHING, INC.

8418) is the kind of place where the signature dish is biscuits and gravy, and everybody orders it. It's a cozy restaurant, with walls covered with memorabilia, collectible kitchen gadgets, and country art. Open daily 6 A.M.–2 P.M.

Kyoto Kafe

The buzzword here is Japanese "home" cooking, which means this isn't a sushi place. Kyoto (40423 Hwy. 41, Oakhurst, 559/692-2400) serves a variety of soups and ramens, as well as teriyaki entrées and a dozen different types of donburi (rice bowls). Prices are low enough to make it affordable to feed a family—entrées are $7–10.

Three Sisters Cafe

Count on the Three Sisters (40291 Junction Dr., Oakhurst, 559/642-2253; www.three sisterscafe.com, breakfast and lunch Wed.–Sun. 9 A.M.–1 P.M., dinner Wed.–Sun. 5–8 P.M.) for three first-rate meals a day, but not every day: it's closed on Monday and Tuesday. Still, it's worth getting out your Filofax to plan on having a meal here, considering the Three Sisters' eclectic and appetizing menu. What the menu calls "San Francisco–style cuisine" includes breakfasts like crab cake eggs Benedict or a smoked salmon and brie omelette ($8) and dinner entrées like crab-stuffed veal, or chicken and walnut crepes ($15–21). This is sophisticated food served in a casual, relaxed atmosphere. The restaurant isn't right on the main drag—it's tucked in between a bowling alley and the Sears building just off Highway 49, a block from its junction with Highway 41. And three sisters don't run the place, it's a husband-and-wife team with a long history of restaurant expertise in the San Francisco area.

Oka Japanese Restaurant

If you're craving sushi and feeling panicked because the ocean is several hundred miles away, relax. Order all the tekka maki you want at Oka (40250 Junction Dr., Oakhurst, 559/642-4850), or try the donburi (hot boiled rice topped with meat, fish, chicken, or vegetables) or udon noodle dishes. Plan on spending $15–20 per person here, no matter what you order.

Erna's Elderberry House

If you think there is no such thing as an upscale dining experience in Oakhurst, think again. Erna's Elderberry House (559/683-6800, chateausureau.com) is the restaurant connected to the fabulous Château du Sureau, and it shares the same elegant country estate atmosphere. Divided into three lavishly furnished dining areas, the restaurant features a six-course, fixed-price dinner each night. A typical dinner costs just shy of $100 per person and might include an array such as poached salmon, braised Sonoma duck, roast beef tenderloin, a salad of local greens, and dessert. To be able to consume six courses, you must show up hungry. The food is wonderful, and the restaurant itself is a feast for the eyes, with antique French furnishings and walls adorned with tapestries and original oil paintings. There are very few places like this anywhere in the United States, and certainly none other in the foothills near Yosemite.

Cactus Jacks Longbranch Saloon

Coarsegold is an Old West kind of town and Cactus Jacks (35364 Hwy. 41, Coarsegold, 559/641-2025, entrées $9–15) is an Old West kind of restaurant. Sit out on the patio and get messy eating baby back ribs, barbecued chicken, pulled pork, southern-style okra, or an array of other traditional smokehouse barbecue foods. Live music is offered every Friday and Saturday. A kids' menu features "kids' ribs" and miniature corn dogs. Whatever you order, bring an appetite. Cactus Jacks is also open for breakfast. If you're craving chicken-fried steak, this is your place.

BASS LAKE

Ducey's on the Lake

Ducey's (Pines Village, Bass Lake, 559/642-3121) is the classiest restaurant at Bass Lake, offering fine dining with a lake view. You won't find any entrées here for less than 20 bucks. If you have money to blow, go ahead and order the Australian lobster tail ($46). If you don't, stick to the appetizers—crab cakes, artichoke hearts, and calamari—which are all less than $10. Or eat at Ducey's Bar and Grill upstairs, which serves proletarian fare like burgers, soft tacos, and salads, all priced under $10. Breakfasts at Ducey's include the usual array of omelettes, plus French toast, eggs Benedict, and quiche.

The Forks Resort
There's nothing fancy about the cafe at The Forks Resort (39150 Road 222, Bass Lake, 559/642-3737), and maybe that's why it's so likable. You can come inside in your fishing or hiking clothes and sit down to a hearty stack of pancakes, a double cheeseburger, or a grilled ham and cheese. "The home of the world-famous Forks Burger" is the kind of place where the waitresses might all be named Thelma. It's right out of the 1950s. Your meal is only going to cost about six bucks, so go ahead and add on a milk shake or a root beer float.

East of the Park: U.S. 395

LEE VINING AND VICINITY

Tioga Pass Resort Cafe
The historic Tioga Pass Resort (Hwy. 120, two miles east of Tioga Pass, 209/372-4471, www.tiogapassresort.com) came under new ownership in 2001 and many changes were made. Nonetheless, inside the lodge's main building, everything is basically the same as it ever was at the Tioga Pass Resort Cafe. The small lunch-counter-style cafe still serves hearty, delicious, simple food 7 A.M.–9 P.M. as long as Tioga Pass Road is open. A favorite meal here is breakfast. It's just what you want in the mountains—big fluffy pancakes, oatmeal, and huge omelettes. An espresso cart outside the lodge makes a variety of coffee drinks. For lunch, choose from a variety of hot sandwiches, including Tioga burgers and tuna melts ($6–10). Different dinner specials are served every night of the week: chicken pot pie, ravioli with artichoke sauce, and beef stew ($12–13). For dessert, the resort's fresh-baked pies are legendary.

Saddlebag Lake Resort Cafe
The "cafe" at Saddlebag Lake Resort is more like a bait and tackle shop with a tiny lunch counter, but if you need some last-minute grub before heading out fishing or hiking for the day, you can get it here. Offerings are slim— sandwiches, breakfast items, chips, coffee, and sodas—but everything comes with a heaping serving of opinions about the weather and the fishing. The cafe is located at the end of Saddlebag Lake Road, which is two miles east of Tioga Pass.

ⓜ Tioga Gas Mart/Whoa Nellie Deli
It's not often that people plan on heading to a gas station to eat dinner, but in Lee Vining, hundreds of people do just that every day. The Tioga Gas Mart (junction of Highway 120 and U.S. 395, Lee Vining, 760/647-1088) isn't any ordinary gas station—it's also a huge gift shop and the home of the Whoa Nellie Deli, which makes truly outstanding fast food for breakfast, lunch, and dinner. Are you hungry? Imagine portions big enough for a pack of rock climbers. Are you craving fast food with real flavor? Try the lobster taquitos on a bed of black beans with tomatillo pineapple salsa ($10). Want a big meal? Order St. Louis ribs with huckleberry barbecue sauce, or buffalo meatloaf with port wine au jus ($14). The deli also makes a wide variety of sandwiches for lunch, plus veggie burgers, hamburgers, hot dogs, and pizza—by the slice or whole. Breakfasts include cowboy steak and eggs, omelettes, and Tioga egg sandwiches ($6–10). For the addicted, espresso drinks are available. The gas station/restaurant is open until 9 P.M. in summer.

Nicely's
Lee Vining's version of a Denny's, Nicely's (U.S. 395, Lee Vining, 760/647-6477, www.sierrahospitality.com) has acceptable but mostly uninteresting food for breakfast,

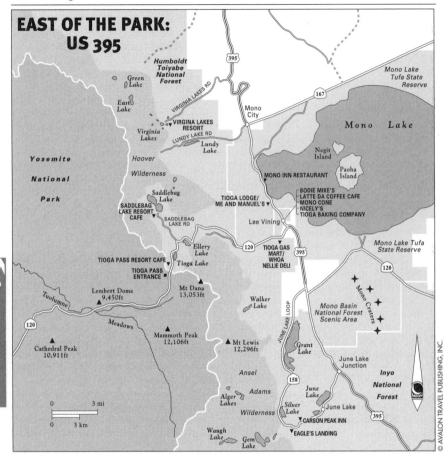

EAST OF THE PARK: US 395

lunch, and dinner. It goes along with the decor, which looks like it hasn't been updated since the 1940s. No matter, though; if you are hungry, you'll be happy to partake in the huge meals at this family restaurant. The pancakes are almost a foot in diameter. Even the menu is large. Lunch includes a variety of salads and hot sandwiches, including classics like the patty melt, chili size, or French dip ($7). Dinners in the $8–15 range include seafood, steaks, fried chicken, and pasta dishes. The homemade pies are always a hit. A children's menu is available. Nicely's is open 6 A.M.–10 P.M. all summer.

Bodie Mike's

Always a happening place on warm summer evenings, Bodie Mike's (U.S. 395, Lee Vining, 760/647-6432, www.sierrahospitality.com) is the place to go when you are craving a big slab of baby back ribs (beef or pork) or half a barbecued chicken ($12–16). Barbecue sandwiches are great for lunch ($7). Beer-battered onion ring appetizers are a real hit here, but after you eat them, you probably won't have room for dinner. A children's menu allows the little ones to eat for about $4.

Diners can sit indoors or outside on the deck overlooking Lee Vining's main drag, and drinkers can hang out at the bar. Besides the relaxed atmosphere and the finger-licking food, a highlight is a display by the cash register that shows two dozen different types of barbed wire, with their respective names. Choose your favorite and then go home and fence in those dang wanderin' cattle.

Latte Da Coffee Cafe

A cheerful little espresso cafe is a recent addition to the ages-old El Mono Motel in Lee Vining. The offerings at Latte Da (51 U.S. 395, Lee Vining, 760/647-6310) are limited—a variety of espresso drinks and exotic teas, plus a few tasty baked goods—but the atmosphere is everything. Buy a book at the neighboring Mono Lake Visitor Center and sit at one of the handful of tables for a good read and some local gossip.

Tioga Baking Company

A recent addition to Lee Vining is the Tioga Baking Company (U.S. 395, Lee Vining, 760/647-6470), a genuine fresh-from-scratch bakery that produces breads, muffins, and an assortment of pastries. The kitchen and the storefront are one and the same, so you can watch everything being made. Coffee and espresso drinks are available, too. Make sure you try the bran muffins.

Mono Cone

They might as well call this place "Mondo Cone." The portions, and the menu itself, are as big as the neighboring saline lake. Mono Cone (U.S. 395, Lee Vining, 760/647-6606) serves an amazing array of burgers (blue cheese, bacon, guacamole, ortega chili, you name it), fries, and ice cream. Just the list of possible milk shake options will leave you shaking your head. A full meal here will cost you $6–8. Indoor and outdoor seating is available. Open 11 A.M.–8 P.M. in summer.

Tioga Lodge/Me and Manuel's

Finally the Lee Vining area has a restaurant that comes close to equaling the quality of the Mono Inn. Me and Manuel's (U.S. 395, two

miles north of Lee Vining, 760/647-6423) is located at Tioga Lodge in a 100-year-old building that has been completely refurbished to create a bright and inviting space. The wood plank floor under the dining tables looks like an antique, but in fact the owners had to remove the original floor due to rot and old age. They photographed it first, though, and had a nearby mill make identical-sized boards out of the same type of lumber. These were then carefully installed to create an exact duplicate.

Tioga Lodge's owners put the same kind of painstaking effort into their restaurant's food. Having opened in 2001, Me and Manuel's is a winner for breakfast or dinner. Breakfast entrées include omelettes stuffed with a variety of fillings and French toast made with Hawaiian egg bread ($5–9). Dinner could be smoked trout, roasted garlic and spinach ravioli, or grilled shrimp ($13–16). Don't miss out on the hearty onion soup ($6).

Mono Inn Restaurant

The views of Mono Lake from the Mono Inn Restaurant (55260 U.S. 395, Lee Vining, 760/647-6581) will blow you away. But the food is even more surprising at this unlikely spot five miles north of Lee Vining. The inn has been serving a prime rib special on Friday and Saturday nights for 50 years ($24), but it's worth trying any of the other menu items, many of which have a California/Mexican slant. Appetizers are $5–10; entrées are $17–26 and run to roasted venison medallions, porterhouse steak, border carnitas, braised lamb shanks, or grilled duck breast medallions. Everything is served with black beans, pico de gallo, and homemade jalapeño bread, so you get a lot of food for your meal, and it's worth every penny. The restaurant is open 5–10 P.M. for dinner every night except Tuesday, and reservations are more than just a good idea. If you have to wait to be seated, you can relax in the window seat in the upstairs lounge, which has a mesmerizing view of Mono Lake's huge, blue expanse. A small art gallery is open alongside the lounge, with prints by Ansel Adams and others for sale. The inn's owner is a relative of the great photographer.

Virginia Lakes Resort

You might not think of eating at Virginia Lakes Resort (at the end of Virginia Lakes Road, six miles west of U.S. 395 and 12 miles north of Lee Vining, 760/647-6484) unless you happen to be staying there, but it's worth the 25-minute drive from Lee Vining to bite into their ortega Spanish omelette ($7) or French toast made with sheepherder bread ($6). For lunch, try the Fisherman Special (grilled cheese on sheepherder bread, $5) or the Campground Favorite (hamburger and fries, $6). The food is dependably good, but even better is the view of Virginia Lake from the deck (not from the cafe itself) and the friendly demeanor of everybody who works here.

JUNE LAKE

Carson Peak Inn

Diners in June Lake have been heading to the Carson Peak Inn (Highway 158, June Lake, 760/648-7575) for as long as anybody under 45 can remember. The inn first opened its doors in 1966, and the owners haven't missed a beat since then. Portions are huge at the cozy, old-fashioned dinner house, even if you choose the "regular appetite" entrées instead of the "hearty appetite" ones. All the standards are done well here: prime rib, filet mignon, king crab legs, lobster tail, trout, and scallops ($11–20). A few oddball items are found on the menu, like chicken livers. All dinners come with soup and salad (not soup *or* salad), a baked potato, and garlic bread. You'll have to roll yourself out of here when it's all over. The Carson Peak Inn prides itself on being open 365 days a year, no matter what the weather. Thanksgiving and Christmas dinners are a big event.

Eagle's Landing

The finest dining establishment in June Lake is found at the Double Eagle Resort's restaurant, Eagle's Landing (Highway 158, June Lake, 760/648-7004). You don't need to stay at the resort to eat here; just stop in. Sit indoors and gaze out the floor-to-ceiling windows at Carson Peak and Reversed Creek, or sit outdoors on the deck and enjoy the warm Sierra sun. Breakfast includes a lobster frittata, steak and eggs, or prime rib hash ($8–12), plus a selection of omelettes. Dinner entrées include orange-glazed salmon, New Zealand rack of lamb, and macadamia-crusted halibut ($14–24). All entrées come with soup or salad and fresh vegetables. In addition to the regular menu, the restaurant offers a "spa menu," just in case you're taking this fitness thing seriously. Open daily 7 A.M.–9 P.M. If it's a quiet night, it might close earlier.

Know
Yosemite

The Land

⚑ GEOLOGY

The tale of Yosemite began about 400 million years ago when the land that is now the Sierra Nevada Mountains lay quietly beneath an ancient sea. This land mass was made up of thick layers of sediment that were piled thousands of feet deep. As the number of layers continued to build, pressure caused the bottom layers to be folded, twisted, and compressed into rock forms. Eventually these massive rocks were thrust upward above the sea's surface by movements of the Pacific and North American continental plates. In the process, a mountain range was formed—what would eventually become the **Sierra Nevada,** the longest and highest single mountain range in the contiguous United States.

As the mountains rose, molten rock welled up from deep within the earth and cooled slowly beneath the layers of rock and sediment, forming the substance we know as granite. Over eons of time, erosion gradually wore away almost all the overlying sediment and exposed the granite underneath. Most of the rock we see today in Yosemite is granite, although some of the original sedimentary rock can still be viewed in the western foothills of the Sierra Nevada. (Easy to distinguish from other types of rock, **granite** bears a salt-and-pepper appearance, created by a random distribution of light- and dark-colored minerals.)

Next, around 20 million years ago, the entire block of the mountain range was uplifted and tilted to the west, creating the long, gentle slope of the foothills to the west and the steep escarpment of the Sierra's east side. Fast-flowing water and snowmelt worked to cut deep river channels into the gentle western slope. The major structure of the Sierra was now formed and only required a few finishing touches.

Those final touches came about two million years ago, when the planet cooled, the Ice Age descended, and the entire mountain range was engulfed in snow and ice. **Glaciers** went to work on the exposed granite, moving slowly down established river valleys and carving Yosemite's landmark shapes and forms. Softer, weaker rock was chiseled away and ground into rubble by the fierce power of the glaciers' grinding ice and rock. Valleys were rounded out from a sharp V-shape to a more gentle U-shape. Lake basins were formed at the bases of towering peaks. Only the sturdiest chunks of granite withstood the glaciers' onslaught—monoliths like **El Capitan,** at 3,000 feet the tallest unbroken cliff in the world. What we see is only the tip of the iceberg—El Cap's solid granite sinks 7–10 miles into the earth.

It is uncertain how many times glacial ice moved through Yosemite, advancing and then retreating, although there is evidence in other areas of the Sierra Nevada that at least three major glaciations occurred, perhaps as many as 10. The last passage of glaciers in Yosemite, called the Tioga glacial period, ended only about 10,000 years ago.

Another process was also taking place as the softer rock was being eroded and carried away. With the top layers of rock removed, the bottom layers were under much less weight and pressure, and so began to expand. As they expanded, their surfaces cracked, and the top layers of rock peeled off in sheets, like layers from an onion.

Slowly, through this process known as **exfoliation,** irregularities in the rock were removed and all that remained were smooth, rounded surfaces. This is one reason for the number of bald **granite domes** we see in Yosemite today, such as Half Dome, Sentinel Dome, and North Dome. A good example of granite in the midst of the exfoliation process is the Royal Arches in the Valley, on the canyon wall behind the Ahwahnee Hotel.

The Sierra Nevada's geologic upheaval isn't over. On a broad scale, the Sierra Nevada Mountains are still rising, although only at about one foot every thousand years. On a more noticeable scale, weathering and erosion continue to shape

© ANN MARIE BROWN

Glacial erratics are large boulders that were dropped in place by the retreating glaciers.

the face of Yosemite. A few small glaciers still exist within the park borders (the Lyell Glacier is the most famous) and are still grinding away. At the same time, another geologic agent is always at work, continually changing the face of Yosemite: gravity. Landslides and rockfalls are common occurrences in the park, particularly in Yosemite Valley with its sheer vertical walls, many of which are severely fractured both on the surface and underneath.

The most famous **rockslide** in Yosemite Valley's recent history occurred in the Happy Isles region on July 10, 1996, when an 80,000-ton slab of granite broke off the southeast side of Glacier Point and fell 1,000 feet. The impact created 160-mph winds and devastated 10 acres of forest. When it was all over, nearly everything in the Valley was covered by two inches of dust. This massive slide made the evening news all over the country, yet smaller rockslides are a common occurrence in the Valley. Almost every year Northside Drive is closed for some period of time due to falling rocks near the Three Brothers.

Although the glacial theory is now the accepted story of Yosemite's geologic past, it wasn't always so. Naturalist **John Muir** first put forth the glacial theory around 1870, after spending years studying Yosemite's rocks and landscape up close. The famous geologist **Josiah Whitney,** the director of the California Geological Survey, thought Muir's theory was ludicrous; he called Muir an "ignoramus." Whitney argued that Yosemite Valley was formed by a single, great cataclysmic event, which caused the bottom to drop out of its mighty rocks, forming the Valley floor. According to Whitney, that same event would have created Half Dome by shearing a much larger dome in half.

One of Whitney's assistants, Clarence King, disagreed with his superior, and discovered glacial scars and other evidence of glaciation in the park. Later Muir came upon small glaciers still in existence in remote areas of Yosemite, adding strength to his and King's glacial theory.

As many as a dozen other theories as to Yosemite Valley's origin persisted until 1930, when **François E. Matthes** settled the matter by synthesizing many of them but in essence siding with John Muir. Matthes was a cartographer and geologist with the U.S. Geological

GEOLOGY DEFINITIONS

Arête: A narrow, jagged ridge, usually between two cirques.

Cirque: A bowl-shaped basin in which a glacier was formed. Water expands as it freezes, eventually digging out rock to form a large basin. These basins often contain lakes; May Lake off Tioga Pass Road is a classic glacial cirque lake.

Erratics: Large boulders that were left behind by retreating glaciers. As the glaciers melted, big rocks that were carried along in their midst were dropped in place like pebbles. Two easy places to see glacial erratics are at Olmsted Point and in the stretch of Tioga Pass Road near Tenaya Lake.

Exfoliation: The process by which concentric sheets of granite fracture and "peel off" from the surface of a rock formation. The rock layers, which can be more than 100 feet thick, crack and then strip off, as if the rock is shedding an outer shell.

Glacier: A mass of rock and ice formed by the freezing and refreezing of snow crystals. The mass moves forward, or flows, pushed by the force of gravity, at the snail-like pace of a few inches per day.

The 3,000-foot-high granite cliff of El Capitan was left untouched by the fierce grinding action of glaciers.

© ANN MARIE BROWN

Hanging valley: While a large glacier was busily scouring the main channel of Yosemite Valley, smaller streams of ice were at work in the Valley's feeder streams and tributaries. These smaller glacial extensions could not cut as deeply as the large Valley glacier, and so when the ice retreated, tributary valleys were left "hanging" above the low Valley floor. Bridalveil Creek flows through a hanging valley to create spectacular 620-foot Bridalveil Fall.

Roche moutonnée: A granite dome that has a smooth, gentle slope on one side and a steep, vertical slope on the other side. Lembert Dome and Pothole Dome, on the east and west ends of Tuolumne Meadows, respectively, are prime examples of roches moutonnées (a French term that roughly means "sheeplike rock"). You can walk right up one side of a roche moutonnée, but the other side is the playground of elite rock climbers.

Talus: A pile of rough, angular rock fragments deposited at the base of a cliff or steep slope. Talus fields can be seen all over Yosemite and are easily viewed along Northside Drive in Yosemite Valley in the vicinity of the Three Brothers.

Terminal moraine: A mix of rubble, rock, and sand pushed ahead of the advancing glaciers and then left in place when the glaciers melted, usually forming a ridge.

Survey who wrote the definitive *Geologic History of the Yosemite Valley*. Geologists continue to study Yosemite and the Sierra Nevada today. Certainly all its ancient secrets have not yet been revealed.

CLIMATE

Yosemite National Park encompasses a wide swath of the slope of the Sierra Nevada Mountains, with elevations that range from 4,000 feet in Yosemite Valley and Hetch Hetchy Valley to 13,000 feet in the high country. Given that range, the climate change within the park is dramatic. Summertime temperatures can reach 100°F in Yosemite Valley or Hetch Hetchy, but it can snow in any month of the year in the high country.

Generally, the climate is quite mild year-round in the Valley, with daytime temperatures in the 80s or 90s (Fahrenheit) in summer and nighttime temperatures in the 50s or 60s. Spring and fall are somewhat cooler. Winter days average 30–55°F, and nights will often drop below freezing. Snow falls in Yosemite Valley a few times each winter, but it usually does not last more than a week or two. Accumulations above one or two feet are rare. Rain is fairly common in winter, but quite rare between May and October.

In the high country—at Glacier Point or even higher along Tioga Pass Road—snow as deep as 10 feet closes the roads most years from late October until early June. Summer in Tuolumne Meadows and on top of Glacier Point is usually dry and cool, with temperatures rarely reaching higher than 75°F. Night temperatures often drop to the 40s, and by September can approach freezing. Afternoon thundershowers are common throughout Yosemite's high country in August and September, when the Central Valley's temperatures are consistently high.

Flora

The wide range of elevation and climate in Yosemite produces an incredible variety of flora, from chaparral plants that only survive in hot, dry areas, to subalpine plants that grow only at 12,000 feet during the few short weeks of summer. The park contains 37 kinds of native trees, from the grand giant sequoia to the delicate dogwood, and 1,400 species of flowering plants. The vegetation changes with elevation and occurs in broad bands called life zones. Four main life zones are found in the park. They are most easily understood by considering the places where park visitors would encounter them and what major species are indicative of each zone.

LOWER MONTANE LIFE ZONE

In Yosemite Valley and Hetch Hetchy Valley lies the lower montane life zone. Elevations range from 3,500 to 6,000 feet. These two valleys are filled with dense mixed forests of ponderosa pine, sugar pine, Douglas-fir, incense-cedar, white fir, and giant sequoia. Mixed in with the conifers are leaf trees like black oak, bigleaf maple, dogwood, and cottonwood. These deciduous trees create a fine color show in the Valley in autumn. Visitors from the East Coast won't find that it competes with fall in Vermont, but for California, this is a good autumn display.

The conifers of this region can be identified by a few easy-to-remember characteristics. The **ponderosa pine** is known by its clearly delineated, jigsaw puzzle–like bark and long needles (4–10 inches). The **sugar pine** is the tallest and largest of more than 100 species of pine trees in the world—old trees frequently reach seven feet in diameter and 200 feet tall. This venerable pine has unmistakable cones, befitting a tree this size: they are 10–18 inches in length, the longest cones of any conifer. The cones hang down like Christmas ornaments off the tips of the sugar pine's long branches. While they are still green, they weigh up to five pounds. The **Douglas-fir** is also easily spotted by its cones, which hang downward while those of true firs sit upright, and its needles, which grow out in all directions from its branches. The tree is actually not a fir at all, which is why its name must be correctly spelled with a hyphen—indicating that "fir" is not the species but simply a moniker. The tree is not a pine, either, or any other commonly known tree, but rather a species unto itself. Because of its fast-growing nature, the Douglas-fir has the unhappy distinction of being the most important lumber tree in the United States. In Yosemite, of course, Douglas-firs are protected from logging.

The **incense-cedar** can be identified by its lacy foliage and unusual needles, which are completely flat at the ends, as if they have been ironed. Its bark is shaggy in appearance, and the tree emits a slight spicy odor (some people think its scent is reminiscent of pencils). Like Douglas-fir, the incense-cedar's name is hyphenated because it is not a true cedar.

The sturdy **white fir** has a white-gray trunk, and the tree commonly reaches a width of five feet. It has needles that grow in flat sprays that are distinctly two-dimensional. White firs are easily spotted in Yosemite's three sequoia groves, where their seeds germinate in the thick duff that covers the ground beneath the giant sequoias. Most people recognize white firs because the young ones look like little Christmas trees; indeed, this is a commonly marketed Christmas tree in California. Older trees easily attain heights of 150 feet.

The last of the conifers in the lower montane life zone is the **giant sequoia,** which is well known not just for its gargantuan height and girth, which combine to make this tree the largest living thing on earth, but also for its distinctive cinnamon-colored bark. Three native groves of these amazing tree giants exist in Yosemite—Mariposa, Merced, and Tuolumne—and a few planted sequoias live in Yosemite Valley, near the Ahwahnee Hotel and at the Yosemite Cemetery.

Among the deciduous trees of the lower montane life zone, the **black oak** was the most prevalent species in the Valley prior to

© ANN MARIE BROWN

The giant sequoia is the largest living thing on earth by volume, a combination of height and girth.

the 1850s. The activities of white settlers in the last 150 years, particularly efforts designed to reduce flooding and a long-standing policy of fire suppression, have caused the Valley's stands of black oaks to dwindle to about 10 percent of their past size. In their place, a greater number of conifers have taken over. Through replanting efforts, the National Park Service is working diligently to restore black oaks to Yosemite Valley. Seedlings and young trees are fenced off to prevent trampling by humans and browsing by animals. The black oaks are an important food source for deer and squirrels, as they once were for the Native Americans who lived in the Valley. Grinding rocks or *morteros* can be found throughout Yosemite, upon which American Indian women ground acorns into meal.

One of the showiest tree species of the lower montane life zone is the **western dogwood.** If you visit Yosemite Valley in May, you will be delighted by the sprays of white blossoms on this small, delicate tree that grows under the canopy of large conifers. The dogwood's five-inch-wide blooms are not truly flowers, but rather petal-like bracts that surround the true flowers—a dense, yellow cluster in the middle of the bracts. One of the most beautiful evening sights in Yosemite Valley is that of flowering dogwoods lit up by the full moon. The tree also develops attractive red berries in the fall, a favorite food of robins.

In the understory of this wide variety of deciduous trees and conifers lives a low-growing shrub that, despite its small size, garners its share of attention in the lower montane life zone. It's a plant with three common names: **mountain misery,** bear clover, or kit-kit-dizze. Visitors may not know it by any of its names, but they will certainly recognize its scent; the fern-like shrub emits a strong, sweet, evocative odor. Once you smell mountain misery, you will always associate its scent with the lower Sierra Nevada. Many visitors encounter the plant for the first time as they drive into the park on Highway 41 from Oakhurst. Both sides of the road are carpeted with mountain misery for several miles south and north of the park's southern entrance station. The scent follows you past Wawona, up to the entrance to Glacier Point Road, and down to the Valley at Bridalveil Fall.

Other chaparral plants common in the lower montane life zone include several species of manzanitas, currants, yerba santa, ceanothus, deerbrush, and buckbrush.

UPPER MONTANE LIFE ZONE

On Glacier Point and along the west end of Tioga Pass Road lies the upper montane life zone, at 6,000–8,500 feet in elevation. Tuolumne Meadows is just on the edge of this life zone, at an elevation of 8,600 feet. It straddles the border of the upper montane life zone and the next higher life zone, the subalpine.

At these elevations, massive red firs and lodgepole pines predominate. The deeply shaded forests in this zone also contain western white pine, Jeffrey pine, and western juniper. Wet mountain meadows are common, and within them bloom a variety of wildflowers in early summer: pink shooting stars, red

and yellow western columbine, bright yellow coneflowers, red or orange paintbrush, and false hellebore (corn lilies), among others.

Western white pines are gray-barked pines with blue-green needles in bundles of five. The tree has nine-inch-long cones that are often slightly curved. Visitors can see many large examples of the tree in the stretch of road between Porcupine Flat Campground and Tioga Pass. Western white pines rarely exceed 100 feet tall, but their long limbs curve gracefully upward.

Red firs are easy to identify because of their reddish-brown bark. They can grow up to six feet in diameter and are often seen in pure groves made up of only their own kind. The area of Tioga Pass Road near the Lukens Lake Trailhead shows off some remarkably large red firs growing in close proximity. Depressions at the bases of the biggest trees are sometimes used by bears as winter dens (the same is also true for white firs).

Red firs played a large role in the early popularization of Yosemite Valley as a tourist attraction; the wood and bark of these trees was lit on fire and pushed off the top of Glacier Point to create a nightly spectacle in Yosemite Valley known as **Firefall.** The sight of the tumbling, burning embers dropping 1,000 feet to the Valley floor was an event witnessed by millions of eager visitors between 1900 and 1968. Eventually the National Park Service discontinued the show, rightly deciding that it was an inappropriate activity for a national park. The crowds that gathered for Firefall each evening damaged meadows, trampled plants, and created traffic jams in the Valley. Cascading embers burned off fragile lichen growth on the cliffs of Glacier Point. And the red fir bark was growing scarce and needed to be gathered at much greater distances from Yosemite Valley.

Lodgepole pines are the only two-needled pines in the Sierra. They earned their name because Native Americans used their dependably straight trunks as poles for their teepees and lodges. On Tioga Road, especially near Tuolumne Meadows, lodgepole pines do not grow very tall—most are in the 20- to 40-foot range. Throughout history the tree has been mistakenly called a tamarack, which is actually a deciduous conifer that does not live anywhere in the Sierra. The lodgepole pine's mistaken identity is the reason for the place names Tamarack Lakes and Tamarack Flat we find in Yosemite and beyond.

Currently, lodgepole pines along and near Tioga Pass Road are suffering from an attack by the **needleminer moth,** an insect whose larvae obtain food and shelter by hollowing out the lodgepole pine's needles. This ultimately kills the tree, and large stands of pines in the Yosemite high country are dead or dying from this insect's activities. However, because the attack of the needleminer moth is a natural occurrence that happens every 100 years or so in a lodgepole pine forest, the National Park Service is allowing Mother Nature to run her course. In the long term, the moth may actually be good for the lodgepole pine forest because it takes out some of the older trees and allows younger, healthier stands to grow in their place.

The **Jeffrey pine** is a favorite of many Sierra tree lovers because of the unique scent of its bark, which smells quite sweet, like vanilla or butterscotch. Hungry hikers sometimes liken the smell of the Jeffrey pine to a breakfast of pancakes and maple syrup. The side of the pine that is warmed by sunlight generally emits the strongest scent. Sometimes the odor is so strong it wafts over to you from several feet away; other times you must put your nose right up to the tree's bark crevices to smell it.

Like the ponderosa pine, the Jeffrey has jigsaw-puzzle bark (it's especially pronounced on older, wider trees). The two species are sometimes confused, but if you know at what elevation the tree sits, you can usually identify it correctly. Jeffrey pines are rarely seen below 6,000 feet, and ponderosa pines are rarely seen above it. The Jeffrey pine is a rugged tree often seen growing on high granite domes and slopes, seemingly without the aid of soil. A very famous and much-photographed Jeffrey once lived on top of the bald summit of Sentinel Dome in Yosemite, but it finally died of old age in 1979. Other Jeffrey pines still eke out a wind-sculpted living on the dome's bald surface.

Another unique feature of the Jeffrey pine is that its cones are not prickly to the touch because their spines point downward, not outward. This feature has earned the tree the nickname "gentleman Jeffrey." The ponderosa pine's cones, by way of contrast, can be remembered as "prickly ponderosa."

Western juniper (also called Sierra juniper) is another distinctive Sierra tree, and an easy one to identify because of its bluish-green, scale-like needles and its spiraling trunk, which makes it appear as if the tree twisted in circles as it grew. The roots of this hearty tree will tunnel through crevices in granite, making it seem as if the Western juniper is growing right out of rock. Western junipers in Yosemite and elsewhere in the Sierra can live as long as 2,000 years. As the juniper ages, its trunk becomes stripped of bark and bleached to a light blond. The juniper produces an abundance of blue "berries" in the summer months, which are well loved by birds. These are actually not berries at all but the juniper's cones.

Aside from the big conifers, one small plant common in the upper montane life zone is worth a special mention. It is the **snow plant,** a red, thick, asparagus-like plant that has no green leaves. It is one of the first flora to make an appearance as the snow melts; early-season hikers will often see it protruding from the forest floor amid piles of melting snow. A member of the heath family, snow plant is so tough and determined to sprout that it can sometimes push up through asphalt.

SUBALPINE LIFE ZONE

Still higher, between Tuolumne Meadows and 9,945-foot Tioga Pass, only two hardy trees survive: whitebark pine and mountain hemlock, both of which are usually low-growing. Elevations in this subalpine life zone range from 8,500 to 10,500 feet. The **whitebark pine** often looks more like a shrub with multiple small trunks than a single tree; at its tallest it grows to about 35 feet. Its cones are purple and two inches long, with seeds that are highly coveted by Clark's nutcrackers, chickarees, and chipmunks.

The **mountain hemlock** is easily spotted by its uppermost branches, which droop downward or sideways, as if they are taking a bow. Naturalist John Muir was a great fan of the mountain hemlock and wrote a lengthy ode to them in his first book, *The Mountains of California*. The hemlock has greenish-blue foliage that is distinct when viewed close up; its needles are dense and completely cover the stems they grow on, like a coat of fur. The tree can be viewed from Tioga Pass Road in the high region between Tenaya Lake and Tioga Pass.

The dominant plants that grow in the high meadows of the subalpine life zone are **sedges,** not the grasses found in lower-elevation meadows. Wildflowers at these elevations include many of the same species of the upper montane life zone, although the higher the elevation, the more likely the plants will be of a smaller, more compact variety.

ALPINE LIFE ZONE

Finally, at 10,500 feet and above lies the region that only hikers in Yosemite will see: the alpine life zone that is found above the timberline, where trees are rare to nonexistent. Plants that grow here are typically very small, mainly because of harsh winds. The growing season is very short, making these alpine environments extremely fragile and easily disturbed by human presence. Cushions or mats of colorful flowers like penstemon and phlox brighten the generally stark landscape of gray, rocky slopes. Some of the loveliest of these matlike plants are the mountain heaths or heathers. John Muir wrote lovingly of the white, bell-shaped flowers of cassiope, which he described as "the most beautiful and best loved of the heathworts... ringing her thousands of sweet-toned bells." Cassiope can be seen today along high lakeshores and on Cathedral Peak.

Fauna

Many visitors travel to American national parks in the hopes of seeing wildlife. In this regard, Yosemite often delivers, although you never know which of the park's 76 mammal species, 247 bird species, and 29 reptile and amphibian species will make an appearance at any given time. Although it's unlikely you'll get to see any of Yosemite's 15 species of bats, most park visitors will make the acquaintance of at least one of the park's 17 species of mosquitoes (although this is generally not a welcome meeting). Fortunately, only three of those 17 mosquito types feast on the flesh of humans, and those pesky critters are generally limited to the early summer season—typically in the three weeks following snowmelt at any given location. The general rule is that if the wildflowers are blooming in an area, the mosquitoes will be there, too. Once the flowers die back, the mosquitoes largely disappear.

The following is a brief guide to some of Yosemite's most commonly seen, or most notable, animal denizens.

LARGE MAMMALS
Black Bear

The only kind of bear that lives in Yosemite, or anywhere in California, is the black bear. Although the fearsome grizzly bear once roamed the state and is immortalized on the California flag, grizzlies have been extinct in Yosemite since 1895 and in the rest of California since 1924. Black bears have a somewhat misleading name, as they are commonly brown, blond, or cinnamon-colored—rarely pure black. Often they have a white patch on their chest. The smallest of all North American bears, they weigh as much as 400 pounds, can run up to 30 miles per hour, and are powerful swimmers and climbers. Despite the adult bear's enormous size, bear cubs weigh only a half pound at birth.

Black bears will eat just about anything, but their staple foods are berries, fruits, plants, insects, honeycomb, the inner layer of tree bark, fish, and small mammals. Contrary to popular

SAVING THE LIVES OF BEARS

There's only one important fact to remember about Yosemite's bears: They love snacks. The average black bear must eat 20,000 calories a day to sustain its body weight. Because its natural diet is made up of berries, fruits, plants, fish, insects, and the like, the high-calorie food of human beings seems very appealing to a bear. (A box full of candy bars is a lot easier to swallow than 1,500 acorns or 10,000 pieces of grass.)

Unfortunately, too many Yosemite campers have trained Yosemite's bears to crave the taste of corn chips, hot dogs, and soda pop. As a result, bears have become less wild, more aggressive, and largely unafraid of humans. Some bears will break into cars and buildings in the hopes of finding food, and they teach their young the same bad habits. The result is hundreds of thousands of dollars in property damage. Ultimately, in the conflict between bears and people, bears lose. In Yosemite and other California parks, bears that develop a reputation as "problem bears" are put to death. Transporting the bear to another area is ineffective. Once a bear has developed a taste for human food, there is no turning back.

Any time you see a bear, it's almost a given that it's looking for food. If it is in a meadow or forest foraging for berries or grubs, that's good news. If it is near a campground or picnic area, that's very bad news. That's why it is essential that Yosemite visitors keep their food packed away in bearproof storage containers when they are camping or staying in Yosemite's more rustic lodgings, like tent cabins, which bears can easily break into. The bearproof brown metal boxes should be closed and latched at all times.

Storing food or any item with a scent a bear might mistake for food (soap, cosmetics, perfume, insect repellent, sunscreen, empty bottles of soda, pots or pans that were used for cooking) in your automobile is simply asking for trouble. Bears are remarkably strong, and they can use their claws and muscles to "peel back" the windows and doors of cars. Once a bear breaks into your car, you can plan on not being able to drive it home. Plan on a long discussion with your insurance agent. Plan on getting a ticket from the rangers for improper food storage. Plan on possibly being responsible for ending a bear's life. In the year 2000, five "problem bears" were put to death in Yosemite. Although that num-

---

belief, black bears do not hibernate. A pregnant female will "den up" in winter and usually give birth while she is sleeping, but this is not true hibernation. Male black bears are often seen roaming for food in winter.

Mule Deer

Frequently seen in Yosemite Valley and crossing roads elsewhere in the park, the mule deer is one of our largest American deer and can weigh up to 450 pounds. The deer gets its name from its ears, which are large and rounded. Mule deer in the Sierra have a white patch on their rumps and a black-tipped tail. The antlers on the bucks, which develop in summer, are usually an elegant, matched set of four points on each side.

Sierra Bighorn Sheep

The last of the native bighorn sheep vanished from Yosemite's high country in 1914. The mighty bighorn was reintroduced in the Yosemite region in 1986. Members of this small, relocated herd are sometimes seen just east of Tioga Pass. Its numbers have dropped from approximately 90 bighorns in the early 1990s to approximately 20 in 2002, most likely due to predation from mountain lions. The sturdy sheep, with their signature thick, backward-curved horns, are listed as a federally endangered species. The Sierra bighorn prefers elevations above 10,000 feet and can travel up and down steep, rocky slopes with amazing speed and grace. John Muir called them "the greatest of all Sierra mountaineers." The males use their horns in the autumn to butt heads and establish the chain of command; a contest between two males can last for more than a day.

ber was unusually high, of the roughly 300 to 500 bears that live in Yosemite, at least two or three are put to death every year because they have become accustomed to human food and are considered dangerously aggressive as a result. In a loosely related issue, humans are also a menace to bears because we often drive too fast on mountain roads. In 2005, 10 bears were hit and killed by cars on Yosemite's roads.

Backpackers should always use plastic bear canisters to store their food for overnight trips. Hanging food from a tree is ineffective in Yosemite, where the bears have long since smartened up to that routine. In certain areas of the park, bear canisters are required: anywhere above 9,600 feet, in the Rancheria Falls area of Hetch Hetchy, and at High Sierra Camps if a bearproof box is not used. If you're going out for a backpacking trip, you can borrow, rent, or buy a bear canister in the park (at Curry Village Mountain Shop, Yosemite Village Sports Shop, Tuolumne Meadows Store, Wawona Store, Crane Flat Store, and Hetch Hetchy Entrance Station). Canisters weigh about three pounds and will store three to five days' worth of food. Renting a bear canister will cost you a mere $5 per trip and ensure that you do not lose all your food to a bear. Canisters can be rented and returned at different locations in the park for no extra charge.

Bears are sometimes encountered by day hikers and backpackers on trails, although not as frequently as by campers in campgrounds. When you are hiking, bears will most likely hear you coming and avoid you. Black bears very rarely harm human beings, but you should never approach or feed a bear, or get between a bear and its cubs or its food. If provoked, a bear could cause serious injury. If a bear approaches while you are eating, pick up all your food and walk away with it. Bears respect possession and will not take food away from you. If a bear approaches while you are in camp, yell, throw small rocks or pine cones, and try to frighten the bear away. A bear that is afraid of humans is a bear that will stay wild and stay alive.

To report improper food storage, trash problems, or other bear-related trouble, call the Save-a-Bear Hotline at 209/372-0322. Your call can be made anonymously, and it may save the life of a bear.

Mountain Lion

The most reclusive of all of Yosemite's creatures, the mountain lion is the largest cat in North America and is best distinguished from afar by its two- to three-foot-long tail. The adult cat's body minus its tail is often six feet long; a male cat typically weighs 250 pounds. The mountain lion is tawny except for its underside, which is white. It usually lives where deer, its main food source, are plentiful. Mountain lion sightings in Yosemite were extremely rare until 1994, when an abnormally high number were reported. There have been no mountain lion attacks on visitors in Yosemite, although a few attacks have occurred elsewhere in California. Although you probably won't see a lion, you may be lucky enough to find its tracks. The large, cat-like footprints are easy to distinguish; they are four-toed prints that do not show claws.

Coyote

Many Yosemite visitors report seeing a wolf or a fox near one of the park roads, but what they have usually seen is a coyote. (Wolves do not live in the Sierra; foxes are quite small and rarely seen during the day.) The coyote is a dog-like animal with a grayish-brown coat; its back slopes downward toward its tail. An average-size coyote weighs about 30 pounds and stands about two feet tall. Coyotes can run as fast as 40 miles per hour and make a series of "yip" cries, often followed by a howl. Across California, the coyote has acclimated well to the presence of humans and is generally unafraid of them.

SMALL MAMMALS
Bobcat

A stocky feline about twice the size of a house

Know Yosemite

cat, the bobcat is easily recognized by its short, "bobbed" tail, only four inches long. Bobcats are mostly nocturnal but are sometimes seen hunting during the day. Their coats are gray-brown in winter and reddish-brown in summer, marked with black spots and bars. The bobcat's ears have short tufts above them.

Raccoon

This black-masked invader is sometimes seen scavenging in park campgrounds, particularly in the evenings. The raccoon has distinctive rings around its tail and a large, gray-brown body that can weigh as much as 40 pounds. Despite its girth, the raccoon is a good swimmer and climber and can run as fast as 15 miles per hour. Its fingerlike toes are useful for washing its food, as well as prying open campers' coolers and food stores.

Porcupine

Only the rare and fortunate Yosemite visitor gets to see the elusive porcupine, a mammal famous for its body covering of thousands of quills—sharp, hollow spines. The porcupine's quills lay

back flat when the animal is relaxed, but they stand straight up when it is threatened. Porcupines spend most of their time high in trees, where they eat twigs and bark, but are sometimes seen crossing meadows or forests in search of a new feeding tree. Porcupine tracks face forward and inward; the animal walks pigeon-toed.

Yellow-bellied Marmot

This largest and most curious member of the squirrel family is frequently seen in Yosemite's high country, particularly in rocky areas like Olmsted Point or on the borders of Tuolumne Meadows. About seven inches tall and as long as two feet, the bold marmot has no enemies and is frequently seen sunning himself on high boulders. The marmot's coat is buff to brown and its belly characteristically yellow. If you see two or more marmots together, they are often wrestling or chasing each other. You may hear them make a high-pitched whistling sound.

Pika

A frequently seen resident in alpine environments higher than 8,000 feet, the pika is a

Yellow-bellied marmots are a common sight in Yosemite's high country.

© ANN MARIE BROWN

small relative of the rabbit that busily collects green grasses, then stacks them in the sun and dries them for winter food and insulation. The creature does not hibernate, so it needs to keep a full stock of dried grasses for its winter nourishment. The diminutive pika is most often seen on talus-lined slopes or rocky hillsides; it is easily recognized because of its small, rounded ears and absence of a tail.

Chipmunks

Not one but eight kinds of chipmunks are found in Yosemite. Most common are the lodgepole chipmunk, alpine chipmunk, yellow-pine chipmunk, Allen's chipmunk, and Merriam's chipmunk. All chipmunks are colored in various shades of brown and have a distinctive stripe on their body and face. The yellow-pine is the most boldly striped. Generally chipmunks at higher elevations hibernate and those at lower elevations do not. Like their cousins the squirrels, chipmunks eat nuts, seeds, and fungi.

Squirrels

The number and variety of squirrels and their close relations in Yosemite can be quite daunting to the amateur naturalist trying to identify them. One of the easiest-to-spot species is the golden-mantled ground squirrel, a common sight at elevations above 6,000 feet. Frequently mistaken for large chipmunks, these cute squirrels can be correctly identified by the fact that they lack the chipmunk's facial stripe. Otherwise, they look much the same, with one white stripe on each side of their brown bodies, bordered by a heavy black stripe. The golden-mantled ground squirrel must fatten himself up all summer to prepare for winter hibernation.

The western gray squirrel is the common gray-coated squirrel we see throughout California, with a long bushy tail and white belly. Western gray squirrels are great tree climbers and are mostly seen below 6,000 feet. In contrast, the Douglas squirrel (also called a chickaree) is much smaller than the western gray, and colored a mix of brown and gray. This constantly chattering and highly active squirrel is a key player in the giant sequoia forest, where it cuts thousands of seed-bearing cones per hour from the high branches of a sequoia. The cones drop to the ground, the chickaree scrambles down the tree and gnaws on their meat, and the sequoia seeds fall to the earth to regenerate.

Two additional types of ground squirrels are also seen in Yosemite, and both types hibernate in winter. The Belding ground squirrel is a high-country dweller that is brown or gray with a reddish tail; it is often spotted in meadows standing upright on its back legs. The California ground squirrel is seen at lower elevations and is best identified by a silver, V-shaped pattern on the shoulders of its brown-spotted coat.

BIRDS

Steller's Jay

Nobody visits Yosemite without seeing the Steller's jay—he is bold and raucous and makes his presence known. The western cousin of the East Coast's blue jay, the Steller's jay has a distinctive black topknot of feathers that point backward, affording him a regal look. The jay's body is about 10 inches in length and a deep, pure blue. When on the ground, the Steller's jay hops, it does not walk. If you are eating a sandwich when one is near, keep a vigilant guard; the jay has no qualms about stealing food.

Clark's Nutcracker

Similar in size and behavior to the Steller's jay (noisy, cantankerous, and often seen scouting at campgrounds and picnic areas for food), the Clark's nutcracker is light gray with white and black patches on its tail and wings. A group of them are often seen and heard among the upper branches of whitebark pine trees, where they quarrel with each other as they collect pine nuts. The bird stores nuts and seeds for the winter in massive granaries, usually located on south-facing slopes. One pair can cache as many as 30,000 nuts and seeds in the fall. In the spring, the birds recall the placement of every single one and retrieve them to feed their young.

Know Yosemite

© ANN MARIE BROWN

Acorn woodpeckers use oak trees and other natural and manufactured wooden structures as granaries for storing acorns.

Raven

Frequently mistaken for the smaller crow, the common raven is a remarkably intelligent bird often seen scrounging for leftovers near campgrounds and picnic areas. Ravens are about two feet long, with glossy black feathers and a curved beak, and a strange call that sounds something like a croaking noise. In the spring, the male raven performs a spectacular aerial dance for its mate—swooping, diving, and barrel-rolling while it cries out loudly. The raven figures prominently in the legends of the Native Americans of Yosemite Valley.

Woodpeckers

Plentiful in Yosemite, a variety of woodpeckers are frequently seen and heard amid the Valley's tall trees. With some variation, they are all black and white with a dash of flaming red on their heads (although in some species only the males bear the red patch). Most common is the acorn woodpecker, which lives in colonies of up to two dozen birds and caches acorns in tree trunks, posts, or other wood structures (sometimes even in the roofs of buildings). A well-stocked granary may hold as many as 10,000 acorns, lined up in

neat rows of individually drilled holes. Called *el carpintero* by the Spanish, the acorn woodpecker outwits marauding squirrels from stealing its stash by pushing the acorns into the holes pointed end first. The wide end of the acorn sits flush with the surface of the tree trunk, giving squirrels nothing to get their paws on.

The downy woodpecker, the smallest woodpecker in North America at about six inches long, is also seen in the Valley, usually in streamside forests. In contrast, the white-headed woodpecker is seen mostly in pine forests, where it eats pine nuts and insects. White-headed woodpeckers do not drill like most woodpeckers; instead they look for food by pulling bark off trees with their beaks. The white-headed woodpecker is all black except for its white head. The male has a small red head patch.

The pileated woodpecker is the largest woodpecker in North America at 16–19 inches in length. Its loud, slow drilling can be heard from a mile away under the right conditions (smaller woodpeckers drill with a faster cadence). The pileated woodpecker, with its black body, white underwings, and bright red crest, is sometimes spotted in the Mariposa Grove of Giant Sequoias.

Peregrine Falcon

Having been almost completely wiped out by the pesticide DDT in the 1950s and 1960s, the peregrine falcon is on the comeback in Yosemite and elsewhere, although it is still listed as an endangered species. This remarkable raptor can fly faster than 200 miles per hour. The adult is blue-gray with a whitish breast; its legs and underparts are striped gray. The peregrine falcon nests on the ledges of near-vertical cliffs; several popular rock climbing sites in Yosemite Valley are closed seasonally to protect nesting sites. When a peregrine falcon hunts, it will circle high until it spots a smaller bird flying below, then plummet downward at breakneck speed and attack it in flight. The female falcon is noticeably larger than the male.

Blue Grouse

This chickenlike bird is curious and virtually unafraid of humans. Frequently seen around Glacier Point, often in groups of six or more, the blue grouse pecks at the ground for conifer needles, buds, and seeds. The grouse is not blue but rather brown-gray. Young grouse are able to walk and feed themselves immediately after they hatch out of their eggs. You may hear but not see the blue grouse while hiking in the high country; the male attracts the female with a strange hooting sound that is amplified by inflating the air sacs on both sides of his neck. The effect sounds something like a hollow drumbeat echoing through the forest.

American Dipper

One of John Muir's favorite birds, the dipper (also called the water ouzel) is an unusual songbird often seen amid the spray of waterfalls—even those as powerful as Yosemite Falls and Bridalveil Fall. Although it is colored a nondescript gray, the dipper lives an extraordinary life, diving underwater to feed on insects and larvae. The bird has a third eyelid that closes over its eyes to protect it from spray, a flap of skin that closes over its nostrils to keep out water, and an extra-large oil gland that waterproofs its plumage. It often builds its nest behind a waterfall, then flies back and forth through the torrent to feed its young. When searching for food in a stream, it can walk underwater.

California Gull

Many a first-time Yosemite visitor has wondered why gulls—a species associated with the seashore—are frequently seen in the high country of Yosemite, especially around Tioga Lake, Ellery Lake, and Tenaya Lake. The reason is the proximity of Mono Lake, located a few miles from the eastern border of the park. The lake is the second largest breeding colony in the world for California gulls. Approximately 90 percent of the gulls seen at the California coast were born at Mono Lake.

Great Gray Owl

An endangered species in California, the great gray owl is thriving in Yosemite probably better than anywhere else in the state, although here they are at the southernmost end of their habitat range. The great gray owl is the largest species of North American owl, reaching more than two feet tall. It hunts for voles and mice in the daytime as well as at night, usually in meadows surrounded by forest. The great gray owl has a memorable face, with dozens of concentric rings around its small, yellow eyes. An estimated 40 great gray owls live within the park's borders; one of the best places to see one is near Crane Flat at dusk.

FISH

Rainbow Trout

Of the five trout species found today in Yosemite—brown, brook, rainbow, cutthroat, and golden—only the rainbow trout is native. The rest were introduced through fish planting programs in the late 19th and 20th century. Although lakes and streams in the park are no longer stocked with fish, an estimated 50 park lakes have self-sustaining populations of non-native trout. The colorful rainbow trout, with its signature pink stripe on its side and black spots on its back, was a favored food of Native Americans in Yosemite Valley.

History

Know Yosemite

NATIVE AMERICANS

It is believed that Native Americans first came to live in Yosemite Valley about 4,000 years ago. Of the original tribes, the only one we know much about was the most recent, the **Ahwahneechee,** a sector of the Southern Sierra Miwok tribe.

The last Ahwahneechee tribe to live in Yosemite, led by **Chief Tenaya,** moved in to the Valley after it had been vacant for some years. Stories are told of a fatal disease that swept through the Valley, probably around the beginning of the 1800s, killing most of its inhabitants and forcing the rest to abandon the area. These tales align with the fact that around that same time, Native American tribes throughout California were afflicted with the diseases of the Spanish missions.

Chief Tenaya, a Yosemite Miwok Indian by descent, was raised in the Mono Lake area with the Paiute tribes. He had heard stories from his people about the glorious Valley, and when he reached adulthood, he traveled to see it. Finding it apparently free of disease, he and about 200 other Indians resettled the Valley. They called it Ahwahnee and themselves the Ahwahneechee.

The Ahwahneechee were skilled hunters, who snared birds, netted and speared trout, and hunted deer, bear, and squirrels with bow and arrow. They gathered acorns from the black oaks and ground them into meal, dug plant bulbs in the spring, and set the Valley's grasses on fire each fall to encourage better seed production the following year. They were also skilled craftspeople, making colorful baskets from willow, redbud, ferns, and strips of bark, and practical tools like knives and scrapers from antlers and bones. They traded with other bands of Indians, particularly the Mono area Paiute Indians, for salt, pine nuts, and insect protein.

The Ahwahneechees invented stories about their Valley as a way of understanding its prominent features, such as El Capitan and Yosemite Falls. Even Half Dome had a story: An Indian woman named Tis-sa-ack and her husband, Nangas, decided to travel to the beautiful Valley they had heard so much about. Along the way, they quarreled, and Tis-sa-ack ran off from her husband. When she got to Mirror Lake, she was so tired and thirsty that she knelt down and drank all its water. Her husband caught up with her at the lake's edge, and when he saw that it was dry and there was nothing left for him, he struck her.

The gods became so angry at these two for disturbing the peace of the Valley that they decided to transform them into granite cliffs that face each other from opposite sides of the Valley, so they could never again be together. Nangas was changed into Washington Column and Tis-sa-ack became Half Dome. The dark streaks on the dome's face are said to be Tis-sa-ack's tears.

As far as anyone knows, the Ahwahneechees lived for many years without any contact with white people. The Valley's sheer walls made it an impenetrable fortress. Although a few explorers, including members of the **Joseph Walker** party, had seen the Valley from its high north rim as early as 1833, none had found a way to enter it. Even other Miwok tribes avoided the Valley; many had heard rumors of the "black sickness" that had swept through it in the past, and they also knew it was carefully guarded by the Indians who lived there. Yosemite Valley was the exclusive territory of the Ahwahneechee tribe.

THE MARIPOSA BATTALION

When the cry for gold rang out across California in the mid-1800s, the Ahwahneechees' future was suddenly and irrevocably altered. Unbeknownst to them, they were on the verge of losing their exclusive domain over Yosemite. **Gold seekers** swarmed over the entire Sierra Nevada, and it was only a matter of time before they entered Yosemite Valley. The various

YOSEMITE'S PLACE NAMES

Many of Yosemite's place names were given by the men of the Mariposa Battalion, who entered Yosemite Valley in 1851 to round up the Ahwahneechee Indians and deport them to a reservation. Dr. Lafayette Bunnell, who traveled with the Battalion, questioned the captured Ahwahneechees about their names for the Valley's natural features. Some of their words he found too difficult to pronounce, so he substituted a Spanish or English word with roughly the same meaning. Other names were invented in a more random fashion. Here are the sources of a few of Yosemite's place names:

Yosemite: From the Indian word "uzumate," which meant grizzly bear. The Indian tribe that lived in the Valley were called Yosemites by white men, and by other Indian tribes, because they lived in a place where grizzly bears were common and they were reportedly skilled at killing the bears. The Mariposa Battalion named the Valley after the "Yosemite Indians" whom, ironically, they'd been sent there to evict. In a further twist, the Indians didn't call themselves Yosemites; they called themselves Ahwahneechees, and they called the Valley "Ahwahnee" or "place of a gaping mouth."

El Capitan: The Ahwahneechees named this granite monolith for the chief of the first tribe of Yosemite Indians, Too-tok-ah-noo-lah. Bunnell substituted the Spanish word for chief, or *el capitán*.

Royal Arches: This impressive granite cliff, found behind the Ahwahnee Hotel, was named by one of the men in the Mariposa Battalion in honor of his Masonic membership.

Bridalveil Fall: The Ahwahneechees called it "pohono" or evil wind. The name Bridalveil was given by the editor of the Mariposa newspaper in the 1850s because of the fall's white, cascading appearance.

Hetch Hetchy: The Miwok Indians named this valley "Hatchatchie" for a type of grass with edible seeds that grew here.

Illilouette: Although it sounds French, Illilouette was a rough translation of the Indian word "Too-lool-a-we-ack," which meant a good place for hunting.

Vernal Fall: This waterfall reminded Bunnell of springtime. He called the cataract "an eternal April."

Wawona: The Indian word for "big tree." Wawona is an imitation of the hoot of an owl, the guardian spirit of the sequoias.

Tenaya Lake: Named for Chief Tenaya, the last chief of the Ahwahneechee Indians. When told that the lake had been named for him, Chief Tenaya replied that the lake already had a name: Pywiack, or "Lake of Shining Rocks." The name Pywiack now refers to a granite dome near Tenaya Lake.

---

mountain and foothill Indian tribes looked upon these fortune-hunting invaders with distrust, and while some chose to ignore the white man's presence, others raided their outposts and settlements, preyed upon their horses and cattle, and stole their food. Trouble was brewing, and before long the miners and settlers demanded that the U.S. government place the estimated 10,000 Native Americans living in California on reservations, where they could be no trouble.

In response to what was termed the "Indian War," federal commissioners were appointed and sent to the Sierra Nevada to convince the local tribes to sign treaties, cede their lands, and settle on established reservations. Some tribes agreed, but many others resisted. The white settlers believed that stronger action needed to be taken, especially in places like the outskirts of Yosemite, where skirmishes with Indians were becoming commonplace.

By January 1851, the state-sanctioned **Mariposa Battalion** was formed. This band of volunteer soldiers planned to enter Yosemite Valley and round up the Indians who lived there. The leader of the battalion was **James Savage,** a miner who ran a trading outpost farther down the Merced River canyon. He knew several Miwok Indian languages and had employed Indians in his business operations. Savage had a personal interest in catching the Yosemite Indians, as two of his outposts had been attacked and some of his men were killed by Indians.

Soon after starting out on their mission, Savage and the Mariposa Battalion met up with the leader of the Ahwahneechee tribe, Chief Tenaya, somewhere in the vicinity of Wawona. Tenaya at first refused to move his tribe out of the Valley, but when Savage told him that if he didn't agree, all of Tenaya's people would be killed, the chief relented. Still, three days went by without any sign of the Ahwahneechees making their way out of the Valley, so the battalion decided to push on through the winter snow and remove the Indians by force.

The Mariposa Battalion made it to the Valley's high southern rim in late March 1851. Although some 72 Ahwahneechees, mostly women and children, were discovered along the way and surrendered easily, more than 100 tribespeople were believed to be hiding in the Valley. Although the men of the battalion had only rousting Indians on their minds, they were taking a journey of major historical significance, being the first white men ever to set foot in Yosemite Valley. At least one member of the party stopped along the rim trail, awestruck at his first vision of the Valley. This was **Lafayette Bunnell,** the battalion doctor, who kept a detailed account of the entire journey. His book, *Discovery of the Yosemite,* lives on as one of the only accounts of Yosemite Valley in its Edenlike early days.

Upon their descent to the Valley floor, the Mariposa Battalion found no Indians. Presumably, the Ahwahneechees had seen them coming and fled to the high country. The battalion did find the Ahwahneechees' shelters, tools, clothing, and other belongings. The soldiers set fire to the dwellings, caches of acorns, and other food stores, figuring that if the Indians returned, they would be starved out. Soon after the battalion left the Valley, Chief Tenaya and most of the 72 captured Indians escaped.

Because the first Mariposa Battalion did not succeed at rounding up the Ahwahneechees, a second expedition was organized in May 1851. This band of militiamen, led by **Captain John Boling,** was more effective: Five Yosemite Indians were captured, including three of Tenaya's sons. They were held hostage until Chief Tenaya could be brought to the battalion's camp in the Valley. One of Tenaya's sons was killed as he tried to escape.

Forcing Tenaya to serve as guide, Captain Boling then pursued the remainder of the Yosemite Indians into the high country. His soldiers surprised the Ahwahneechees on the shore of Tenaya Lake, where they had made camp. The Indians, who were exhausted and hungry, surrendered. But they asked their captors two haunting questions: "Where can we go that the Americans will not follow us? Where can we make our homes that you will not find us?" The answer, sadly, was the Fresno reservation.

THE END OF THE AHWAHNEECHEES

Tenaya and his people did not fare well in the hot Central Valley. They were unaccustomed to the government food they were given and did not get along with other relocated tribes. The U.S. government never ratified the treaty necessary to close the land deal with the Indians, so in less than a year, after Tenaya promised to create no more trouble, he was allowed to leave the reservation and return to Yosemite. He was soon joined by other Ahwahneechees.

But the tribe's troubles were not over. In May 1852, two prospectors were killed near Bridalveil Fall by a group of Indians. This time the U.S. Army pursued the Ahwahneechees into the high country; five of them were killed along the way in Bloody Canyon. Tenaya and the few remaining members of his band fled to live among the Pauite Indians near Mono Lake.

Still there would be no peace. Accounts vary as to how exactly it occurred, but a common story is that in the summer of 1853, members of the two tribes were engaged in a gambling game. It became competitive, and at some point a fight broke out. Chief Tenaya and several members of his tribe were killed.

Tenaya's death signaled the end for the Ahwahneechees. The last remaining members of his tribe dispersed, some joining the Paiutes and others joining Miwok tribes along the Tuolumne River. Although a few Ahwahneechee descendants continued to live in Yosemite Valley over the next several decades, their numbers were few, and their culture was forever altered by the arrival of the white people.

YOSEMITE'S FIRST TOURISTS

Although the first Mariposa Battalion did not succeed in rousting the Indians, they did arouse public interest with their descriptions of this wondrous valley with its high granite walls and amazing waterfalls. Tourists began flowing into Yosemite Valley as early as 1855, following old Indian trails on horseback.

One of the earliest visitors was **James M. Hutchings,** publisher of the much-read *California Magazine.* Hutchings became so enamored with the Valley that he soon moved there to open a hotel near the base of Sentinel Rock. His magazine published favorable stories about the area, and more and more visitors came. Fortunately, among them were some early-day conservationists—men like **Frederick Law Olmsted,** the man who designed New York's Central Park. Olmsted and others recognized the precious nature of the resources in Yosemite Valley and the nearby Mariposa Grove of Giant Sequoias, another major attraction. They appealed to the U.S. Congress to protect these places from exploitation.

CREATION OF A NATIONAL PARK

In 1864, Senator John Conness introduced a bill to the U.S. Congress that would require

Know Yosemite

GALEN CLARK: YOSEMITE'S FIRST GUARDIAN

After the Yosemite Grant became federal law, Yosemite Valley and the Mariposa Grove of Giant Sequoias came under the management of a board of California commissioners. They hired homesteader Galen Clark, who ran the stagecoach stop at Wawona, as the first guardian of Yosemite Valley and the Mariposa Grove.

Among men whose names will forever be associated with Yosemite National Park, Clark stands out. He had come to California in 1854 to search for gold, but a lung ailment sent him to the mountains, where he expected to live out his final days. Apparently the fresh air was good for him, because he survived another 50 years until just four days before his 96th birthday.

Clark set up a stagecoach station and inn at Wawona in 1857 and acted as a guide to visitors to Yosemite Valley and the Mariposa Grove. He was known as "Mr. Yosemite" and was well respected for his knowledge and love of the park. As official park guardian, he performed largely the same tasks that he had been doing as a volunteer who simply loved the area. He worked to relocate homesteaders, improved facilities for travelers, and most of all, did whatever was necessary to protect the giant sequoias and Yosemite Valley. John Muir called him "one of the most sincere tree-lovers I ever knew."

Clark selected his own grave site in the Yosemite Valley Cemetery, where he is now buried. His grave lies beneath five giant sequoia trees that he planted himself, with seeds transported from the Mariposa Grove.

LEAVE NO TRACE

When hiking in Yosemite, follow the Leave No Trace Principles of outdoor ethics:

Plan Ahead and Prepare
- Prepare for extreme weather, hazards, and emergencies.
- Schedule your trip to avoid times of high use.
- Visit in small groups. Split larger parties into groups of 4–6.

Travel and Camp on Durable Surfaces
- Durable surfaces include established trails and campsites, rock, gravel, dry grasses or snow.
- Protect riparian areas by camping at least 200 feet from lakes and streams.
- Good campsites are found, not made. Altering a site is not necessary.
- Concentrate use on existing trails and campsites.
- Walk single file in the middle of the trail, even when wet or muddy.
- Keep campsites small. Focus activity in areas where vegetation is absent.

Dispose of Waste Properly
- Pack it in, pack it out. Inspect your campsite and rest areas for trash or spilled foods. Pack out all trash, leftover food, and litter.
- Deposit solid human waste in catholes dug 6 to 8 inches deep at least 200 feet from water, camp, and trails. Cover and disguise the cathole when finished.
- Pack out toilet paper and hygiene products.
- To wash yourself or your dishes, carry water 200 feet away from streams or lakes and use small amounts of biodegradable soap. Scatter strained dishwater.

Leave What You Find
- Preserve the past: examine, but do not touch, cultural or historic structures and artifacts.

the state of California to protect Yosemite Valley and the Mariposa Grove of Giant Sequoias and preserve them undisturbed. Despite the fact that the Civil War was in progress and the government's attention was on more pressing matters, President Abraham Lincoln signed the bill into law on June 30, 1864. This act, called the **Yosemite Grant,** had much greater significance than just protecting portions of what is now Yosemite. It was also the first application of a new concept, that of the U.S. government preserving and protecting a wild place as a "park," for public use and recreation. Although the law actually created a California state park, not a national park, this single legislative act ultimately paved the way for our great chain of National Parks.

While visitation of the new park was reaching an all-time high, so was use of land surrounding the protected Valley and Mariposa Grove. The High Sierra region that is now part of Yosemite National Park was seen as a free resource to be exploited. Cattle and sheep ranchers used the high, fragile meadows to graze their stock in the summer. Hundreds of sawmills were built on the west side of the Sierra Nevada, as loggers moved in to fell giant sequoias and other big conifers. Silver and gold mines sprung up in even the most remote areas, and with them the need for lumber and fuel.

- Leave rocks, plants and other natural objects as you find them.
- Avoid introducing or transporting non-native species.
- Do not build structures, furniture, or dig trenches.

Minimize Campfire Impacts
- Campfires can cause lasting impacts to the backcountry. Use a lightweight stove for cooking and enjoy a candle lantern for light.
- Where fires are permitted, use established fire rings, fire pans, or mound fires.
- Keep fires small. Only use sticks from the ground that can be broken by hand.
- Burn all wood and coals to ash, put out campfires completely, then scatter cool ashes.

Respect Wildlife
- Observe wildlife from a distance. Do not follow or approach them.
- Never feed animals. Feeding wildlife damages their health, alters natural behaviors, and exposes them to predators and other dangers.
- Protect wildlife and your food by storing rations and trash securely.

Be Considerate of Other Visitors
- Respect other visitors and protect the quality of their experience.
- Be courteous. Yield to other users on the trail.
- Step to the downhill side of the trail when encountering pack stock.
- Take breaks and camp away from trails and other visitors.
- Let nature's sounds prevail. Avoid loud voices and noises.

This copyrighted information has been reprinted with permission from the Leave No Trace Center for Outdoor Ethics. For more information or materials, please visit www. LNT.org or call 303/442-8222.

Another early conservationist came to the aid of Yosemite: a young Scotsman by the name of **John Muir,** who made his first trip to Yosemite in 1868, then kept coming back for another 40 years. Muir was greatly concerned with the destructive activities taking place in the region surrounding the land protected by the Yosemite Grant. He wrote articles about it for *Century* magazine, an influential publication edited by **Robert Underwood Johnson,** who was also interested in preserving Yosemite. With prompting by Muir, Johnson, and other far-thinking Yosemite advocates, Congress was pushed to further action. On October 1, 1880, it passed a law that created Yosemite National Park and preserved the areas surrounding Yosemite Valley and the Mariposa Grove. President Benjamin Harrison put his signature on the law.

To protect this newly created federal park, the **U.S. Army Cavalry** arrived in the high country and worked to stop all grazing activities, remove illegal homesteaders, fight forest fires, and chase out poachers. In 1906, the State of California ceded its control of the Valley and the Mariposa Grove to the federal government. Those regions, too, now fell under the cloak of the national park. In 1916 the U.S. Army Cavalry was relieved of its duties when the national parks were placed under civilian management through the Department of the Interior, and the **National Park Service** was born.

THE POPULARIZATION OF YOSEMITE

By 1874, a half-dozen toll roads had been built into Yosemite Valley. Since visitors could now travel via stagecoach instead of horseback, more and more tourists came to see the famous Valley. Still, travel was far from easy. From Wawona, the trip via a rocky, dirt toll road into Yosemite Valley took about eight hours. It was dusty and sometimes treacherous—stagecoach holdups were not uncommon, and the horses were skittish on the narrow, steep roads. Once they made it to the Valley, travelers were surprised to find none of the fancy accommodations they were accustomed to in other places—only rustic cabins and tents.

In short order, Yosemite Valley went from being an exotic destination only visited by the very wealthy or adventurous to a place where tourists of every ilk had access. In 1886, the California state legislature made all privately owned toll roads and trails free and open to the public. **Camp Curry** (now Curry Village) opened in Yosemite Valley in 1889. In 1907, the Yosemite Valley Railroad was completed all the way to El Portal, where riders transferred to a stagecoach for the final passage up the Merced River canyon. This mountain railroad remained in operation until 1945 but was little used after 1926, when Highway 140, the "All-Year Highway," was completed.

Although the first two automobiles—a Stanley Steamer and a Locomobile—had entered Yosemite Valley in 1900, it wasn't until 1913 that the first park entrance fee was paid. Automobiles were banned from Yosemite after 1906, when Yosemite Valley became a part of the national park. The policy at that time was that autos were not allowed in any federal park, but in 1913, the new Secretary of the Interior relented, recognizing that automobiles were the way of the future. By 1917, enough people were traveling to Yosemite by car that the Park Service saw the need to build paved roads. By

1920, two-thirds of all Yosemite visitors were arriving by car. From then until World War II, Yosemite saw its years of greatest development, from roadways to sewer and garbage systems to luxury hotels.

A side note: The first vehicle entrance fee was $5, good for seven days. This same fee remained in effect from 1913, when it was a sizable sum, to the tail end of the 20th century, when it was equal to the price of a sandwich. The only fee hike in the history of the park occurred in 1997, when it was raised from $5 to the current $20, still good for seven days.

THE PARK TODAY

Ironically, but also fortunately, after so many years of efforts to change Yosemite from its primitive state to a more developed, visitor-friendly park, the current trend is a move in the opposite direction. The Park Service released the **General Management Plan** for Yosemite in 1980. It was designed to strike a balance between preservation and protection of the park on the one hand, and public enjoyment on the other.

The original plan called for removing all parking lots and automobiles from the Valley and the Mariposa Grove, and moving most of the park's development and services out of the Valley. Shuttles would carry visitors into the Valley and Mariposa Grove from outlying parking lots.

As of 2006, none of those actions have been taken. Although the General Management Plan created a lot of heated debate, it didn't produce much noticeable change in the park. In the years after 1980, political winds shifted in Washington, less funding was available for national parks, and the General Management Plan was shelved until 1992, when it was altered and amended after the completion of an environmental impact statement. Two somewhat more workable documents were completed in 2000—the Yosemite Valley Plan and the Merced River Plan.

Both plans are quite ambitious. The **Yosemite Valley Plan** alone calls for 250 separate ac-

THE GREAT FLOOD OF 1997

Wandering around Yosemite Valley, you see the 10-foot-high signs at strategic points: outside the Yosemite Chapel, and along the road near the Pines Campgrounds. The signs read, "Flood water level, January 2, 1997, 11 P.M." They are a reminder of the biggest flood in Yosemite Valley's recorded history.

Floods, like rockslides and earthquakes, are natural occurrences in Yosemite. They have happened before; they will happen again. Until the 1997 flood, the biggest flood on record in the Valley was in 1955. Another massive flood occurred in 1937. But the 1997 flood was several feet higher than any that had occurred previously and served to dramatically alter the face—and the future—of Yosemite Valley.

The torrential rainstorm began on New Year's Eve and didn't stop for three days. A warm front moved in. The temperature rose until it was so unseasonably warm that at 9,000 feet in elevation it was raining instead of snowing. Existing snow began to melt from the high rim above the Valley, filling creeks and streams. Yosemite Falls roared with such a torrent that windows and walls rattled in the homes below it. Trees, brush, and boulders clogged the Merced River. The river swelled to a lake that flooded the Valley as high as 10 feet in places.

Nearly 2,000 people were stranded in Yosemite Valley and forced to camp out on the upper floors of buildings. Employees' quarters, campgrounds, and several Yosemite Lodge buildings were destroyed. The sewer system was knocked out. Picnic tables and fire grills were picked up and floated to new locations. Even after the rain stopped, the Valley was closed to visitors for more than two months during the cleanup.

In the end, the National Park Service used the great 1997 flood as an opportunity to make some dramatic changes in the Valley. Several campgrounds that were situated in the flood plain were cleared out, reducing the total number of Valley campsites by nearly half. Other buildings, including visitor lodgings and employee housing, were also permanently removed. While some people perceived this loss of visitor facilities as a negative, it was in fact a push in a positive direction, toward decreasing traffic and congestion in the Valley.

Know Yosemite

---

tions, which will take more than a decade to complete. These include moving the Valley Visitor Center to a more accessible location, building more pedestrian and bicycle trails, and removing road segments from Ahwahnee and Stoneman Meadows. More controversial measures include limiting day-use parking in the Valley to a 550-space parking lot and creating an out-of-Valley parking area with shuttle bus service into the Valley. Day visitors could still choose to drive into the Valley, but with the understanding that they may not be able to park. Overnight visitors would be able to drive in and park at their lodging or campsite.

Also under the Yosemite Valley Plan, more emphasis would be placed on rustic accommodations befitting a national park. Some motel-style units of Yosemite Lodge would be removed, and Housekeeping Camp would be reduced to 100 units that are set back farther from the Merced River. Campgrounds would be redesigned to include a greater variety of sites, including some walk-in tent sites and utility hookup RV sites, to reduce noise from generators. Showers would be added at some camps.

It is uncertain how much of the Yosemite Valley Plan will ever be implemented. As political moods swing, and as lawsuits get filed, plans for Yosemite Valley will probably be made, altered, revised, and re-made.

Some of the intentions of the original General Management Plan were given a helping hand by Mother Nature in 1997, when she delivered a devastating flood that wiped out 350 campsites and dozens of lodging units from the Valley. Yosemite has also been helped by the fact that since the mid-1990s, when visitation hit an all-time high of four million people per year, that number has dropped to about 3.4 million. Many who work in or near

Yosemite believe that visitation has fallen because people were scared off by rumors about the implications of the proposed General Management Plan. Hotel and inn managers report that some visitors, especially those from outside California and the United States, believe they must have reservations to enter Yosemite or that they cannot drive their cars in the park.

A few good changes have been accomplished or are in the works. One is the **YARTS** bus system, which is a voluntary-use bus line that carries visitors into the park from various pickups outside the park. The bus system started running in May 2000 and currently serves towns in Mariposa, Merced, and Mono Counties. (For more information on YARTS, call 877/989-2787 or visit www.yarts.com.) In time, this bus system will probably be expanded, perhaps to the point of carrying out the mandate of the Yosemite Valley Plan.

Clearly, change is in the wind for Yosemite Valley, and perhaps for other areas of the park as well. But as the more than 20 years since the General Management Plan was released have proven, change will not happen overnight.

Tips for Travelers

FOREIGN TRAVELERS
Entering the United States and California

Generally, citizens of foreign countries who wish to visit the United States must first obtain a visa. To apply for a visa, applicants must prove that the purpose of their trip to the United States is for business, pleasure, or medical treatment; that they plan to remain for a limited period of time; and that they have a residence outside the United States as well as other binding ties that will guarantee their return abroad.

However, under the Visa Waiver Program, citizens of 28 foreign countries do not need a visa for travel to the United States, provided they are staying no more than 90 days. The countries are: Andorra, Austria, Australia, Belgium, Brunei, Denmark, Finland, France, Germany, Iceland, Ireland, Italy, Japan, Liechtenstein, Luxembourg, Monaco, The Netherlands, New Zealand, Norway, Portugal, San Marino, Singapore, Slovenia, Spain, Sweden, Switzerland, the United Kingdom, and Uruguay.

As part of the customs process, the United States Department of Agriculture screens all foreign visitors at their first point of arrival in the United States (usually, at the airport). Foreigners must declare, in writing, all fruits, vegetables, fruit and vegetable products, meat, meat products, and dairy products that they have brought from another country. Failure to declare an apple or orange, or a leftover sandwich containing meat, can lead to a major delay in getting through customs.

Once a foreign visitor is inside the United States, he or she may travel freely from state to state. However, all visitors (foreign or not) are subject to additional agricultural inspections when entering California by automobile from bordering states. A California Department of Food and Agriculture (CDFA) officer may stop your car momentarily to ask you where you've been traveling and if you are carrying any fruits, vegetables, or plants from other states. In rare cases, vehicles are searched. Most out-of-state produce and plants should be kept out of California. For more information on current regulations, phone the CDFA consumer help line at 800/675-2427.

Finally, there is no compulsory or government insurance plan in the United States. Foreign travelers are advised to purchase travel and health insurance in case of an emergency.

Money and Currency Exchange

Most large banks in the United States exchange major foreign currencies. Large international airports such as San Francisco have currency exchange offices in their international terminals. If you are traveling to Yosemite, you should exchange your money before you head into the small-town regions surrounding the park. The areas around Yosemite, as well as the developed areas inside the park, are not large enough to offer currency exchange.

While traveling in California, your best bet is to use traveler's checks and credit cards for purchases (both are accepted widely in Yosemite), and use an ATM (automated teller machine) to get cash. ATMs are found at various business establishments in the park.

Electricity

Electrical current in the United States is 110 volts. A hair dryer or electric shaver from Europe won't work here without an adapter, which is available at most travel stores.

Foreign Language Assistance

Within the United States, you may phone 888/US1-INFO for free access to emergency services and travel assistance in more than 140 languages.

California Laws

You must be 21 years of age to purchase and/or drink alcohol in California. Drinking and driving is a serious crime in this state; the simple act of having an open container of alcohol in your car, even if it is empty, is punishable by law. If you are arrested for driving under the influence of alcohol, you must submit to a chemical test to determine blood alcohol content.

Smoking is prohibited on public transportation and in all public buildings in California. Most restaurants and bars have no-smoking policies. For the most part, you aren't allowed to light up unless you are in a private space or outside in an open area. If someone asks you to put out your cigarette, it's best to do so. Chances are, they have the law on their side. You must be 18 years of age to purchase tobacco products in California.

Taxes and Tipping

The California state sales tax is 7.25 percent. Local taxes may be as much as 1.25 percent, adding a total 8.5 percent to almost everything

you buy. At sit-down restaurants, it is customary to tip 15 percent on top of the bill. The tip is your payment to your food server for good service—and in the United States, most servers count on your tip as part of their day's pay.

TRAVELING BY RV

Recreational vehicles (RVs) are welcome in Yosemite, except for the very biggest of the rigs: RVs over 40 feet long are not permitted in Yosemite Valley, and RVs over 35 feet long are not permitted in other areas of the park.

Certain roads in the park are not accessible to smaller RVs as well. The Hetch Hetchy Road is closed to all vehicles longer than 25 feet. The Mariposa Grove Road is closed to RVs and trailers longer than 23 feet 9 A.M.–6 P.M. in summer, but you can park your rig at Wawona and ride a free shuttle bus to the grove. The five-mile access road to Yosemite Creek Campground is closed to RVs or trailers longer than 24 feet. The road to Tamarack Flat Campground also is not recommended for large RVs.

If you are visiting Yosemite Valley for the day in your RV, you would be well advised to enter the park early in the morning, park your rig as soon as possible, and then ride the free Valley shuttle bus to all of the Valley's sites (or join an organized tour, or rent a bike and ride, or walk around the Valley on foot).

If you are planning to camp in your RV, know in advance that there are no utility hookups in Yosemite. Park regulations permit the use of generators 7 A.M.–7 P.M. only. Dump stations are available at three locations in the park: Upper Pines Campground, Wawona Campground, and Tuolumne Meadows Campground.

TRAVELING WITH CHILDREN

Families and national parks are a perfect match. Yosemite and other national parks are ideal places to teach kids about nature and the environment, and to let them experience a world without television sets and video games.

Kids invariably have fun in the outdoors, and with all the kid-friendly activities in the park, parents are never left wondering what to do with their charges. In Yosemite, kids can go for hikes, attend a campfire talk led by a park ranger, climb on rocks, help with camp chores, learn about animals that reside in the park, ride bikes, toast marshmallows, go rafting, ride horses, learn photography skills, or just hang out in a meadow and be kids. The list of possible activities for kids in Yosemite is endless—just as it is for adults.

Visit the **Nature Center at Happy Isles.** Kids can play in the children's corner or check out wildlife exhibits. A few short trails lead from the center.

Go to an **evening campfire program** and enjoy songs and stories with a ranger. Campfire programs are held at Crane Flat and Wawona

Campgrounds; check the free Yosemite newspaper for dates and times.

The **Explore Yosemite Family Program,** run by Yosemite Concession Services naturalists, is designed for children of any age. Each half-day session is limited to 20 participants (adults and children) and departs from Curry Village in the morning and afternoon. Areas of study might include geology, wildlife, or Yosemite history. Sign up at any tour desk or phone 559/252-4848 for reservations.

LeConte Memorial Lodge in Yosemite Valley (shuttle bus stop number 12), run by the Sierra Club, has a **children's center** with a variety of rotating programs for kids. Phone 209/372-4542 for more information, or check the schedule in the park's free newspaper.

The **Junior Ranger program,** popular at national parks across the country, is open to kids

CAN I BRING MY DOG TO YOSEMITE?

Fido isn't going to like hearing this, but dogs in Yosemite are a really bad idea. Dogs are not permitted on Yosemite's trails, although they are allowed in parking lots, picnic areas, paved roads, and some campgrounds. (They are not allowed at Camp 4, Tamarack Flat, Porcupine Flat, and all group campsites.) Dogs may not be left unattended at campsites or anywhere else in the park. At all times, they must be physically restrained or attached to a leash six feet long or shorter. They are not permitted at any of the park's accommodations (except some campgrounds), and they are not allowed on shuttle buses.

Although as a general rule dogs are not allowed on trails, there are a few rather confusing exceptions: Dogs are allowed on "fully paved" trails, such as the path to Lower Yosemite Fall or Bridalveil Fall and the Yosemite Valley Bike Path. However, they are not allowed on "poorly paved" trails, such as the trail to the base of Vernal Fall.

To add to the confusion, dogs are permitted on a few old dirt roads that are now trails: the Meadow Loop and the Four Mile Fire Road across from the Wawona Hotel (not the Four Mile Trail in the Valley), the Carlon Road near Big Oak Flat, and the Big Oak Flat Road between Hodgdon Meadow and Hazel Green Creek.

Yosemite Valley has a dog kennel near the horse stables where you can board your dog, but this is a terribly sad place where dogs sit glumly in cages while their owners go off for great hikes around the Valley. To put your dog in the kennel, he or she must be at least six months old and 10 pounds in weight and have written proof of vaccinations (rabies, distemper, parvo, and Bordetella). The kennel is open only from May to September (209/372-8348).

On top of all that, here's one more doggone rule to keep in mind: If you insist on bringing your dog to Yosemite, you are responsible for cleaning up after him or her, and you must deposit all "deposits" into the nearest trash receptacle.

7–13. They earn a certificate and a patch as they learn about the wonders of Yosemite. For more information, check the park's free newspaper, or ask in any visitor center. Younger kids (3–6) can join in the Little Cubs program.

Kids with cameras can join a Kodak photographer for a **one-hour workshop.** Each morning lesson starts at the Ahwahnee Hotel and is open to shutterbugs ages 7–12. Check the park's free newspaper for more details, or ask at the Ahwahnee front desk.

TRAVELING WITH PETS

Traveling with your pet to Yosemite, or any national park in the United States, is a difficult proposition. Pets are not allowed in any lodging in Yosemite, and they are not allowed on the vast majority of trails. Pets are permitted in some campgrounds and in all parking lots and picnic areas. In campgrounds, they must be in your tent, RV, or car at night, or you risk having your pet tangle with a bear or other wild animal. Pets should never be left unattended at any time.

SENIORS

If you are 62 years of age or older and a U.S. citizen or permanent resident, you can purchase a Golden Age Pass for $10. This is a one-time fee that is good at all U.S. national parks for the rest of your life. If you are blind or permanently disabled and a U.S. citizen or permanent resident, you can receive a Golden Access Pass at no cost. This, too, is good at all U.S. national parks for life.

ACCESSIBILITY

People with permanent disabilities are entitled to a Golden Access Passport, which provides free access to all federal fee areas, including all U.S. national parks and national forests. It also allows for discounted camping fees at some campgrounds. Golden Access Passports are available at no cost from Yosemite visitor centers and entrance stations.

A free brochure on accessibility for wheelchair users and other physically challenged visitors is available by contacting the park. Wheelchair rentals are available at the Yosemite Medical Clinic (209/372-4637) and at the Yosemite Lodge bike rental kiosk (209/372-1208).

For hearing-impaired visitors, a sign language interpreter is available in the park in the summer months. To request in advance that the interpreter is available at a certain park event or activity, contact the rangers in any visitor center. All requests are filled on a first-come, first-served basis. Park orientation videos and slide shows in the Valley Visitor Center are captioned.

For visitors who are sight-impaired, tactile exhibits are found at the Yosemite Valley Visitor Center, Happy Isles Nature Center, Indian Cultural Museum, and Mariposa Grove Museum.

People with handicapped placards in their cars are allowed driving access on the Happy Isles Loop and paved road to Mirror Lake (east of Curry Village). Disabled visitors who don't have a handicapped placard may obtain a temporary one from park visitor centers.

In spring through fall, disabled people who are unable to board the Mariposa Grove Tram may drive behind the tram and listen to a cassette tape tour of the grove.

For additional information on disabled visitors services, phone the Yosemite Medical Clinic at 209/372-4637 or the Accessibility Coordinator at 209/379-1068.

HEALTH AND SAFETY

If you should happen to have a medical problem while you are visiting Yosemite, you'll be happy to know that the Valley Medical Clinic can handle most big and small emergencies. Located on Ahwahnee Drive in Yosemite Valley, the clinic has an experienced nursing staff, emergency physicians, a nurse practitioner, and support staff on duty (209/372-4637). Emergency care is available 24 hours a day; drop-in and urgent care are available daily 8 A.M.–7 P.M. The nearest hospitals are in Sonora, Oakhurst, and Mammoth Lakes.

By far the biggest dangers to be faced in Yosemite are those created by visitors who don't follow posted rules and regulations. If a sign says Stay Back from the Edge, obey it. Be wary of waterfalls, slick hiking trails, and cliffs and ledges with steep drop-offs. Remain on the trails to avoid getting lost or getting yourself into a hazardous situation. Always carry a good map. If you are heading out for a hike, tell someone where you are going and when you will be back. Carry a day pack with the essentials for a day out and a few emergencies.

A few more rules to live by: Don't drink water from streams and lakes without purifying it; carry and use a filter for purifying water from natural sources, or pack along bottled water. While you're at it, take along extra water and food; if you don't need it, you can give it to someone else who does.

While hiking, be aware of your surroundings: Pay attention to the direction you've traveled and landmarks you've passed. Keep an eye out for approaching storms, and stay off exposed ridges and peaks if a thunderstorm is threatening. Watch yourself and your companions for symptoms of altitude sickness and problems encountered from high elevation.

Getting There

ORIENTATION

Yosemite National Park is on the western slope of the Sierra Nevada mountains, approximately 180 miles east of San Francisco and 400 miles north of Los Angeles. Driving time from San Francisco is approximately four hours. A large chunk of the drive is on two-lane highways where you can't drive faster than 45 mph. Driving time from Los Angeles is about seven hours. Most of that time is spent on major freeways where you can drive 65 mph or faster. The vast majority of Yosemite visitors enter the park in a private automobile or RV, either their own or one they have rented. Taking public transportation to the park is possible, although it requires some careful planning. But once in the park, you will probably want to have a car anyway, unless you plan to spend your time in Yosemite Valley, where free shuttle buses make cars unnecessary.

By Air

The closest airport to Yosemite is in Fresno, California, a two-hour drive from Yosemite's South Entrance at Wawona. Because of its proximity, the **Fresno-Yosemite Airport** is an excellent choice for Yosemite travelers, but the small airport has only limited service.

Yosemite-bound travelers can also fly into

San Francisco International Airport (SFO), which is served by all major international and domestic airlines. The San Francisco Bay Area's two other major airports, in Oakland and San Jose, are also worth checking out. Flights into Oakland or San Jose are often less expensive than flights into SFO. It is a four-hour drive from SFO to either the Arch Rock Entrance on Highway 140 or the Big Oak Flat Entrance on Highway 120; Oakland and San Jose are both about half an hour closer. Yosemite visitors should also look into flights into **Sacramento International Airport,** which is a three-hour drive from the Big Oak Flat entrance on Highway 120, or a four-hour drive from the Arch Rock Entrance on Highway 140.

In the summer months only, Yosemite visitors can fly into **Reno, Nevada,** then make a three-hour drive to Yosemite's Tioga Pass Entrance on Highway 120 off U.S. 395. Tioga Pass is usually open from June through October each year, depending on snow.

Smaller airports are located at Merced, Mammoth Lakes, and Modesto, California, but they do not offer commercial passenger service.

By Train and Bus

The nearest train station (Amtrak, 800/USA-RAIL, www.amtrak.com) is in Merced, California, more than an hour's drive from the park. Visitors riding Amtrak will need to board a bus or rent a car to get to Yosemite.

Bus transportation is available year-round from Merced on VIA Bus Lines, 209/384-1314 or 888/727-5287, www.via-adventures.com. Reservations for VIA bus service to Yosemite should be made 24 hours in advance. VIA makes four trips daily to the Amtrak station in Merced and connects for direct service with trains.

Rental cars are available in Merced from Aide Rent A Car, 1530 W. 16th St., 209/722-8084; or Enterprise Rent A Car, 1334 W. Main St., 209/722-1600.

FROM FRESNO
Airport

The single terminal at Fresno-Yosemite Airport (559/498-4095, www.flyfresno.org) is served by these airlines: Air Wisconsin, Alaska, Allegiant, America West/Mesa Airlines, American, Continental, Delta, Hawaiian, Horizon, Northwest, Skywest, and United. Because Fresno-Yosemite isn't a "major" airport, flying here usually requires making a connection through larger airports in other cities. Currently, service is offered to and from Boise, Idaho; Denver and Colorado Springs, Colorado; El Paso and Dallas/Fort Worth, Texas; Des Moines, Iowa; Las Vegas, Nevada; Los Angeles, San Francisco, and Palm Springs, California; Memphis, Tennessee; Phoenix, Arizona; Portland, Oregon; Salt Lake City, Utah; Seattle, Washington; and Guadalajara and Mexico City, Mexico.

There is virtually nothing to do for entertainment at the diminutive Fresno airport. You can have a meal at the lone coffee shop/restaurant, or get a haircut at the airport barbershop, or buy a souvenir in the solo gift shop. Otherwise, be sure you have a good book to keep you company while you wait for your plane.

Car Rentals

Several major car rental companies are located at Fresno-Yosemite Airport: Avis (559/251-5001 or 800/331-1212, www.avis.com), Budget (559/253-4100 or 800/527-0700, www.budget.com), Dollar (866/434-2226 or 800/800-4000, www.dollar.com), Hertz (559/251-5055 or 800/654-3131, www.hertz.com), and National (559/251-5577 or 800/227-7368, www.nationalcar.com).

RV Rentals

RV rentals in Fresno cost about the same as elsewhere in California. Expect to pay about $500 for three nights in the low season (October to April) or $650 in the high season (May to September) for an RV that can sleep six people. On a night-by-night basis, you can save a little money by renting an RV for a week. Seven nights' rental will run about $1,000 during the low season, $1,400 during the high season. But don't forget to tack on the mileage fee. Most companies allow 100 free miles per day, and then charge a flat rate for extra mileage (typically about 29 cents per mile).

Also, plan to spend a small fortune on gasoline—most RVs get 6–10 miles to the gallon. The smallest rigs may get a whopping 14 miles per gallon.

A local company that rents RVs in Fresno is **A-Class RV Motorhome Rental,** 559/264-1920. A large national company also has a rental office in Fresno: **Cruise America,** 4325 W. Shaw Ave, Ste. D, 559/498-8445 or 800/327-7799, www.cruiseamerica.com.

Accommodations

Because Fresno-Yosemite Airport is only a two-hour drive from Yosemite, it's unlikely you'll spend much time in Fresno. It's not that the region doesn't have its charms (hey, it's the number one farm county in the nation); it's just that it pales when compared to Yosemite. But if your flight gets in late and you need a place to stay, four good overnight choices are located near the airport, all of which offer free shuttle service to Fresno-Yosemite and room rates of less than $100 per night.

Try the 210-room Holiday Inn, 5090 E. Clinton Way, 559/252-3611 or 800/465-4329. It has all the Holiday Inn amenities: heated pool, televisions and telephones in the rooms, and an on-site restaurant and cocktail lounge. Or try the 116-room Courtyard by Marriott/ Fresno Airport, 1551 N. Peach Ave., 800/321-2211; or the 78-room Chateau Inn by Piccadilly Inn Hotels, 5113 E. McKinley Ave., 559/456-1418 or 800/445-2428. Right next door to the Chateau Inn, but with more amenities and a higher price tag, is the Piccadilly Inn by the Airport at 5115 E. McKinley Ave., 559/251-6000 or 800/468-3587.

Suggested Driving Routes

Of the five entrance stations to Yosemite, visitors coming from the south (Fresno, Los Angeles, Oakhurst) generally use the **South Entrance** on Highway 41. The Mariposa Grove of Giant Sequoias is found within two miles of the South Entrance. This is also the easiest access point for Glacier Point and Badger Pass Ski Area. Yosemite Valley is a one-hour drive from the South Entrance.

From Fresno, simply take Highway 41 north for 65 miles. Plan on two hours on this winding highway to reach Yosemite. The road is usually open year-round, although chains may be required during snowy periods in the winter months.

Gateway Towns

Yosemite visitors driving from Fresno to Yosemite will find that **Oakhurst** is the last major town before the park. This large commercial center is the biggest of any of the towns located near Yosemite's five entrances. The town is completely lacking in charm but extremely handy if there is anything you forgot to pack for your trip. In addition to a multitude of chain motels and restaurants (see the *Lodging* and *Dining* chapters for details), Oakhurst is home to the excellent Yosemite Sierra Visitors Bureau (41969 Highway 41, 559/683-4636, www.yosemitethisyear.com). Several large grocery store chains are located here—Albertson's and Raley's among them. Pretty much anything you could possibly need or want for your Yosemite vacation can be purchased somewhere in town.

Farther north on Highway 41 and much closer to Yosemite's southern entrance, the little hamlet of **Fish Camp** has a few visitor services (a gas station and small grocery store) as well as several motels, bed-and-breakfasts, and other lodgings. The Yosemite Mountain Sugar Pine Railroad (56001 Hwy. 41, Fish Camp, 559/683-7273, www.ymsprr.com), with its historic logging trains, is located here. For a short, easy hike outside of Yosemite's boundaries, take a walk on the Lewis Creek Trail (trailhead is located along Hwy. 41, five miles south of Fish Camp).

FROM SAN FRANCISCO
Airport

San Francisco International Airport (SFO) has three main terminals plus an international terminal, which are shared by most major international and domestic carriers. Don't expect to find cable cars or barking sea lions anywhere nearby, because SFO is not located in San Francisco proper, but rather 15 miles south of the city near the town of Millbrae in San Mateo County (650/876-7834, www.flysfo.com). Do expect to find within SFO's hallowed halls just about every imaginable kind of gift shop and ethnic food restaurant, as well as an excellent series of rotating art exhibits as intriguing as anything you'll find at a major city museum. SFO is not a bad place to kill a few hours.

The San Francisco Bay Area has two other major airports: Oakland International (www.oaklandairport.com) and San Jose International (www.sjc.org). At both airports "international" means primarily Mexico, although San Jose does have flights to and from Tokyo as well. Travelers coming from cities within the United States, especially the western states, should check fares and flight times into San Jose and Oakland as well as San Francisco. Most Bay Area locals prefer the ease of travel at smaller Oakland and San Jose airports over mammoth SFO (and the commute to Yosemite is about 30 minutes shorter!). Visitors arriving from other countries will most likely fly into SFO.

Car Rentals

All the major companies have rental counters at San Francisco Airport, although none are in the terminals. Instead, SFO has an off-airport Rental Car Center that houses all the car companies' rental counters. Travelers get to the Rental Car Center from any of the airport terminals by taking an automated light rail system, the AirTrain Blue Line. AirTrain operates 24 hours a day.

You can have your pick of the car rental companies at SFO: Alamo (650/347-9911 or 800/462-5266, www.alamo.com), Avis (650/877-3156 or 800/331-1212, www.avis.com), Budget (650/877-0998 or 800/527-0700, www.budget.com), Dollar (650/244-4131 or 800/800-4000, www.dollar.com), Enterprise (650/697-9200 or 800/736-8222, www.enterprise.com), Hertz (650/624-6600 or 800/654-3131, www.hertz.com), National (650/616-3000 or 800/227-7368, www.nationalcar.com), and Thrifty (650/259-1313 or 800/847-4389, www.thrifty.com).

RV Rentals

There are no RV rental outlets located in San Francisco proper, but a few are found in outlying cities. **Cruise America,** is located at 796 66th Ave. in Oakland (510/639-7125 or 800/327-7799, www.cruiseamerica.com).

El Monte RV, another big national chain that rents RVs, has a location near Oakland Airport (4901 Coliseum Way, Oakland, 510/532-7404 or 800/367-3687, www.elmonterv.com). A big advantage to renting here is its "fly and drive" service, with transfers to and from Oakland airport.

Smaller RV rental companies include California Campers (1692 Tacoma Way, Redwood City, 650/216-0000 or 877/894-7368) and Family RV (2828 Monterey Rd., San Jose, 408/365-1991 or 800/201-1991, www.familyrv.com).

Accommodations

San Francisco International Airport is approximately 180 miles from Yosemite, so depending on your flight times, you may need to spend a night somewhere near the airport.

A word of caution: Unless you possess an endless amount of patience, don't even think of driving into or out of the Bay Area toward Yosemite between the hours of 3 and 7 P.M. on weekdays. (On Fridays, that window is even larger—say 1–7 P.M.) Traffic heading eastward at rush hour from San Francisco and its environs is hellish at best. If your plane lands at 4 P.M. and you set out for Yosemite immediately after picking up your rental car, your five-hour drive to the park could easily extend to seven hours. It might be better to wait until the morning, when most of the traffic heads in the opposite direction.

You'd be hard-pressed to find any motels or hotels near San Francisco in the "budget" category. The following seven establishments, all within a few miles of SFO and with free shuttle service to and from the airport, will rent you a room with all the standard amenities for $80–130 per night. Phone around to get the best deal, and don't forget to request an automobile club or other discount.

Holiday Inn Express, 1250 Bayshore Hwy., Burlingame, 650/347-2381.

Travelodge Airport, 110 S. El Camino Real, Millbrae, 650/697-7373.

Best Western Airport Grosvenor Hotel, 380 S. Airport Blvd., South San Francisco, 650/873-3200.

Holiday Inn San Francisco International Airport, 275 S. Airport Blvd., South San Francisco, 650/873-3550.

La Quinta Inn, 20 Airport Blvd., South San Francisco, 650/583-2223.

Hyatt Regency San Francisco Airport, 1333 Bayshore Hwy., Burlingame, 650/347-1234.

Clarion San Francisco Airport, 401 E. Millbrae Ave., Millbrae, 650/692-6363.

Suggested Driving Routes

Visitors coming from the west (San Francisco, Oakland, Sacramento) generally access Yosemite by using the Big Oak Flat Entrance on Highway 120 or the Arch Rock Entrance on Highway 140. The Arch Rock/Highway 140 entrance boasts the easiest access to Yosemite

Valley and also has the best winter access to the park because it rarely receives any snowfall. The Big Oak Flat/Highway 120 entrance is the closest western access to Tuolumne Meadows and Tioga Pass, and it also provides fairly easy year-round access to Yosemite Valley. Highway 120 is the shortest and most direct route to Yosemite from the San Francisco Bay Area.

To reach the **Arch Rock Entrance** from San Francisco, take I-80 East across the San Francisco/Oakland Bay Bridge, then head south and east on I-580. Stay on I-580 for 55 miles, passing through Livermore, then take I-5 south. Drive 30 miles and turn east on Highway 140. Drive 40 miles east to Merced, then continue east on Highway 140 for another 35 miles to Mariposa (last chance for supplies), then another 30 miles to the Arch Rock Entrance. The entire drive will take about 4.5 hours, unless you run into traffic in the San Francisco Bay Area. Avoid driving during commute hours if at all possible.

To reach the **Big Oak Flat Entrance** from San Francisco, take I-80 East across the San Francisco/Oakland Bay Bridge, then head east on I-580. Stay on I-580 for 45 miles, passing through Livermore, then continue east on I-205. In 15 miles, connect to Highway 120 East in Manteca. Stay on Highway 120 heading east for the remaining 85 miles to the Big Oak Flat Entrance. Total driving time is about four hours if you are not stopped by traffic. If your destination is Yosemite Valley, you have another 45 minutes of driving after the Big Oak Flat Entrance.

If you want to visit **Hetch Hetchy,** the access road to this region of the park begins one mile from the Big Oak Flat Entrance station, so you should use Highway 120 as your driving route.

Gateway Towns

If you are traveling to Yosemite via Highway 120, the Gold Rush–era town of **Groveland** is your last chance for services before entering the park. The entire town is about 400 yards long, and, although decidedly quaint, it has little to offer in the way of shops and services. A handful of excellent lodgings and restaurants serve Yosemite visitors; see the *Lodging* and *Din-*

ing chapters for details. Main Street Market (19000 Hwy. 120, 209/962-7452) on the east end of town is a good place to buy last-minute groceries. At Mountain Sage (18653 Hwy. 120, 209/962-4686), you can pick up a pair of convertible hiking pants or snowshoes. Nine miles east of Groveland in the hamlet of Buck Meadows is the Stanislaus National Forest Groveland Ranger District office (209/962-7825), a useful stop for information about Yosemite or the surrounding national forest. A hiking trail leads from the campground near the ranger station to the fire lookout atop Smith Peak.

A good source of additional information on the area is the Groveland Chamber of Commerce, 209/962-0429 or 800/449-9120, www.groveland.org. Or contact the Tuolumne County Visitor Center, 800/446-1333, www.thegreatunfenced.com. For lodging information near Groveland and Yosemite, go to www.staynearyosemite.com.

For more serious grocery or other shopping than what is available in Groveland, you might stop sooner along Highway 120 in **Oakdale,** about 45 minutes before Groveland. Several large grocery chains are found there, as well as numerous fast-food chains and a Big 5 Sporting Goods (209/847-2537). For caffeine junkies, Oakdale is your last chance for a vente latte at Starbucks. If you are looking for a reason to get out of the car for a while, stop in at the Cowboy Museum (355 E. F Street, 209/847-5163, www.oakdalecowboymuseum.org) or the Oakdale Visitors Bureau (590 N. Yosemite Ave., 209/847-2244, www.yosemite-gateway.net).

Visitors traveling to Yosemite via Highway 140 out of Merced will find that **Mariposa** is the last chance for supplies before driving the final stretch along the Merced River to the Arch Rock entrance. Much like Groveland, the small town doesn't offer much besides lodgings and restaurants, but both of those are plentiful. See the *Lodging* and *Dining* chapters for details. The Pioneer Market (209/742-6100), a large grocery store on the eastern edge of town, has enough foodstuffs and supplies to stock your trip, plus a supply of "variety" items like beach towels, miscellaneous camping supplies, and the like. If you are staying in town, two museums are worth a look: the California State Mining and Mineral Museum at the fairgrounds and the Mariposa County Museum and History Center in downtown. The well-stocked Mariposa County Visitor Center is located at the junction of Highways 140 and 49 (5158 Hwy. 140, Mariposa, 209/966-7081 or 866/425-3366, www.homeofyosemite.com).

FROM RENO

Airport

Reno/Tahoe International Airport is an ideal choice for summer visitors who want to see the high country of Yosemite along Tioga Pass Road and perhaps also visit Lake Tahoe, Las Vegas, Death Valley, or other destinations in and around the state of Nevada or the east side of California's Sierra Nevada mountains. Tioga Pass Road (Highway 120) where it enters Yosemite at Tioga Pass, elevation 9,945 feet, is usually open from mid-June to late October each year, but if you are planning your trip far in advance, be cautious about choosing dates on either end of that window. Getting through Tioga Pass cannot be guaranteed in June or October.

The medium-sized airport has two main terminals that serve Alaska, America West, American, Continental, Delta, Frontier, National, Northwest, Skywest, Southwest, and United airlines. Scattered among the gates are the usual cabal of airport shops: a Starbucks, Pizza Hut, Taco Bell, Burger King, golf shop, frozen yogurt shop, and several gift shops and newsstands.

Car Rentals

Several major car rental companies are located at Reno/Tahoe International Airport: Advantage (800/777-5500, www.arac.com), Alamo (800/462-5266, www.alamo.com), Avis (800/984-8840, www.avis.com), Budget (800/527-0700, www.budget.com), Dollar (800/800-4000, www.dollar.com), Hertz (800/654-3131, www.hertz.com), National (800/227-7368, www.nationalcar.com), and Thrifty (800/367-2277, www.thrifty.com).

Additionally, Enterprise Rent-A-Car is located near the airport (3002 Mill St., Reno, 775/329-3773, www.enterprise.com).

RV Rentals

The biggest and oldest RV rental company in Reno is **Sierra RV** (9125 S. Virginia St., Reno, 775/324-0522 or 800/972-8760, www.sierrarv.com). It rents RVs of all shapes and sizes, from 20-foot Class B motor homes that sleep only two to 35-foot motor homes that sleep eight. All are fully contained models with kitchen, bath, color TV, CD player, generator, and microwave. Pets and smoking are not permitted. The daily rate for three to six days is $120–195 (depending on the size of the rig); the weekly rate is $700–1,260. Keep in mind that as with most RV rental companies, you get only 100 free miles per day (not even enough to get from Reno to Tioga Pass). You'll pay 29 cents per mile for the first 2,000 extra miles.

If you'd rather go with a national chain, try **Cruise America** (85 Gentry Way, Reno, 775/824-0576 or 800/327-7799, www.cruiseamerica.com).

Accommodations

Reno calls itself "the biggest little city in the world," for reasons that are altogether unclear. Despite its best efforts to publicize and promote its gambling casinos and nightlife, Reno has remained the poor cousin to much more glamorous Las Vegas in southern Nevada. Nonetheless, the town has a great location vis-à-vis the Eastern Sierra and Lake Tahoe, which serves to keep its hotels and motels in business. It's unlikely you'll want to spend much time in Reno, except perhaps to pull the lever on a few one-armed bandits, but if you need a place to stay near the airport, here are four good choices in the under-$100 category. Each is less than two miles from Reno-Tahoe International Airport:

Best Western Airport Plaza, 1981 Terminal Way, 775/348-6370.

La Quinta Reno Airport, 4001 Market St., 775/348-6100.

Plaza Resort, 121 West St., 775/786-2200.
Reno Hilton, 2500 E. 2nd St., 775/789-2000.

Suggested Driving Routes

Visitors heading to Yosemite from the east (Reno, Mammoth Lakes, Death Valley, Bishop) generally use the **Tioga Pass** Entrance on Highway 120. Note that this road is only open in the summer months; it is usually closed from November until early June. The Tioga Pass Entrance delivers you to Yosemite's high country, only a few miles from famous Tuolumne Meadows. If you're heading straight for Yosemite Valley, it is a 1.5- to 2-hour drive from Tioga Pass, through some of the loveliest scenery you can imagine.

To access Tioga Pass from Reno, Nevada, take U.S. 395 south for 135 miles (through Bridgeport, California) to Lee Vining. This small town is your last chance for supplies. Turn west on Highway 120 on the south side of Lee Vining and drive 13 miles to the Tioga Pass Entrance.

One note: When crossing into California by automobile, all visitors are subject to agricultural inspections. These inspections are run by the California Department of Food and Agriculture (CDFA). The inspection may be as simple as an officer stopping your car momentarily to ask you where you have been traveling and if you are carrying any fruits, vegetables, or plants from other states. Be sure to declare anything you are carrying. In very rare cases, vehicles are searched. As a general rule, most out-of-state produce and plants should be kept out of California, unless they have been properly inspected by the CDFA. For more information on current regulations, phone the CDFA consumer help line at 800/675-2427.

Gateway Towns

Driving from Reno to Yosemite, the small town of **Lee Vining** is your last chance to stock up on supplies before entering the park. Several motels and restaurants are found here; see the *Lodging* and *Dining* chapters for details. A small grocery store on the main drag, the Mono Market, (760/647-1010) can supply you with any last-minute foodstuffs. Numerous campgrounds are found in both Lee Vining Canyon and Lundy Canyon to the north (see the *Camping* chapter).

Aside from being only a few miles from Yosemite, Lee Vining has its own major natural attraction—700,000-year-old Mono Lake, with its strange tufa spires and saline waters. It is one of the greatest bird-watching spots in the entire Sierra. The Mono Lake Committee (760/647-6595, www.monolake.org) has an information center and well-stocked bookstore in downtown Lee Vining. Their office shares space with the Lee Vining Chamber of Commerce (760/647-6629 or 760/647-6595, www.leevining.com).

FROM SACRAMENTO

Airport

Sacramento International Airport (www.sacairports.org) is served by these airlines: Alaska, Aloha, America West, American, Continental, Delta, Frontier, Hawaiian, Horizon, Jet Blue, Mexicana, Northwest, Southwest, United, and United Express. Travelers arriving from other U.S. cities will often find that airfare is less expensive to Sacramento than it is to San Francisco Bay Area airports. The usual array of airport restaurants and shops can be found here: a Starbucks, Cinnabon, Burger King, several bookstores and souvenir shops, and the like.

Car Rentals

Several major car rental companies are located at Sacramento International Airport: Alamo (800/462-5266, www.alamo.com), Avis (559/251-5001 or 800/331-1212, www.avis.com), Budget (559/253-4100 or 800/527-0700, www.budget.com), Dollar (866/434-2226 or 800/800-4000, www.dollar.com), Hertz (559/251-5055 or 800/654-3131, www.hertz.com), and National (559/251-5577 or 800/227-7368, www.national car.com).

RV Rentals

RV rentals in Sacramento cost about the same as elsewhere in California. Expect to pay about $500 for three nights in the low season

(October to April) or $650 in the high season (May to September) for an RV that can sleep six people. On a night-by-night basis, you can save a little money by renting an RV for a week. Seven nights' rental will run about $1,000 during the low season, $1,400 during the high season. Expect to pay extra in mileage fees. Most companies allow 100 free miles per day, and then charge a flat rate for extra mileage (typically about 29 cents per mile).

Plan to spend a small fortune on gasoline—most RVs get 6–10 miles to the gallon; smaller rigs may get up to 14 miles per gallon. **Cruise America,** a large national company, has an RV rental office in Sacramento (B&L RV Parts and Service, 11 Quinta Court, 800/671-7839, www.cruiseamerica.com).

Accommodations

If your flight gets in late and you need a place to stay, more than a dozen hotels are located near the airport. Those listed here have free shuttle service to and from the airport. Room rates are $100–150 per night.

Try the 154-room Hilton Garden Inn (2540 Venture Oaks Way, 916/568-5400, www.hiltongardeninnsacramento.com). It's located only nine miles from the airport, and all rooms have microwaves and small refrigerators. A restaurant is on-site. Or try the Governors Inn (210 Richards Blvd., 916/448-7224 or 800/999-6689,

www.governorsinn.net). Located midway between the airport and downtown Sacramento, the hotel is conveniently located near the shops of Old Sacramento and the city's downtown plaza. Other options include the Residence Inn (Sacramento Airport/Natomas, 2410 W. El Camino Ave., 916/649-1300, www.marriott.com) or the Hawthorn Suites Sacramento (321 Bercut Dr., 916/441-1200, www.hawthorn.com).

Suggested Driving Routes

Of the five entrance stations to Yosemite, visitors coming from the north (Sacramento and Northern California) generally use the **Big Oak Flat** Entrance on Highway 120. This entrance has the most convenient access to Tuolumne Meadows and Tioga Pass Road and is a 30-minute drive from Yosemite Valley.

From Sacramento, take Highway 99 south for 58 miles to Manteca. Take the Yosemite Boulevard/Highway 120 East exit in Manteca. Follow Highway 120 East for 85 miles all the way to the Big Oak Flat entrance to Yosemite. The road is usually open year-round, although chains may be required during snowy periods in the winter months.

Gateway Towns

If you are traveling to Yosemite from Sacramento, **Oakdale** and **Groveland** are your last stops for groceries and supplies.

Getting Around

DRIVING

Except on crowded summer days in Yosemite Valley, driving a car around Yosemite National Park is quite easy. More than 200 miles of roads lace the park, and parking is not usually difficult—again, except in the Valley in summer. If you are visiting Yosemite Valley in summer, consider leaving your car in one of the day-use parking areas and riding the free shuttle bus or taking an organized tour.

Remember to always follow bear precautions when leaving your car parked anywhere in Yo-

semite, especially at night—this means nothing scented should remain inside the car, including food and toiletries.

When visiting Yosemite from November to April, know that chains may be required on any park road at any time. You are least likely to need chains on Highway 140, the "all-weather highway," but it is always possible.

MAPS

Park maps are available at Yosemite's five entrance stations and four visitor centers or by contacting

Yosemite National Park at 209/372-0200. A more detailed map, better suited for people who want to explore beyond the park roads, is available for a fee from Tom Harrison Maps at 415/456-7940 or 800/265-9090, www.tomharrisonmaps.com. This company publishes a general Yosemite National Park recreation map, which shows all the major park trails, and also specialized maps showing greater detail of Half Dome, Yosemite Valley, and the Yosemite High Country. Trails Illustrated (www.trailsillustrated.com) also publishes a Yosemite National Park map.

SHUTTLE BUSES

Free shuttle buses run year-round in Yosemite Valley, and along a stretch of Tioga Pass Road in summer. A free shuttle bus also runs from the Wawona Store to the Mariposa Grove of Giant Sequoias in the summer months. Unlike the shuttle buses in the rest of the park, this one is mandatory (it is intended to relieve traffic on the Mariposa Grove Road).

For visitors staying in towns just outside the park borders, YARTS (Yosemite Area Regional Transit System) buses run from gateway towns outside the park into Yosemite Valley. YARTS buses travel on Highway 120 East and West and Highway 140. The bus system provides an option for visitors who would rather not drive and park in Yosemite Valley. For schedules and information, phone 877/989-2787 or visit the website www.yarts.com.

Suggested Reading

GEOLOGY

Huber, N. King, *The Geologic Story of Yosemite National Park.* Yosemite Association, 1989. The authoritative guide to the complexities of Yosemite's geology, intended to be read by the layman. For the most part, this book succeeds in making the mysteries of glacially carved and polished rock accessible even to non-geology majors. Color photographs and maps aid the process.

Matthes, François E., *The Incomparable Valley: A Geologic Interpretation of the Yosemite.* University of California Press, 1950. For geology fans, this is the must-read classic of the genre, detailing the formation of domes, spires, cliffs, hanging valleys, and their brethren in Yosemite's granite landscape. Ironically, the book was not actually written by the world-famous geologist Matthes, but rather by his colleague Fritiof Fryxell after Matthes died of a heart attack. Fryxell worked from Matthes' decades of research and study in Yosemite, as well as his private notes and unpublished lectures.

HUMAN HISTORY

Belden, L. Burr, and DeDecker, Mary, *Death Valley to Yosemite: Frontier Mining Camps and Ghost Towns.* Spotted Dog Press, 2000. For treasure seekers and history lovers, this collection of mining town stories sheds some light on the histories of long-gone but once bustling communities such as Dogtown, Lundy, and Bennettville. Little of the book pertains to Yosemite proper, except for the story of the old Tioga Road, but the mining towns of the nearby Eastern Sierra are described in detail. Worth a look for the old photographs alone.

Browning, Peter, *Yosemite Place Names.* Great West Books, 1988. If you are wondering why that big meadow is called Tuolumne, or Hetch Hetchy's waterfalls are Tueeulala and Wapama, this is your resource. A great way to learn about Yosemite's history without actually reading a history book.

Browning, Peter, Ed., *John Muir in His Own Words: A Book of Quotations.* Great West Books, 1988. The cogent sound bites of

John Muir make enjoyable reading around a campfire. The editor pulls "Muirisms" from 14 of the great naturalist's books.

Bunnell, Lafayette Houghton, M.D., *Discovery of the Yosemite*. Yosemite Association, 1990. The only first-hand account of European-Americans' first view of Yosemite Valley in March, 1851, when the Mariposa Battalion arrived to round up the Ahwahneechee Indians. Bunnell, who served as the battalion's company doctor, writes in extensive detail and with great depth of feeling for both the scenery and the people of Yosemite.

Chase, J. Smeaton, *Yosemite Trails: Camp and Pack-Train in the Sierra Nevada*. Tioga Publishing Company, 1988. A British gentleman who moved to California in the early 20th century, the author explored the Golden State on horseback from 1911 to 1918. Often described as California's first outdoor writer, Chase's descriptions of Wawona, Hetch Hetchy, and Tuolumne Meadows are still compelling today.

Godfrey, Elizabeth, *Yosemite Indians*. Yosemite Association, 1977. This diminutive. 36-page "booklet" was first published in 1941 and includes an intriguing summary of the history of the Ahwahneechee Indians in Yosemite, with descriptions and photographs of their way of life, from clothing and hair dress to hunting and fishing methods.

Johnston, Hank, *Ho! For Yo-semite*. Yosemite Association, 2000. A collection of 11 original accounts of early day travel to Yosemite Valley by various means of transportation: on foot, horseback, stagecoach, horseless carriage, bicycle, and steam locomotive. The writers include Thomas A. Ayres, later famous for his drawings of Yosemite, Captain John A. Lockwood, a member of the U.S. Cavalry who was assigned to protect the newly founded national park, and Oliver Lippincott, the driver of the first automobile to enter Yosemite Valley in 1900.

Johnston, Hank, *Yosemite's Yesterdays, Volume I and Volume II*. Flying Spur Press, 1989 and 1991. Historian Hank Johnston searched out newspaper and magazine articles, letters, and personal accounts to compile these two collections on Yosemite history. Chapters cover topics such as early logging operations in the park, the building of the first roads into Yosemite and their subsequent and frequent stagecoach holdups, and the long imagined but never constructed Glacier Point Tramway. Filled with black-and-white photographs showing a Yosemite of yesteryear that is hard to imagine today.

McDonald, Douglas, *Bodie: Boom Town, Gold Town! The Last of California's Old-Time Mining Camps*. Nevada Publications, 1988. If your curiosity has been stimulated by a trip to Bodie State Historic Park, check out this short book filled with 1878 black-and-white photographs of the rough-and-tumble mining town.

Meyerson, Harvey, *Nature's Army: When Soldiers Fought for Yosemite*. University of Kansas Press, 2001. This book documents the period from 1890 to 1916, when Yosemite National Park was first created but the National Park Service was not yet in existence. The U.S. Army was given the task of protecting the new national park—a job well out of their normal scope. The author describes the Army's admirably competent efforts at stewardship.

Muir, John, *My First Summer in the Sierra*. Penguin Books, 1997. For fans of Yosemite, this Muir classic is a must-read. Written 40 years after his "first summer," Muir pulled together detailed notes from his initial Yosemite explorations to create an enthusiastic and uplifting story of his love affair with the mountains.

Muir, John, *The Mountains of California*. Sierra Club Books, 1988. More of a naturalist's guide to the Sierra than the novelistic *My First Summer in the Sierra,* this book includes

Muir's detailed observations of creatures like the water ouzel (or dipper bird) and the Douglas squirrel. Even so, Muir's attempts at hard science are always mitigated by his lyrical writing style and unbridled exuberance about the natural world.

Muir, John, *The Yosemite*. Sierra Club Books, 1988. Many of Muir's Yosemite-specific writings are compiled in this one volume, including chapters on the Big Trees (giant sequoias), South Dome (now called Half Dome), and the damming of Hetch Hetchy Valley. An especially good read for Yosemite travelers is the chapter entitled "How Best to Spend One's Yosemite Time," which includes suggested one-, two-, and three-day excursions in the park (circa 1890).

Sanborn, Margaret, *Yosemite: Its Discovery, Its Wonders, and Its People*. Yosemite Association, 1989. This fascinating collection includes 23 separate historical accounts of Yosemite's history, including stories about Ahwahneechee Chief Tenaya, photographer Carleton E. Watkins, scientist Joseph LeConte, and showman and bear tamer Grizzly Adams.

Vale, Thomas and Geraldine, *Walking with Muir Across Yosemite*. The University of Wisconsin Press, 1998. A husband-and-wife team set out to walk in the footsteps of John Muir, following the route he describes in his book *My First Summer in the Sierra*. This personal account, written by two non-Californians, makes a fun companion book to Muir's, especially for first-time visitors to Yosemite.

NATURAL HISTORY

Arno, Stephen F., *Discovering Sierra Trees*. Yosemite Association and Sequoia Natural History Association, 1973. Beautifully illustrated, this brief, 89-page tree guide gives thorough and easily digestible descriptions of 19 conifers and 17 broadleaf trees of the

Sierra. The author's lyrical writing is a pleasure even if you are far from the nearest giant sequoia or mountain hemlock.

Blackwell, Laird R., *Wildflowers of the Sierra Nevada and Central Valley*. Lone Pine Publishing, 1999; and *Wildflowers of the Eastern Sierra and Adjoining Mojave Desert and Great Basin*. Lone Pine Publishing, 2002. These two indispensable wildflower guides, written by a professor at Sierra Nevada College, detail the colorful blooms of the west and east sides of the Sierra. High-quality color photographs and descriptive text make it easy to identify flowers.

Botti, Stephen J., *An Illustrated Flora of Yosemite National Park*. Yosemite Association 2001. This huge coffee-table book is a treasure to own, but you can't take it with you on the wildflower trail. The volume weighs in at more than eight pounds and costs more than $100. This amazingly comprehensive book took 20 years to create and is beautifully illustrated with more than 1,000 watercolor paintings of flowers.

Harvey, H. Thomas, *The Sequoias of Yosemite National Park*. Yosemite Association, 1978. A brief handbook to Yosemite's three giant sequoia groves as well as general information on the life cycle and ecology of the giant trees.

Haulenbeck, Rod, *Tree Adventures in Yosemite Valley*. Wide-Eyed Publications, 1994. Tree and nature lovers might want to get their hands on this paperback to carry on walks in Yosemite Valley. The author provides eight different "tree adventures" that can be experienced in the Valley, from a tour of the garden behind the Yosemite Museum to a hunt for 47 planted giant Sequoias.

Horn, Elizabeth L., *Sierra Nevada Wildflowers*. Mountain Press Publishing Company, 1998. Good photographs accompany descriptions of more than 300 species of flowering plants and shrubs. Unlike most flower identification guides, this one is organized alphabetically (not by color of flower), which could prove problematic. Still, the photographs and descriptions are useful.

Morgenson, Dana C., *Yosemite Wildflower Trails*. Yosemite Association, 1988. More of a narrative than traditional wildflower guides, this book was originally written in the 1970s by a naturalist who led photography walks in Yosemite. Only a few park trails are described, but in exhaustive depth and detail.

Paruk, Jim, *Sierra Nevada Tree Identifier*. Yosemite Association, 1997. This practical guide to the Sierra's 20 conifers and 24 broadleaf trees provides useful tips on tree identification as well as an interesting natural history of each species.

Stokes, Donald and Lillian, *Field Guide to Birds: Western Region*. Little, Brown, and Company, 1996. Utilizing more than 900 full color photographs (not illustrations, as in the popular Peterson Field Guides) the Stokes have created a non-intimidating bird guidebook respected by novice and expert birders alike. General identification information is provided for each species, as well as feeding, nesting, and other characteristic behaviors.

Wiese, Karen, *Sierra Nevada Wildflowers*. Falcon Publishing, 2000. This wildflower guide is loaded with clear, easy-to-see photographs of more than 230 wildflowers specific to the Sierra Nevada Mountains. In addition to the usual descriptive information, each listing includes an explanation of the flower's genus or species name and other interesting facts.

Wilson, Lynn and Jim; and Nicholas, Jeff, *Wildflowers of Yosemite*. Sierra Press, 1998. Gorgeous photographs and helpful descriptions of 224 flower species found throughout Yosemite. A separate section describes what

flowers can be seen in what areas of Yosemite and provides a driving tour of several park regions with flower identification stops along the way.

OUTDOOR RECREATION AND TRAVEL

Beck, Steve, *Yosemite Trout Fishing Guide*. Frank Amato Publications, 1995. An extremely detailed full-color guide to fishing in and around Yosemite, including the Eastern Sierra. The author appears to have left no waters unfished.

Brown, Ann Marie, *Foghorn Outdoors 250 Great Hikes in California's National Parks*. Avalon Travel Publishing, 2004. An extensive guide to the trails of California's 14 national parks, including 50 day-hiking trails in Yosemite. Includes details on mileage, elevation gain, crowd levels, directions to trailheads, and trail recommendations for hikers of every level of ability.

Ditton, Richard P., and McHenry, Donald, *Yosemite Road Guide*. Yosemite Association, 1989. This short guidebook is keyed to roadside markers throughout the park, providing details about what drivers can see from the road. It's an excellent introduction to Yosemite for first-time visitors, especially those who are making a quick tour of the park.

Giacomazzi, Sharon, *Trails and Tales of Yosemite and the Central Sierra*. Bored Feet Press, 2001. A hiking trail book with a twist—each trail has been chosen for its interesting historical context, which is described at length. Readers can learn history while hiking the route of the old Yosemite Mountain-Sugar Pine Railroad or the Old Big Flat Road, or visiting the Merced Grove of Giant Sequoias via the Coulterville Road. Includes not just Yosemite National Park but also portions of the Gold Country, Eastern Sierra, and Sierra National Forest south of Yosemite.

Messick, Tim, *Cross Country Skiing in Yosemite*. Chockstone Press, 1995. A round-up of ski trails leading from Badger Pass, Yosemite Valley, Crane Flat, Tuolumne Meadows, and the Tioga Pass area. Each trail description includes topographical graphs showing changes in elevation, plus ratings for mileage, time, and difficulty.

Roper, Steve, *Camp 4: Recollections of a Yosemite Rock Climber*. Mountaineers Books, 1998. More of a history book than a recreation guide, this volume tells the story of the golden age of Yosemite rock climbing in the 1960s and 1970s. The author, a veteran of 400 Yosemite ascents, is surprisingly honest in his account—these pages contain much more than mere tales of machismo and bravery.

White, Michael C., *Snowshoe Trails of Yosemite*. Wilderness Press, 1999. Snowshoe trips for all levels of ability, including two-hour jaunts for beginners and multi-day trips for skilled snowshoers.

Internet Resources

www.nps.gov/yose

This official National Park website for Yosemite provides up-to-date information on current road and weather conditions, lodging and camping options, park rules and regulations, and wilderness permits. (The same information ican be obtained by phone at 209/372-0200.) A printable travel guide is available, and you may request to have maps and information about Yosemite mailed to your home. In addition to plentiful visitor data, the site also has online exhibits on Yosemite's natural history, human history, and geology, as well as information on jobs in Yosemite, current management plans for the park, and a wide range of related links.

www.yosemitepark.com

The park concessionaire, Delaware North Companies (DNC), handles all of Yosemite's in-park accommodations, tours, events, and organized activities, which are described on this site. You can make reservations here or contact DNC by phone at 559/252-4848. DNC handles all reservations for the Ahwahnee Hotel, Yosemite Lodge, Curry Village, Housekeeping Camp, White Wolf Lodge, Tuolumne Lodge, and Wawona Hotel, as well as special events like the Bracebridge Dinner at the Ahwahnee Hotel, and a wide range of park activities from camera walks to open-air tram tours of Yosemite Valley. Badger Pass skiing and snow-related information can also be found at this website.

reservations.nps.gov

Visitors seeking to camp in Yosemite can make campground reservations at this site, or by phoning 800/436-7275 (or 301/722-1257 from outside the United States). Reservations are available up to five months in advance at one of three reservable campgrounds in Yosemite Valley or one of four reservable campgrounds elsewhere in the park.

www.yosemitesites.com

If you get frustrated trying to navigate your way through reservations.nps.gov, go to this site, which acts as a search engine for the official campground http://reservations site. Take the guess-work out of making reservations by checking this site's month-by-month calendars, which tell you which campgrounds have campsites available on which days. When you see what you have to choose from, proceed to http://reservations.nps.gov to make your reservation. This can be a real time-saver.

www.reserveusa.com

Visitors planning to camp near Yosemite but not within the park borders can reserve campsites at several national forest campgrounds through this website (or by phoning

877/444-6777). It helps to know the name of the campground where you'd like to stay (see the *Camping* chapter of this book).

www.yosemite.org

The official website of the Yosemite Association (YA), a nonprofit organization dedicated to supporting the park through visitor services, sales of books and maps, and membership activities. YA operates visitor center bookstores throughout the park and offers a wide range of educational courses through Yosemite Outdoor Adventures. The website provides information on becoming a YA member, current Yosemite weather conditions, upcoming seminars and events, news stories, and the Yosemite Live Web Cam with live shots of Yosemite Valley.

www.yosemitefund.org

The nonprofit fundraising arm of Yosemite National Park, the Yosemite Fund grants money for managing wildlife, restoring habitat, creating educational exhibits, and repairing trails in the park. Since its inception in 1988, the fund has granted over $20 million for more than 150 different Yosemite projects. The website provides information on current and past projects, how you can contribute to the fund, and how to purchase a Yosemite license plate for your vehicle.

www.yosemite.com

Yosemite visitors planning to stay outside the park but still within easy driving range should check out this site. Camping, dining, hiking, and other information is sketchy, but the lodging links for the four main Yosemite entrances (Highway 120 East and West, Highway 140, and Highway 41) are useful.

www.staynearyosemite.com

For Yosemite travelers planning to enter the park on Highway 120 from the San Francisco Bay Area, Sacramento, or elsewhere in Northern California, this site has information on lodgings specific to the Highway 120/Groveland-area park gateway.

www.yosemitethisyear.com

For Yosemite travelers planning to enter the park on Highway 41 from Fresno, Los Angeles, or elsewhere in Southern California, this site has information on lodging, dining, and activities specific to the Highway 41/Oakhurst-area park gateway.

www.yosemitebnbs.com

For Yosemite travelers planning to enter the park on Highway 140 from the Central Valley/Merced area, this site has information on bed-and-breakfast lodgings specific to the Highway 140/Mariposa-area park gateway.

www.anseladams.com
www.adamsgallery.com

Both of these web addresses lead you to the online store of the Ansel Adams Gallery in Yosemite Valley, a great source for artistic gifts (including posters, special edition photographs, books, reproductions) and also for information on photography workshops in Yosemite.

www.yni.org/yi

Yosemite National Institutes is a private, nonprofit organization dedicated to nature education. The institutes are located in Yosemite and Olympic National Parks and in the Marin Headlands in Golden Gate National Recreation Area. The program in Yosemite serves more than 40,000 children and adults annually through National Park Service partnership projects, a field science school program, and scholarship opportunities.

www.yosemite.national-park.com

This website is a general compilation of Yosemite information. It is organized in such a straightforward fashion that you may be able to get your questions answered here sooner than anywhere else. The home page lists an alphabetical table of contents with topics ranging from bear safety to shuttle bus service. Click on a topic and you'll get brief, summarized facts that may be just what you wanted to know.

www.395.com

If you plan to spend some or all of your vacation around Tioga Pass or in the Eastern Sierra, go to this site for information on lodging, camping, local businesses, and the like. It contains pages with local news, an interactive message board, High Sierra video streams, and current road conditions.

www.yarts.com

YARTS is the voluntary-use bus system that carries visitors into Yosemite Valley from various locations outside the park. The bus system currently serves towns in Mariposa, Merced, and Mono counties, and can be very convenient for travelers staying in lodgings in these towns. YARTS can also be reached by phone at 877/98-YARTS.

www.yosemitevalleyrr.com

Everything you ever wanted to know about the Yosemite Valley Railroad, the 77-mile passenger train that provided the main access to Yosemite National Park before the All-Year Highway (Highway 140) was built in 1926.

www.supertopo.com

A website dedicated to a wealth of rock climbing "beta" (or inside information) on Yosemite's big walls, the Tuolumne Meadows Area, and other regions of the High Sierra. Approach and descent facts, route histories, and lots of other details about the popular climbs.

www.hetchhetchy.org

The website of the nonprofit organization Restore Hetch Hetchy offers updates on the quest to drain Hetch Hetchy Reservoir and restore the valley to its pristine state.

Index

Hiking

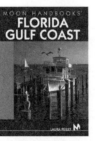

U.S. ~ Metric Conversion

1 inch = 2.54 centimeters (cm)
1 foot = .304 meters (m)
1 yard = 0.914 meters
1 mile = 1.6093 kilometers (km)
1 km = .6214 miles
1 fathom = 1.8288 m
1 chain = 20.1168 m
1 furlong = 201.168 m
1 acre = .4047 hectares
1 sq km = 100 hectares
1 sq mile = 2.59 square km
1 ounce = 28.35 grams
1 pound = .4536 kilograms
1 short ton = .90718 metric ton
1 short ton = 2000 pounds
1 long ton = 1.016 metric tons
1 long ton = 2240 pounds
1 metric ton = 1000 kilograms
1 quart = .94635 liters
1 US gallon = 3.7854 liters
1 Imperial gallon = 4.5459 liters
1 nautical mile = 1.852 km

To compute Celsius temperatures, subtract 32 from Fahrenheit and divide by 1.8. To go the other way, multiply Celsius by 1.8 and add 32.

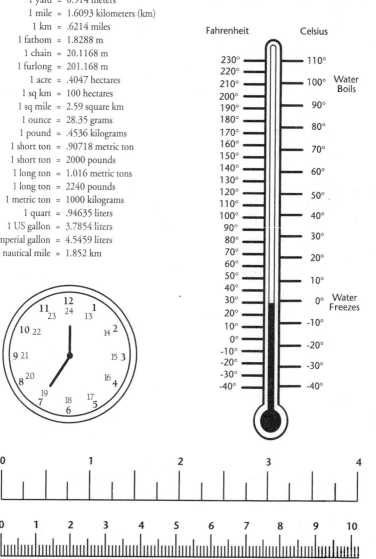

Keeping Current

Although we strive to produce the most up-to-date guidebook humanly possible, change is unavoidable. Between the time this book goes to print and the moment you read it, a handful of the businesses noted in these pages will undoubtedly change prices, move, or even close their doors forever. Other worthy attractions will open for the first time. If you have a favorite gem you'd like to see included in the next edition, or see anything that needs updating, clarification, or correction, please drop us a line. Send your comments via email to feedback@moon.com, or use the address below.

Moon Handbooks Yosemite
Avalon Travel Publishing
1400 65th Street, Suite 250
Emeryville, CA 94608, USA
www.moon.com

Avalon Travel Publishing
An Imprint of
Avalon Publishing Group, Inc.

AVALON
publishing group incorporated

Editor: Sabrina Young
Series Manager: Kathryn Ettinger
Acquisitions Editor: Rebecca K. Browning
Copy Editor: Valerie Sellers Blanton
Graphics Coordinator: Tabitha Lahr
Production Coordinator: Darren Alessi
Cover Designer: Kari Gim
Interior Designers: Amber Pirker
Map Editor: Kat Smith
Cartographers: Kat Bennett,
    Christine Markiewicz, Landis Bennett
Cartography Manager: Mike Morgenfeld
Indexer: Judy Hunt

ISBN-10: 1-56691-875-8
ISBN-13: 978-1-56691-875-6
ISSN: 1542-3972

Printing History
1st Edition—2003
2nd Edition—March 2006
5 4 3 2 1

Some photos and illustrations are used by permission and are the property of the original copyright owners.

Front cover photo: Half Dome, © John Elk III

Printed in Canada by Transcontinental